MASS EFFECT 2

PRIMA Official Game Guide

Written by:

Catherine Browne

Prima Games
An Imprint of Random House, Inc.

3000 Lava Ridge Court, Suite 100
Roseville, CA 95661
www.primagames.com

© 2010 EA International (Studio and Publishing) Ltd. Mass Effect, Mass Effect logo, BioWare and BioWare logo are trademarks or registered trademarks of EA International (Studio and Publishing) Ltd. in the U.S. and/or other countries. All Rights Reserved. EA and EA logo are trademarks or registered trademarks of Electronic Arts Inc. in the U.S. and/or other countries. All other trademarks are the property of their respective owners.

Senior Product Manager: Mario De Govia
Associate Product Manager: Shaida Boroumand
Design & Layout: Bryan Neff & Jody Seltzer
Manufacturing: Stephanie Sanchez & Suzanne Goodwin
Copy Editor: Deana Shields
Map Editor: David SJ Hodgson

Important:

Prima Games has made every effort to determine that the information contained in this book is accurate. However, the publisher makes no warranty, either expressed or implied, as to the accuracy, effectiveness, or completeness of the material in this book; nor does the publisher assume liability for damages, either incidental or consequential, that may result from using the information in this book. The publisher cannot provide any additional information or support regarding gameplay, hints and strategies, or problems with hardware or software. Such questions should be directed to the support numbers provided by the game and/or device manufacturers as set forth in their documentation. Some game tricks require precise timing and may require repeated attempts before the desired result is achieved.

ISBN: 978-03074-6706-5
Library of Congress Catalog Card Number: 2009913508
Printed in the United States of America

10 11 12 13 LL 10 9 8 7 6 5 4 3 2 1

Author Bio

Catherine grew up in a small town, loving the proverbial "great outdoors." While she still enjoys hiking, camping, and just getting out under the big sky, Catherine also appreciates the fine art of blasting the Covenant in *Halo* as well as arranging a perfect little village in *Animal Crossing*. (Seriously, you cannot just plant apple trees all willy-nilly. Neat rows, people!)

We want to hear from you! E-mail comments and feedback to cbrowne@primagames.com

CONTENTS

MASS EFFECT

Introduction

Training

Upgrades and Research

Walkthrough

Special Assignments

Planetary Database

Appendix

HOW TO USE THIS GUIDE

Welcome back to the galaxy, Commander. Though you are considered the beacon of humanity for your bravery against the rogue Spectre Saren and for stopping the Reaper attack on the Citadel, the galaxy has not become much friendlier. Humans are still not completely respected, so some alien species remain skeptical if not outright hostile to humanity. There are rival mercenary bands terrorizing planets and trade routes. And if politics and criminal activity weren't bad enough, a new threat has surfaced in the galaxy, and it has humankind in its crosshairs.

This guide will help you neutralize the threats you encounter while trying to save humanity from extinction. Every enemy you face is detailed. Every weapon is explained. We've assembled strategies, tactics and tricks to help you successfully complete every single mission you undertake in your push to stop this frightening new threat. Though the goal is singular, the route is not. This is a galaxy full of choices, from those you recruit to the words uttered in conversation. No two trips from here to there (and back again) are the same. So let us offer this guide that shows you the consequences of your words and deeds. Knowing what's in store around every corner will help you in matters of war... and love.

Introduction

A sudden and violent attack on the *Normandy* leaves Commander Shepard's fate in question.

Training

Use this chapter to get acquainted with basics like character creation, classes, and controls. This chapter also details all of the powers Shepard and the squad can acquire, from tech powers to biotic attacks. Combat is detailed here, too, including a list of all weapons.

Upgrades and Research Projects

Once the professor has been recruited, Shepard can research special upgrades to weapons, the ship, armor, and powers. This chapter details all research projects available from Cerberus including the costs in minerals like element zero and iridium, which must be recovered on missions or mined from planets.

Awakening

Shepard wakes up inside a Cerberus medical facility. This chapter helps you through the in-game tutorial and introduces you to Jacob and Miranda, two companions that stay with Shepard for the entire adventure.

Freedom's Progress

A human colony has just gone offline. Use this chapter to help discover what happened and how you can prevent another disaster.

Normandy SR2

This chapter will familiarize you with your new ship, and help you get to know the *Normandy*'s crew.

The Citadel

The Citadel figures into the main plot during two primary missions. However, you can optionally visit the Citadel at any time after you take command of the *Normandy*. This chapter explains the optional assignments and exploration available on the Citadel.

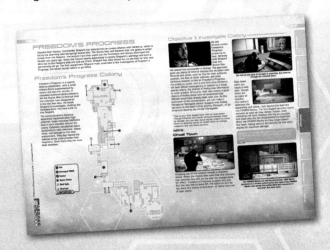

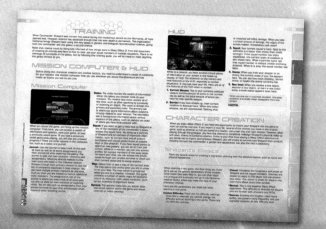

MASS EFFECT 2

Introduction

Training

Upgrades and Research

Walkthrough

Special Assignments

Planetary Database

Appendix

> The mission titles in this section are, in a way, **spoilers** themselves. If you absolutely want to avoid any hint of events in the game, don't read the descriptions of any missions on this page. That's when story elements will be revealed, although not explicitly.
>
> **NOTE**

Dossiers

Jacob and Miranda are great squad members, but Shepard needs even more talented fighters and biotics to round out the team. A new world, Omega, and the missions to recruit four individuals—Mordin, Subject Zero, Archangel, and a krogan warlord—are detailed in this chapter.

Horizon

Another human colony is under attack, but this time Shepard can actually intercept the assailants. Use this walkthrough to confront the terrifying Collector threat and pick up a very powerful new weapon.

Dossiers, Part 2

Continue building the team with the three individuals outlined in this chapter: an engineer, a justicar, and an assassin. Shepard needs at least two of these recruits, but follow the walkthrough to enlist all three and increase the potency of the team. This chapter also introduces Illium, a new planet full of exploration and special assignments.

Collector Ship

Cerberus scientists have located a damaged Collector ship. This is a perfect opportunity to gather intel on the enemy. Explore the ship via this chapter to pick up all of the new upgrades and strike a blow against the Collectors.

Loyalty

The mission to stop the Collectors threatens to be a one-way trip. Help the team settle old scores and put lingering matters to rest to ensure their absolute dedication to the mission. There is one loyalty mission per team member. Completing loyalty missions unlocks a special power in the team member if their mission ends in success. The krogan homeworld Tuchanka is also detailed in this chapter.

Derelict Reaper

An abandoned Reaper could be the tool that helps Shepard take the fight to the Collectors beyond the Omega 4 relay. Explore this Reaper and unlock its secrets, including a surprise addition to the team.

Normandy Attacked/Legion

The Collectors do not turn the other cheek. After the Collectors attack the *Normandy* (while Shepard and the squad are not aboard), Shepard returns to the vessel to either finish off outstanding loyalty missions, take on the loyalty mission of its newest recruit, or continue on to the Omega 4 relay.

Endgame

This is it. Shepard and the squad brave the relay to strike the Collector homeworld. Follow the strategies in this chapter to minimize casualties (seriously, squad members will die if Shepard is not careful) and learn the shocking final plot of the Collectors.

Special Assignments

While chasing down the Collector threat, Shepard and the team are offered a host of small assignments in cities like Nos Astra on Illium and the Citadel, which are detailed in this chapter. Shepard can also pursue a series of N7 assignments by scanning planets and finding new ports of call and other sites of interest. All of the assignments in this chapter are optional, but most result in experience, credits, minerals, or a combination of the three.

Planetary Database

The galaxy is vast, hosting dozens of clusters and hundreds of planets. This database helps not only make sense of the galaxy, but also offers up a full chart of mineral richness so Shepard wastes little time excavating barren worlds. With the minerals this chapter exposes, Shepard can complete more research projects and unlock powerful upgrades.

Appendix

All achievements for the Xbox 360 edition of the game are listed here, as well as the full inventory of all stores in the galaxy.

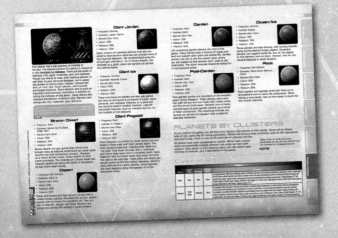

INTRODUCTION

HUMANITY'S ASCENSION

Before there was history, there were the Protheans.

The Protheans were an ancient race of beings that vanished from the Perseus Arm of the galaxy 50,000 years ago. However, they did not disappear without a trace. The Protheans left behind a series of relics and artifacts for the galaxy's future beings to discover. When a race finally achieved space travel proficiency and discovered a marker left behind by the Protheans, they were directed to a mass relay—a piece of alien technology that allows faster-than-light travel.

Over the eons, more and more races evolved and expanded, eventually discovering what is believed to be Prothean technology. When they followed the trail left behind by the ancients, they rocketed to the Citadel in the Serpent Nebula. The Citadel is a massive space station, a wonder of technology that managed to survive while the Protheans themselves did not. As more races reached the Citadel, it became the central hub of government and order in the Perseus Arm.

Humans found their first Prothean beacon on Mars. This directed them to a mass relay that allowed them to become the newest member of the galactic community. The galaxy was not exactly happy to see humankind, though. Humans developed a reputation for arrogance and aggression because they did not merely accept their lowly station as newcomers. Though the Council that oversees all order in the galaxy did indeed welcome the humans, skepticism of humankind reached all the way to the top.

But now the galaxy owes a debt to humanity and, more importantly, to Commander Shepard. The commander is almost single-handedly responsible for unraveling a tapestry of deceit that would have led to the destruction not just of humankind, but of all life in the galaxy.

A rogue Spectre named Saren, an agent of the ruling Council, commandeered an army of artificial beings called geth to annihilate the Citadel. The geth were created over 300 years ago by the quarians as laborers, but they rose up against their masters. A long, costly war between the geth and quarians resulted in the eventual banishment of the geth to a sector of the galaxy beyond the Perseus Veil. But a dark nebula of opaque gas obscured the actions of the geth.

Why would Saren turn on the Council he was sworn to protect? Saren knew of the Reapers, an ancient race of beings that are hell-bent on wiping out all organic life—like they had done once before with the Protheans. And a race before them. And before them. In fact, the Reapers have been repeating a cycle of allowing life in the galaxy to evolve to a certain point and then crushing it again. The Citadel is just a tool of the Reapers' wicked plans.

Saren hoped that by helping the Reapers, he would be spared the inevitable. But he was tragically wrong. A powerful Reaper called Sovereign was revealed to be controlling Saren, using the former Spectre to gain access to the Conduit so the Reapers could take over the Citadel and its citizens.

Defying the Council, which refused to believe Shepard's findings about the Reapers, Shepard raced to the Conduit to stop Sovereign. Through skill and sacrifice, Shepard and his crew were able to stop Sovereign from taking the Citadel and destroying all life in the galaxy. As a result of Shepard's heroism, the Council recognized the worth of humanity. The human race was accepted into the Council and began the next chapter in its seemingly unending ascension.

But Sovereign was only one of the Reapers.

Long Live the *Normandy*

One month has passed since the failed geth attack on the Citadel. The galaxy is now rebuilding, and the Council has turned to the resilient humans, once regarded with barely veiled scorn by some races because of their dogged pursuit of destiny, to lead the way back into the light.

Rather than bask in glory, Shepard remains on active duty aboard the starship *Normandy* as it continues to comb the cosmos for signs of a threat against humanity, the Council, and the Citadel.

The crew of the *Normandy* does not need to wait very long to encounter danger. On an assignment to investigate the disappearance of three human ships, the *Normandy* is intercepted by an unidentified vessel. The enemy is massive, blocking out a sinister outline against the planet below. Despite the *Normandy*'s stealth measures, the enemy ship draws a bead on its location and opens fire.

As Shepard approaches the cockpit, a massive hole opens in the fuselage, exposing the interior to the hostilities of space. It's almost peaceful to watch bits and pieces of the *Normandy* escape the ship's gravity field and float away. Finally, Shepard reaches Joker and drills the direness of the situation into his head: Give up. Don't go down with the ship.

No amount of ace piloting from Joker can evade the attack. The *Normandy* is torn to pieces by searing laser blasts. Fire breaks out on all levels as the *Normandy*'s hull is compromised.

Shepard orders immediate evacuation, accepting that the *Normandy* is lost. But Shepard also knows that its pilot, Joker, will be the last to recognize the sad fate of his beloved ship and heads to the cockpit to pry him from the controls.

Shepard places Joker in an escape pod as the unknown enemy comes around to deliver the killing blow. Just as Joker's pod is safely jettisoned, a laser blast shatters the *Normandy*. Shepard is violently thrown into space as the *Normandy* explodes. Shepard's suit is losing oxygen. And the gravitational pull of the planet is about to pick up the commander's broken body. Soon, Shepard breaches the upper atmosphere and begins heat entry. No human could ever survive planetfall. Not even the Spectre who stopped the Reapers from destroying all life in the galaxy.

The beacon of humanity goes out.

It goes out bright.

But it goes out nonetheless.

An old friend assists Shepard with the evacuation. If you selected a male Shepard, you are assisted by Ashley Williams. If you chose a female Shepard, Kaidan Alenko helps with the evacuation. If you imported Shepard from the original *Mass Effect*, and had a romance with Liara T'Soni, she assists with the evacuation.

NOTE

Introduction

Training

Upgrades and Research

Walkthrough

Special Assignments

Planetary Database

Appendix

TRAINING

When Commander Shepard was thrown into space during the mysterious attack on the *Normandy*, all hope seemed lost. However, science has advanced enough that not even death is permanent. The organization Cerberus brings Shepard back using the very latest in genetic and biological reconstruction science, giving both the commander and the galaxy a second chance.

Make that chance count by being fully informed of how things work in *Mass Effect 2*, from the essentials of creating an entirely new hero to how to best use your squad members in combat situations. There is no shortage of curveballs in the galaxy, but by following this training guide, you will be ready to meet anything the galaxy throws at you.

MISSION COMPUTER & HUD

Before diving into character creation and combat tactics, you need to understand a couple of constants for your mission: the mission computer that you use whenever you pause the adventure and the heads-up display you see as you play.

Mission Computer

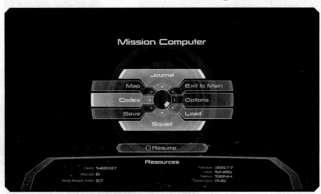

When you pause the game, you bring up the mission computer. From here, you can access a wealth of information and updates, save your game, or load a previously saved game. (If you load a previously saved game while playing, you will lose any unsaved progress.) There are other options in the computer, too, such as a journal and a codex.

Journal: Use the journal to keep track of the task at hand as well as all extra assignments you uncover while exploring the galaxy. The journal is split into two sections—missions and assignments. Missions directly related to the main story are listed in the missions section. Browse through each primary mission to see the list of uncovered objectives in that mission. You can have multiple primary missions at one time, such as when you are tasked to recruit additional squad members. The assignments tab of the journal is where you keep track of all small jobs you pick up while on main missions or exploring cities. You will also pick up assignments from your private terminal on your ship and discover short missions when scanning worlds.

Codex: The codex stores the wealth of information about the galaxy you uncover while on your missions. You receive new codex entries all of the time, such as after speaking to somebody or scanning an object. The codex is divided into primary and secondary tabs. The primary tab is where you store information about subjects directly related to your mission. The secondary tab is background information about various aspects of the galaxy, such as planets you scan or aliens you have little contact with.

Squad: If you want to get a close look at Shepard or any of the members of the commander's team, access the squad here. You bring up a portrait of Shepard and an overview of important information, such as current level and all powers purchased with squad points (more on powers later in this chapter). If you have squad points to spend on new powers, you can do so from this screen. While on a mission, you can only access profiles for current members of the away team. On board your ship, you can access the entire squad through your private terminal to check out their current state and to allocate points toward powers.

Map: Select this to see a map of the current area. The map option only works when you are in cities or on your ship. The map option is grayed out when you are on a mission. However, this guide contains a number of useful maps for locations visited on missions, with useful notations, such as the locations of important items.

Options: The options menu lets you adjust video and sound options within the game, adjust controls or online settings, or quit your game.

HUD

While on a mission, you have several critical pieces of information on your screen in the heads-up display, or HUD. Pay attention to the meters and intel featured on the HUD, especially in combat situations—it may just save your life. Here are all of the features of the HUD when in combat:

1. **Current Weapon:** This is your currently selected weapon and the amount of ammo in the current clip as well as the total amount of ammo you have for that specific weapon.

2. **Shields:** If you have shields up, their current condition is displayed here. When this meter empties, you are unprotected. Getting shot or smashed will inflict damage. When you take a critical amount of damage, the edges of the screen redden. Immediately seek cover!

3. **Squad:** Your current squad is here. Next to the portraits is a meter that shows their shield strength. If the squad member has biotic capabilities, the current state of cooldown is also shown here. When a portrait turns red, that squad member is without shields and being attacked. When it is gray, the squad member has fallen.

4. **Enemy:** When you train your weapon on an enemy, the current state of your foe appears here. You can see how much shielding, barrier, armor, or health the enemy currently has.

5. **New Intel:** When you receive a new object, discover a new object, or learn a new codex entry, a small notice appears down here.

> When you are not in a combat situation, the biotic cooldown and shield meter disappears from the screen.
>
> **NOTE**

CHARACTER CREATION

When you begin *Mass Effect 2*, you have the opportunity to import your Shepard into the game or start an entirely new one. If you import a save file, several of the choices you made in the original game, such as whether or not you saved the Council, carry over into this next mission. However, after playing through the prologue, you have the chance to completely redesign Shepard's physical make-up and class, thanks to Cerberus science. If this is your first time playing a *Mass Effect* adventure or you decide not to import your previous Shepard, you will create an entirely new Shepard from scratch, including not just the commander's gender and appearance, but also the hero's backstory.

Shepard's Basics

There are several steps to creating a character, starting with the absolute basics, such as name and physical appearance.

Start-up

When starting a new game, the first thing you must do is set up the general parameters of the mission. Once these have been filled in, you can then begin the prologue and eventually end up in the Cerberus medical facility, where you make the rest of your character choices.

Here are the parameters you must set when starting a new game:

Combat Difficulty: There are five difficulty settings. Once one is selected, you cannot change the difficulty without starting a new game. These are the difficulty settings:

- **Casual:** Increases the toughness and power of Shepard and the squad members. Enemies are slower to react to the player and use powers less often. This option is great for players who care more about story than combat.

- **Normal:** This is the baseline *Mass Effect* experience. This difficulty is intended for players who are familiar with shooters and RPGs.

- **Veteran:** Enemies are tougher, react more quickly, use powers more frequently, and use upgraded weapons at this difficulty level.

- **Hardcore:** This difficulty is intended for players who have already beaten *Mass Effect 2* and want a bigger challenge. Enemies are extremely tough, use upgraded weapons, and are aggressive with their powers.

- **Insanity:** This level is intended for players who have beaten the game on hardcore and want the ultimate challenge. Enemies are exceedingly aggressive and use their powers mercilessly.

Auto Level Up: Turning this off lets you manually assign points every time Shepard or a squad member gains a level.

Subtitles: You can turn subtitles on or off during dialog scenes. This can be changed later in options from the mission computer.

Squad Power Usage: Enabling this feature allows your squad members to make their own calls in combat in regards to using powers. Turning it off means your squad members will also use powers defensively. Otherwise, you must deploy powers for them.

Autosave: Choose whether or not the game autosaves for you on a regular basis.

Quickstart or Custom?

If you just want to get into the game, you can choose a quickstart Shepard. Shepard's appearance is predetermined, as is the commander's backstory. A quickstart Shepard is always a soldier. If you decide to make your own Shepard, select Shepard's name. You can only choose Shepard's first name. The last name is a constant.

Appearance

After selecting Shepard's name, you enter the facial customization tool. From here, you can completely design (or redesign in the case of an imported Shepard) the commander's face. If you are happy with the default options, then keep moving. If you want to make changes to Shepard's face, then comb through the different categories of facial features. There are multiple options within each

category. For the nose, you can select different shapes, adjust bridge width, change height, etc. Here are the available categories:

- **Facial Structure:** Select a baseline face to work with.

- **Head:** Change the general shape of the commander's head.

- **Eyes:** Adjust the eye color, shape, and placement.

- **Jaw:** Adjust the commander's jaw line and chin.

- **Mouth:** Select the shape of Shepard's mouth, lip size, and mouth depth.

- **Nose:** Adjust the nose shape, height, and depth.

- **Hair:** Select from different hairstyles and colors.

- **Makeup** (female only): Adjust lip color and add eye shadow or blush.

Personal Background and Profile

After selecting Shepard's appearance, you can choose the commander's class (soldier, vanguard, etc.). However, before we explain the strengths and benefits of all of the different classes, let's just

finish up the basics of creating a new character. You must give Shepard a personal background that broadly defines the commander's personality. There are three choices:

Spacer: Both of your parents were in the Alliance military. Your childhood was spent on ships and stations as they transferred from post to post, never staying in one location for more than a few years. Following in your parents' footsteps, you enlisted at the age of 18.

Colonist: You were born and raised on Mindoir, a small border colony in the Attican Traverse. When you were 16, slavers raided Mindoir, slaughtering your family and friends. You were saved by a passing Alliance patrol, and you enlisted with the military a few years later.

11

Introduction

Training

Upgrades and Research

Walkthrough

Special Assignments

Planetary Database

Appendix

Earthborn: You were an orphan raised on the streets of one of the great cities covering Earth. You escaped a life of petty crime and underworld gangs by enlisting with the Alliance military when you turned 18.

After selecting the commander's personal backstory, you then select a psychological profile. There are three options:

Sole Survivor: During your military service, a mission went horribly wrong. Trapped in a life-threatening situation, you had to overcome physical torments and psychological stresses that would have broken most people. Everyone around you fell, and you alone survived to tell the tale.

War Hero: Early in your military career, you found yourself facing an overwhelming enemy force. You risked your own life to save your fellow soldiers and defeat the enemy despite the impossible odds. Your bravery and heroism earned you medals and recognition from the Alliance fleet.

Ruthless: Throughout your military career, you held fast to one basic rule: Get the job done. You've been called cold, calculating, and brutal. Your reputation for ruthless efficiency makes people wary of you. But when failure is not an option, you are the one to call.

The background choices you make are more than just window dressing. These choices affect the overall morality of your hero. The morality system in *Mass Effect 2* is explained a little later in this chapter, but here are the morality benefits of each choice:

- Paragon Bonus: Earthborn, War Hero
- Renegade Bonus: Spacer, Ruthless

These bonuses give a slight bump to the number of morality points you earn when making choices during the mission. For example, a Ruthless Spacer would earn extra Renegade points when being hard on somebody, whereas an Earthborn Sole Survivor would earn just a few less.

Character Classes

When creating a hero or redesigning an imported Shepard, no decision is more important or has a more far-reaching effect on your adventure than class. There are six classes you can choose from, each with strengths and weakness that will shape your combat options and style. Do you want to take the galaxy at the end of a gun? Then look into the soldier class, which is heavily geared toward developing weapon expertise. If you want to charge headlong into danger, flinging biotic attacks at your foes, then consider the adept.

Each class has three defining factors—power training, weapon training, and ammo training. These three factors shape your character right out of the gate. Weapon training determines what kind of weapons your hero can use. Ammo training determines what special ammunition your character

is able to use. Power training lists the powers the character can immediately start developing. Now, none of these are set in stone. As you level up and earn more squad points, you can apply them to additional powers.

Each class also has a mastery power that only a hero in that class can develop and use. For example, the Infiltrator Mastery power improves an infiltrator's sniping skills, while the adept's Biotic Mastery shortens the cooldown period between unleashing biotic attacks.

> For a complete list of all powers, what they do, and how they change as you apply squad points to them, please see the "Powers" section of this chapter.
>
> **NOTE**

Soldier

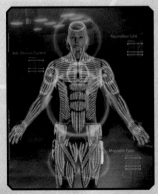

Soldiers are pure combat specialists. No one is tougher or more effective at taking down enemies with gunfire. Soldiers have the most thorough weapons training and can use all special ammo types.

- **Power Training:** Adrenaline Rush, Concussive Shot
- **Weapon Training:** Assault Rifle, Heavy Pistol, Shotgun, Sniper Rifle
- **Ammo Training:** Cryo, Disruptor, Incendiary

> Soldiers start out with more health than the other classes.
>
> **TIP**

> The soldier class is designed for players who want an action-oriented experience full of heavy gunplay.
>
> **TIP**

Infiltrator

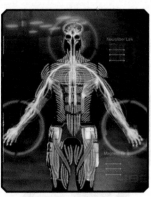

Infiltrators are tech and combat specialists with the unique ability to cloak themselves from visual and technological detection. Infiltrators are deadly at any range, with a wide variety of weapons, equipment, and powers that can take down any enemy.

- **Power Training:** AI Hacking, Incinerate, Tactical Cloak
- **Weapon Training:** Heavy Pistol, Sniper Rifle, Submachine Gun
- **Ammo Training:** Cryo, Disruptor

> **TIP**
> Players who want to rely on sniping for taking down targets should pick the Infiltrator class.

> **TIP**
> Tactical Cloak is a lifesaver. If you use guns to dish out damage and then use Tactical Cloak to save yourself in emergencies, you will be extremely hard to kill.

Vanguard

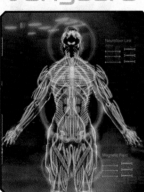

Vanguards are feared for their high-risk, high-reward combat style, closing quickly on enemies and destroying them at close range with weapons and biotic abilities.

- **Power Training:** Charge, Pull, Shockwave
- **Weapon Training:** Heavy Pistol, Shotgun, Submachine Gun
- **Ammo Training:** Cryo, Incendiary

> **TIP**
> Vanguard is the class for players who relish close-range combat. The combination of Charge with a shotgun follow-up is the vanguard's style of lethality.

> **TIP**
> Charge is not just an offensive move. Use Charge to replenish barriers as you rush away from a fight.

Sentinel

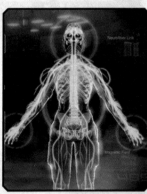

Sentinels are unique, bringing both tech and biotic abilities to the battlefield. While they lack the focus of adepts and engineers, they are versatile and can handle any situation.

- **Power Training:** Cryo Blast, Overload, Tech Armor, Throw, Warp
- **Weapon Training:** Heavy Pistol, Submachine Gun
- **Ammo Training:** None

> **TIP**
> Sentinels get to use both biotic and tech powers, expanding your options on the battlefield.

> **TIP**
> Develop Tech Armor and deploy it whenever possible. You will be tough to kill.

Adept

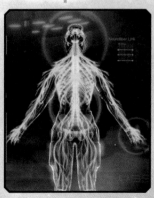

Adepts are biotic specialists, capable of disabling and killing enemies with raw biotic power. While they lack advanced combat training, they are the best at defeating enemies without firing a shot.

- **Power Training:** Pull, Shockwave, Singularity, Throw, Warp
- **Weapon Training:** Heavy Pistol, Submachine Gun
- **Ammo Training:** None

> **TIP**
> Singularity, when developed, is a devastating power that can bring down even the mightiest enemies.

MASS EFFECT

Engineer

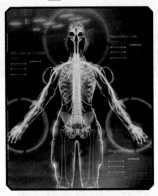

Engineers are tech specialists, the only class able to employ combat drones on the battlefield. Engineers are the most effective class at blasting through enemy defenses and disabling opponents.

- **Power Training:** AI Hacking, Combat Drone, Cryo Blast, Incinerate, Overload
- **Weapon Training:** Heavy Pistol, Submachine Gun
- **Ammo Training:** None

CHARACTER MANAGEMENT

Experience and Level Progression

As you cross the galaxy, defeat enemies, and complete both missions and assignments, you earn experience points. Experience points accumulate over time. When your experience points reach specific thresholds, you earn a new level. Each new level awards you talent points, which you can spend on developing powers for both yourself and the other members of your squad. You do not earn talent points at the same rate for yourself and your squad, though. Squad points for the team lag behind points earned for yourself.

With each new level, you are awarded two squad points for yourself. You can immediately assign these points to powers, or you can hold on to them and use them later. When you develop powers to their third level, you need more than two squad points to move to the fourth level.

> Advancing levels does not directly unlock any powers or skills. You must apply those squad points to unlock new powers to later develop.

NOTE

Use this level chart to see how many experience points are required for each level as well as the awarded points for yourself and the squad.

Level	Experience Points	Talent Points	Squad Talent Points
1	0	2	1
2	1,000	4	3
3	2,000	6	5
4	3,000	8	7
5	4,000	10	9
6	5,000	12	9
7	6,000	14	11
8	7,000	16	11
9	8,000	18	13
10	9,000	20	13
11	10,000	22	15
12	11,000	24	15
13	12,000	26	17
14	13,000	28	17
15	14,000	30	19
16	15,000	32	19
17	16,000	34	21
18	17,000	36	21
19	18,000	38	23
20	19,000	40	23
21	20,000	41	24
22	21,000	42	24
23	22,000	43	25
24	23,000	44	25
25	24,000	45	26
26	25,000	46	26
27	26,000	47	27
28	27,000	48	27
29	28,000	49	28
30	29,000	50	29

Introduction

Training

Upgrades and Research

Walkthrough

Special Assignments

Planetary Database

Appendix

Morality

Your hero has a sense of morality that follows them through the adventure. How you choose to interact with squad members, enemies, and even complete strangers affects your hero's morality, which in turn defines their personality in a more active manner than their backstory (which does affect morality). Morality is expressed in two forms: Paragon and Renegade. Paragon and Renegade sound like absolutes, but as you know, life is never quite that black and white. So many choices deal in the gray area between the absolutes.

Paragons are largely considered good people. They charm. They flatter. And when given a choice between doing the right or wrong thing, they choose the former even if it makes the task ahead harder to complete.

Renegades are not wicked, but they could be considered intimidating or selfish. Renegades look out for themselves and are not always considerate of the feelings of other people, especially when such consideration stands between them and getting the job done.

When you choose a Paragon action or conversation topic, you earn Paragon points. Conversely, choosing a Renegade action results in Renegade points. Over time, these points accumulate. Having more points on either end of the morality scale affects choices you have during your adventure. If you are trending toward Paragon, you will have more Paragon conversation choices, such as the ability to charm people into doing what's right or agreeing with you.

> In conversations, Paragon options appear in blue. Renegade options appear in red. If you do not have a high enough Paragon or Renegade rating to use one of these options, it will appear in gray.
>
> **NOTE**

> There are powers and talents that affect the number of morality points earned when making either Paragon or Renegade actions.
>
> **TIP**

So, does it pay then to walk the line between Paragon and Renegade? Not necessarily. Although there will be times when a Paragon wants to take a Renegade action (Renegade actions sometimes shorten battles thanks to underhanded moves) and vice versa, it pays to trend toward one or the other over the course of the adventure. The higher your rating in either Paragon or Renegade, the more options you will have. If morality points are spread across both evenly, you will miss out on some of the more extreme morality options. Furthermore, a high Paragon or Renegade rating may also affect which allies you can recruit. Your Paragon or Renegade rating also affects your appearance: as you earn more Renegade points, your facial scars worsen; scars improve as you earn more Paragon points.

Interrupts

During conversations, you may see a Paragon or Renegade symbol appear on-screen. The Paragon symbol always appears on the left side of the screen. The Renegade symbol always appears on the right side. This signals an opportunity for an interrupt that results in morality points. When you see the symbol, press the associated button to take the interrupt.

Interrupts let you take charge of a situation. For example, let's say a krogan warrior is rambling on and on about his master plan to make his clan the most powerful in the galaxy. While talking, the krogan does not realize he's standing on an explosive tank. The Renegade interrupt appears. If you act fast and take it, you shoot the tank under the krogan's feet. The tank explodes, killing the krogan warrior. The battle that would have taken place after the conversation happens anyway, but thanks to your move, the krogan warrior is already out of the equation. Now, killing the krogan while he's just talking isn't exactly the honorable thing to do, so you take on Renegade points for doing so.

> Paragon and Renegade interrupts are available to you regardless of your current morality score.
>
> **NOTE**

Introduction

Training

Upgrades and Research

Walkthrough

Special Assignments

Planetary Database

Appendix

Dialog

While a gun is an extremely effective communication tool, it's not the only one at your disposal. You will talk to friends, enemies, and strangers while traveling the galaxy. When you enter into a conversation, you direct your responses or line of questioning with the dialog wheel located on the bottom of the screen. Move the arrow in the center of the wheel to the desired conversation option and select it to speak or end a conversation (sometimes you end conversations wordlessly—nothing says goodbye like a bullet).

The dialog wheel always has different options on it, but the structure of the wheel itself is universal. Options on the left side of the wheel draw out a conversation—these are investigative topics. Options on the right side of the wheel steer a conversation toward its conclusion.

The position of an option on either side of the wheel is also important—these are tonal. Options in the upper corner of the wheel are largely considered

friendly or positive. An option in a lower corner is hostile or dismissive. Guiding a conversation through positive or negative channels can result in Paragon or Renegade points, so if you are playing to a particular morality end, keep these positions in mind when using the dialog wheel.

As mentioned in the "Morality" section, if you have a high enough Paragon or Renegade ranking, you unlock additional conversation options. Just as there are different degrees of Paragon and Renegade, there are conversation options that do not open until you are high enough in either morality category. If you are merely trending toward Paragon, for example, you will easily be able to charm shopkeepers into giving you a discount. You need to be quite the Paragon, though, to talk a disgruntled crew member into rejoining the social structure of the team. Without a high enough Paragon or Renegade ranking, some dialog avenues will just never be open for you.

Fraternization and Loyalty

When a crew goes through extreme situations together, it is impossible not to feel great bonds with each other. Nothing sparks and eventually solidifies a relationship quite like staring death in the face. While Cerberus does not exactly condone relationships between team members, the Illusive Man is not about to board the ship and tell two team members to take a cold shower. And so you can pursue deep friendships with members of the team, including romantic relationships.

Not every relationship with a team member has the potential to turn romantic. Some relationships will always remain just friendships—perhaps even close ones. To develop a relationship, you need to talk to team members—and then keep talking to them. Check in with team members between missions. Kindle relationships by choosing positive dialog. Show compassion. Don't be afraid to be tender or even flirt a little. However, there are always risks involved when building relationships. Say the wrong thing to the wrong person and you will turn someone off. Some will be turned off permanently. They won't bail out the nearest air lock, but they will keep things strictly business from then on out. Gaining the loyalty of your crew is important to your overall mission, so it's a good idea to keep everyone happy.

Gender does affect some potential romantic subplots. Jacob, for example, is only interested in a female Shepard, while Miranda is only romantic with a male Shepard. Some shipmates will consider a relationship regardless of gender.

NOTE

Developing relationships is exciting. It adds a personal level to an adventure that's bigger than life. You may not want to spoil how relationships unfold if you prefer to tackle them organically and let the chips fall where they may. Relationships with team members all start out the same. You have generic questions you ask them once they are aboard the ship to get a little backstory on them and establish a baseline friendship. However, team members hold a lot back in the very beginning of their service on your ship. To draw them out and build the relationship, you must keep talking to them. Over time, you will nurture a relationship unless you say something absolutely terrible. That shuts down a relationship, and it's very difficult to recover from it without a high Paragon or Renegade rank. Some relationship killers can never be overcome, so consider the potential effects of your dialog before opening your mouth.

All members of the crew have personal situations that they need help dealing with—these are called loyalty missions because once you complete one, that team member is considered loyal to you, which unlocks not only relationship potential, but also a special power. The loyalty mission is a pivotal moment in a relationship and is crucial to completing the main story line of the game. Prior to the loyalty missions, you can speak to team members once or twice to get a little conversation out of them. You must let a little time pass between conversations to keep building the relationships. Passing time is equivalent to going on a mission.

However, once a loyalty mission has been successfully completed (you can fail three of the loyalty missions, which also shuts down a potential relationship), the relationship enters its next phase. Speak to the team member following the loyalty mission and be positive. At this point, a friend is turning into either a romantic interest or a trusted ally.

After undertaking another mission following the completion of the loyalty mission, return to the team member and talk again. If this conversation is positive and successful (meaning, you don't say anything rude or untoward), the relationship reaches its highest level. If the relationship is a romance, then you will see a special scene between you and the team member prior to going on the final mission. And by special, we mean…well, you know what we mean.

Now, because you can nurture relationships with all team members, you need to realize you cannot carry every relationship to the penultimate scene. You must choose which team member you want to be exclusive with. If you try to be romantic with another team member, they will let you know that they wish to be exclusive. You now have the option to go to the team member you have set up for the special moment and let them down either easy or hard. If you break off the romance with tact and grace, the team member remains loyal. If you are harsh, you lose the spurned team member's loyalty, but they still stay on the team. Breaking off a romance is always private. This is a no-drama crew.

TRANSPORTATION AND COMMERCE

Interstellar Travel

Shepard is the commanding officer on the *Normandy SR2*, a re-creation of the *Normandy SR1* ship that helped the Alliance defeat Saren and save the Citadel. The *Normandy SR2* includes all of the systems of the original, including a mass effect FTL drive that allows it to use mass relays to travel between distant points in the galaxy almost instantaneously. Although the *Normandy* has a dedicated pilot, you are the final call when it comes to navigation.

You set the course for the ship all across the cosmos via the galaxy map, the central feature in the combat information center (CIC) of the ship. This multi-level map allows you to start with a galaxy view of known space and then drill down through various tiers, including clusters and systems, until eventually deciding on a specific planet to orbit.

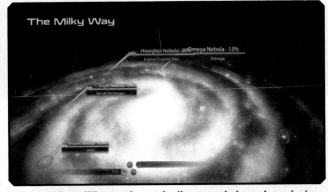

Galaxy View: *When a cluster is discovered through a mission or the purchase of a star chart, it appears on the galaxy view. If the cluster has an active mission, the name of the mission appears on the cluster and on every level down.*

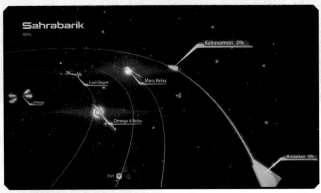

System View: *This view shows all planets within a system, orbiting around a central star. The number of planets explored/scanned is noted with a percentage. Other systems within the cluster can be accessed by traveling to the edge of the system. This returns you to cluster view.*

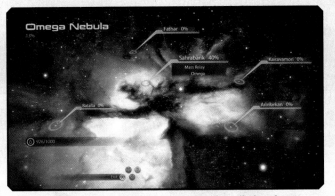

Cluster View: *A collection of systems is called a cluster. Cluster view is actually bypassed when selecting a cluster; instead you drill down to the system within the cluster that contains the mass relay. This view is only seen when you exit a system by traveling to the edge of the map.*

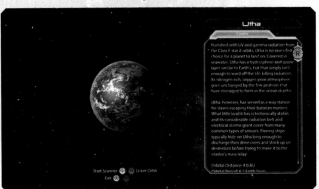

Orbital View: *From this view, you can either scan a planet for resources or land on a hospitable planet with a landing zone. Just dropping into orbital view adds a planet to your "known" registry and counts toward the percentage of the system considered explored.*

> For more on scanning and mining planets, please see the "Mining" section of this chapter.

NOTE

Travel Between Systems

When you select a cluster from the galaxy map, you bypass the cluster view and instead enter the system with the mass relay within that cluster. Each cluster has a single mass relay, which is the "warp" point you access when using the mass relay network. To travel to another system within a cluster, you must physically steer the *Normandy* to it. To travel to another system within a cluster, direct the *Normandy* to the arrow marked with the name of the system. This sends you to cluster view. Steer the *Normandy* to the desired system and then select it to drop into system view again.

Traveling within a system does not consume any fuel. However, traveling across the void between systems does. You must purchase fuel from Fuel Depots. There is a Fuel Depot in every system with a mass relay. At first, the *Normandy* can only hold 1,000 units of fuel. With an upgrade, though, you can double the ship's fuel capacity, allowing for longer periods of travel.

> If you run out of fuel, you will be "towed" back to the system with the mass relay in that cluster and suffer a financial penalty.

CAUTION

Introduction · Training · Upgrades and Research · Walkthrough · Special Assignments · Planetary Database · Appendix

You can also buy probes from Fuel Depots; they are critical for mining operations.

NOTE

Commerce
Mining

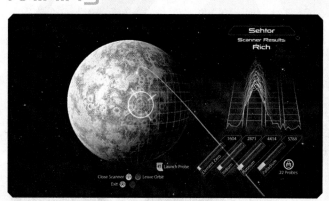

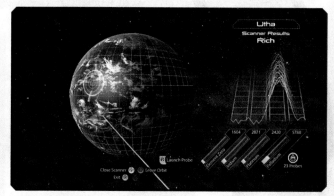

There are two commodities of immediate value to you during this adventure: credits and minerals. Minerals are discovered while undertaking a mission (usually found within crates) or by scanning planets. There are four types of minerals: platinum, palladium, iridium, and element zero. Element zero (eezo) is the rarest and most valuable of the four minerals. These minerals are essential for carrying out research projects aboard the *Normandy*, which result in useful upgrades for you and your squad, such as weapon and biotic boosters.

You cannot excavate minerals without probes. You purchase probes at a Fuel Depot for 100 credits each. At first, the *Normandy* can carry 30 probes, but an upgrade raises the capacity to 60.

To mine a planet for resources, you must drop into orbital view. From orbital view, choose "scan." This view drops a grid over the planet's surface. The planet automatically rotates, but you can speed the rotation one way or the other by moving the cursor on it either left or right to the edge of the planet view. Place the scan cursor over the part of the planet you wish to scan and then select "scan" again. Hold scan and move the cursor around to scan a larger area.

While scanning, pay attention to the scanner on the right side of the screen, directly above the four wells—each well is assigned to one of the minerals. The scanner shows just noise when you are moving the cursor over an empty area. However, when you direct the cursor to an area with a mineral deposit the scanner jumps over one or more of the wells. The height of the peak reveals the richness of the cursor site. When you find a rich vein, tap the "probe" button to launch a probe down to the planet surface. The impact of the probe immediately results in the acquisition of minerals.

There are multiple mineral deposits on planets. However, when you probe an area, you drain it of minerals. So, make sure you are sending a probe down over the richest spots, because even if the scanner would have shown a higher peak just to the south of the probe site, the area around the probe dries up.

You cannot scan planets you explore for missions in the main story line. However, you can scan planets with special assignments.

CAUTION

For a complete index of all planets in the galaxy and the minerals you will find on each of them, please see the "Planetary Database" in the back of this guide.

NOTE

Credits

Credits make the galaxy go round. They are the universally accepted currency throughout Citadel space (and beyond). Credits are primarily used to purchase items from shops, but there are a handful of situations where you may part with some credits to gamble or even spread a little good around.

To spend credits, you have to earn credits. Completing missions is the primary way to bank large amounts of credits. Completing small special assignments pays credits, too, but not as much as completing a mission from the main plot. You will find credits in safes, crates, hackable datapads, and computers. You can earn credits by salvaging spare parts and scanning technology valuable to Cerberus. At the end of each mission, you also receive a lump sum payment from Cerberus.

Shopping

After speaking to a shopkeeper, use the nearby kiosk to buy goods.

When you visit one of the hub worlds—Illium, the Citadel, or Omega—you will typically locate at least one or two shops. Shops sell weapons, armor, upgrades, and nonessential items (such as decorations for your private quarters aboard the ship). Buying from stores is not required, but as the old saying goes: You can't take it with you. Spend big on useful upgrades to increase your chances of success in future combat situations.

Each shop has a set inventory that remains constant throughout the entire adventure. However, the prices of goods are not set in stone. If you use Paragon or Renegade conversation options with a shopkeeper upon meeting them, you can sometimes wrangle a discount.

All store inventories are located in the appendix.

NOTE

Hacking and Decryption

When you encounter a wall safe or terminal that is locked or encrypted, you must hack it. With the exception of locked doors or computer terminals that are linked directly to the mission, you only have one shot at hacking something. You can make three mistakes while performing the hack, but if you fail out of the hack or are attacked while hacking (always make sure the coast is clear before attempting a hack), the object remains locked until the next time you visit that planet.

Hacking minigames are timed. If the treasure inside the container being hacked is credits, the amount of credits recovered starts dropping when time runs out. If the container holds an upgrade, the upgrade is locked back up when time runs out. There is an upgrade, though, that grants you extra time for hacking.

There are two hacking games. The first is a matching minigame. The circuit board has eight nodes with four matching pairs. You must match the pairs. However, when you select one-half of the match, a circle around the node starts to fill. You must select the matching node before the circle is complete. When you finish the fourth pair, the hack is complete.

The second hacking minigame requires you to match three pieces of code to replicate a security protocol. Each piece of the protocol is shown

at the top of the screen. You must scroll through a field of code snippets and select the exact match. Avoid the red squares in the field. Use the layout of orange, white, and blue lines of code to make fast matches. Many pieces of code look alike, but if you pick out a defining feature, such as a block of white code, you may have an easier time finding the match within the time limit.

COMBAT

Following the disastrous prologue, you wake up in a medical bay and must escape a frenzied attack on the facility. This mission acts as an in-game tutorial that goes over the essentials of combat, such as how to take aim at enemies, the fine art of slamming into cover to avoid incoming fire, bringing up the Power Wheel, and how to use medi-gel to heal wounded squad members.

So, instead of going over the basics of movement and shooting, let's instead focus on the assembly of a squad and how those decisions affect your success on a mission. How you lead a squad in the field is also exceedingly important. Weapon choice and power development are also critical for success.

TIP If you're badly wounded, take cover. Avoiding damage for a few seconds regenerates your health and shields.

Squad

Shepard cannot save the galaxy alone. The commander needs to recruit a coterie of the most talented individuals—personally selected by Cerberus's top man—to join the crew. Once recruits have been convinced to join the crew, they are available to use when designating an away team for a mission. You must select a squad to accompany you whenever you disembark from the *Normandy*, even if it is just to explore a city.

You must select two squad members for the away team. An outline of a person indicates the recruit has not been convinced to join you yet. You can take a quick look at each potential squad member's current weapons and powers from the squad selection screen to help you make a decision.

CAUTION If a squad member appears in red, that means the squad member is dead.

TIP As soon as new members join the team, immediately start assigning talent points you have collected to them. If you ignore this, they will go into battle unprepared and potentially drag a mission down.

Each squad member has individual strengths you must consider before finalizing an away team. Sometimes you will simply go with personal preference because it's quite difficult not to develop some level of attachment to the team members you recruit. They may have personalities that will engage you, but try to be cold and calculating when designating an away team. Use these factors to make your decision:

- **Mission Objectives and Enemies:** Some squad members have powers that are useful against specific enemies, such as AI Hacking when going into a battle with geth.
- **Shepard's Class:** Balancing against your class will create a well-rounded squad. However, consider that a squad biased toward certain strengths—guns, biotics, tech—is actually useful in certain situations.
- **Squad Member's Powers:** Expert commanders will issue orders to squad members to use their powers and not just rely on the away team's own choices. Look at the squad member's available powers and weigh whether or not you would find a personal use for them.
- **Upgrades:** There are many upgrades you can find while on missions; they affect things from shield strength to the damage done by a specific class of weapons. If you have greatly increased the damage of submachine guns, perhaps you should consider taking squad members that specialize in submachine guns to capitalize on that extra damage.

With up to 10 potential squad members (and you must recruit at least eight of them for the main plot), you can create away teams that are guaranteed to tackle any situation and come out on top.

NOTE One more thing about the powers of your team: Each squad member also has an additional power that is only unlocked after you complete their loyalty mission. You can see this power while looking at a squad member's profile, via either the private terminal on the *Normandy* or the squad option while pausing during a mission. This talent is more powerful than those the team member possesses when they are initially recruited.

Balanced Squads

Shepard's Class	Squad Member 1	Squad Member 2	Squad Description
Soldier	Jack	Tali	Jack's high-powered biotics and Tali's tech talents complement a weapons expert.
Adept	Grunt	Mordin	Your adept needs firepower and brute strength for balance. Mordin completes the squad via his tech abilities.
Engineer	Thane	Samara	You have tech expertise. What you need now is a strong biotic like Samara and a crack shot, which you find in Thane.
Vanguard	Garrus	Mordin	The biotic-combat combination of the vanguard can be complemented by the long-range specialties of Garrus and Mordin's tech.
Infiltrator	Miranda	Grunt	You have no problem taking down an enemy from a distance. You need a brute like Grunt for the close-up work and Miranda for her biotics.
Sentinel	Jacob	Grunt	Sentinels are decent with tech and biotics. Jacob's combat and biotic strengths are a good match, while Grunt's force is great for hairy situations.

Combat Squads

Shepard's Class	Squad Member 1	Squad Member 2	Squad Description
Soldier	Grunt	Jacob	Your weapons expertise mixed with Grunt's brutality and Jacob's combat readiness makes a solid combat-oriented squad.
Soldier	Grunt	Garrus	Grunt's close-up game and Garrus's long-distance killing power neatly complement each other.
Vanguard	Thane	Grunt	Vanguards have a nice split of combat and biotic powers. Grunt adds the "tank" factor this squad needs, and Thane snipes.
Infiltrator	Jacob	Grunt	Infiltrators need close-up experts like Grunt to get their hands dirty.

Biotic Squads

Shepard's Class	Squad Member 1	Squad Member 2	Squad Description
Adept	Samara	Jack	Samara and Jack are the purest biotics on the crew. Together with an adept, the trio is the most powerful biotic squad in the galaxy.
Vanguard	Samara	Miranda	The combat skills of a vanguard are complemented by Miranda's skills. Adding a pure biotic to the squad fills in any holes in the vanguard's biotic talent library.
Sentinel	Jack	Miranda	Sentinels do not have the strongest combat skills. Miranda's gunplay addresses that, while Jack's awesome biotics address any potential shortcomings.

Tech Squads

Shepard's Class	Squad Member 1	Squad Member 2	Squad Description
Engineer	Tali	Legion	This squad of hackers is brilliant against synthetics.
Sentinel	Mordin	Miranda	Miranda's biotic abilities add some versatility to this tech-heavy squad.
Infiltrator	Mordin	Legion	Legion and your infiltrator are a pair of deadly distance killers, while Mordin's tech expertise keeps the squad alive.

Jacob

Jacob is a former Alliance corsair, now in the employ of Cerberus. He is a dependable, resolute member of the team. He's good with a gun and has decent biotic skills.

- **Weapon Training:** Heavy Pistol, Shotgun
- **Standard Powers:** Cerberus Operative, Incendiary Ammo, Pull
- **Loyalty Power:** Barrier

> **TIP**
> Jacob's Incendiary Ammo power is great for taking down organic enemies. It is not at all effective against synthetics like geth.

Miranda

Miranda may have a cold exterior, but her steely resolve is critical for the success of this mission. She possesses biotic and tech powers.

- **Weapon Training:** Heavy Pistol, Submachine Gun
- **Standard Powers:** Cerberus Officer, Overload, Warp
- **Loyalty Power:** Slam

> **TIP**
> Miranda's Overload and Warp are useful for dropping enemy barriers and shields so you can use your own powers effectively.

Mordin

Mordin Solus is a brilliant salarian scientist who is needed to overcome a serious threat to the mission. His brain sometimes

gets ahead of his words, and he speaks in a halting manner. He is recruited on Omega.

- **Weapon Training:** Heavy Pistol, Submachine Gun
- **Standard Powers:** Incinerate, Cryo Freeze, Salarian Scientist
- **Loyalty Power:** Neural Shock

> Mordin's Incinerate power is exceptional at shutting down organic enemies like krogan and vorcha.
>
> **TIP**

Garrus

Shepard has a history with Garrus—they fought Saren and the Reaper called Sovereign together in the battle for the

Citadel. Garrus is an excellent shot, and his combat skills will make any squad stronger.

- **Weapon Training:** Assault Rifle, Sniper Rifle
- **Standard Powers:** Concussive Shot, Overload, Turian Rebel
- **Loyalty Power:** Armor-Piercing Ammo

> Garrus's combination of assault rifle for midrange combat and sniper rifle for killing at range makes him a strong squad member.
>
> **TIP**

Subject Zero (Jack)

Jack is considered the most powerful human biotic in the galaxy. Her violent history makes her cagey and difficult to approach, but she

loves a good fight and is tenacious in battle.

- **Weapon Training:** Heavy Pistol, Shotgun
- **Standard Powers:** Pull, Shockwave, Subject Zero
- **Loyalty Power:** Warp Ammo

> Jack's biotics are incredible, but if the enemies have shields or barriers, she struggles to make the most of her powers.
>
> **TIP**

Grunt

Grunt is a powerful krogan warrior who has little to offer in the way of tech or biotics. Instead, he brings his might

to the team, quickly becoming the go-to "tank" for combat-heavy missions.

- **Weapon Training:** Assault Rifle, Shotgun
- **Standard Powers:** Concussive Shot, Krogan Berserker, Incendiary Ammo
- **Loyalty Power:** Fortification

> Grunt is tough and resilient on his own, but if you max out the Krogan Berserker power, he is nearly unstoppable.
>
> **TIP**

Tali

The quarian Tali'Zorah is another familiar face for Shepard—they also served together in the battle against

Saren and Sovereign. Tali is a tech expert with strengths in AI programming.

- **Weapon Training:** Heavy Pistol, Shotgun
- **Standard Powers:** AI Hacking, Combat Drone, Quarian Machinist
- **Loyalty Power:** Energy Drain

> Combat drones are great for distracting enemies so the rest of the squad can clean up.
>
> **TIP**

Samara

Samara is a justicar, an asari warrior dedicated to bringing the wicked and evil to justice—and she will use extreme violence to achieve

that goal. Samara is a powerful biotic like Jack.

- **Weapon Training:** Assault Rifle, Submachine Gun
- **Standard Powers:** Throw, Pull, Asari Justicar
- **Loyalty Power:** Reave

> Biotic powers and assault rifle training are rare combos in this galaxy—use Samara well to get the best of both worlds.
>
> **TIP**

Thane

This drell assassin is one of the last recruits to join your team. Thane is a crack shot with good anti-defense measures, making him an effective crowd control agent.

- **Weapon Training:** Submachine Gun, Sniper Rifle
- **Standard Powers:** Throw, Warp, Drell Assassin
- **Loyalty Power:** Shredder Ammo

> Make Thane loyal to the team to access his Shredder Ammo. It slices through organic targets, doing extra damage.
>
> **TIP**

Legion

Legion is an unexpected member of the team (a geth working with a human for a common goal?), acquired toward the end of the main story. Legion is full of surprises, though, and becomes a valuable squad member thanks to its resilience in combat situations.

- **Weapon Training:** Assault Rifle, Sniper Rifle
- **Standard Powers:** AI Hacking, Combat Drone, Geth Infiltrator
- **Loyalty Power:** Geth Shield Boost

> Legion's shields are more powerful than yours, so it can withstand greater damage in combat and keep firing. Its AI Hacking talent is also great to use against geth, as it temporarily turns them against each other.
>
> **TIP**

There is actually one more potential squad member. Rather than spoil it up front, though, we'll introduce the mystery member in the walkthrough for the moment in the game when you can make a dramatic switch for the new squad member.

NOTE

Squad Commands

Without any direction from you, squad members will do their best in battles to help you accomplish the current mission. However, expert players will want to take a more hands-on approach with the squad, exerting greater control over weapon choice, power usage, and battlefield position.

The Power Wheel and Weapon Wheel are explained in greater detail in the "Weapons and Armor" and "Powers" sections of this chapter. However, using them on a regular basis to keep tabs on your squad will make sure they are performing at the top of their game. Tali, for example, may be fighting well in a battle against some mercenaries, but she could probably deploy combat drones more often. So, when you see a crowd of mercs gathering, drop into the Power Wheel and select the combat drone on her behalf. Tali will follow the order and you will benefit from the combat drone exactly when you want it.

Controlling the positions and targets of your squad is also critical for setting up tactics that may prove advantageous in certain circumstances. You can direct each squad member to a specific location in your line of sight. If the squad members can reach the designated spots without putting themselves in the way of a bullet, they will follow the order. You can order squad members to focus their fire on a specific target, which is useful for keeping a large enemy busy or creating a distraction.

Introduction · Training · Upgrades and Research · Walkthrough · Special Assignments · Planetary Database · Appendix

Squad Commands (continued)

Directing your squad members to designated positions is how to set up effective crossfires. Crossfires are deadly gauntlets that can trap enemies and cut them down within seconds. By directing yourself and your teammates to equal points around a target, you make it extremely difficult for the enemy to select a target. They are getting shot at from all angles. When they pick a target, they end up exposing themselves to two other fighters.

Crossfires are good for taking down enemies that are dug in, too. If you set up your squad to bear down on an enemy effectively using cover, you can keep that enemy busy while you flank to deliver the kill.

Position your squad members on either side of a chokepoint in a battlefield, such as a door or a bridge, to create an ambush for enemies. Your squad members will instinctively seek cover and pop out when an enemy approaches. If you find that enemies are not falling for the ambush, use yourself as bait. Attack from a distance and draw the enemy into your trap. When the enemy is within firing range of the ambush, your squad engages.

One more thing about squad placement: Don't ever be too proud to retreat and regroup. You will face some incredibly powerful enemies and occasionally feel in over your head. Rather than hold untenable ground and take losses that consume all of your medi-gel, order your squad to fall back from a battle. As they recover, you can decide on a new tactic for the troublesome battle.

Weapons and Armor

When a peaceful resolution to a problem cannot be reached, then you must resort to violence. There are many conventional weapons you can use in battles, but not every squad member can use all of the weapons. When you chose your class, you saw that you were limited to specific weapons (although you can acquire weapons training while on a specific mission near the halfway point of the story). Team members must follow the same rules.

There are several weapon classes available to you and your team, with at least two weapon variations in each class:

- **Assault Rifles:** These automatic weapons strike a good balance between stopping power and accuracy. Assault rifles are commonly used by soldiers, but you can train Shepard on this weapon if the commander selects a different class.

- **Heavy Pistols:** These handguns are all-purpose weapons that are effective even at long range. They are the most accurate and powerful weapons outside of sniper rifles Heavy pistol clips are small, though, and need to be reloaded often.

- **Shotguns:** Shotguns are brute force weapons that deal tremendous damage at close range. They may have a slow rate of fire, but if a shell is delivered point blank, you may need only one squeeze of the trigger.

- **Submachine Guns:** Submachine guns benefit from a fast rate of fire that can chew up a target's armor or shields. However, submachine guns are the least accurate of all weapons.

- **Sniper Rifles:** Sniper rifles combine long-range killing power with lethal accuracy. The trade-off is that they have a slower rate of fire.

- **Heavy Weapons:** If enemy strength is the question, heavy weapons are the answer. This class of weapon delivers incredible firepower, but ammo is very limited. You must constantly seek out power cells to replenish heavy weapons.

> **CAUTION**
> You can take only one heavy weapon on a mission. Visit the *Normandy* armory to choose your loadout.

> **NOTE**
> Rapid-fire guns such as submachine guns and assault rifles are less accurate than other weapons, but reliably inflict damage.

Call up the Weapon Wheel to select the current weapons for you and your squad. Monitor the situation and adjust for the enemy.

All weapons can overheat after firing multiple times. When a weapon overheats, you must switch to another or rely on alternative attacks, such as biotic powers or melee strikes. There is a universal thermal clip that all weapons except heavy weapons use. You will spot thermal clips on your missions on shelves or desks—look for the reflection of the clip in the light to easily spot them in intense situations. Fallen enemies also drop thermal clips. When you pick up a thermal clip, all weapons are partially replenished, not just the weapon you are holding.

Introduction

Training

Upgrades and Research

Walkthrough

Special Assignments

Planetary Database

Appendix

Aside from thermal clips, some squad members, including you, have special ammunition they can use that has an added benefit, such as fire damage, or is powerful against a specific type of enemy. Here are the six different ammunition types you can use:

- **Armor-Piercing Ammo:** This round cuts through armor so you can deliver the killing shot.

- **Cryo Ammo:** Multiple shots with cryo ammo slowly freeze an enemy. Frozen enemies take more physics damage from melee attacks, but they cannot take more damage from weapon attacks or most powers.

- **Incendiary Ammo:** Incendiary ammo catches a target on fire, doing damage beyond the initial shot. Synthetic enemies such as mechs do not suffer from the extra effects of incendiary ammo.

- **Disruptor Ammo:** This class of ammunition is strong against shields and synthetic enemies, such as mechs and geth.

- **Shredder Ammo:** Shredder ammunition rips through organic enemies, doing extra damage. No extra damage is done against synthetics.

- **Warp Ammo:** Warp ammo transforms biotic energy into heavier damage against barriers and armor.

TIP

If it's available to your squad, always use special ammo. There is no cost and the extra damage to specific targets is always beneficial.

TIP

Cryo ammo is truly deadly in the right hands. If you freeze an enemy and rush in close to deliver a smashing attack (the Charge power is perfect in this situation), you can thin a herd within seconds.

NOTE

You can upgrade many of your weapons, so do not consider them static. Consult the upgrade tables in the "Upgrades and Research Projects" chapter to chart the effects of upgrades and pursue those that best serve your class and your squad.

NOTE

Do not underestimate the usefulness of a melee attack. If enemies get close, bash them with your elbow or shoulder to push them back. As they reel from the attack, unload a clip into them or hit them with a power.

Arsenal

Assault Rifles

Weapon	Description	Used By
M-8 Avenger Assault Rifle	Accurate when fired in short bursts, and deadly when fired on full auto. Effective against shields, armor, and biotic barriers.	Soldiers, Legion, Samara, Grunt, Garrus
M-15 Vindicator Battle Rifle	Fires five-round highly accurate bursts, and can be pulsed for rapid fire. Deadly at any range, and effective against armor, shields, and biotic barriers.	Soldiers, Legion, Samara, Grunt, Garrus
M-76 Revenant Machine Gun	Unleashes a storm of deadly high-velocity slugs. Less accurate than an assault rifle, but deals much more damage.	Soldiers
Geth Pulse Rifle	Fires a rapid stream of high-energy phasic slugs. Very effective against shields and biotic barriers.	Soldiers, Legion, Samara, Grunt, Garrus

Heavy Weapons

Weapon	Description	Used By	Research Project?	Tip
M-100 Grenade Launcher	Rapid-fire grenade launcher. Effective against armor, shields, and biotic barriers.	Shepard (any class)	No	Fire at your target's feet for maximum impact.
ML-77 Missile Launcher	Rapid-fire missile launcher with seeking projectiles. Effective against armor, shields, and biotic barriers.	Shepard (any class)	Yes	Can be fired around corners; arc your shots!
M-622 Avalanche	Fires a freezing blast that hits targets within a five-meter radius. Effective against armor, shields, and biotic barriers.	Shepard (any class)	Yes	Frozen enemies take more damage, so follow up with a power or direct your teammates to attack.
M-920 Cain	High damage with a large area of effect. Very effective against armor, shields, and barriers.	Shepard (any class)	Yes	Very powerful, but uses a lot of ammo with each shot. Reserve for tough boss battles.
Collector Particle Beam	High-damage particle beam with laser-like accuracy. Very effective against armor, shields, and barriers.	Shepard (any class)	No	Find this weapon in the Horizon mission.

Heavy Pistols

Weapon	Description	Used By
M-3 Predator Heavy Pistol	Reliable, accurate sidearm. Effective against armor. Weak against shields and biotic barriers.	Infiltrators, vanguards, adepts, engineers, sentinels, Jacob, Miranda, Tali, Mordin, Jack
M-6 Carnifex Hand Cannon	Highly accurate and lethal sidearm. Effective against armor but weak against shields and biotic barriers.	Infiltrators, vanguards, adepts, engineers, sentinels, Jacob, Miranda, Tali, Mordin, Jack

Shotguns

Weapon	Description	Used By
M-23 Katana Shotgun	Common military shotgun. Deadly at short range, but ineffective at long range. Very effective against shields and biotic barriers, but weak against armor.	Soldiers, vanguards, Jacob, Tali, Jack, Grunt
M-27 Scimitar Assault Shotgun	Rapid-fire shotgun. Deadly at short range. Ineffective at long range. Effective against shields and biotic barriers. Weak against armor.	Soldiers, vanguards, Jacob, Tali, Jack, Grunt
M-300 Claymore Heavy Shotgun	Rare krogan shotgun. Deals high damage at short range. Less effective at long range. Effective against armor, shields, and biotic barriers.	Soldiers, vanguards, Grunt

Sniper Rifles

Weapon	Description	Used By
M-92 Mantis Sniper Rifle	Powerful sniper rifle. Accurate at long range, but has a slow rate of fire. Very effective against armor, but weaker against shields and biotic barriers.	Soldiers, infiltrators, Legion, Garrus, Thane
M-97 Viper Sniper Rifle	Accurate and deadly at long range. Highly effective against armor. Somewhat effective against shields and biotic barriers.	Soldiers, infiltrators, Legion, Garrus, Thane
M-98 Widow Anti-Material Rifle	Deadly accurate anti-material rifle. Especially effective against armor, but also against shields and biotic barriers.	Soldiers, infiltrators, Legion

Submachine Guns

Weapon	Description	Used By
M-4 Shuriken Machine Pistol	Fires three-round bursts. Very effective against shields and biotic barriers. Weak against armor.	Infiltrators, vanguards, adepts, engineers, sentinels, Miranda, Mordin, Samara, Thane
M-9 Tempest Submachine Gun	This submachine gun is deadly at short range but inaccurate at long range, effective against shields and biotic barriers but weak against armor.	Infiltrators, vanguards, adepts, engineers, sentinels, Miranda, Mordin, Samara, Thane

Armor

When you begin your mission, you are given standard-issue Cerberus armor. While it's effective in battle, there are better pieces of armor you can acquire while traveling across the galaxy. Each piece of armor, such as a helmet or gauntlets, offers a special benefit. These benefits include special protection from incoming fire, increased accuracy for headshots, or extra health. The effects of the armor are only available when that piece of armor is in use. You may not stack multiple pieces of armor in the same category; for example, you cannot wear two chest plates at the same time.

> You buy armor only for Shepard. You do not need to purchase armor for your squad.
>
> **NOTE**

> Armor pieces can be used by any class.
>
> **TIP**

Use the locker in your private quarters aboard the Normandy to change out your armor after acquiring new pieces.

Here is a full list of armor options available to you, including the effects of each piece of armor:

Helmet

Armor Piece	Effect
Death Mask	Increases negotiation success chance by 10%.
N7 Breather Helmet	Increases health by 5%.
N7 Helmet	Increases health by 5%.
N7 Visor	Increases headshot damage by 10%.

Chest

Armor Piece	Effect
Aegis Vest	Increases health by 5%.
Capacitor Chestplate	Reduces shield delay by 10%.
N7 Chestplate	Increases power damage by 3%.
Shield Harness	Increases shields by 5%.

Shoulders

Armor Piece	Effect
Amplifier Plates	Increases power damage by 5%.
Asymmetric Defense Layer	Increases health by 5%.
N7 Shoulder Guards	Increases weapon damage by 3%.
Strength Boost Pads	Increases melee damage by 25%

Arms

Armor Piece	Effect
Heavy Damping Gauntlets	Increases shields by 5%.
N7 Gauntlets	Increases health by 3%.
Off-Hand Ammo Pack	Increases spare ammo capacity by 10%.
Stabilizing Gauntlets	Increases weapon damage by 5%.

Legs

Armor Piece	Effect
Life Support Webbing	Increases health by 10%.
N7 Greaves	Increases shield strength by 3%.
Stimulator Conduits	Increases storm speed by 10%.

Powers

Powers are special skills that augment the character's area of expertise, such as biotic attacks or combat talents. These powers are used in battles to destroy the enemy or provide defense for the squad. All powers have four levels of development. You spend squad points to develop powers. The more you develop a power, the more effective it is.

When you max out a power to level 4, you may then "evolve it" to obtain an extra benefit. To do this, you must choose between two evolutionary options that add even greater effect to the power. For example, when you master the Adrenaline Rush power, you must choose between Hardened and Heightened. The Hardened Adrenaline Rush reduces damage taken while the power is engaged, while Heightened boosts combat awareness to the point where enemies seem temporarily frozen in time. Once the evolution of a power is selected, there is no going back. You may not re-evolve a power.

> You are much better served by maximizing a few powers rather than spreading your squad points across multiple powers. Mastering a power grants awesome extra benefits. Plus, by mastering a talent, you make it much easier to create balanced squads that do not have talent overlaps.
>
> **TIP**

Use the Power Wheel to direct your squad mates to use their powers. While the Power Wheel is active, the

action stops. You can still look around, though, which allows you to pick a target for an aggressive power, such as Pull or Overload.

> Be sure to map your powers to hot buttons so you can quickly access them in battle without having to bring up the Power Wheel.
>
> **TIP**

> Most powers have cooldown periods between use. When a power is in cooldown, the icon on the Power Wheel is dark. The closer you are to being able to use that power again, the more the icon fills back up. Using any power makes all your other powers unavailable during the brief cooldown period.
>
> **CAUTION**

Every single power you can acquire, develop, and master is listed in the following charts. Each chart details who may use a power, the benefits of developing the power, and the final evolution of the power.

Class

Class powers are associated with each specific class. Only somebody within that class, such as a vanguard or adept, can develop this power. These powers are designed to increase the hero's mastery of the class talents, such as the infiltrator power, Operative. Operatives can have more health, inflict more weapon damage, and need less cooldown time for powers.

> Passive class powers improve combat capabilities and increase the rate at which you gain Paragon and Renegade points.
>
> **NOTE**

Adept							
Power	Description	Evolution 1	Evolution 1 Description	Evolution 2	Evolution 2 Description	Tip	
Singularity	A dark energy sphere dangles your enemies helplessly, leaving them wide open to attack.	Heavy Singularity	Your singularity sphere can hold numerous enemies helpless for a long period.	Wide Singularity	The radius of your singularity sphere's gravitational pull increases.	Park your singularity where you think reinforcements will come from.	
Biotic Mastery	Unleashes your biotic power faster, quicker, and with more intensity.	Bastion	All your powers last longer and take less time to recharge. Paragon/Renegade scores increase.	Nemesis	Your biotic powers do more damage and take less time to recharge.	Points in this power are required to access the most critical Paragon and Renegade conversation options in the game.	

Engineer							
Power	Description	Evolution 1	Evolution 1 Description	Evolution 2	Evolution 2 Description	Tip	
Combat Drone	Command your very own battle robot.	Attack Drone	You have upgraded the combat drone so its electric shock damages health, armor, and biotic barriers.	Explosive Drone	Your combat drone is rigged to explode when destroyed, pulsing energy that inflicts high damage on all nearby enemies.	Keep your combat drone up at all times; it's great for distracting enemies.	
Tech Mastery	Makes your creative powers faster, flashier, and more frequent.	Operative	Specializing in combat operations, you reduce recharge time on all powers and receive a bonus to their damage.	Mechanic	Your powers are incredibly efficient. They recharge faster and last longer. Your Paragon and Renegade scores receive their final bonus.	Points in this power are required to access the most critical Paragon and Renegade conversation options in the game.	

Infiltrator

Power	Description	Evolution 1	Evolution 1 Description	Evolution 2	Evolution 2 Description	Tip
Tactical Cloak	To your enemies, you're invisible.	Assassi-nation Cloak	You are a master of the hidden strike, gaining a huge bonus to damage if you attack while cloaked.	Enhanced Cloak	You have modified your cloak's power cells to stay hidden for extended periods, useful for bypassing enemies or setting up a strike.	Use this power defensively. Keep this power available for emergencies and you'll be incredibly hard to kill.
Operative	Your weapon damage is more punishing and frequent, and targeting enemies is easier.	Assassin	Your focus in sniper zoom is enhanced, and you receive a damage bonus to all weapons and powers.	Agent	Your endurance and mental fortitude reduce the recharge time of powers and give a bonus to their duration. Your Paragon and Renegade scores reach their highest level.	Want to be a master sniper? This power is a must; it makes it much easier to hit enemies.

Sentinel

Power	Description	Evolution 1	Evolution 1 Description	Evolution 2	Evolution 2 Description	Tip
Defender	Fine-tunes your brain, making your powers more potent and efficient.	Guardian	You excel under stress, reducing your recharge time as far as it will go, and your forceful personality takes your Paragon and Renegade scores to the maximum level.	Raider	You specialize in using your engineering and biotics as weapons, reducing recharge time a small amount further and giving a bonus to your powers' damage.	Points in this power are required to access the most critical Paragon and Renegade conversation options in the game.
Tech Armor	Energy-charged armor boosts your shields and detonates a damaging energy wave when destroyed.	Assault Armor	The armor is now rigged for maximum pulse when it is destroyed, increasing its damage, force, and radius. In case any enemies still survive, it gives an additional shield boost after the detonation.	Power Armor	The armor's deflection capability is now at maximum, and the armor can channel its energy into biotic amps and weapons, increasing the damage of all your powers.	Keep this power active all of the time and you'll be incredibly hard to kill.

Soldier

Power	Description	Evolution 1	Evolution 1 Description	Evolution 2	Evolution 2 Description	Tip
Adrenaline Rush	Hyper-accelerates your reflexes, giving you time to line up the perfect shot.	Hardened Adrenaline Rush	Your endorphins block out pain and trauma in addition to speeding your reaction time. Health damage is reduced for the power's duration.	Heightened Adrenaline Rush	Your reaction time is the stuff of legends. When you are "on," enemies seem to stand still.	Your shots do more damage when you use Adrenaline Rush; go for an accurate headshot for an easy kill.
Concussive Shot	A massive blast that propels enemies with bone-crushing force.	Heavy Concussive Shot	A more powerful concussive blast that knocks down enemies.	Concussive Blast	High-energy explosive charges give your shot an impact radius large enough to knock down multiple enemies.	Blast away your enemy's shields with your weapon, then take them down with concussive shot.
Combat Mastery	Makes you tougher, stronger, faster, and more charismatic.	Commando	Your killing intent is ever-present, increasing weapon damage and storm speed, and giving a damage bonus to powers.	Shock Trooper	Your survival instinct grants you an intense concentration that further increases weapon damage and storm speed, and gives a duration bonus to powers.	Points in this power are required to access the most critical Paragon and Renegade conversation options in the game.

Vanguard

Power	Description	Evolution 1	Evolution 1 Description	Evolution 2	Evolution 2 Description	Tip
Charge	Using a damaging shockwave, ram into an enemy with incredible force.	Heavy Charge	Your biotic focus is so intense that not only does the charge flatten enemies, but also your reaction speed is increased, slowing the world around you as you come out of the charge.	Area Charge	Your mass effect field now bursts on impact, sending out energy that can damage multiple opponents and knock them off their feet.	Use Charge defensively to recharge your barrier, or to charge away from a dangerous enemy.
Assault Mastery	Be faster, fiercer, and more powerful on the battlefield.	Destroyer	Your weapon inflicts even more damage, and you receive a damage bonus to biotic powers.	Champion	Your staying power lets you survive marathons of combat. Power-recharging time and Paragon and Renegade scores are improved still further, and you receive a bonus to biotic power duration.	Points in this power are required to access the most critical Paragon and Renegade conversation options in the game.

Combat

Combat powers are advanced military training that helps warriors focus their minds in battle situations, use special ammunition, and increase damage.

Power	Description	Evolution 1	Evolution 1 Description	Evolution 2	Evolution 2 Description	Used By	Tip
Incendiary Ammo	Burns through armor, sets enemies on fire, and damages health.	Inferno Ammo	An explosive charge spreads the ammunition's payload on impact, potentially igniting the target and all nearby enemies.	Squad Incendiary Ammo	Your entire squad gains the effect of your incendiaries, allowing you to spread pain and panic in a very literal crossfire.	Vanguards, soldiers, Jacob	Stops krogan and vorcha from regenerating.
Cryo Ammo	Freezes enemies, allowing you to shatter them with gunfire or biotics.	Improved Cryo Ammo	The apex of cryogenic rounds, this ammunition freezes targets more frequently and for a longer duration.	Squad Cryo Ammo	Your entire squad gains the cryo ammo's effects, letting you incapacitate large groups or relentlessly hammer one target.	Vanguards, soldiers	This is a good general-use power; freezing an enemy is always useful.
Concussive Shot	A massive blast that propels enemies with bone-crushing force.	Heavy Concussive Shot	A massive blast that propels enemies with bone-crushing force.	Concussive Blast	High-energy explosive charges give your shot an impact radius large enough to knock down multiple enemies.	Soldiers, Garrus, Grunt	Knock enemies off of ledges with Concussive Shot.
Disruptor Ammo	Rips through shields and shreds synthetic targets.	Heavy Disruptor Ammo	This ammunition's electro-magnetic properties can cause synthetics to critically overload and explode.	Squad Disruptor Ammo	Your entire squad gains the Disruptor Ammo's effects, allowing you to catch synthetics in deadly crossfires.	Soldiers, infiltrators	Good against synthetic enemies and enemies with shields.

Biotic

Biotic powers are generated through bio-amp technology that allows the user to the generate mass effect fields. By manipulating mass effect fields, biotic users can move enemies independent of gravity, tear enemies to pieces with the powerful Singularity attack, and generate protective barriers.

> Use biotic attacks in conjunction with gunplay. For example, if you have Pull, lift enemies into the air and then shoot them to either deplete their health or push them over an empty space. When Pull wears off, the enemy falls into the void.
>
> **TIP**

> Throw and Concussive Shot are more effective on a weightless target; for maximum effect, use Pull on your enemy first.
>
> **TIP**

Arc powers around obstacles to hit enemies trying to hide from you. Just target the enemy (you will see its name on-screen) and then deploy the power. With practice, you can fire around corners or over cover. Arcing powers around obstacles is a great way to pull an enemy out of cover!

Power	Description	Evolution 1	Evolution 1 Description	Evolution 2	Evolution 2 Description	Used By	Tip
Throw	Hurls enemies through the air using a powerful biotic field.	Heavy Throw	Fling a single enemy with unparalleled momentum, smashing it against walls with hurricane force.	Throw Field	Your mastery of biotic throws allows you to hurl multiple targets into the air simultaneously.	Adepts, sentinels, Samara, Thane	Throw enemies off of cliffs or ledges for an instant kill.
Warp	Rips enemies apart at the molecular level and stops health regeneration. Effective against armor and biotic barriers.	Heavy Warp	Your Warp damage is hugely increased.	Unstable Warp	Increases the blast radius when Warp detonates biotic effects.	Adepts, sentinels, Miranda, Thane	Warp is super-effective versus armor and barriers.
Pull	Levitates enemies, rendering them helpless while they drift toward you.	Heavy Pull	Your levitational abilities keep your target suspended longer.	Pull Field	Affects all nearby targets, suspending entire groups in the air.	Adepts, vanguards, Jack, Jacob, Samara	Aim to the side of an enemy to pull your target off a cliff or ledge.
Shockwave	Biotic shockwaves topple enemies in your path.	Heavy Shockwave	Your Shockwave's power strengthens to become a biotic freight train, swatting aside everything in a long path.	Improved Shockwave	Your Shockwave now has a wide impact radius, taking out everything in a broad strip in front of you.	Adepts, vanguards, Jack	Use shockwave on close enemies and you will get devastating results.

Introduction

Training

Upgrades and Research

Walkthrough

Special Assignments

Planetary Database

Appendix

Tech

Tech powers are different from biotics. These powers include boosting shields, hacking AI, and engaging a tactical cloaking mechanism.

Power	Description	Evolution 1	Evolution 1 Description	Evolution 2	Evolution 2 Description	Used By	Tip
Incinerate	Exploding flame damages the health and armor of anyone nearby.	Heavy Incinerate	This advanced plasma round melts or burns nearly anything it hits.	Incineration Blast	The splash zone on this plasma round is increased, allowing you to scorch multiple targets.	Infiltrators, engineers, Mordin	Organic enemies will panic if you set them on fire.
AI Hacking	Turns synthetic enemies (mechs, geth) against their own allies.	Improved AI Hacking	Your AI Hacking provides the ultimate in shield strength and maintains it for a very long hack duration.	Area AI Hacking	Your wireless signal is boosted in strength, affecting a wide area to hack multiple robots.	Infiltrators, engineers, Legion, Tali	When you hack an enemy you also put a defensive shield on it, so its friends can't dispatch it quickly.
Overload	Massive energy blasts overpower shields and synthetic enemies.	Heavy Overload	Your pulse now damages synthetic enemies so brutally that they explode on "death."	Area Overload	You have increased your pulse's strength to cover a wide area, making it easy to hit multiple targets.	Engineers, sentinels, Garrus, Miranda	Does massive damage against shields and synthetic enemies.
Combat Drone	Command your very own battle robot.	Attack Drone	You have upgraded the combat drone so its electric shock damages health, armor, and biotic barriers.	Explosive Drone	Your combat drone is rigged to explode when destroyed, pulsing energy that inflicts high damage on all nearby enemies.	Engineers, Legion, Tali	Target a specific enemy when you cast a combat drone and it will attack that enemy.
Cryo Blast	Snap-freezes your targets.	Full Cryo Blast	The blast potency and freeze duration is much longer than the initial blast.	Deep Cryo Blast	This cryo weapon's fluid dynamics are engineered to maximize your chances of freezing multiple targets in the immediate area of the initial blast.	Engineers, Sentinels, Mordin	Frozen enemies are more vulnerable to damage.

Squad Member

Most squad member powers are specific to one member of the team. Shepard can learn certain active squad powers (such as Barrier or Slam) through research.

Jacob						
Power	Description	Evolution 1	Evolution 1 Description	Evolution 2	Evolution 2 Description	Tip
Barrier	Creates a shield that soaks up huge amounts of damage.	Heavy Barrier	Your barrier is nearly impenetrable, shrugging off even heavy weapons.	Improved Barrier	Your barrier lasts a few critical seconds longer.	Heavy Barrier is great in tough boss battles.
Cerberus Operative	Boosts Jacob's combat skills, weapon damage, and health	Cerberus Veteran	Jacob's experience surviving gunshot wounds and other traumas increases Jacob's health.	Cerberus Specialist	Jacob's expertise in neutralizing hostiles increases his weapon damage.	Using too much medi-gel on Jacob? Choose the Cerberus Veteran evolution.

Miranda						
Power	Description	Evolution 1	Evolution 1 Description	Evolution 2	Evolution 2 Description	Tip
Cerberus Officer	Hones Miranda's combat skills, weapon damage, and health. The entire squad receives a combat bonus.	Cerberus Leader	Miranda's coordination of the fire team gives an increased bonus to squad weapon damage.	Cerberus Tactician	Miranda's leadership tactics leave no one behind, giving an increased bonus to squad health.	Turn Miranda into a team player with the Tactician evolution.
Slam	A biotic body-slam that inflicts massive damage.	Heavy Slam	Miranda's Slam force is prodigious and causes grievous bodily harm.	Crippling Slam	Miranda forgos brute force and instead Slams the target on its most vulnerable points, incapacitating the opponent for some time after impact.	All classes can actually learn this power.

Mordin

Power	Description	Evolution 1	Evolution 1 Description	Evolution 2	Evolution 2 Description	Tip
Neural Shock	Cripple an organic enemy with pain.	Heavy Neural Shock	Mordin's shock strength on a single target is so severe that multiple shocks can be chained together to deny an enemy any chance of action.	Neural Shockwave	Mordin's shock capacitors are greatly increased, allowing a wide area of effect to hit multiple targets.	All classes can learn this power.
Salarian Scientist	Strengthens Mordin's combat skills, weapon damage, health, and shields.	Salarian Genius	Mordin's technical breakthroughs further increase the strength of his shields.	Salarian Savant	Mordin's studies of ballistics, physics, and shock trauma increase his weapon damage.	Is Mordin using up medi-gel? Evolve to Salarian Genius to boost his shields.

Garrus

Power	Description	Evolution 1	Evolution 1 Description	Evolution 2	Evolution 2 Description	Tip
Armor-Piercing Ammo	Increases damage to armor and health.	Tungsten Ammo	Advanced tungsten carbide rounds in discarding sabots increase the damage done by Armor-Piercing Ammo.	Squad Armor-Piercing Ammo	Time spent custom gunsmithing allows the entire squad to gain the effects of Armor-Piercing Ammo.	Choose the group version of this power if you don't have any weapon powers, and you can use this on your own weapons!
Turian Rebel	Enhances Garrus's combat skills, weapon damage, and health. Makes his powers more damaging.	Turian Renegade	If it can be fired, Garrus knows how to use it. His weapon and power damage increase dramatically.	Turian Survivor	Long hours alone against impossible odds have conditioned Garrus's health and kept his powers sharp.	If Garrus falls often, use Turian Survivor to give his health an extra boost.

Grunt

Power	Description	Evolution 1	Evolution 1 Description	Evolution 2	Evolution 2 Description	Tip
Krogan Berserker	Enhances Grunt's weapon damage and health. Gives him krogan health regeneration.	Krogan Pureblood	Grunt's mastery of his blood rage increases his already fantastic regeneration rate, letting him survive wounds that would kill other krogan.	Krogan Warlord	Grunt can go berserk without losing his lethal focus, increasing his weapon damage.	Evolve Krogan Berserker and Grunt will be nearly unstoppable.
Fortification	A brief but massive boost to Grunt's armor.	Improved Fortification	The armor is more resilient and reacts better to multiple hits, increasing its duration.	Heavy Fortification	By altering the chemistry of the prime ingredients of the armor, it now absorbs even more damage.	Heavy Fortification boosts Grunt's armor rating.

Jack

Power	Description	Evolution 1	Evolution 1 Description	Evolution 2	Evolution 2 Description	Tip
Warp Ammo	Transforms absorbed biotic energy into heavier damage against health, armor, and biotic barriers.	Heavy Warp Ammo	Further increases damage done by warp ammo, which now tears flesh and metal like a miniature disruptor torpedo. Effective against barriers.	Squad Warp Ammo	In an impressive feat of sustained biotic concentration, you can grant the effects of Warp Ammo to the entire squad.	Choose the group version of this power to share its effects with the entire squad.
Subject Zero	Enhances Jack's weapon damage and health. Improves her power recharge time.	Primal Adept	Jack can push her biotic abilities to the limit, greatly reducing the recharge time of her powers.	Primal Vanguard	Jack focuses her ruthless energy into combat, heightening her weapon damage.	Jack is a powerful biotic, but with Primal Adept, she's even more of a biotic killer.

Tali

Power	Description	Evolution 1	Evolution 1 Description	Evolution 2	Evolution 2 Description	Tip
Energy Drain	Drains enemies' shields in order to boost your own shields.	Heavy Energy Drain	Your energy drain is much more disruptive to synthetics and shields, causing unparalleled damage.	Area Drain	You can greatly widen your energy drain's radius to easily hit multiple targets.	Area Drain is better suited for crowd control situations. Against lone targets, it is not as powerful.
Quarian Machinist	Sharpens Tali's combat skills and weapon damage. Lengthens her power duration.	Quarian Engineer	Tali is operating at peak efficiency, increasing the duration of her powers. Modest cybernetics and immuno-enhancers increase her health.	Quarian Mechanic	Tali's expertise in engineering firearms of all kinds increases her weapon damage. Modest cybernetics and immuno-enhancers increase her health.	Tali's great with a submachine gun. She'd be even better with Quarian Mechanic.

Introduction

Training

Upgrades and Research

Walkthrough

Special Assignments

Planetary Database

Appendix

Samara

Power	Description	Evolution 1	Evolution 1 Description	Evolution 2	Evolution 2 Description	Tip
Reave	Damages the nervous or synthetic system to prevent target from healing. Restores the biotic's health when power is used against organics.	Heavy Reave	The biotic focuses on snuffing out a single target's life, increasing the Reave's strength, duration, and damage.	Area Reave	The biotic becomes a vortex of life, increasing the Reave's radius to affect multiple targets.	Don't even bother using Reave against geth or mechs.
Asari Justicar	Increases Samara's combat skills, weapon damage, and health. Improves her power recharge time.	Sapiens Justicar	Samara's biotic abilities now rival those of an asari matriarch, further reducing the recharge time of her powers.	Caedo Justicar	Samara's time is spent honing her lethal skills, increasing her weapon damage.	Evolve to Sapiens Justicar to unleash more biotic powers more often.

Thane

Power	Description	Evolution 1	Evolution 1 Description	Evolution 2	Evolution 2 Description	Tip
Drell Assassin	Increases Thane's combat skills, weapon damage, and health.	Drell Marksman	Thane's anatomical expertise and unerring aim increase his weapon damage beyond its already extraordinary level.	Drell Veteran	Thane's experience surviving life-threatening wounds increases his effective health.	Combine Drell Marksman with Heavy Shredder Ammo to create an ultimate warrior.
Shredder Ammo	Increases damage to health of organic targets.	Heavy Shredder Ammo	Your ammo now delivers the ultimate in grievous wounds to fleshy targets.	Squad Shredder Ammo	The entire squad now gains the effects of Shredder Ammo, making short work of organic opponents.	This is a great power to share with the whole squad.

Legion

Power	Description	Evolution 1	Evolution 1 Description	Evolution 2	Evolution 2 Description	Tip
Geth Shield Boost	Co-opt geth shield technology to deflect attack damage.	Heavy Geth Shield Boost	The shield's increased strength enables it to absorb impacts from even heavy weapons.	Improved Geth Shield Boost	Re-routing the shield generator into your weapons' power source can boost their damage for the duration of the shield.	Power up Legion's weapons with Improved Geth Shield Boost.
Geth Infiltrator	Augments Legion's combat skills and weapon damage. Improves its power recharge time.	Geth Assassin	Legion has become an expert at disassembling organics and synthetics alike, increasing Legion's weapon damage.	Geth Trooper	Legion has created redundant systems for its critical functions, increasing its health.	Save on medi-gel by evolving into Geth Trooper.

Enemies

Naturally, not every being you encounter in the galaxy greets you with an open hand. Those aligned with evil will attack at a moment's notice, from lowly mercenaries to advanced robots programmed to kill on sight. When you do find yourself in a combat situation, your second-best weapon is knowledge (it's hard to argue that the gun at your side is not the best). Profiles of the enemies you encounter throughout your adventure are placed throughout the walkthrough section of this guide so you know how to deal with them when you meet them for the first time.

However, there is a standardized approach for detailing your enemies found in each profile. Each enemy profile includes listings for the foe's carried weapon and any special powers or defenses. The profile also lists a classification for the enemy so you have intel on how much resistance to expect from the target.

- Minion: A low-level enemy with average intelligence.
- Elite: An intelligent enemy with good attack strength and use of powers.
- Sub-boss: A very intelligent enemy with good defenses, powerful weapons, and aggressive use of powers.

When you target an enemy, you immediately see the current condition of its defenses beneath its name. This information is located along the top of the screen. The base of the enemy information is its health, which is indicated by a red bar. If the enemy has shields, armor, or barriers, meters for those defenses appear over the health bar.

Enemy Health: Health is the baseline of enemy vitality. Once health has been reduced to zero, the target dies.

Enemy Armor: Enemy armor is shown with an orange bar. Armor can be removed by shooting the enemy or using powers on it, even if the power itself does not have the desired effect on the target. The best powers for breaking through armor are Warp and Incinerate. Heavy pistols, sniper rifles, and assault rifles are good for depleting armor, especially if equipped with incendiary ammo.

Enemy Shields: Tech-based shields are displayed as a blue bar. Like armor, shields prevent most powers from having the desired effect, but casting a power on a shielded enemy still does damage to the shields. The best weapons to use against shields are rapid-fire ones, such as the submachine gun or assault rifle. Disruptor ammo is effective against shields, and the Overload power can dismantle a shield.

Enemy Barrier: Biotic-based barriers are noted with purple bars. You can weaken a barrier by shooting it or casting a power on it, although the barrier will thwart the main effect of the power. The best weapons against barriers are submachine guns, shotguns, and assault rifles. Concussive Shot and Warp are useful against barriers, too.

> Not all enemies have health bars. Enemies that are defeated by depleting their armor have the armor bar at the base of their defense information.
>
> **NOTE**

> Some enemies can replenish lost health, shields, and barriers. Krogan and vorcha enemies have regenerative health. If you leave them with even a sliver of health, they can take cover and replenish their health. Enemies with tech or biotic skills, such as mercenary engineers, can replenish depleted shields or barriers if they are allowed to fall back and recover.
>
> **CAUTION**

> Enemy engineers use combat drones and powers to attack from afar.
>
> **TIP**

Bonus Power

Each time you successfully complete a loyalty mission, your newly loyal squad member will earn a loyalty power, and you will earn a loyalty Achievement. The loyalty Achievements you earn will grant you a special option if you replay the game. After completing the character creation using a new or imported character, you will be able to select a single bonus power for Commander Shepard before any experience has been gained. Here is the full list of bonus powers you may choose from and the Achievement you must earn to make that power available:

Possible Bonus Powers	
Power	Related Achievement
Armor-Piercing Ammo	Fade Away
Barrier	Ghost of the Father
Dominate	???
Energy Drain	Treason
Fortification	Battlemaster
Geth Shield Boost	A House Divided
Neural Shock	The Cure
Reave	Doppelganger
Shredder Ammo	Cat's in the Cradle
Slam	The Prodigal
Warp Ammo	Catharsis

A full explanation of each power is found in the "Squad Powers" table in this chapter.

> You don't have to finish the entire game to access bonus powers. As soon as you earn one of the loyalty Achievements, research Advanced Training and you will get a bonus power.
>
> **TIP**

Introduction

Training

Upgrades and Research

Walkthrough

Special Assignments

Planetary Database

Appendix

UPGRADES AND RESEARCH PROJECTS

Commander Shepard can improve the mission's chances for success by pursuing more than just weapons and powers. Upgrading the squad's weapons and armor, building special prototype upgrades, and pursuing new technology via research projects is essential for keeping the squad ready for the growing threats in the galaxy.

> **TIP**
> Upgrading the *Normandy* will improve Shepard's chance of surviving his final mission.

There are two categories of upgrades and improvements that Shepard must keep track of: upgrades and research projects. These are intertwined. Many research projects require that you already possess a specific upgrade that you acquired in the field or purchased from a shop. For example, you won't be able to access the Tungsten Jacket research project until you have upgraded your assault rifle to Damage Level 2.

UPGRADING TECHNOLOGY

Upgrades make your equipment and abilities more powerful. There are three ways to acquire upgrades: Spend credits to purchase them in stores. Find them during missions by scanning technology with the omni-tool. Or, complete research projects.

Almost all upgrades have multiple levels. The benefits of upgrades are largely multiplicative. When Shepard discovers the first biotic damage upgrade, it offers 10 percent additional damage from biotic attacks at level 1. Acquiring level 3 increases the additional damage to 30 percent.

You can keep track of all acquired upgrades in the lab on the *Normandy*, which is available once you convince the professor to join your team. Shepard's private terminal in the CIC or inside the commander's personal quarters charts all of the upgrades acquired, and can help reveal deficiencies. Using the information provided by the terminal (and these upgrade charts), you can make educated moves toward gathering more upgrades, which in turn can affect which research projects you pursue.

> **NOTE**
> Check the inventories of shops in the appendix to locate where you can purchase many upgrades.

Research Projects

As soon as you have located and recruited the professor, Mordin Solus, you can begin discovering research projects. Research projects consist of everything from new weapons, such as the cryo blaster, to the Microfiber Weave upgrade, which increases the ferocity of Shepard's melee attacks.

> **NOTE**
> Not all research projects are immediately available, though. As you finish missions, new research projects open up in the lab.

The most powerful upgrades in the game are built in the lab, and become available to you when you acquire enough weaker upgrades. For example, purchasing or researching assault rifle upgrades will unlock research projects for powerful addtional assault rifle upgrades.

Discover research projects by scanning unique technology (such as computer terminals or discarded weapons) on missions. Scanning this technology with the omni-tool automatically sends data back to the *Normandy* for analysis. Once analysis is complete, research projects become available; you can view your research projects at the research computer in the *Normandy*'s lab.

In the lab, spend minerals to turn research projects into upgrades. Minerals can be found in storage crates while on a mission or through mining operations via probes.

> **NOTE**
> Be sure to reference the "Planetary Database" chapter to see which worlds are more likely to have the best element deposits.

> **TIP**
> As soon as a weapon, armor, or prototype upgrade is acquired, the entire squad immediately benefits from it.

Sometimes when you obtain an upgrade, your scientists will have a research breakthrough and a brand-new research project will become available. The upgrades produced from these research breakthroughs are the best upgrades in the game. It can't be stressed enough: Researching upgrades is critical to success in *Mass Effect 2*. It's recommended you obtain enough minerals to obtain all useful research upgrades as they will greatly improve your capabilities.

Use the tables and charts in this chapter to take the guesswork out of acquiring upgrades and research projects. By knowing exactly which upgrades are out there and which research projects you may want to complete, you can prioritize which upgrades Shepard pursues. Upgrade tables note when an upgrade can only be acquired via a research project, and if so, how much the project will cost.

Stores and Upgrades

Stores on galactic hub worlds are an excellent way of acquiring upgrades. Upgrades can be purchased from stores with credits. Obtain credits on missions by finding them and by receiving a bonus from Cerberus for completing missions.

Upgrades purchased from stores can help your science team discover new research projects for more powerful upgrades.

Weapons Found on Missions

Shepard will sometimes obtain new weapons while on missions. Once these weapons are obtained, Shepard's entire squad will immediately start using the new weapon if possible. New weapons are always upgrades over stock Cerberus weapons.

If you obtain a new weapon but would prefer to use a previous weapon, access a weapons locker to switch back to your old weapon.

Weapon Upgrades

Weapon upgrades improve the quality of Shepard's existing weapons. The most common upgrades are damage upgrades, but more advanced upgrades can be developed with research. Most weapons have five damage upgrades available and two advanced upgrades that improve the weapon on a more fundamental level.

All upgrades are cumulative. For example, if you have two assault rifle damage upgrades you will get

+20 percent assault rifle damage. If you acquire a third the bonus increases to +30 percent.

Upgrades affect all weapons of the appropriate type in Shepard's squad.

Obtain upgrades that improve Shepard's weapons and the weapons of favored squad members, and you will have a better chance at success on missions.

Technology Name	Upgrade	# of Upgrade Levels	Found/ Research Project	Upgrade Level Required	Research Cost	Description
Tungsten Jacket	Assault Rifle Penetration	1	Research	Assault Rifle Damage Level 2	15,000 Iridium	Provides +25% assault rifle damage against armor, shields, and biotic barriers. Upgrades the assault rifles, battle rifles, and machine guns for your entire squad. The slugs' tungsten content is increased, and the weapon's computer is recalibrated, improving penetration of heavily armored targets. A phasic envelope surrounds each slug before it is fired at a target. This disrupts any mass effect field protecting the target, resulting in better penetration.
Targeting VI	Assault Rifle Accuracy	1	Research	Assault Rifle Damage Level 3	25,000 Iridium	Your entire squad's assault rifles are now much more accurate. Upgrades assault rifles, battle rifles, machine guns. A smart targeting module calculates and compensates for minute barrel movements, weather, and the environment. Firing on a target in a howling gale feels the same as it does on a calm day on a practice range. Smart targeting does not mean the bullet will automatically find the mark every time the trigger is pulled; it only makes it easier for the marksman to aim.
Kinetic Pulsar	Assault Rifle Damage	5	2 Found, 3 Research	None	2,500/ 5,000/ 7,500 Iridium	Provides +10% assault rifle damage. Upgrades assault rifles, battle rifles, and machine guns for your entire squad. This upgrade strengthens a weapon's mass effect field generator, increasing the velocity of each slug fired.

Technology Name	Upgrade	# of Upgrade Levels	Found/ Research Project	Upgrade Level Required	Research Cost	Description
Phasic Jacketing	Submachine Gun Penetration	1	Research	Submachine Gun Damage Level 2	15,000 Iridium	Provides +50% submachine gun (SMG) damage against shields and biotic barriers. Upgrades SMGs for your entire squad. A module in the mass effect field generator creates a phasic envelope around each slug before it is fired at a target. This disrupts any mass effect field protecting the target, resulting in superior penetration.
Heat Sink Capacity	Submachine Gun Extra Rounds	1	Research	Submachine Gun Damage Level 3	25,000 Iridium	Adds 10% more submachine gun (SMG) rounds. Improves SMGs for your entire squad. More efficient heat-sink materials improve the absorption and dissipation of heat. Allows for smaller, easier-to-carry heat sinks.
Microfield Pulsar	Submachine Gun Damage	5	2 Found, 3 Research	None	2,500/ 5,000/ 7,500 Iridium	Squad bonus +10% submachine gun damage. Upgrades the submachine guns of your entire squad. This upgrade improves a weapon's mass effect field generator, increasing the velocity of each slug fired.
Sabot Jacketing	Heavy Pistol Penetration	1	Research	Heavy Pistol Damage Level 2	15,000 Palladium	Provides +50% heavy pistol damage against armor. Upgrades heavy pistols and hand cannons for your entire squad. Increasing the tungsten content of slugs and recalibrating the weapon's computer improves penetration of heavily armored targets.
Smart Rounds	Heavy Pistol Critical	1	Research	Heavy Pistol Damage Level 3	25,000 Palladium	Heavy pistols sometimes deal double damage. Upgrades the heavy pistols and hand cannons of your entire squad. Normandy's scientists have prototyped a modification to the traditional smart-targeting module commonly incorporated into high-end weaponry. While this technology is commonly used to compensate for wind and recoil, it was adapted to slightly deflect rounds to strike a more vital part of an enemy.
Titan Pulsar	Heavy Pistol Damage	5	2 Found, 3 Research	None	2,500/ 5,000/ 7,500 Palladium	Provides +10% heavy pistol damage. Upgrades heavy pistols and hand cannons for your entire squad. This upgrade improves a weapon's mass effect field generator, increasing the mass and acceleration of each slug fired.
Microphasic Pulse	Shotgun Penetration	1	Research	Shotgun Damage Level 2	15,000 Platinum	Increases damage by +50% against shields and biotic barriers. Improves shotguns, heavy shotguns, and assault shotguns for your entire squad. With the addition of a phasic module to the mass effect field generator, each slug is encased in a phasic envelope before it is fired at a target. This disrupts any mass effect field protecting the target, resulting in superior penetration.
Thermal Sink	Shotgun Extra Rounds	1	Research	Shotgun Damage Level 3	25,000 Platinum	Shotguns, heavy shotguns, and assault shotguns double their rounds. This bonus affects the entire squad. More efficient heat-sink materials improve the absorption and dissipation of heat. Allows for smaller, easier-to-carry heat sinks.
Synchronized Pulsar	Shotgun Damage	5	2 Found, 3 Research	None	2,500/ 5,000/ 7,500 Platinum	Provides +10% shotgun damage. Improves shotguns, heavy shotguns, and assault shotguns. This upgrade improves the weapon's mass effect field generator, increasing the mass and acceleration of each round fired.
Tungsten Sabot Jacket	Sniper Rifle Penetration	1	Research	Sniper Rifle Damage Level 2	15,000 Platinum	Increases damage by +50% against armor. Improves sniper rifles for entire squad. Increasing the tungsten content of slugs and recalibrating the weapon's computer greatly improves penetration against heavily armored targets.
Combat Scanner	Sniper Headshot Damage	1	Research	Sniper Rifle Damage Level 3	25,000 Platinum	Sniper rifles deal +50% headshot damage. This bonus affects the entire squad. Normandy's scientists have prototyped a modification to the traditional smart-targeting module commonly incorporated into high-end weaponry. While this technology is normally used to compensate for wind and recoil, it was adapted to slightly deflect rounds to strike a more vital part of an enemy's head.
Scram Pulsar	Sniper Rifle Damage	5	2 Found, 3 Research	None	2,500/ 5,000/ 7,500 Platinum	Provides +10% sniper rifle damage. Improves sniper rifles for your entire squad. This upgrade improves the weapon's mass effect field generator, increasing the mass and acceleration of each slug fired.

Armor and Biotic Upgrades

Armor upgrades improve the defensive and medical capabilities of Shepard's squad. They also can upgrade biotic and tech powers by improving biotic implants and omni-tools. This category of upgrade affects your biotic powers (damage, cooldown), shield strength, and medi-gel usage. Many upgrades in this category have cumulative effects.

There are five basic upgrades for each armor component and two advanced upgrades.

Biotic and tech upgrades are extremely valuable in increasing the offensive abilities of biotic and tech squad members and Shepard (unless the commander is a soldier).

MASS EFFECT

Technology Name	Upgrade	# of Upgrade Levels	Found/ Research Project	Upgrade Level Required	Research Cost	Description
Hyper Amp	Biotic Damage	5	2 Found, 3 Research	None	500/ 1,000/ 1,500 Element Zero	Provides +10% biotic damage. Standard firmware shipping with bio-amps is designed to work with a variety of alien races and nervous systems. By hacking this firmware to relax built-in safety protocols, more powerful mass effect fields can be generated. Each hack must be done carefully, tuned to the individual's nervous system, or there's risk of nervous system damage, sensation loss, or blindness.
Neural Mask	Biotic Duration	1	Research	Biotic Damage Level 2	3,000 Element Zero	Provides +20% biotic power duration. Maintaining a single mass effect field requires continual concentration. By measuring and replicating neural system activity, this upgrade enables the user to maintain mass effect fields with less effort.
Smart Amplifier	Biotic Cooldown	1	Research	Biotic Damage Level 3	5,000 Element Zero	Provides 20% faster biotic cooldowns. Generating a mass effect field requires significant concentration. After generating a field, all biotics require some rest before they have the mental focus and clarity to generate another. By tracking neural activity and recognizing the individual patterns of the user, the amp can better interpret the kind of field the biotic wishes to generate. This requires less focus when generating fields and reduces cooldown time.
Microscanner	Medi-gel Capacity	5	2 Found, 3 Research	None	2,500/ 5,000/ 7,500 Platinum	Medi-gel capacity is increased by 1. All modern combat armor incorporates a first-aid interface. Microprocessors in this interface monitor vital functions and release small localized doses of medi-gel to accelerate the healing process. Manually timed heavy doses of medi-gel can be released in response to major trauma. However, the efficiency of this depends on proprietary medical software that cannot be copied and is prohibitively expensive. Cerberus has developed its own software and is actively working to impove its efficiency.
Trauma Module	Unity Increase	1	Research	Medi-gel Capacity Level 2	15,000 Platinum	Unity heals your squad to full health. A standard first-aid interface can stabilize a badly wounded soldier, preventing death from all but the most serious wounds. The base technology, however, is ineffective on conscious soldiers who are currently taking fire, as each pain signal resets the process. A trauma module separates the medi-gel administration into two layers: active and passive. The active layer constantly distributes small amounts of medi-gel to fresh wound sites. The passive layer handles major deployments to incapacitating wounds. When large amounts of medi-gel are deployed to incapacitated squad members, fighting members are also healed.
Shield Harmonics	Emergency Shielding	1	Research	Medi-gel Capacity Level 3	25,000 Platinum	Unity restores squad member shields to full strength. Shield emitters are optimized to produce a strong, reliable kinetic barrier that can be active for hours. Because of the potential for interference, it is nearly impossible to run two active emitters simultaneously. When one kinetic barrier is down, it's possible to activate a second, but this will generally interfere with the reactivation of the primary barrier. With precise timing, a short-term kinetic barrier can be made that seamlessly retracts when the primary barrier regenerates.
Ablative VI	Damage Protection	5	2 Found, 3 Research	None	2,500/ 5,000/ 7,500 Palladium	+10% to shields, barriers, and armor. This comprehensive systems upgrade offers improved protection for all squad members, regardless of team members' individual defensive strategies.
Burst Regeneration	Redundant Field Generator	1	Research	Damage Protection Level 2	15,000 Palladium	Sometimes when Shepard's shields go down, they are instantly fully restored. Kinetic barriers have improved the survival rate of individual soldiers against modern weapons, but attempts to reinforce failing shields with backups have traditionally failed due to interference. This area has remained an active topic of research for Cerberus, and a prototype redundant field generator has been created. With the proper investment, this can be miniaturized for personal use.
Nanocrystal Shield	Hard Shields	1	Research	Damage Protection Level 3	25,000 Palladium	Shepard's shields take 20% less damage. Cerberus has achieved limited success in studying geth shield technology. Its scientists don't completely understand why, but it seems geth shields are not as vulnerable to incoming projectiles. A breakthrough is imminent, however, and it is possible to make a modified mass effect field generator that mimics this technology.
Multicore Amplifier	Tech Damage	5	2 Found, 3 Research	None	500/ 1,000/ 1,500 Element Zero	Provides +10% tech power damage. Standard omni-tools are calibrated with a wide neural input tolerance range so they can be used effectively by any race. By tuning the inputs of the omni-tool to match the specific neural patterns of the user, responsiveness and power can be greatly increased. Once tuned in this manner, the omni-tool is almost unusable by anyone but the wearer, and it must be constantly recalibrated to subtle neural shifts.

Introduction

Training

Upgrades and Research

Walkthrough

Special Assignments

Planetary Database

Appendix

Technology Name	Upgrade	# of Upgrade Levels	Found/ Research Project	Upgrade Level Required	Research Cost	Description
Custom Heuristics	Tech Duration	1	Research	Tech Damage Level 2	3,000 Element Zero	Provides +20% duration for all tech powers. Traditional omni-tools are tuned for precise and delicate work. Eclipse engineers tune their omni-tools in an opposite manner, focusing on quickly releasing raw energy, but rendering them incapable of performing delicate work without swapping in an alternative tool. Cerberus has prototyped a multiple-operating-system approach that should allow one omni-tool to run dozens of configurations, with instantaneous swapping as the user switches tasks. This should result in better performance at each individual task.
Hydra Module	Tech Cooldowns	1	Research	Tech Damage Level 3	5,000 Element Zero	Provides +20% faster cooldown on tech abilities. Most omni-tools are tuned to have an effective life span of 10 years or more for precision work and up to 50 for more general tasks. Disabling most safety protocols and installing an experimental power core improves efficiency but reduces the expected operating life span by a factor of 20.

Prototype Upgrades

Most upgrades can be mass-produced in the *Normandy*'s lab. Prototype upgrades are experimental technology that can only upgrade a single squad member.

Examples of prototype upgrades include building heavy weapons, building a unique weapon for a specific squad member, or tuning a squad member's implants.

Investing in prototype upgrades for Shepard and your favorite squad members will dramatically increase their combat capabilities.

Technology Name	Upgrade	# of Upgrade Levels	Found/ Research Project	Upgrade Level Required	Research Cost	Description
Microfusion Array	Heavy Weapon Ammo	5	2 Found, 3 Research	None	2,500/ 5,000/ 7,500 Iridium	Provides +15% heavy weapon ammo capacity. The power cell technology used by heavy weapons is fairly old but can be improved by rebuilding the core with more modern components. These improvements allow standard power cells to yield more shots per power cell and allow for more total shots to be fired.
ML-77 Missile Launcher	New Heavy Weapon	None	Research	Heavy Weapon Ammo Level 1	5,000 Iridium	This is a rapid-fire missile launcher with seeking projectiles. It's effective against armor, shields, and biotic barriers. Missile launchers are surfacing with increasing frequency among mercenary bands in the Terminus Systems, but their origin is unknown. Each projectile features a friend-or-foe recognition system, ensuring it will find a hostile target—though not necessarily the one in the crosshairs. In urban situations, it is useful for taking out snipers and other entrenched enemies, so it is popular with the Blue Suns mercenary band. It is nearly impossible to duplicate, as it uses Fabrication Rights Management (FRM) technology.
M-622 Avalanche	New Heavy Weapon	None	Research	Heavy Weapon Ammo Level 2	15,000 Iridium	Cryo round technology is used to modify standard weapon slugs. A cooling laser collapses the ammunition into Bose-Einstein condensate, a mass of super-cooled subatomic particles capable of snap-freezing impacted objects. *Normandy*'s scientists have found a way to apply this technology on a large scale: By generating a mass effect containment "bubble," this proof-of-concept large weapon technology is effective against armor, shields, and biotic barriers. It is nicknamed the "cryo blaster."
M-920 Cain	New Heavy Weapon	None	Research	Heavy Weapon Ammo Level 3	25,000 Iridium	The effectiveness and efficiency of mass-effect-based weapon technology has rendered large-scale deployment of highly explosive weaponry all but obsolete in infantry weapons. *Normandy*'s scientists have prototyped a modified version of traditional high-explosive rounds that is applied to a 25-gram slug. When accelerated to 5 km per second, the round is devastating. Though a technically inaccurate label, this prototype weapon is nicknamed the "nuke launcher," and its high-explosive matrix generates an archetypical mushroom cloud on impact. Inflicts high damage with a large area of effect. Very effective against armor, shields, and barriers.
Lattice Shunting	Health Increase	5	2 Found, 3 Research	None	2,500/ 5,000/ 7,500 Palladium	Shepard gets +10% health. Strong synthetic fibers can be woven through the skin, dramatically reducing damage taken from most attacks. These fibers also act as a medi-gel conduit, improving healing.
Skeletal Lattice	Melee Defense Boost	None	Research	Lattice Shunting Level 2	15,000 Palladium	Shepard takes 50% less damage from melee attacks. By reinforcing the skeleton with a synthetic weave, bones can be made almost unbreakable. In the event of bone trauma, medi-gel conduits allow for bone regeneration in a matter of days.

Technology Name	Upgrade	# of Upgrade Levels	Found/ Research Project	Upgrade Level Required	Research Cost	Description
Microfiber Weave	Melee Attack Boost	None	Research	Lattice Shunting Level 3	25,000 Palladium	Shepard's melee attack is now more powerful. Perforating the muscles with micro-fibers increases overall strength and decreases the potential for muscle damage from exertion.
Microfiber Weave	Krogan Vitality	2	1 Found/1 Research	None	5,000 Platinum	Grunt gets +25% health. A scientist named Okeer designed a retrovirus that matches the krogan genetic code. Modifying the gene sequence of the virus and injecting a small amount into a krogan can introduce a change in that genetic code.
Custom Claymore	Krogan Shotgun	None	Research	None	15,000 Platinum	Grunt gets a Claymore heavy shotgun. Armory scientists produced a single prototype for Grunt that appears to be unbalanced.
Cyclonic Particles	Geth Shield Strength	2	1 Found/1 Research	None	5,000 Platinum	Legion gets +25% shield strength. Geth and Alliance technology diverged when the geth migrated beyond the Veil. While geth technology is wholly incompatible with Alliance technology, this upgrade improves on geth shield strength.
Custom Widow Rifle	Geth Sniper Rifle	None	Research	None	15,000 Platinum	Legion gets an M-98 Widow anti-material rifle. With enough raw resources and access to the armory lab, an advanced sniper rifle compatible only with Legion can be produced.
Multicore Implants	Subject Zero Biotic Boost	None	Research	None	3,000 Element Zero	Subject Zero gets +20% biotic damage. Subject Zero's vital signs show progressive neural degeneration, which would normally decrease her potential ability to generate mass effect fields. Instead, her ability appears to be increasing. Replacing the power module in her bio-amp with a higher-capacity prototype module would dramatically increase the strength of her biotics.
Custom Tech Upgrade	Mordin Omni-Tool	None	Research	None	3,000 Element Zero	Mordin gets +20% tech power damage. Mordin built his own omni-tool and can make significant upgrades given the proper materials.
Tactical Shift	Retrain Powers	None	Research	None	3,750 Element Zero	Advanced training allows Shepard to re-allocate points to powers. No additional points are granted.
Tactical Mastery	Advanced Training	None	Research	None	7,500 Element Zero	Through intensive training, Shepard can learn to use a single bonus power. Obtaining more loyal squad members will increase the number of powers available for Shepard.

Normandy Upgrades

The *Normandy* is the most technologically advanced Cerberus ship in the galaxy, but improvements are always possible. Upgrades to the *Normandy* will improve her combat capabilities, increasing the chance of success in Shepard's final mission. Other upgrades will aid in exploration or improve the ship's medical capabilities.

All ship upgrades must be researched. To obtain these research projects, talk to your crew members and ask them about research or ship upgrades.

Without any ship upgrades, you will be in extreme peril if you ever confront an enemy Collector ship.

> **TIP**
> The weapon and shield upgrades for the *Normandy* have a serious effect on Shepard's success in the final mission.

Technology Name	Upgrade	Found/ Research Project	Upgrade Level Required	Research Cost	Description
Argus Scanner Array	Advanced Mineral Scanner	Research	None	15,000 Iridium	The Ayndroid Group's proprietary Argus Planet Scan Technology has been integrated into the ship's systems. This will greatly speed up the planet-scanning process.
Cyclone Shield Tech	Shielding	Research	None	15,000 Palladium	The rapidly oscillating kinetic obstructions of Cyclonic Barrier Technology (CBT) are added to the ship. This should help the ship survive blasts like those that destroyed the first *Normandy*.
Dermal Regeneration	Med-Bay Upgrade	Research	None	50,000 Platinum	This upgrades the *Normandy*'s medical facilities with an advanced dermal regeneration unit. Using this unit will immediately and completely heal your scars. Further scarring will not occur regardless of the actions you take.
Helios Thruster Tech	Extended Fuel Cells	Research	None	3,000 Element Zero	*Normandy* now has 50% additional fuel cell capacity.
Modular Probe Bay	Probe Booster	Research	None	15,000 Iridium	*Normandy* now has 100% extra probe capacity; 30 survey probes are added to ship's complement.
Silaris Armor Tech	Heavy Ship Armor	Research	None	15,000 Palladium	The asari-made Silaris armor upgrade is attached to the ship's superstructure. This will help the ship hold together if hit by a blast powerful enough to penetrate its shields.
Thanix Cannon	Particle Cannon	Research	None	15,000 Platinum	The turian-designed Thanix Magnetic-Hydronamic Cannon is now installed on the *Normandy*. This cannon is powerful enough to destroy a Collector ship with repeated hits.

WALKTHROUGH

AWAKENING

Commander Shepard was lost following the unexpected and devastating attack on the *Normandy*. But science has advanced far enough that not even death is final. The commander is about to return to duty and resume the mission to rid the galaxy of the Reaper threat. But Shepard will need to find new allies to win this fight.

Medical Facility

The medical facility is part of a space station not under control of the Alliance or the Council. There is an air of mystery to the station, which seems intentionally nondescript. What could be happening aboard the station that would make its owners wish to remain as inconspicuous as possible?

Spoils of War
- **Credits: 7,500**

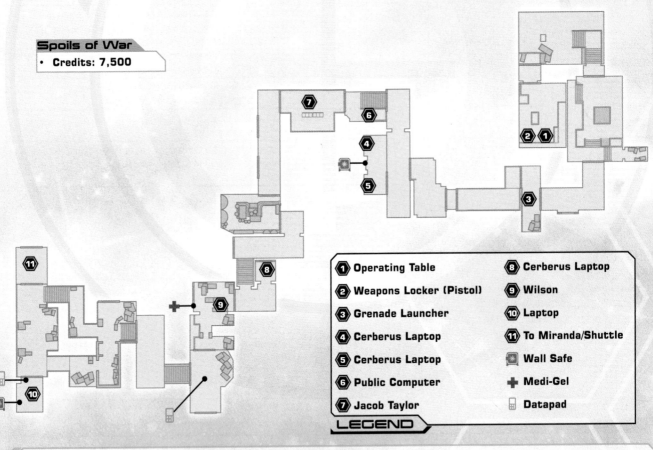

LEGEND

1. Operating Table
2. Weapons Locker (Pistol)
3. Grenade Launcher
4. Cerberus Laptop
5. Cerberus Laptop
6. Public Computer
7. Jacob Taylor
8. Cerberus Laptop
9. Wilson
10. Laptop
11. To Miranda/Shuttle
- Wall Safe
- Medi-Gel
- Datapad

Glossary

Spectre: Spectre stands for Special Tactics and Reconnaissance. The Spectre is a special class of agent that works directly for the Council and outside of all galactic laws that otherwise govern the accepted races that occupy the Citadel. Spectres are the best of the best, lethal in both intelligence and might. Commander Shepard was the first human Spectre.

Council: The Council is the governing body within the Citadel, responsible for dictating and upholding the law within Council space. Prior to the geth attack on the Citadel, the Council comprised only three races: asari, turian, and salarian. But now humanity is represented on the Council, a major step for the reputation of humankind in the galaxy.

Cerberus: Cerberus is a splinter group with a humans-first philosophy and a checkered history. Cerberus is responsible for conducting a series of questionable experiments—often on humans—such as luring the huge, violent thresher maws to marines to gauge the resulting fight. Cerberus is also responsible for the breeding of the near-extinct and feared rachni, a race that once threatened the galaxy, which Shepard had to deal with during the previous mission to stop Saren.

Objective 1: Project Lazarus

You wake inside a laboratory. Faces blur in and out of focus. Though it is difficult to understand what the people hovering over you are saying, you realize that you are being operated on and that you really should not be awake right now. After your vitals are stabilized, you slip back into slumber and the technicians above you resume their work.

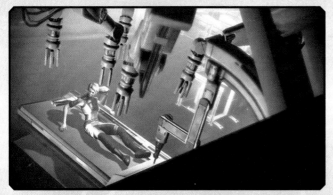

Welcome to Project Lazarus. Here, you discover that Commander Shepard is not as dead as you may have believed. Inside this medical facility, technicians and scientists have labored to reconstruct the broken Shepard. The fallen Spectre has been put back together not just in body (through the use of cybernetics and other required upgrades to replace ruined body pieces and augment others) but in spirit. Project Lazarus allows you to reconstruct Shepard's visage and core personality; your actions later in the adventure will determine Paragon and Renegade status.

If you imported Commander Shepard from your original *Mass Effect* save, you can keep everything as is or make some physical changes to Shepard.

NOTE

When you exit Project Lazarus, Shepard's appearance is final. You cannot make any more changes, so be sure you are happy with the commander's mug before continuing.

NOTE

Project Lazarus ends a little earlier than intended. Shepard wakes again to the sounds of combat. As Shepard rises from the operating table, the voice of Miranda—one of the voices heard during that brief episode of consciousness during the procedure—comes over the comm. She doesn't have time to tell Shepard much. Questions must wait until after she can guide Shepard out of the area before hacked security drones called LOKI Mechs burst into the facility. The mechs seem hell-bent on bringing Shepard down.

This part of the game is a tutorial designed to teach the player some of *Mass Effect 2*'s controls. Follow Miranda's orders to successfully move through the medical bay. She directs Shepard to a machine pistol and then to some thermal clips. Soon, though, the first of the mechs appears on the stairs and she can only hope Shepard's combat acumen survived the project.

Follow the doors with green lights on them to make it through the tutorial. Green signals that a door is unlocked. A red light on a door means it cannot be opened.

TIP

Shoot the mech in the head before it is fully activated.

Most weapons require a steady supply of thermal clips to keep them from overheating. Thermal clips are dropped by destroyed mechs and left behind by fleeing facility personnel.

NOTE

Enemy Profile: LOKI Mech

- **Classification:** Minion
- **Powers:** Taser Blast
- **Defenses:** —
- **Weapons:** Machine Pistol

LOKI Mechs are designed as inexpensive, expendable security drones. These mechs are typically programmed to patrol sectors and, when ordered, act to keep the unauthorized out. LOKI Mechs attack with standard-issue machine pistols at long to medium range. Up close, the mech uses a taser blast to incapacitate a target.

Because LOKI Mechs are built to be cheaply replaced, they are easy to take down. A single blast to the head causes the mech to explode. Alternatively, a mech can be disarmed by shooting off its appendages, particularly the arm holding the machine pistol.

Storm through the flame jets to emerge unscathed.

In the next room, Miranda directs Shepard to use the nearby cover before a batch of hacked mechs storm toward the commander. Use the cover to block the mechs' shots while returning fire. After dropping the mechs, check the room to the left to pick up some refined iridium and thermal clips. The path leads to a fallen human. Pick up his M-100 Grenade Launcher (this is a new weapon for Shepard, noted by a codex entry) and then use it on the three hacked mechs that push through a door on the landing below. Use the nearby elevator to drop down, and continue moving through the station under Miranda's orders.

Although the situation is hectic, take a moment to enter the room with the two mechs crawling through the door. Check the terminals inside the room. These terminals add critical information to the codex. There is also a safe in the wall.

Bypass the safe's lock to pocket 3,000 credits. Those will be useful later.

> Iridium is one of four valuable commodities (along with platinum, palladium, and element zero) you can collect throughout the game. Eventually, you can spend these resources to acquire upgrades.
>
> **NOTE**

Objective 2: Rendezvous with Jacob Taylor—

Jacob Taylor

Someone pointing a gun in a direction other than Shepard's is a small comfort in this deteriorating situation. Shepard meets Jacob in the D wing's giant courtyard. Jacob is pinned down by a wave of hacked mechs streaming through a door on the opposite side of the chamber. Before agreeing to join the fight with Jacob, Shepard has a moment to get some much-needed answers.

According to Jacob, you've been out of commission for over two years as Project Lazarus literally brought you back from the dead. Jacob also lets slip that you are not in an Alliance facility. This is third-party, which makes Shepard suspicious. At least Jacob can confirm that your friends made it off the *Normandy* before it was vaporized. The rest of your questions will have to wait until the combat subsides.

This is as good a time as any to learn how to use the Power Wheel in combat. Bring up the wheel and select Jacob's Pull biotic power to yank the mechs off their ledge.

Following the fight, Jacob agrees to answer the rest of your questions as best as he can. You can pursue a line of questioning about your crew from the *Normandy*, but don't leave the dialog without finding out more about the situation in the medical facility. Jacob has no idea why the mechs started the attack, but he assumes that it's all an inside job. Only somebody close to the project could get the needed access to hack and reprogram all of the mechs to attack—especially just as you woke up. There are other topics to pursue:

- **Miranda:** Miranda Lawson is the station's ranking officer and Jacob's boss. There's not much more he is willing to say about her at this point.
- **Jacob:** Jacob is Miranda's top lieutenant. He served five years in the Alliance before leaving and accepting this job.
- **Project Lazarus:** Project Lazarus was a two-year operation that brought you back from the dead.

Wilson

Before long, Wilson comes over the comm. He is holed up in the network control room and in serious trouble. Wilson needs Jacob and Shepard to rescue him before the mechs locate him. The transmission is cut off just as mechs burst into the control room.

Jacob directs you through a series of service tunnels to find the control room.

Use Miranda's terminal to learn more about Project Lazarus and add relevant information to your codex.

In a Hurry?

The service tunnels lead to Wilson in room B. He survived the mech attack but was shot in the leg (why would mechs

aim for the leg?). There is a medi-gel station on the wall. Grab a medi-gel pack from the station and then use Unity to heal Wilson (Unity is on your Power Wheel). After Wilson rises, you can talk to him about the current situation in the facility. Jacob and Shepard lean toward finding Miranda, but Wilson is convinced she's dead due to the mech attacks. Wilson seems eager to leave Miranda behind.

NOTE

This is one of those classic Paragon or Renegade dialog trees that you encounter over the course of the mission. Choosing to tell Wilson you want to look for Miranda results in Paragon points while agreeing that it is best to leave her behind adds Renegade points. Not all of the Paragon/Renegade conversation options are this obvious. As the galactic intrigue increases, so does the opacity of good versus evil.

As the conversation continues, Jacob admits that the station—and Project Lazarus—is controlled by Cerberus. That's a familiar name. Shepard had heard of Cerberus during previous missions, and that adds to Shepard's suspicions. Cerberus is a pro-human splinter group that is often at odds with the Alliance. Jacob says there is somebody who can provide answers: the mysterious Illusive Man.

The conversation is cut short by the arrival of more hacked mechs. Use Wilson's Overload power on nearby crates to detonate them and stop the mechs.

Look for a datapad on a fallen Cerberus employee in the next hall. If you successfully hack it, you pocket more credits.

Miranda

The battle spills into a warehouse that is crawling with mechs. With Wilson and Jacob at your side, push into the warehouse and pick apart the mechs. Jacob and Wilson help you out with biotics and weapons.

PRIMA Official Game Guide | primagames.com

As you pursue the mechs, you approach the facility exit. When the exit door opens, you see a familiar face: Miranda.

It's also the last face Wilson will ever see.

Miranda explains that Wilson was a double-crosser and responsible for the mech attacks. You must decide just how troubled Shepard is by her killing Wilson without a single question. How you answer determines whether you earn Paragon or Renegade points. No matter how skeptical you choose to be of Miranda, your options for getting off this compromised station are limited. You must go with Jacob and Miranda. Miranda leads you to a shuttle and promises to take you to see the Illusive Man.

Playing with the Past

On the shuttle, Miranda and Jacob ask you a few questions about Shepard's past. These questions are designed to fill in some decisions that were made at the end of the original *Mass Effect*. For example: Who was appointed to the Council? Anderson or Udina? Did you save the Council or not? If you imported your Shepard character from *Mass Effect*, these decisions will be based on your last imported save game.

The Illusive Man

After the shuttle docks at the Cerberus outpost, Shepard finally has a chance to get some answers with the Illusive Man. Don't expect any face time, though. Security is paramount. So, as Shepard enters the chamber where the commander thinks the Illusive Man is supposedly waiting, Shepard is scanned into a hologram projector. The commander will speak to the Illusive Man via some serious long-distance.

The Illusive Man goes over some of the things Shepard missed over the last two years, including the disturbing trend of human colonies vanishing and a lack of action by the Council. Shepard points out that if the Illusive Man wanted to take on the Reapers, he could have trained an entire army for the cost of the Project Lazarus. The Illusive Man's reasoning is simple: Shepard killed a Reaper. He is unsure if the Reapers feel fear, but the Reapers must respect Shepard at least. And that's a good foundation for instilling fear. Is it the geth? The Reapers? The Illusive Man believes the best way to investigate the situation is to go hands-on. A shuttle will take Shepard to Freedom's Progress, the latest human colony to go offline.

> This is a great time to scroll through your codex and investigate the information you picked up during this initial leg of the mission.

NOTE

Use the armor locker in the bay above the hologram chamber to outfit Shepard.

Talk to Miranda and Jacob to learn more about them and potentially earn more Paragon/Renegade points.

When you are ready to ship out to Freedom's Progress, use the door next to the armor locker. Shepard, Jacob, and Miranda all enter a shuttle and plot a course for the vanished human colony. What horrors befell these colonists? And whatever took them—is it still there, just waiting for new arrivals?

Introduction

Training

Upgrades and Research

Awakening

Walkthrough

Special Assignments

Planetary Database

Appendix

FREEDOM'S PROGRESS

Despite their history, Commander Shepard has entered into an uneasy alliance with Cerberus, which is led by the charming (and intriguing) Illusive Man. The Illusive Man still believes that the galaxy is under threat from the Reapers, the ancient race that wiped out the Protheans and almost destroyed the Citadel two years ago. Since the Council seems determined to ignore Shepard's warnings and turn a blind eye to the Reapers that are still out there, Shepard has little choice but to see how far this new partnership will go. The first assignment Shepard must undertake is the investigation of Freedom's Progress, the latest human colony to go offline.

Freedom's Progress Colony

Freedom's Progress is a typical Alliance settlement, with a small military force supplemented by mechs and security drones. A complete communications blackout led the Illusive Man to find out that the colonists have disappeared in the last few days. He sends Shepard to investigate, thinking the disappearance may have a link to the Reapers.

The communications blackout apparently happened after high-powered, lower-mounted GARDIAN lasers were installed around the colony. Colonists complained about construction cost overruns, delays, noise, and damage to the local environment. They also feared the defense array could provoke their neighbors. Such fears may not have been baseless.

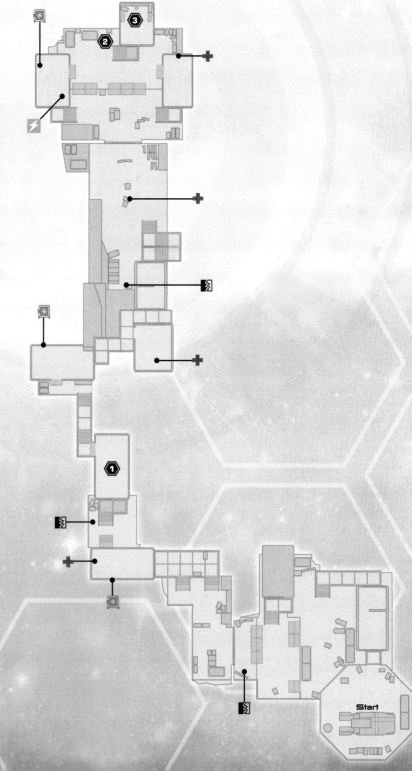

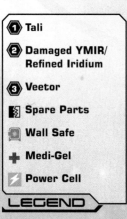

LEGEND

- **1** Tali
- **2** Damaged YMIR/ Refined Iridium
- **3** Veetor
- **Spare Parts**
- **Wall Safe**
- **Medi-Gel**
- **Power Cell**

Start

Objective 1: Investigate Colony

As the shuttle circles Freedom's Progress, preparing to land, Miranda tells Shepard that the Illusive Man has placed the commander in charge. The approach gives you plenty of time to discuss the situation with Miranda and Jacob, such as how far that authority extends, the fate of other colonies, and what Cerberus expects to find at Freedom's Progress. According to Jacob, this is the first time Cerberus will beat official investigators or looters to a disappeared colony; the chance of finding new information is much greater. Of course, that also means a good chance of finding some form of resistance that officials would have already dealt with, too. At the conclusion of the conversation, you can make a Paragon or Renegade choice: suggest that finding survivors is the team's first priority (Paragon), or go in hard to destroy any threat (Renegade).

> **NOTE**
>
> This is your first assignment with an away team. Though Miranda and Jacob will automatically react to danger, you can also issue squad orders to move them to advance points or direct them to change weapons and use biotic powers.

Ghost Town

Stepping out of the shuttle reveals a desolate scene. When the Illusive Man said that the colonists had vanished into thin air, he was not exaggerating for effect. Freedom's Progress is silent and still. But the last one to leave left the lights on and did not place the colony on lockdown, so follow the trail of open doors.

The lack of any signs of struggle is unnerving, but press on through the unlocked doors.

Slow down when you reach a wide door. Though there are no signs of humans, the colony's defenses are apparently still online. Just beyond the door are two FENRIS Mechs. The four-legged security mechs activate as soon as they detect motion, their unblinking red optic displays offering an unsubtle hint that they are not programmed to negotiate. Blast the FENRIS Mechs as they lunge toward the team, taking care to aim directly for the optic display for maximum damage.

> **TIP**
>
> Use zoom to target the mechs. Shooting from the hip reduces accuracy, which burns through thermal clips faster.

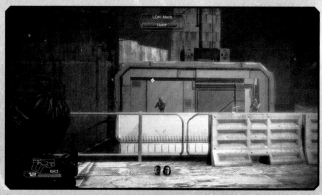

The FENRIS Mechs are not the only threat. LOKI Mechs stationed on a landing behind and to the right of the FENRIS Mechs also spring into action when your movement is detected. Cut them down.

Introduction

Training

Upgrades and Research

Walkthrough

Freedom's Progress

Special Assignments

Planetary Database

Appendix

Watch the door at the top of the landing to the right. When it opens, look out for FENRIS Mech reinforcements to bound into the area.

Enemy Profile: FENRIS Mech

- **Classification: Minion**
- **Powers: —**
- **Defenses: —**
- **Weapons: Taser Bite**

FENRIS Mechs are common security mechs. Their four-legged design reminds many humans of attack dogs seen in old films. The design allows the FENRIS Mech to spring toward a target with its back legs, quickly closing distances while knocking the target down with the two front legs. The FENRIS Mech's taser bite is then used to incapacitate. While FENRIS Mechs under Alliance control are often left factory-standard, many mercenaries hack the mech and upgrade it with a more powerful taser bite that can do significant damage.

Incendiary ammo does not do extra damage to mechs—only organic beings.

CAUTION

After taking down the mechs, investigate the building behind them to locate medi-gel and a wall safe that is loaded with credits. After emptying the building of useful items, move on to the next cluster of colony structures.

Objective 2: Find Veetor

The Illusive Man believed his team would be the first on the scene. He was wrong. A quarian patrol has already reached the colony and is conducting its own investigation. But why would quarians be interested in the disappearance of humans?

Tali

The quarians are surprised by your presence. They meet your raised weapons with their own, spurred on by the seemingly trigger-happy quarian Prazza. Prazza has zero trust for Cerberus operatives, but he is ordered to stand down by a familiar voice in the group: Tali'Zorah vas Neema, whom Shepard knows as Tali.

Small galaxy.

After you choose exactly how happy you are to be greeted with guns, Tali directs Prazza and the other quarians to definitely back down. Prazza is unhappy with the situation but dutifully obeys, giving Shepard a chance to explain the newfound partnership with Cerberus. Tali is skeptical, and understandably so. For one thing, you are supposed to be dead. For another, you and Tali fought Cerberus together. But Tali gives you the benefit of the doubt and allows you to form a truce.

Tali explains why she and the other quarians are at Freedom's Progress. One of their own was on his Pilgrimage: Veetor. While Tali describes Veetor as nervous, Prazza offers a less charitable adjective: unstable. When the quarians arrived to help Veetor, he fled into a warehouse and activated the security mechs to protect himself from the next wave of intruders. Veetor survived while everyone else disappeared. This leads to a bigger question: Why did the force that swallowed up the human colonists leave behind a quarian?

Tali and Shepard draw up a plan: Shepard and squad will investigate the warehouse in the center of the colony. Tali and her team will circle the far side of the colony and draw away security defenses.

Glossary

Quarian: A nomadic race of beings, the quarians are known for their skill with technology. They live aboard the Migrant Fleet—a huge collection of starships that travel together and spread out across the galaxy. Quarians are rarely seen without their masks, which spurs speculation that the quarians are not entirely organic beings.

Quarians have earned a mixed reputation in the galaxy. Through their Pilgrimage rite of passage, they often do good deeds. But the quarians are also responsible for the creation of the geth. Though the quarians tried valiantly to put down the geth resistance, they ultimately failed. Now the quarians must live with the repercussions of unleashing such a deadly force into the galaxy.

Drones

After splitting with Tali, lead the team through the next building and pick up any additional medi-gel packs you may need by this point, you are likely at capacity, but there's an upgrade to increase your capacity.

Just beyond the next building is a pair of Alliance Assault Drones. Stationed across a wide chasm, the drones open fire as soon as Shepard and the team step back out into the colony's open space. Turn to the left and return fire on the drones, using the

half-walls along the catwalk as cover against the incoming fire. Chew through the drones' shields and then pick apart the exposed hull to put the turrets down.

Enemy Profile: Alliance Assault Drone

- **Classification: Minion**
- **Powers: —**
- **Defenses: Shields**
- **Weapons: Assault Gun**

Assault drones are not intelligent AI creatures like the geth. Instead, these drone turrets run on very specific programs or are operated by remote control. The turrets can be programmed to recognize allies as well as enemies. The assault drone is armed with an assault gun that has a high rate of fire.

Prazza's Choice

Following the destruction of the drones, Tali comes over the comm. Prazza has broken rank with Tali and rushed ahead to seize Veetor before you can find him. If you want to get any information out of Veetor about the colonists, you'd better hurry. Push through the next series of small buildings and back outside in an attempt to intercept Prazza before he reaches Veetor.

Tali helps open a large bay door that will let you reach Veetor. Prazza is closing in, but his team is tangled up with a huge security mech.

Prazza's team is shredded by a YMIR Mech. Hopefully you will have better luck.

There is a lot of cover in the courtyard with the YMIR Mech, but some of the crates crumble under fire. Be mindful of ducking behind these fragile crates, which are noted by yellow trim.

Enemy Profile: YMIR Mech

- **Classification: Boss**
- **Powers: Death Explosion**
- **Defenses: Heavy Shields, Heavy Armor**
- **Weapons: Minigun, Heavy Rocket Launcher**

YMIR Mechs are large-scale security droids that dwarf LOKI and FENRIS models. The giant is armed to the teeth with a rocket launcher on one arm and a minigun on the other. These weapons are designed to tear up infantry and disable vehicles. The YMIR is also fitted with both shields and armor, so before you can rip into its hull, you must take down these two defenses.

As threatening as the YMIR is, certain design flaws can be exploited by crack shots. First, the arms can be blasted off the mech. Depending on which arm you remove, the mech loses access to one of the weapons. If both arms are disabled, then the only weapon the YMIR has left is a brute force charge. Second, the YMIR can be destroyed by targeting a weak spot on its head. Shooting the head causes the mech to overload. The resulting explosion is substantial; fall back so as not to be caught in the blast radius.

The YMIR Mech wastes little time charging into the courtyard to challenge Shepard's team. The quarians did not put up much of a fight, but your team has biotic powers and superior weapons. The YMIR has a real scrap on its hands. Use cover to avoid detection and then lean out to pop off shots on the mech.

Miranda's Overload technique chips away at the YMIR Mech's shields. Normally, biotics are blocked or negatively impaired by shields, though.

The YMIR is protected by shields and armor. If you do not keep on top of the mech, it will regenerate those shields and extend the fight.

As cruel as it sounds, you can use your team as decoys. Direct Miranda or Jacob to a point in the courtyard that the YMIR will notice. As the mech turns to fire upon your squad mate, blast it in the back. (Don't worry! You can heal your squad mates with Unity should the YMIR actually land a shot.)

Following the fight, scan the damaged YMIR Mech in the courtyard to pick up the Microfusion Array. This adds 10 percent more heavy weapon ammo capacity to your squad.

Explore all of the buildings around the courtyard to locate medi-gel and hackable wall safes.

Finding Veetor

You locate Tali in one of the small structures surrounding the courtyard. Tali is busy tending to the wounded but suggests you use this opportunity to find Veetor without any further resistance from the rest of her quarian associates. Investigate the building directly above the wreckage of the YMIR Mech (you did scan it with your omni-tool, yes?) to finally catch up with Veetor.

Veetor has had better days. The quarian is in a state of paranoid panic, feverishly hovering over a command center and watching all activity at the colony. He is mumbling something about monsters and swarms. You have to approach Veetor and extract whatever information you can get out of him. How you choose to start the conversation sets the tone for the rest of the exchange. If you use compassion and understanding to draw Veetor out and let him know he is safe, you earn Paragon points. If you choose to be more ruthless and demand answers from Veetor, you earn Renegade points.

> If the quarian must be snapped out of his paranoia, use an interrupt when prompted to shut off the displays.
>
> **NOTE**

Veetor finally turns away from the monitor bay and to your team. He is surprised to see humans. All the humans in the colony were taken away by what he calls the "monsters." Veetor calls up a video file on the monitors to explain what he means by "monsters." The footage is startling. There was a swarm moving through the colony, with colonists screaming as they ran, going into stasis as they were overtaken. But far more disturbing is the alien being with multiple eyes pushing what looks like a cocoon through the colony. Miranda calls this being a Collector. If the Collectors are involved in wiping out human colonies, then the threat to humankind just got much worse.

Glossary

Collector: Almost mythical in stature because so few have ever seen one and lived to tell about it, the Collectors are a species from beyond the unmapped Omega 4 mass relay. Collectors are known to work with intermediaries and mercenaries in their efforts to seek out rare or genetically mutated species. Collectors rarely do their own dirty work at first, but when they do get directly involved, they are accompanied by seeker swarms that spread out across a designated area and seek out targets. These targets are put in stasis so the Collectors can take them away without resistance.

Mass Relay: Mass relays enable near-instant travel to multiple points within the galaxy. The discovery of the Charon mass relay near Pluto is what allowed humanity to join the galactic community and eventually become one of its leading lights.

The fact that Veetor was able to survive the Collectors' sweep through Freedom's Progress leads Miranda to wonder if the Collectors are using technology that singles out humans. The quarian was not part of the Collectors' mission, which allowed him to watch and learn. If you compassionately end the conversation with Veetor, you will learn that Veetor used his omni-tool to scan the monsters and picked up dark energy readings.

Introduction

Training

Upgrades and Research

Walkthrough

Freedom's Progress

Special Assignments

Planetary Database

Appendix

Tali finally catches up to Shepard, just in time to overhear Miranda's desire to take Veetor with them. The quarian refuses to let even Shepard take away Veetor. He obviously needs help, and she wants to take him back to the fleet so his people can care for him. How you approach this minor standoff will earn you Paragon or Renegade points. You can implore Tali to join you on this mission and peacefully allow her to take Veetor back to the fleet (to Miranda's chagrin). This will earn you Paragon points, as well as Tali's gratitude. Or you can demand that Veetor come with you and your squad so you can question him further. This will earn you Renegade points.

Illusive Man

The Illusive Man is impressed with Shepard's performance on Freedom's Progress. Cerberus is known for being ruthless, so your actions affect how the Illusive Man perceives Shepard. It turns out that the Illusive Man suspected the Collectors were involved in the disappearance of the human colonies, and Veetor's data provided the necessary proof. Continue your conversation with the Illusive Man to gather additional intel about the Collectors and the mysterious, unreachable Omega 4 relay. No non-Collector ship has ever been able to successfully use that relay.

The Illusive Man sees a connection between the Reapers and the Collectors. He wants you to continue investigating but understands that you will need resources beyond just Miranda and Jacob. The Illusive Man has prepared dossiers on notable soldiers and scientists that could prove beneficial for the mission. Shepard would rather have the original team back, but the Illusive Man reminds the commander that two years have passed and offers updates on the whereabouts of old friends.

The last advice that the Illusive Man has before you depart to begin the process of assembling a new team is to seek out the salarian scientist Mordin Solus on Omega. Having a scientist on the team will open up research options aboard your ship. New ship?

The Illusive Man introduces Shepard to the new pilot: Joker. And Joker only looks good in the cockpit of one ship...

NORMANDY SR2

The original *Normandy* was shattered by an unknown assailant in the same incident that nearly eliminated Shepard. However, considering that Cerberus has the technology and wherewithal to bring Shepard back from the dead, rebuilding Shepard's ship was not nearly as difficult. Christened *Normandy SR2*, the ship will be Shepard's main transportation through the galaxy as the commander chases down leads on the Collectors and investigates their connection with the Reapers.

Again piloted by Joker, the *Normandy SR2* was improved during the construction process. Joker approves of Cerberus's replica—well, almost all of it. While he appreciates upgrades like leather seats (as well as an upgraded FTL drive), he resents the installation of an advanced AI system to monitor the mission.

> There are no mission objectives aboard the *Normandy*, but in addition to overall story missions, there are special missions you can accept before moving out across the galaxy.
>
> **NOTE**

Boarding the *Normandy*

Ever since Shepard woke up in the Cerberus facility, life has been moving pretty fast. Surviving a mech attack. Meeting the mysterious Illusive Man. Investigating a human colony stripped bare by the Collectors. Though the fate of the galaxy hangs in the balance, this is the first time Shepard actually gets to call the shots and determine the next course of action.

Touring the *Normandy* is entirely optional; Shepard can immediately plot a course to the next planet. However, walking around the new ship and meeting the new crew has real merit. There are special missions to accept, for example, and there are plenty of new codex entries to log through scans of the *Normandy*'s facets and conversations. Conversing with the crew can also result in morality points and potentially more—much more.

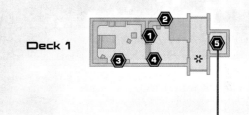

Deck 1

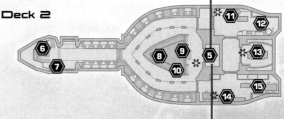

Deck 2

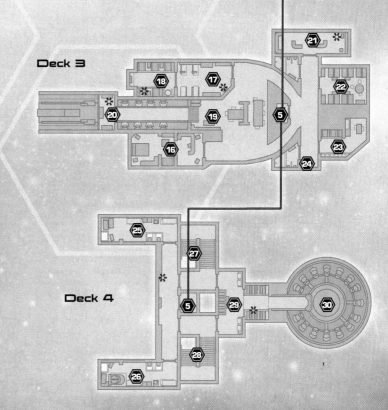

Deck 3

Deck 4

LEGEND

1. Personal Terminal
2. Medals Case
3. Armor Locker
4. Fish Tank
5. Elevator
6. Joker
7. EDI
8. Normandy Hologram
9. Galaxy Map/ Yeoman Chambers
10. Personal Terminal
11. Research Terminal
12. Lab
13. Briefing Room
14. Weapons Locker
15. Armory
16. Miranda's Office
17. Medical
18. AI Core
19. Mess Hall
20. Main Battery
21. Starboard Observation Deck
22. Crew Quarters
23. Life Support
24. Port Observation Monitoring Station
25. Starboard Cargo/ Surveilance
26. Port Cargo
27. Sub-Deck Stairwell
28. Sub-Deck Stairwell
29. Engineering
30. Engine Core
* EDI Hub

Introduction · Training · Upgrades and Research · Walkthrough · Normandy SR2 · Special Assignments · Planetary Database · Appendix

Miranda and Jacob

As soon as Shepard sets foot on the *Normandy*'s flight deck (the second deck of the ship), Miranda and Jacob flank the commander to talk about the next step of the mission. Miranda has her suggestion ready: immediately seek Dr. Mordin Solus on Omega. The brilliant salarian scientist is critical to developing a countermeasure to the Collectors' incapacitating swarm attacks. Without some means of neutralizing the swarm, there is no hope of getting close to the Collectors and discovering their link to the Reapers.

The order of seeking recruits is ultimately up to Shepard, who might even need to remind Miranda exactly who is in charge on this mission. However, EDI—the *Normandy*'s new AI system—chimes in to back up Miranda. Without the professor, the mission simply cannot go on. This is a good opportunity to initially greet EDI (which stands for Enhanced Defense Intelligence), although Shepard can interact more with the AI in the cockpit during a general tour of the ship.

Four recruits can be pursued at this point, each recommended by the Illusive Man and backed up by the dossiers he offered at the conclusion of Freedom's Progress. Here are the four possible recruitment missions:

- Dossier: The Professor
- Dossier: Archangel
- Dossier: The Convict
- Dossier: Dr. Okeer

Of these possible four recruits, the professor is the one that most directly advances the mission. It is always good to have additional friends at Shepard's side for the struggles ahead, but recruiting the professor not only unlocks the tech lab aboard the *Normandy* (allowing Shepard to direct research projects and improve tech), it also starts the development of the critical Collector countermeasures. Once they have been completed, Shepard and the team can actually start their chase in earnest.

The locations of these four recruits have been marked on the galaxy map. Use the galaxy map on deck 2 to plot a course.

As soon as you finish looking around the *Normandy*, you can head out to chase down these potential recruits. You can track your recruits in any order, but the only one required (at this point) is the professor.

NOTE

After this initial conversation, Miranda and Jacob fan out to their respective stations on the *Normandy*; Miranda's office is on deck 3, and Jacob's is the armory on the main deck, deck 2. Shepard can continue talking to them at their stations.

There are four decks to the *Normandy* that Shepard can explore, although not every door is open to the commander at this point, such as the tech lab.

- Deck 1: Captain's Cabin
- Deck 2: Command Information Center (CIC)
- Deck 3: Crew's Quarters
- Deck 4: Engineering

Deck 1

Captain's Quarters

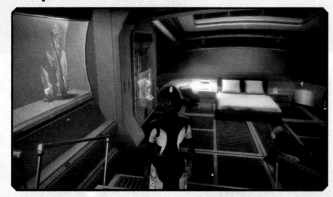

When you buy ship replicas in shops, they appear on the display case above Shepard's desk.

Shepard's private quarters occupy deck 2, directly above the flight deck. The spacious quarters contain a private terminal, just like the terminal next to the galaxy map.

There is an armor locker in the captain's quarters, too. From the armor locker, Shepard's outfit can be modified, just as in the armor locker at the Cerberus outpost just prior to leaving for Freedom's Progress. There is not much to do with the armor part of this locker just yet. However, as Shepard acquires more pieces of armor during missions or from shops, return to this locker to outfit the commander with better defenses, such as helmets or chest plates.

Right now, though, Shepard can change casual wear for non-mission dress. Select from different outfit pieces and tints.

The Medal of Honor display next to the private terminal shows off all collected achievements.

> **NOTE**
>
> Please refer to the "Training" chapter for detailed explanations of how armor works and what is available.

Deck 2

Combat Information Center (CIC)

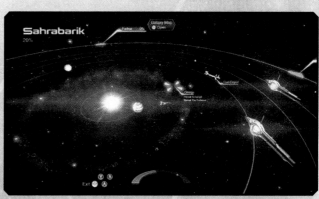

The galaxy map is your launch pad to the galaxy. As soon as you are done exploring the Normandy, return here and plot a course for the first desired recruit.

The largest feature of the flight deck is Shepard's command center and the galaxy map. From the galaxy map, Shepard can launch missions and direct Joker to pilot the ship to any available planet. As the mission expands, more and more planets become available on the galaxy map.

Next to the galaxy map is Shepard's private terminal. Access the private terminal to read incoming messages meant only for Shepard's eyes, to investigate the crew's specializations (when Shepard collects enough minerals and tech, specialization upgrades can be reviewed and ordered from this terminal), and to get a report on the team's status.

> **NOTE**
>
> Some of the incoming messages are informal, but the terminal is also a good place to check for special assignments from Cerberus.

Also next to the galaxy map is Yeoman Kelly Chambers, who has been assigned as Shepard's administrative assistant. Chambers is in awe of Shepard and is obviously excited to be working for the commander. As Shepard's assistant, she is something like traffic control. When the crew needs to speak to Shepard, Chambers will alert the commander. Any outstanding missions or appointments? Chambers will be there with a reminder or update.

Chambers is more than just Shepard's assistant, however; she has also been tasked with keeping an eye on the mental health of the crew. This role as crew psychologist is unofficial, though: Chambers believes she will be far more effective in this role if she appears more as an informal confidante than a Cerberus-sanctioned head doctor.

Yeoman Kelly Chambers

How Shepard interacts with Chambers during this initial conversation can start a potential love story.

If Shepard keeps it all business, the chance for this relationship to be anything but professional is snuffed out. But selecting flirty replies to Chambers's questions or statements ignites a spark, which can grow into romance or friendship depending on how Shepard responds to Chambers's leading statement about closing her eyes and falling back into Shepard's arms. If you'd like to pursue a good friendship with Kelly, let her know Shepard would catch her instead of embrace her. If you are interested in a romance with Kelly, tell her that Shepard might do more than catch her... Chambers almost shimmers at the come-on.

Whenever you return to the *Normandy* after completing a mission, check in with Chambers. There are multiple opportunities to flirt or just get to know Kelly better. If you really want to pursue a relationship, then talk to Chambers often and keep up the coy talk.

Bridge

Just beyond the galaxy map is the bridge of the *Normandy SR2*. As Shepard walks through the hall leading up to Joker's position, scan the terminals to log two codex entries. Once in the cockpit, Shepard can either speak to Joker or get to know more about EDI.

Conversing with EDI leads to additional information about the role of the AI's routine. Press EDI about her ability to run electronic and cybernetic warfare defenses to prevent any intruders into the *Normandy*'s systems during an attack. EDI also monitors shipboard activities and reports certain information back to the Illusive Man.

> EDI's physical core is located in a quantum blue box behind the ship's medical bay.
>
> **NOTE**

EDI is also up front about having additional functions that are currently locked and unknown. Only when the time is right will these new functions be revealed.

> EDI can also elaborate on Cerberus's command structure, letting Shepard know exactly how the group operates, from the Illusive Man on down to individual cells. However, some of EDI's conversation options must be unlocked later, after the "Save the *Normandy*" mission.
>
> **TIP**

> EDI's main interface is on the bridge, but you can speak with EDI in many of the ship's compartments. Look for EDI terminals on the walls to get a deeper tour of the *Normandy*.
>
> **NOTE**

Shepard can also catch up with Joker a little here. Joker—referred to as Mr. Moreau by EDI—is pleased with the new *Normandy*, save for his skepticism of EDI, since, well, AI doesn't have the most sterling reputation in the galaxy thanks to the rise and proliferation of the geth. But Joker thinks that since Cerberus has invested so much in Project Lazarus

and the reconstruction of the *Normandy*, there is little upside to Cerberus betraying Shepard and the team. Joker also has his opinion on the aftermath of the original mission and how both the Alliance and Council cut them adrift in spite of the success against Sovereign.

Keep checking back with Joker between missions. Talk to him and get his feelings and opinions on the crew and the mission. Joker may have a smart mouth, but there is an emphasis on smart. He often has interesting things to say about the crew and the mission.

The Armory

Behind the CIC are the closed-off tech lab and the armory. Inside the armory, Shepard can change the squad's loadout from all available weapons. Jacob is stationed inside the armory, and this is a good chance to speak to him without Miranda. Jacob is honored to be serving with Shepard and actually has

some degree of hope about the mission outcomes despite concerns about Cerberus's past activities.

Enjoying camaraderie with Jacob results in Paragon points.

NOTE

Jacob

While everything is professional with Jacob right now, you can also wear down his "all business" defenses over time.

Repeatedly check in with Jacob and try to initiate personal conversations. He will rebuff some of your efforts. Give him his space when he needs it. But look for openings, such as asking Jacob what he thinks of your Cerberus-rebuilt body. Much as with Chambers, keep checking with Jacob and—if so desired—pry open his heart with a combination of smooth talk and genuine concern. Jacob is only romantically interested in a female Shepard.

Deck 3

When you visit deck 3, expect to find some closed off areas, such as life support. As you add to the crew and progress on your mission, areas of the ship that were closed off open up. When these areas become critical locations, such as the station of a new member, look for an explanation of the area following the acquisition of the recruit.

Mess Area

The mess occupies the open area near the elevator. There are crew sitting around a table visiting, but you should stop by the kitchen to chat up Mess Sergeant Gardner. Gardner is a friendly fellow and quite proud to be serving with the commander, even if it is as a cook and janitor. Talk to Gardner about his job and how he got involved with Cerberus.

Before leaving to explore more of the *Normandy*, be sure to ask Gardner if he needs anything. This

opens up a special assignment: Special Ingredients. Gardner would love better provisions so he can give the crew some quality meals. If you agree to help, Gardner hands over a list. All you need to do at this point is find a place to buy them and bring them back to the *Normandy*.

The provisions for this special assignment are located at the Citadel. You will end up there soon enough, so no hurry right now.

TIP

Medical Lab

There is a familiar face in the medical lab: Dr. Chakwas. She was the medical officer aboard the original *Normandy*, so it is a relief to see that she was able to escape the ship before it was destroyed. You can chat with Chakwas about the mission and Cerberus. Ask Chakwas if she has everything she needs to open up a special mission: Serrice Ice Brandy. It seems that when the *Normandy SR1* was destroyed, her private stash didn't quite merit space in an escape pod. Offering to bring back a bottle places the assignment in your journal.

Introduction

Training

Upgrades and Research

Normandy SR2 | Walkthrough

Special Assignments

Planetary Database

Appendix

TIP

You can fulfill this assignment on Omega by purchasing the special brandy from the bar Afterlife.

Also of note in the medical lab: EDI's AI core is locked behind the rear door in the room. You cannot access EDI right now. But the fact that the door can indeed be opened implies that EDI was built with the recognition that at some point, human hands on the core would be a necessity.

Miranda's Office

Miranda's office is located on deck 3, not too far from the crew's quarters and the mess area. During your first visit, Miranda seems quite accommodating. She is willing to answer your questions about Cerberus, the mission, and the Illusive Man, but she gives you pat answers that seem to serve the best interests of Cerberus. Miranda is a potential romantic partner (for a male Shepard) if you take the time to get to know her.

You can also ask Miranda about herself. She becomes a little more animated in her responses, but these still feel slightly rehearsed. She goes over her augmented form, her cybernetics, and her training. Miranda has a high opinion of herself, that's for sure. But her self-regard is not without merit. She is a highly trained individual with excellent combat skills and an analytical mind.

Miranda's office on deck 3 will be a regular stop. Since she was such a pivotal figure in your resurrection, you will want to talk to her often. But understand that Miranda is not the most forward person. She has a highly polished veneer that she rarely lowers. It will take time and repeat conversations to peek behind it and find out a little more about her, like where she came from and what her family is like. It is also possible to get even closer to her, if you carefully navigate the minefield of conversation. Show genuine sympathy and strength.

Deck 4

Deck 4 is the engineering deck. There is little going on down here on your first trip aboard the *Normandy*, but as you pick up recruits and travel the galaxy, more of the engineering deck opens up.

Engineers

There are two engineers monitoring the *Normandy*'s condition down on deck 4: Engineer Daniels and Engineer Donnelly. Pay a visit to these two. They are quite amenable to company, especially from the commander. Take an interest in what they are doing and listen to them tell their stories. Having the support of your crew is important. You should always make an effort to get along with your crew members. You'll never know what help or insight they can provide on your missions. Donnelly mentions that calibration takes longer with their current equipment. Daniels says that with new couplings, they could really cut down maintenance time.

This conversation opens another special assignment: FBA Couplings. If you can bring back the couplings for the engineers, you will have their gratitude. Furthering your friendship with the pair pays off. Maybe they'll even invite you to a card game later on where you can win some credits.

TIP

The FBA Couplings you need for these engineers are located on Omega.

NOTE

More places inside the *Normandy* are opened as you recruit more squad members. As the squad expands, the size of the rounds you make post-mission increases. Keep talking to squad and crew members to get their take on the mission. And if you desire a relationship, you need to repeatedly check in with potential paramours throughout the adventure to build up the romantic tension.

CITADEL

The Citadel is a massive deep space station originally thought to be constructed by the Protheans and later discovered to be a device of trickery by the Reapers. The Citadel serves as the seat of the Council, which is the governing body of Citadel space. Races that do not sit on the Council still frequent the Citadel because it is a major hub of commerce as well as politics. Most races that use the mass relays at least have embassies on the Citadel.

Although much of the physical damage done to the Citadel by Saren and Sovereign two years ago has been repaired, the psychological effects still linger, even if the Council has been trying to portray the Reaper attack as an isolated incident.

> You can visit the Citadel as soon as you are able to command the *Normandy* and use the galaxy map on the CIC. However, it is not as central to the story as it was in the first *Mass Effect*. Only two primary missions on the Citadel figure into the main plot: Thane's and Garrus's loyalty missions. But there are also optional special assignments on the Citadel that are worth experience points. All of the special assignments on the Citadel are available on your first visit, so stopping by early can really help you gain a level. Otherwise, it is a good place to shop as well as to visit Captain Anderson.
>
> **NOTE**

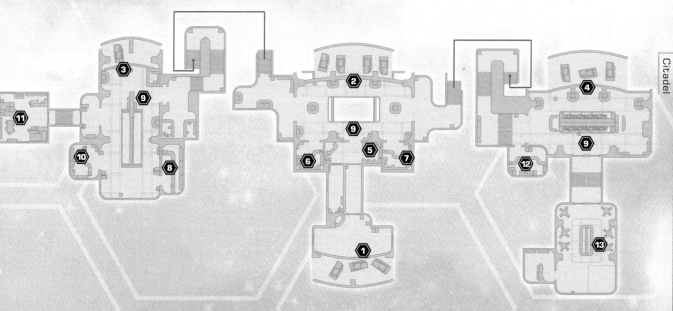

LEGEND

1 Rapid Transit / Normandy	**5** Captain Bailey	**10** Sirta Foundation
2 Rapid Transit	**6** Zakera Café	**11** Warehouse
3 Rapid Transit	**7** Citadel Souvenirs	**12** Rodam Expeditions
4 Rapid Transit	**8** Saronis Applications	**13** Dark Star Lounge
	9 Avina Terminal	

Introduction

Training

Upgrades and Research

Citadel

Walkthrough

Special Assignments

Planetary Database

Appendix

Arrival

Two years after the attack, Shepard visits the Citadel and discovers it has changed noticeably. However, unlike in the original *Mass Effect*, Shepard's activities on the Citadel this time are limited to just a few floors of the Zakera Ward and the Presidium, where Anderson waits to see if the rumors that Shepard is still alive are indeed true. The three floors Shepard can explore are primarily shopping areas, although there is still much to learn about how the galaxy's politics work; there are also a few special assignments, most of which are confined to the Citadel.

When you first stop at the Citadel, you dock at level 27. You should check in with the C-Sec desk. It seems that security measures on the station have been bumped up. The geth attack was a shock, and so to prevent any future infiltration, most visitors are asked to surrender weapons and biotic amps before entering the Citadel.

Glossary

C-Sec: Short for Citadel Security, C-Sec is the internal police force on the Citadel. C-Sec recruits from almost every race in Citadel space, with a few exceptions, such as the krogan and vorcha.

Just beyond the C-Sec desk is a checkpoint. You are stopped by the turian running the checkpoint because the scanner shows that you are dead. The C-Sec guard requests that you check in with his captain, just past the scanners on the right. You can get reinstated in the system there, as well as learn more about changes in the Citadel. Just follow the sound of Captain Bailey's voice. He's loud, even when talking about putting the squeeze on suspects.

Captain Bailey recognizes you right away. He runs through a litany of bureaucratic stuff you will need to do to be reinstated and allowed access to the Citadel, such as stopping by the treasury, since apparently other people have faked their deaths to avoid taxes. However, Bailey is able to fast-track your access right at his terminal. Bailey's description of C-Sec sounds a touch more sinister, almost as if the security force has deeper reach inside the Citadel than before.

Avina, located outside Bailey's office, is a tour guide for the Citadel. The hologram provides additional background on the Citadel.

Galactic News terminals are everywhere. Activate them to listen to news reports about the current state of affairs.

If you imported Shepard into *Mass Effect 2*, the decisions you made at the end of the first game are felt soon enough. If you allowed the Council to be destroyed, for example, Avina warns you that skepticism of humans is rampant on the Citadel since humans benefitted most from the reconstruction of the Council.

NOTE

Rapid Transit

There are three floors of the Zakera block that you can explore on your first visit. Shepard can also visit the Presidium, the location of the human embassy. Stairs connect the three floors of the Zakera Ward, but the easiest mode of travel is via Rapid Transit.

Just approach a Rapid Transit terminal and select the floor you wish to visit. The current floor will be grayed out, as will the Factory District, which does not come into play until later. From the Rapid Transit menu, you can also stop at the Presidium, request a new squad member, or return to the *Normandy*.

Level 27

If you're interested in seeing the sights, listening to conversations, or doing a little shopping, stay to explore level 27 of the ward (the level where you dock). If you want to dive right into some action, head directly to level 26 to begin a special assignment or proceed to the Presidium.

> The Citadel's special assignments are detailed in the "Special Assignments" chapter.
>
> **NOTE**

Citadel Souvenirs

Citadel Souvenirs is run by a friendly asari named Deleia Sanassi. Her shop contains souvenirs for the Citadel and other goods like model ships and fish. You can either lean on Deleia to accept your endorsement for a discount or you can accuse her of classism.

Zakera Cafe

Stop into the Zakera Cafe and browse the kiosk. There are just a handful of things you can buy at the cafe, but if you are searching for the high-quality provisions for Mess Sergeant Gardner back on the *Normandy* (part of the Special Ingredients assignment), this is the place to buy them. You can also buy two historical novels at the cafe, which add entries to your codex.

Level 28

There is more shopping on level 28. In addition to frequenting stores, be sure to listen in at the game kiosk for the latest on video games on the Citadel and to chat with other ward dwellers.

Rodam Expeditions

Rodam Expeditions is a shop owned by turian Etarn Tiron. Etarn is not immediately friendly, but like in most shops, you can choose either Paragon or Renegade options to secure a discount. Rodam Expeditions' inventory includes upgrades, such as the Scram Pulsar, which improves sniper rifle damage for the entire squad, and body armor that ups health by 5 percent.

Introduction

Training

Upgrades and Research

Citadel

Walkthrough

Special Assignments

Planetary Database

Appendix

The News

Remember the news reporter Khalisah al-Jilani? She's still on the Citadel, chasing scoops that sometimes make people look bad. You were once the subject of Khalisah's sensational journalism. Now the reporter wants to talk again. This is another situation where your decisions in the original *Mass Effect* during the geth attack on the Citadel come into play.

If you allowed the Council to fall, for example, Khalisah rubs that in your face. However, you may have an interrupt opportunity that puts her in her place. Regardless of your previous choices on the Citadel, your behavior during this conversation determines whether you walk away with either Paragon or Renegade points.

Level 26

Level 26 is home to more shops, a transport dealership, and more. There are special assignments to undertake down here, too; if you're interested in completing them, check the "Special Assignments" chapter to learn who to contact in this area.

Sirta Foundation

The Sirta Foundation is run by the asari, Kian Louros. There are a few defense- and health-related wares available for purchase, such as the Microscanner medical upgrade to increase medi-gel capacity.

Saronis Applications

Marab, the salarian at the counter of Saronis Applications, is happy to see a human come into the shop. Marab is good for a short chat. Don't leave without inspecting his kiosk, though. Saronis carries tech upgrades, such as the Multicore Amplifier, which increases tech power damage.

The entrance to the Shipping Warehouse is on level 26, too; it is the entrance to Garrus's loyalty mission.

NOTE

Dark Star Lounge

The Dark Star is a lounge where ward dwellers congregate. There is no commerce you can do at the bar, but you should at least talk to characters in the room (the Presidium groundskeeper, for example, is part of one of the special assignments in the Citadel). And why not take a spin around the dance floor? Even formerly dead commanders need to blow off a little steam from time to time.

Presidium

After doing a little shopping, Shepard can stop by the Presidium and pay a visit to the human embassy. Use Rapid Transit to access the Presidium.

Anderson is waiting there to see Shepard. Anderson is awfully glad to see Shepard alive, although his heart is heavy with all the changes that happened while Shepard was away. One of those changes was Shepard falling in with Cerberus.

Shepard talks to Anderson about the Collectors, too. Though Anderson is open to the theory that the Collectors are working with the Reapers to steal away human colonists and are ultimately a threat to the entire Citadel, much work has gone into convincing everyone that Sovereign was a one-off attack by the geth.

The conversation with Anderson may be fulfilling on a personal note, but the fact that Shepard is working with Cerberus now is still a sticking point. There are things Anderson will not tell Shepard because of that. After wrapping up the conversation, do any additional shopping in the ward, finish any outstanding special assignments, and then return to the *Normandy*.

DOSSIERS

After touring the *Normandy* and reading the dossiers on the four possible recruits the Illusive Man recommended, Shepard must make some decisions. Where does the new crew start searching? Does Shepard follow Miranda's advice and immediately set out for Omega to locate the salarian professor, Dr. Mordin Solus? Or should the commander seek out other potential teammates first, like the convict on the prison ship *Purgatory*?

The choice is Shepard's, but without the professor there is no hope of building defenses against the Collector swarms. So at some point in the near future, even if Shepard recruits the other three teammates first, the commander must seek out the professor in the slums of Omega.

There are two recruits on Omega, though: the professor and the merc hunter Archangel. No matter which one Shepard seeks first, the Omega hub world must be explored. So, use the intel on Omega to track down the professor or Archangel. If you choose to go for the convict or the krogan first, skip ahead to those mission briefings and then come back to the Omega hub when you're ready to pursue the Omega-based recruits.

> **NOTE**
> Only after all four recruits are located does the Illusive Man communicate the next step of the mission to Shepard.

Omega

Omega is a hub of criminal activity built on an asteroid once rich with element zero. The asteroid was cracked open in a collision with another asteroid and corporations descended upon it to extract the valuable element zero. After the asteroid was mined out, the huge city erected to support the community eventually became a haven for weapon trafficking, narcotics, and other activities of ill repute.

> **NOTE**
> Both Archangel and the professor are located on Omega, so use the hub world walkthrough to make sure to see all of Omega as you work on these two recruits.

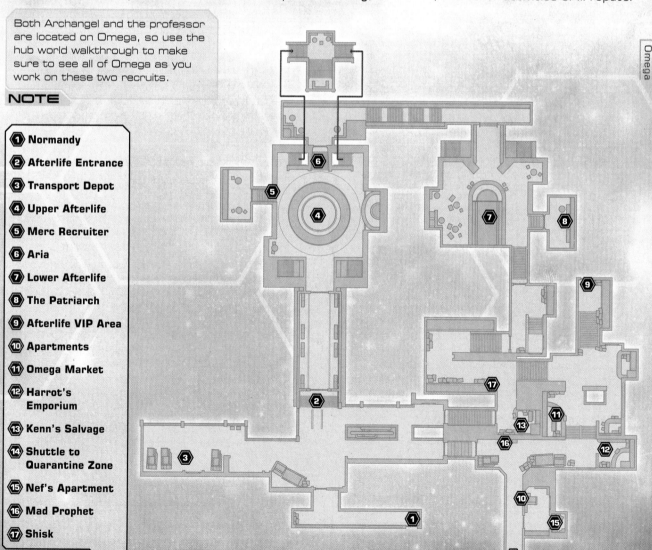

LEGEND

1. Normandy
2. Afterlife Entrance
3. Transport Depot
4. Upper Afterlife
5. Merc Recruiter
6. Aria
7. Lower Afterlife
8. The Patriarch
9. Afterlife VIP Area
10. Apartments
11. Omega Market
12. Harrot's Emporium
13. Kenn's Salvage
14. Shuttle to Quarantine Zone
15. Nef's Apartment
16. Mad Prophet
17. Shisk

Introduction · Training · Upgrades and Research · Omega · Walkthrough · Special Assignments · Planetary Database · Appendix

First Arrival

Omega is divided into a handful of areas: the marketplace, Afterlife, the slums, and the port where Archangel is holed up. The marketplace is available to you right away and you can go shopping any time you wish. The slums are where you should report if you want to chase down the professor. You cannot locate Archangel without paying a visit to Afterlife, the giant nightclub just outside the *Normandy*'s dock. So, make Afterlife your first stop, no matter which recruit you decide to chase down.

Omega is a pretty rough corner of the galaxy. As soon as Shepard steps off of the *Normandy*, the commander is greeted by a batarian with a nasty disposition. The batarian recommends that Shepard check in with Aria, who sounds like the kingpin of Omega—or at least, this month's kingpin. With all of the mercenary gangs, vorcha, and low-lifes running the joint, stable leadership seems like an anomaly rather than a constant.

> Omega never closes down, so you can come back as many times as you like until the story places Shepard beyond the point of no return.
>
> **NOTE**

Glossary

Asari: The asari are one of the four Council races that sit on the Citadel. In fact, they were the first to discover the Citadel and sought to establish the Council once the salarians arrived via their own mass relays. Asari are mono-gendered, with no concept of gender differences. The asari resemble human females, but they can mate with any race and live for up to 1,000 years. Asari go through three stages in their life-cycle: the youthful maiden, the maternal matron, and finally the wise matriarch.

Salarian: The second race to join the Citadel, the salarians have a mixed reputation in the galaxy. Though admired for their intelligence and for bringing the krogan out of their primitive state, the salarians are also judged harshly for their development of the krogan genophage, which the turians used to sterilize the majority of the krogan following the Krogan Rebellions.

Turian: The turians joined the Council 1,200 years ago and are considered the galaxy's peacekeepers, thanks to the sheer size of their fleet and their spread across the stars. They are a militaristic and highly disciplined race who first proposed the idea of the Citadel Security Services. Turians and humans were involved in a conflict called the First Contact War of 2157, although many of those differences have been set aside.

Batarian: The batarians are an aggressive species that withdrew from the Citadel following the Council decision to consider batarian colony space unsettled and open for human development. Batarians have funded a number of criminal enterprises and pirate operations since then to strike human colonies, but humanity was able to push the batarians back into their own systems.

Vorcha: Vorcha are reptilian aliens that are victims of much hostility and racism in the galaxy. Because the vorcha are unable to get a foothold in civilized society, they largely turn to criminal gangs for employment and camaraderie. Vorcha have regenerative bodies that withstand pain and injury, but they have a short life expectancy due to their violent nature.

Krogan: The krogan are a brutal race discovered by the salarians and transformed into a mighty army to help put down the spider-like rachni in the great Rachni Wars. After being brought out of their primitive state, though, the krogan multiplied exponentially and aggressively colonized. The salarians developed a bioweapon (deployed by the turians in the Krogan Rebellions) called the genophage that renders only one in every 1,000 krogan pregnancies viable. As a result, the krogan face eventual extinction unless a cure for the genophage is found.

Afterlife

Afterlife is a two-level nightclub and a central feature of Omega. The bar throbs with the latest dance music. Patrons drown their sorrows and toast their successes at the upstairs bar. The bar is directly in front of you when you enter the long corridor leading to the club interior.

Confront Kylan, a batarian, in the hallway to earn some Paragon or Renegade points.

However enticing the bar looks, the main reason to visit Afterlife is to seek an audience with Aria. She is behind the bar, on a platform that lets her survey her kingdom. She's flanked by heavies, but they will not give you any trouble in her presence. In fact, Aria seems quite content to talk to Shepard.

On the lookout for a bottle of Serrice Ice Brandy for Dr. Chakwas? Pick it up at the small bar inside Afterlife. The special assignment ends when you take it back to the *Normandy*'s medical officer.

TIP

Want to pursue Archangel? Speak to the merc recruiter to the left of the bar.

NOTE

Aria

Aria is the asari in charge of Omega. She oversees all from her perch at the top of this station's food chain. She didn't get there by being nice, so don't be offended if she is a touch brusque when you speak with her.

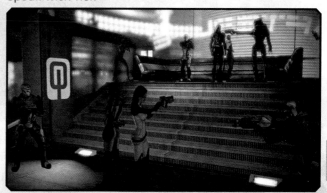

The commander's presence has made Aria's muscle a little jumpy.

Aria has information on Professor Mordin Solus and Archangel, so talk to her about each potential recruit. Aria talks about the professor being both a genius and a madman, taking up residence inside the slums, which are currently under lockdown due to a plague. The plague affects all alien races except vorcha and humans. Meanwhile, Archangel is a thorn in the paw of the mercenary companies doing business on Omega. Aria seems more amused by him than anything, probably because Archangel hasn't directly interfered with her business, which would break Aria's first rule of living on Omega: Don't mess with Aria. (Her phrasing is a touch more colorful...)

You should also use this chance to familiarize yourself with Omega through Aria's eyes, so explore every bit of potential conversation.

Aria gives Shepard information about the professor and Archangel, but she is not directly involved with either of them. However, after completing either of the recruitment missions on Omega, return to Afterlife. Speak to Grizz, the turian watching the stairs to the left of Aria. The turian informs you that Aria has a small side job she needs done. The special assignment involves a local krogan called the Patriarch. The special assignment is called The Patriarch and is explained in the "Special Assignments" chapter following the walkthrough for the main story.

NOTE

Lower Bar

Afterlife's VIP Room is not exactly welcoming to humans. You can enter the lower floor via the entrance inside Afterlife's main floor or seek out the alternative entrance into the lower bar, which is downstairs from the main bar. Head into the marketplace and use the map to wind through the stalls and debris. The secret entrance leads to a long staircase that deposits you right inside the bar.

The lower bar is smaller and more intimate than the main floor. It's just as loud, though. If you like, you can stop by the bar. A batarian is slinging drinks. If you order a drink from the bartender, you open up a small special assignment that you can complete right away: Batarian Bartender.

Special assignments received from citizens of cities and via your private terminal are detailed in the "Special Assignments" chapter. However, we explain this one here so you get an idea of what's involved when you take on a small, local job.

NOTE

Re-enter the lower bar the same way and return to the bar. The batarian will not recognize you right away because he assumes you're already a corpse in the muck under Omega. But once he has poured you a drink, you have two choices. The Renegade route is to force the batarian into drinking his own poison. Or you can opt to raise a little noise about poisoned drinks to get the attention of other patrons. A turian takes particular interest in the situation. So offended by the batarian's alien hate (and the fact that the batarian is likely to transfer his grudge to turians one day), the turian shoots the bartender. This ends the special assignment. The batarian bartender's reign of terror is over. The next time you visit the lower bar, an agreeable salarian is behind the counter and he's been instructed to give you drinks on the house.

Talk to the batarian and order a drink. After slugging it, you collapse to the ground. You wake up just outside the bar. A human local tells you that the bartender has a reputation for hating humans so much that he poisons them. You're the first human to survive the batarian's spiked drinks. If you'd like, you can make sure you are the last.

Shopping

To locate the shopping on Omega, pass through the doors marked "Shopping" or "Apartments" to the right of Afterlife. Both doors lead to the stalls, although from different directions. The shopping area is pretty crowded, so expect to see a solid cross-section of aliens wheeling and dealing.

The ramblings of the Mad Prophet on his soapbox greet you as you walk inside the marketplace via the apartment doors. Stop and have a listen if you'd like, and egg him on to unfurl more of his grand prophecy on humanity being a blight on the galaxy. The Mad Prophet can be left alone, too, without any consequences.

What you really want to do, though, is explore the stalls in the marketplace and see what is for sale. There is also a special assignment available if you visit Kenn's Salvage at the bottom of the marketplace. Some of the stalls refuse to do business with a human, though, and those will offer no options for interactivity when you look at them.

> The entrance to the slums is inside the marketplace, too. It's close to the apartments door, just down the long corridor. You'll spot a turian guard at the slum entrance, turning back anybody who tries to access the plague-ridden district.
>
> **NOTE**

Harrot's Emporium

Harrot's Emporium is on the main floor of the Omega marketplace. The shop is run by an elcor, one of a race of aliens that speak in such a monotone they are forced to declare their inflections before each sentence. Harrot sells useful tech and model ships. When you meet him, he is also treating a young quarian named Kenn shabbily. Talking to Kenn starts a special assignment that involves speaking to Harrot about his actions.

Kenn's Salvage

Kenn is a young quarian who was stranded on Omega when he lost the majority of his savings. He has since taken to selling salvaged tech to make a meager living on Omega. You are able to appeal to Kenn to get a discount on his goods, although he needs to sell his goods for high prices to keep peace with Harrot.

Kenn needs 1,000 credits to get off Omega. You can opt to give him the credits now and free him, or you can go speak to Harrot as part of the Struggling Quarian special assignment. Even if you help Kenn, you can still buy his salvaged tech.

> Buy the FBA Couplings needed for the engineers on the *Normandy* at Kenn's Salvage.
>
> **TIP**

Talk to the vorcha next to Kenn's Salvage to get your first encounter with this alien. The vorcha are...unpleasant.

Omega Market

The Omega Market on the main floor of the marketplace is run by Marsh, a batarian. Batarians are not necessarily partial to humans, but Marsh values business over race relations and is willing to deal with you. Marsh sells a variety of goods, from model ships to useful tech.

Introduction

Training

Upgrades and Research

Omega

Walkthrough

Special Assignments

Planetary Database

Appendix

THE PROFESSOR

The Illusive Man has identified a salarian scientist named Mordin Solus who is intelligent enough to potentially craft countermeasures against the Collector swarms. Mordin is currently operating a clinic inside the quarantined slums of Omega. A plague has ripped through the slums, affecting all races except humans and vorcha. Shepard must find a way into the slums and then locate Mordin. Getting the scientist out, though, will not be easy. The slums are overrun by merc gangs looking for a piece of the action in the wake of the plague.

Spoils of War

- Credits: 50,000
- Element Zero: 1,000
- Palladium: 2,000
- Platinum: 2,000
- Iridium: 2,000

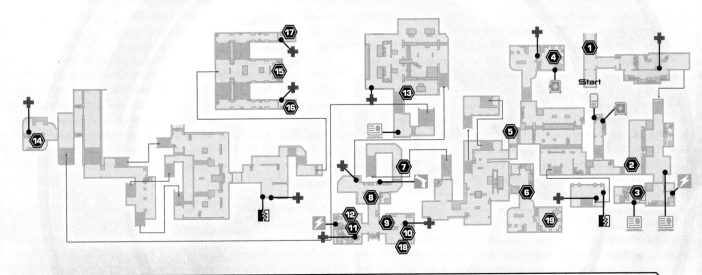

LEGEND

1 Refined Element Zero	8 Mordin's Clinic	14 Daniel	Spare Parts
2 Batarian Victim	9 Refined Platinum	15 Power Startup	Wall Safe
3 Turian Plague Victim	10 Refined Palladium	16 East Fan Array	Medi-Gel
4 Refugee	11 Mordin	17 West Fan Array	Datapad
5 Modified Assault Rifle	12 Refined Element Zero AND Refined Iridium	18 Research Station (Medi-Gel Capacity Upgrade)	Computer
6 Refined Element Zero	13 Gambling Terminal	19 Human Looters	Power Cell
7 Clinic Guard			Weapon Locker

Objective 1: Locate Mordin Solus

The slums are currently off-limits to Omega residents. The entrance is guarded by an armed turian. When you arrive, he's busy turning away a human female. Despite humans not being susceptible to the plague, the turian still refuses to let the human in, lest she bring it back out with her.

You must talk to the turian in order to enter the slums. The turian is stubborn at first, but use your powers of persuasion to talk the turian into stepping aside. You can tell the turian either that you're on a mission to find Mordin or that you can help clean up the merc problem that's almost as much of a plague in the slums as the Blue Suns and other gangs. Either way, the turian relents and allows you inside, although he warns that the Blue Suns guards enforcing the quarantine inside the slums are likely to open fire as soon as you try to enter the area.

> Even though the plague affects all non-human and non-vorcha races, you can take non-human teammates inside. The plague will not affect them.
>
> **NOTE**

Enter the Slums

The slums seem deserted. There are a few bodies slumped in the corners. Check behind the barricade of crates directly inside the slums to find 250 units of refined element zero. After collecting the element zero, press deeper into the slums.

Sure enough, when you reach the first checkpoint, district guards pop up from behind a barricade and open fire. Pick off the guards from cover. Then, slip through the archway to the right of the checkpoint and move along the corridor. Collect the medi-gel from the station on the nearby wall and then move down to the Gozu District via the door beyond the checkpoint.

Sick Batarian

There is a stack of burning bodies inside the Gozu District—a barbaric way to dispose of the dead in hopes of curtailing the spread of the plague. There is a batarian still alive next to one of the fires. He's fallen victim to the plague and is in really bad shape. Talk to the batarian to learn more about the source of the plague.

The batarian is convinced that because humans are not affected by the plague, humans must have created the plague.

While he is in the middle of a coughing fit, you have the interrupt opportunity to give the batarian medi-gel. The offering of medicine and sympathy changes the batarian's tone. He is willing to talk to you about the plague and conditions inside the slums.

If you ask about Mordin, the batarian paints a picture of a doctor with unorthodox methods. Blue Suns mercs tried to press Mordin for protection money, but the salarian just killed them. After talking to the batarian, it's time to wish him luck and move farther into the slums.

Hack the terminal next to the mechanical services door for 5,000 credits.

Inside the mechanical services room, you can replenish heavy weapons by opening the crate of power cells. Bypass the locks on the door near the crate to enter the tomb of two slum residents. Inspect the body of the turian plague victim and then play the data logs on the nearby console to listen to the unfortunate turian's final plight.

Moving Deeper

Continue down the corridor just behind the batarian. A locked door on the right can be bypassed. At the bottom of the stairs, you find a small room with another plague victim. His datapad reveals that the Blue Suns have been busy locking residents up to die. Check the wall safe for 7,000 credits and then head back up the stairs.

When you inch up to the corner just beyond the locked door, you can hear the grunt of Blue Suns thugs. They have taken up position behind a barricade and will fire on you as soon as they see you. Use cover to inch up to the barricade and fire on the Blue Suns troopers. The troopers are in an ideal spot, so you might be better served firing at them to get a little cover and then running across the hall to flank them from the right.

The Blue Suns at the barricade have multiple reinforcements, including Blue Suns legionnaires. If you flank, you can cut them down with the explosive containers.

Two humans are holed up in their apartment to the right of the Blue Suns barricade. When you enter the apartment, take the medi-gel from the kitchen table and then walk up to the living room. The humans come out of hiding. They explain that because the plague does not affect humans, the Blue Suns also believe that humans are responsible. As a result, they shoot humans on sight.

Talk to the humans about Mordin. They explain that his lab is pretty deep in the slums. Mordin is taking in refugees now but the humans are suspicious. Mordin was able to kill vorcha and Blue Suns without much effort. He must be more than just a doctor—perhaps a former soldier. Return to the barricade when you have exhausted the conversation.

> **TIP**
> There are 8,000 credits in the wall safe to the right of the humans.

Scan the dead Blue Suns soldier behind the barricade for the Kinetic Pulsar tech upgrade. It adds 10 percent damage to assault rifles.

As you move along, you pick up the sounds of a battle. Inch up to the corner where you hear gunshots. The Blue Suns are opening fire, but not on you. Use the stairs to get a top-down view of the scene. The Blue Suns are locked in a gunfight with Blood Pack thugs: krogan and vorcha. And the Blue Suns are losing.

The Blood Pack mercs are moving in on Blue Suns territory. There are Blood Pack troopers, pyros, and warriors. The troopers and pyros are vorcha and so they are aggressive, but they do not charge like the krogan warriors. You must watch for the krogan and not get too close. The krogan will charge, which causes a lot of damage.

Snipe the pyros' flame packs. If you shoot a pack, it explodes in just a few seconds, instantly killing the vorcha.

TIP

The Blood Pack mercs brought varren with them. These war dogs close in fast, so take them down as soon as possible.

CAUTION

Use the explosive containers as makeshift bombs to clear out as many of the Blood Pack as possible.

TIP

You can do a lot of damage from the walkway overlooking the courtyard, but watch out for krogan Blood Pack warriors who storm the stairs so they can charge and use their shotguns up close.

After the battle is won, go through the door down on the main floor. It leads to a storage room with 250 units of refined element zero. Another door inside opens into an apartment. Two human looters are ransacking the place. Have words with them. You can either turn a blind eye or appeal to their dignity.

After leaving the humans, follow the signs to the clinic.

Meeting Mordin

Breathe easy as you walk by the two mechs guarding the clinic. They are not programmed to kill humans, so they leave you alone. Enter the clinic and have a look around. There are a lot of refugees seeking sanctuary at the clinic. A weapons locker near the entrance lets you swap out guns before heading back out into the slums. Medi-gel stations on the wall restock your spent supplies.

Scan the computer in the lab next to Mordin. This scan leads you to find the Microscanner, which increases your medi-gel capacity.

Mordin is friendly to you, which is a nice change of pace from the other aliens in the slums. The salarian talks fast and seems scatter-brained, but that's just his non-linear thinking getting ahead of his mouth. Mordin is a genius and has developed a cure for the plague.

Mordin has heard of the Collectors. He wonders if there might be some connection between the plague—which leaves humans alive—and the fact that the Collectors are seizing only human colonists. Mordin would join your team, but he is too busy at the clinic right now. He still needs to deploy his cure and get the plague under control. He wants to distribute it through the air-cycling system, but the vorcha are guarding it. Mordin needs you to brave the merc-controlled slums again and release the plague cure into the air-cycling system. Once the plague has been cured, Mordin will join your team.

Mordin also requests that you keep an eye out for Daniel, one of his assistants, who went into the slums to help plague victims. Can you please make sure he gets back to the clinic? This is a special assignment: Missing Assistant.

Be sure to tell Mordin about the batarian at the entrance to the slums. Perhaps the salarian can help him?

TIP

Before you leave, Mordin hands over a new weapon: the hand cannon. The handgun holds fewer shots than the heavy pistol, but each shot packs a greater kick. This is a perfect weapon for headshots. You can take down weaker vorcha with a single shot from the hand cannon at medium range. After searching the clinic and making sure you have your preferred weapon, use the door in the back of the clinic to move on to the environmental control center, where you can release the cure into the air-cycling system.

Objective 2: Cure the Plague

Fight to Environmental Control

It doesn't take long to find the Blood Pack. The Blood Pack thugs have set up an ambush behind the clinic. At least the courtyard has enough cover for your team to use when launching a counterattack. Look out for Blood Pack troopers in the rear of the room; they will not get too deep into the fight but instead squeeze off shots from a distance in hopes of killing you with a dozen small wounds.

The width of the courtyard is well suited for flanking. Move along one side of the room to get closer to the Blood Pack and pick them off.

Before long, the weak Blood Pack troopers are reinforced with Blood Pack warriors. These krogan do not believe in staying back.

Running low on thermal clips? With so many enemies killed, there will be plenty of dropped thermal clips on the floor.

Don't leave without hacking the gambling terminal to the left of the courtyard. That's 6,000 easy credits.

There are stairs near the gambling terminal. Head up them and then hack the nearby banking terminal for another 7,500 credits. Continue up the stairs until you reach a hall with two doors. Open the door on the left first; Daniel is behind that door.

Daniel

Daniel has been seized by batarians. The scene turns into a standoff within seconds. Try to convince the batarians that Daniel is not there to spread any more disease. You can end this standoff by either letting the batarians back down, thus earning Paragon points, or you can refuse to let them leave and earn Renegade points. If Daniel survives, he heads back to the clinic, leaving behind a medi-gel crate.

More Blood Pack

The Blood Pack has taken a lot of territory away from the Blue Suns. More Blood Pack troopers wait just inside the door across the hall, but that's the only way to the air systems. Open the door and then immediately fire on the vorcha scum on the other side of the room.

Those Blood Pack troopers were just a couple of advance soldiers. When you try to close in on the air systems, rockets rain down from a Blood Pack boom-squad on a ledge above you. Use the stairs to avoid the rockets or run to the right to flank the Blood Pack and fire at them from an angle. (You can get clean shots at explosive containers on the ledge from here.)

More Blood Pack thugs move through the courtyard directly in front of the environmental control room. Fire on them from above for as long as you can. You will soon have to use the stairs to drop to their level and directly engage.

After cleaning out the Blood Pack, follow the doors to the environmental control center. More Blood Pack foes attack the closer you get.

Salvage the spare parts in the corner of this room for an easy 2,000 credits. There's medi-gel nearby, too.

Introduction

Training

Upgrades and Research

The Professor

Walkthrough

Special Assignments

Planetary Database

Appendix

Environmental Control

Vorcha are guarding the controls for the air systems. The leader of this patrol is talkative. He says that the Collectors are indeed behind the plague. The vorcha are assisting the Collectors. In return, the Collectors will help raise the vorcha's profile in the galaxy. The vorcha doesn't talk forever. His spitting and snarling gives way to gunfire soon enough.

Look for Blood Pack boom-squads to fill the air with rockets, so dive into cover. Pick off the advancing Blood Pack pyro and clear the Blood Pack out of the room. As soon as the Blood Pack opposition is dead, you can approach the central console. Insert the cure and unlock doors to the two fans that will spread it.

As soon as you insert the cure, more Blood Pack members fill the room. You must turn on the fans. There is one on each side of the console, behind doors. As you close in on the doors, though, Blood Pack pyros pop out. Shoot those tanks!

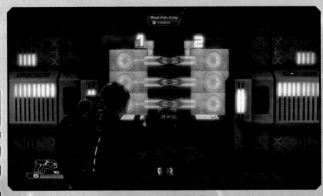

Initialize the first fan and then make your way to the second fan room.

The Blood Pack puts up an even greater fight to keep you out of the second fan room. Not only do Blood Pack troopers fan out, but krogan Blood Pack warriors also try to rush you as you cross the room. Rockets from vorcha heavies streak across the room. You cannot spend much time out of cover as you move on the second fan. Take down as many as you can, but be sure to use your team to keep the Blood Pack busy, too. This isn't a solo operation, after all.

Enemy Profile: Vorcha

Vorcha Thug

- **Classification: Minion**
- **Powers: Vorcha Regeneration**
- **Defenses: —**
- **Weapons: Assault Rifle, Heavy Pistol**

Vorcha Heavy

- **Classification: Minion**
- **Powers: Vorcha Regeneration**
- **Defenses: —**
- **Weapons: Rocket Launcher**

Not all vorcha have enlisted in the Blood Pack. Vorcha thugs and heavies are also working to advance the vorcha position in the galaxy, and this opportunity with the Collectors has brought out some of the deadliest in the species. Do not leave any vorcha with even a sliver of health. They will regenerate if given half a chance, so shoot to kill and do not stop shooting until the vorcha is lifeless on the floor.

Fight your way to the second fan room, chewing through vorcha and krogan. As soon as you activate the second fan, the cure spreads through the slums. It works right away, eliminating the virus causing the plague. You head back to Mordin to reiterate your offer to join the team and take the fight to the Collectors. After all, they were the ones responsible for this plague.

Objective 3: Return to Mordin

Back at the clinic, Mordin is happily noting that the cure is working exactly as it should. Patients are improving. (If you saved Daniel, the assistant is at the doctor's side.) Mordin is happy to join your team now. He's ready to see what he can do to stop the Collectors and agrees to meet you at your ship. You can opt to leave for the *Normandy* right away or look around the clinic. Medi-gel and power cells can be collected, and it's good to catch up with the patients.

If you sent for the batarian plague victim, he is in the clinic now and feeling much better. He is also pleased to see that his assumptions about humans were wrong.

Back on the *Normandy*...

Mordin is ready to work. After a brief conversation aboard the *Normandy* where you and Jacob bring the professor up to speed about the Collector situation, the salarian heads straight for the tech labs. Now that Mordin is on the team, you can access that part of the ship and order up research projects—as long as you have the required minerals.

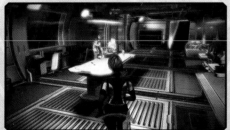

Be sure to go see Mordin right away. Talk to the salarian about his previous work with the krogan genophage. Mordin was very involved in the genophage. He knows an awful lot about it—perhaps too much. This is also a good opportunity to walk the ship and check in with existing crew. If you have recruited others, stop by their quarters for a chat. And be sure to see Joker, too.

> Now is a good time to talk to Miranda in her office; this will unlock the Argus Scanner Array research project. When completed, your planet scans for minerals will be much faster.

TIP

After Recruitment

It should not take Mordin long to develop the means to stop the Collector swarms. As soon as Shepard has all four recommended recruits, the Illusive Man requests that the commander talk to him. Report

to the communications room on deck 2 to speak to the Illusive Man and determine the next course of action.

The Illusive Man informs Shepard that a human colony on Horizon has just gone silent—that's a fingerprint of the Collectors. Hopefully, Mordin's countermeasures will be ready. Illusive Man also informs Shepard that a former *Normandy* crew member is also on Horizon. That's too big of a coincidence. The Collectors have to be aware of Shepard. The Illusive Man gives Joker the coordinates for Horizon. It's time to save some colonists.

Sure enough, Mordin is able to develop the means to stop the swarms right before Shepard goes to Horizon— the salarian seems to work best under pressure. Now that you cannot be stunned by the swarm, Shepard can actually watch the Collectors operate. The commander had better be ready for what is about to unfold.

Introduction
Training
Upgrades and Research
The Professor
Walkthrough
Special Assignments
Planetary Database
Appendix

ARCHANGEL

According to the dossier provided by the Illusive Man, Archangel is a mercenary commander with expertise in small-unit tactics, an omni-tool expert, and a remarkable sniper. Archangel is currently embroiled in a violent war against the gangs of Omega. In order to pull the potential recruit out of Omega alive, Shepard must somehow infiltrate the gangs that are hunting Archangel. To gain access to the mercenary gangs that are targeting Archangel, Shepard must apply for an assignment as a freelancer.

Spoils of War
- **Credits: 40,000**
- **Element Zero: 500**

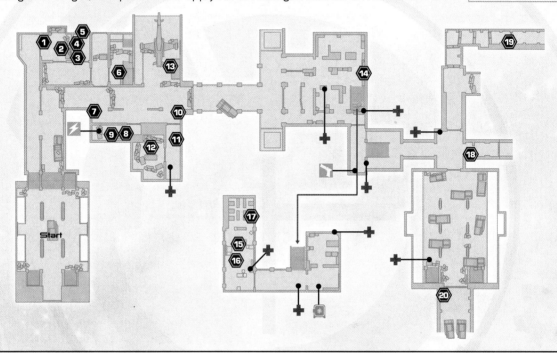

LEGEND

1. Jaroth
2. Message to Tarak
3. Eezo Smuggling Accounts
4. Refined Element Zero
5. Heavy Mech Diagnostic Station
6. Garm
7. 'Protection' Money Accounts
8. Blue Suns Weapon Shipment
9. Blue Suns Gunrunning Accounts
10. Freelancer
11. Blue Suns Troopers
12. Tarak and Jentha
13. Cathka's Assistant (and Cathka)
14. Omni-tool Power Boost X-Mods
15. Archangel (Garrus)
16. Vindicator Battle Rifles
17. Footlocker ($2000)
18. Emergency Shutter Control
19. Emergency Shutter Control
20. Emergency Shutter Control
- Wall Safe
- Medi-Gel
- Power Cell
- Weapon Locker

Objective 1: Join the Mercs

Shepard cannot get close to Archangel without joining up with the mercenary bands that have targeted him: Blue Suns, Eclipse, and Blood Pack. The freelance recruiter is inside the main room of Afterlife. Speaking to the recruiter allows Shepard to go downstairs and formally apply.

If you're playing as a female Shepard, the conversation with the mouthy downstairs Blue Suns merc recruiter leads to a Renegade interrupt opportunity, but no matter how you answer, he isn't about to turn down freelancers with as many weapons as Shepard and the squad have. While accepting the job, talk to the recruiter to get a better handle on the situation. Joining up does not get Shepard a permanent spot with any of the merc gangs hunting Archangel. Archangel has been targeted because he keeps messing with the merc gang activities, such as stealing shipments.

The recruiter spells out the operation: Previous teams have taken out Archangel's crew. Now Archangel is all alone. However, Archangel has positioned himself at quite a vantage point. There is only one bridge leading into the area. This gives the sniper plenty of advance warning of a new assault. Taking the bridge has resulted only in a bloodbath, so the merc bosses' new plan is for Shepard and the freelancers to take point while the merc bosses call in heavy hitters.

On the way out of Afterlife's recruiting office, Shepard passes a kid looking to sign up. Paragons can interrupt the kid and stop him before he throws his life away. Renegades let the kid make his own decision. Live? Die? That's the kid's call, not Shepard's.

Glossary

Blue Suns: Founded by Solem Dal'serah, a batarian slaver, the Blue Suns have grown from a protection racket to a security agency. Though the Blue Suns have the appearance of a legit security provider, it has been claimed that the mercenary force sells its captives into slavery.

Eclipse: This mercenary gang was originally a security company pioneered by an asari named Jona Sederis. While Eclipse is viewed with serious suspicion by the Citadel, the merc band has been welcomed into the Terminus Systems. Eclipse does more than trafficking. It offers out assassination contracts, engages in sabotage, and offers security.

Blood Pack: The Blood Pack was originally a vorcha gang, but a krogan battlemaster named Ganar Wrang turned it into a fearsome mercenary outfit. Wrang was so confident in his outfit that he took the Blood Pack public and made a killing. More krogan joined the Blood Pack, adding to the outfit's expertise at professional violence.

Go to Transit Hub

After leaving the recruiter, Shepard and the crew must make their way to the transports just outside Afterlife. Do any shopping you think is prudent at Omega before heading out. When you're ready, look for the Blue Suns driver waiting by the shuttles to the left of Afterlife (if you are facing the main entrance). Speak to the driver and he'll whisk you away to the outer edge of Archangel's base of operations.

Objective 2: Go to Sergeant Cathka

Once Shepard arrives on location, the Blue Suns dole out a little more information about the operation. The bridge leading to Archangel's position is completely exposed—it's a killing ground. However, they have kept up the attacks for so long that Archangel is getting exhausted. He's making mistakes. The mercs hope Shepard's squad can help them capitalize on those mistakes. If Shepard takes a forward assault position to distract Archangel, the Blue Suns can sneak up on Archangel from behind.

Right now, Archangel is just getting over an attack from a gunship. Archangel took down the gunship, but not before the mercs were able to slip a few men close to the facility. Archangel doesn't know they are there. To help with the attack (and actually make the mission ahead easier), Shepard should locate Sergeant Cathka at the third barricade closest to Archangel's hideout.

Introduction

Training

Upgrades and Research

Archangel

Walkthrough

Special Assignments

Planetary Database

Appendix

First Barricade

Follow the road from the Blue Suns welcome wagon. There is no action en route, but you will see a few mercs holed up at the first barricade, monitoring the situation. Dart inside the nearby door to speak to Jaroth, leader of the Eclipse chapter on Omega.

Talk to Jaroth to gather intel on Eclipse's activities on Omega. They have a corner on the element zero (eezo) market, but Archangel is complicating things. This mission is personal for Jaroth. Apparently Archangel killed Jaroth's brother in an attack.

Grab the datapad off the back table in Jaroth's room. Aria would love to see a message between Jaroth and Tarak that implicates them in a plot on her life. This starts a small special assignment: Deliver Datapad.

TIP

After leaving Jaroth, duck into the small side room. There is some valuable cargo inside the room, such as eezo and credits. The big prize, though, is the dormant YMIR mech. Hack the diagnostics station next to the mech to reprogram it, reversing its friend-or-foe recognition software. This will come in quite handy later when Eclipse tries to use it against Archangel.

Second Barricade

The Blood Pack is stationed just a little farther up the road. Listen for the snarls of a vorcha to find Garm, the krogan leader of the Blood Pack. Garm claims that the Blood Pack mercs are the real muscle on Omega. Garm is looking forward to taking out Archangel. Not only has Archangel been thinning the Blood Pack ranks with his sniper rifle, but Garm has a personal beef with Archangel.

Garm actually cornered Archangel once. They fought, but Archangel slipped away just as Garm's reinforcements arrived. Garm chased Archangel, but he got away. Garm lets slip that Archangel is a turian, which is more information than you received from the Blue Suns earlier.

Leave Garm and follow the road. Hack the datapad next to the dead merc in the corridor for 6,000 credits.

Hack open the locked door near the dead merc to locate a room full of good stuff. There's medi-gel on the wall, a crate of power cells, and a datapad worth 4,000 credits. However, the best pickup is the Microfield Pulsar, which upgrades submachine gun damage. Scan the gun-running accounts to collect it.

Third Barricade

The sight of the gunship indicates that you've closed in on Sergeant Cathka. Speak to Cathka's assistant in front of the gunship to gain an audience with his Blue Suns sergeant. Cathka is busily repairing the gunship for use in the upcoming assault on Archangel but takes a moment to speak with you about the mission.

Cathka informs you that the gunship is not going to be your cover, but instead will be used directly against Archangel. However, the ship is not ready just yet. It still needs work before it can take to the air. In the meantime, you will help the infiltration team get closer to Archangel. In fact, while you speak to him Cathka gets word to send in the bravo team of freelancers.

If you are willing to take on some Renegade points, you can give your team an advantage in the upcoming skirmish. When Cathka bends back over the gunship to do some repairs, hit the interrupt to fry him with the electrical tools. With bravo team rushing in, nobody notices Cathka slump to the ground.

> Now the gunship will not be at full strength later in this mission.
> **TIP**

Objective 3: Go to Archangel

You must now join the assault on Archangel's position. A meter appears on-screen that tracks Archangel's vital signs; if Archangel dies, you fail the mission. The longer you allow the freelancers and mercs to attack, the greater the chance of Archangel falling.

> Now is also a very good time to seek out the tech power upgrade at the base of the stairs leading up to Archangel's perch. Scan the Multicore Amplifier with your omni-tool to raise squad tech damage by 10 percent.
> **TIP**

Turncoat

You got this close to Archangel by being duplicitous. There's no reason not to finally reveal your intentions at this point. Open fire on the freelancers trying to take Archangel's position. (The sooner you do it, the less damage Archangel takes.) The first time you fire on a freelancer, word spreads that you are a traitor and the freelancers will fire on you as well as Archangel.

> Don't shoot the bomb the team is working on. You need that for later.
> **CAUTION**

There are two members of the infiltration team trying to cut through the door protecting Archangel's vantage point up on the second floor. Take them down and then mop up the rest of the freelancers on the main floor and the stairs. After all of the freelancers are down, Archangel opens the door the mercs were trying to cut through. Why would Archangel welcome you?

Introduction

Training

Upgrades and Research

Walkthrough

Archangel

Special Assignments

Planetary Database

Appendix

It turns out that Archangel has a different name, one more familiar to Shepard: Garrus Vakarian.

Garrus came to Omega after your reported death in hopes of doing some good without having to cut through layers of red tape. Out here, he can kill criminals without anybody shaking a finger at him. In fact, some of the locals really appreciate it; that's where the nickname Archangel came from.

But now it's time to go. You and Garrus must make a plan for getting out. Although the bridge let Garrus hold

off mercs, it will also funnel you directly to them. It's too risky to make a break for it right now, so you decide instead to hold the position and pick off incoming mercs until an escape presents itself.

Hold the Fort

A look through Garrus's scope reveals that incoming forces include more than just mercs. LOKI mechs are also on the move and coming across the bridge in great numbers. The goal right now is just to hold off the mechs.

Use the Renegade interrupt to take an early shot at the mechs coming over the barricade.

NOTE

Pick up the M-15 Vindicator near Garrus to add the new assault rifle to your arsenal.

TIP

Join your team as they help take down the mechs from the vantage point. Remember: Aim for the heads!

After you mop up the mechs, a team of Eclipse mercs starts to make a run on Garrus's base. The bomb can come in useful now. Blast it as the mercs try to move into position. The blast radius is good-sized and will drop any merc caught in it.

You cannot just stay on the upper level. You must drop to the main floor to take on the Eclipse thugs directly with your teammates.

Enemy Profile: Eclipses

Eclipse Trooper

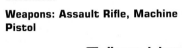

- Classification: Minion
- Powers: —
- Defenses: —
- Weapons: Assault Rifle, Machine Pistol

Eclipse Heavy

- Classification: Minion
- Powers: —
- Defenses: —
- Weapons: Rocket Launcher

Eclipse Engineer

- Classification: Elite
- Powers: Incinerate, Combat Drone, Shield Boost
- Defenses: Shield
- Weapons: Machine Gun, Hand Cannon

Eclipse Vanguard

- Classification: Elite
- Powers: Warp, Barrier
- Defenses: Barrier
- Weapons: Battle Rifle

What the Eclipse mercs lack in battle training they make up for in weapons and gear. Eclipse troopers and heavies do not move in a cohesive unit and attack without much plan, but their weapons (such as the heavy's rocket launcher) can cause real trouble. Look for weak spots like exposed heads to take down the low-level Eclipse thugs right away. Fortunately, most low-level Eclipse troops do not have shields. Watch for the engineers and other higher-ranking mercs, though. These hired guns have shields and barriers.

Remember; you're dealing with organic enemies now. Incendiary ammo is quite effective against fleshy types.

TIP

After you bring down the first wave of Eclipse mercs, Jaroth sends in his YMIR mech. If you reprogrammed the mech earlier, you will gain a real asset in this fight. The YMIR turns away from you and instead opens fire on the Eclipse troopers and heavies that pour over the barricade. You can let the YMIR do a lot of the work. But that's a good way to lose the YMIR assist within just a few moments.

Hold back behind the YMIR mech for cover while picking off Eclipse mercs. The more you take down, the longer the YMIR will last.

The YMIR assist does not last the entire battle. If you keep it "alive" for more than a few waves of mercs, it eventually recovers its original programming and turns on you.

CAUTION

Before too long, Jaroth has lost so many Eclipse mercs that he has no choice but to enter the battle himself. When you see Jaroth come over the barricade, take cover and concentrate your fire on him. Your teammates will get the clue right away and also direct their fire at Jaroth. Use powers to weaken the Eclipse boss, and stay in cover whenever possible to avoid his incoming submachine-gun fire.

Jaroth has barriers and shields, so you must bring those down before using some of your squad's powers against him.

Direct your squad mates to attack Jaroth so that they keep him pinned down, then target the Eclipse boss in the head and use incendiary ammo to drop his health. The Eclipse boss will fall, but that only takes care of one of the three merc gangs after Archangel.

Introduction

Training

Upgrades and Research

Archangel

Walkthrough

Special Assignments

Planetary Database

Appendix

As soon as you bring down Jaroth, return to Garrus. Garrus is pleased to have taken out Jaroth, who was shipping goods made with tainted eezo all over Citadel space. But no sooner than the reunion starts does the building start to shake. Garrus realizes that the mercs have figured out another way in: the basement. Garrus suggests you head down to the basement and seal off the entrances.

Decision time: Do you take the whole team with you or leave one member behind to help fend off attacks with Garrus? Taking the full team will make your job easier, but if Garrus has been weakened by merc attacks, then having an extra gun near him will certainly keep him alive longer. It's your call, but leaving a friend with Garrus does bank Paragon points.

Objective 4: Close Off Basement

Go to Basement

After deciding who to leave with Garrus (if anybody), race downstairs and seal up the basement before the Blood Pack can make it inside. Use the door directly below the stairs. A medi-gel station and a weapons locker are just beyond the door. Raid them both.

It takes 10 seconds for the shutters to seal. As soon as you hit the button, Blood Pack mercs start coming down the hallway ahead of you. You must push them back. If one of them can reach the shutter and stand under it, that resets the shutter. Hold off the Blood Pack thugs at the gate, using the sides of it for cover while picking them off from a distance.

Enemy Profile: Blood Pack Trooper

- **Classification: Minion**
- **Powers: —**
- **Defenses: Vorcha Regeneration**
- **Weapons: Assault Rifle, Heavy Pistol**

Blood Pack troopers are vorcha. These are rank-and-file minions in the merc gang. They have been trained to seek and use cover while allowing heavier forces to storm the enemy. While the enemy is busy fighting off the frontal force, the troopers can attack from a safe distance.

The basement shutters (all three of them) are controlled by green wall switches. Press the button on the nearest shutter to start to lower it.

NOTE

You can close the wall shutters in any order. Doing a particular shutter first does not affect the outcome of the mission. This walkthrough assumes that you start at the shutter nearest the basement entrance (marked Emergency Exit) and move next to the shutters that flank it, starting with the shutter to the right.

Enemy Profile: Blood Pack Warrior

- **Classification: Elite**
- **Powers: Krogan Regeneration, Krogan Charge, Carnage, Incendiary Ammo**
- **Defenses: Heavy Armor**
- **Weapons: Assault Shotgun**

Blood Pack warriors are krogan, making them terribly fearsome in battle. Krogan do not necessarily look for any strategy other than to rush the enemy and attack at close range. Look out for shotgun blasts and charge attacks when a Blood Pack warrior closes the gap. Make sure that when you drop a Blood Pack warrior, it is all the way down. Left with any health, the krogan will use regeneration to replenish spent stamina and get up for another attack.

Once the initial shutter is closed, use the garage door to intercept a Blood Pack squad attempting to infiltrate the building. Use cover inside the room to pick off the Blood Pack thugs as they advance. Watch for them to step near explosive crates. Shoot the crates to detonate them and kill the surrounding vorcha and varren.

The majority of enemies in here are Blood Pack troopers without any shielding. Pick them off with headshots.

The next shutter is on the far side of the room. Take down the Blood Pack mercs then press the button to start the countdown. This wide corridor gives the Blood Pack room to spread out. Take cover and blast the Blood Pack warriors coming through, but save your heavy weapon for a tougher fight coming up. You must keep them back from the shutter or else it will not close.

The final shutter is through the door marked Utility. The door opens into a long corridor with many barricades. Blood Pack troopers stream down the corridor, dropping behind the barricades and slowing your progress. Shoot the troopers and vault over the barricades.

Introduction · Training · Upgrades and Research · Archangel · Walkthrough · Special Assignments · Planetary Database · Appendix

The shutter (number 9 on the map) is just around the corner at the end of the corridor. As soon as the shutter starts to close, more krogan and vorcha fill the hall. The Blood Pack warriors are the greatest threat, as they can rush the shutter with nothing in their way. Cut them down before they reach the shutter or else the countdown will be halted.

> **CAUTION**
>
> Be on the lookout for Blood Pack pyros, too. These thugs wield flamethrowers that cause incredible damage.

Objective 5: Stop Blood Pack

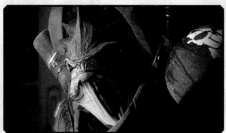

After you close the third shutter, Garrus comes over the comm. He tells you to hurry back as Garm and his thugs have breached the area's defenses and are about to attack. Garrus cannot hold off Garm and his mercs alone.

Hold Off Blood Pack

Garm has every intention of taking down Garrus himself, so he makes a beeline for the stairs. You cannot easily follow. Blood Pack troopers spread out and offer immediate resistance. The longer Garm is upstairs with Garrus, the worse things go for the turian. Direct your team to hold off the Blood Pack near the stairs and chase down Garm.

In addition to the Blood Pack troopers, you must also take down the varren they brought with them. The varren aren't terribly bright, but they are fast and can bite hard. Since the varren move fast, either use a close-range weapon to drop them or try biotics to throw them around the room.

Enemy Profile: Varren

- **Classification: Minion**
- **Powers: —**
- **Defenses: —**
- **Weapons: Bite Attack**

Varren in the wild are fast, brutal war dogs with terrible bites. The Blood Pack mercs train their varren to sniff out enemies using cover and flush them out.

There is likely a Blood Pack warrior flanking Garm that runs interference as soon as it spots you. Watch out for its charge attack. Get out of the way or take him down before you are flattened by the charge.

Garrus and whoever you left behind (provided you actually did) are holding their own against Garm for now, but without you joining the fight, Garrus could be in real trouble. Get Garm in the crossfire and rip his armor apart. With Garm equidistant between you and Garrus, the krogan will not be able to easily pick a target to charge. Lay hard into Garm with weapons and powers.

After Garm is down, Garrus fills you in on his brief history with the krogan. Apparently, Garm put up quite a fight the first time they tangled. But now? Krogan cannot regenerate their way out of being dead. Garrus agrees that it is time to get out of here. All that is left are the Blue Suns. They are the toughest of the three, but if you've broken the Blood Pack and Eclipse, the Blue Suns should be manageable.

Objective 6: Fight Blue Suns

You don't get a chance to make a break for it. Tarak and the Blue Suns charge Garrus's base with the cover of the gunship. The gunship, piloted by Tarak, is a real menace. You must take it down, but dealing with waves of Blue Suns mercs makes it impossible to concentrate solely on the gunship.

> Did you zap Cathka earlier? If so, the gunship will have only half of its armor. Sometimes being a Renegade pays.
>
> **NOTE**

Blue Suns Dawn

The gunship blasts the windows out of Garrus's vantage point, allowing Blue Suns troopers to slip into the building. The gunship swerves away to come at the building from another side. While Tarak flies the gunship around to the side, you must engage the Blue Suns troopers in a firefight. Like Garrus said, they are strong and often attack from cover, so taking them out can be challenging.

Enemy Profile: Blue Suns

Blue Suns Trooper

- **Classification: Minion**
- **Powers: —**
- **Defenses: —**
- **Weapons: Submachine Gun**

Blue Suns Legionnaire

- **Classification: Elite**
- **Powers: Shield Boost, Disruptor Ammo**
- **Defenses: Shields**
- **Weapons: Battle Rifle**

Blue Suns Centurion

- **Classification: Elite**
- **Powers: Shield Boost, Incendiary Ammo**
- **Defenses: Shields**
- **Weapons: Assault Shotgun**

The Blue Suns are not to be underestimated. These are the best-trained mercenaries in the Terminus Systems. They use military tactics against their enemies, such as flanking and using available cover to recover from wounds. The Blue Suns are not biotics, though. But what they lack in powers, they make up for in force, tactics, and weaponry.

Blast the gunship with everything you have. Heavy weapons do the most damage, but even if you only have a machine pistol, empty the clip into the gunship.

The first wave of Blue Suns is led by a mercenary named Jentha. She is a serious threat—lethal with her guns and very smart about maintaining cover until she has a good shot. She has shields and armor, so it will take a lot of hits to bring her down before the gunship swings around for the next assault.

Be mindful of Blue Suns trying to take Garrus's base from the stairs.

While you clean up the stairs, the gunship gets the drop on Garrus. The turian falls to the ground, riddled with bullets and clearly in critical condition. You must eliminate that gunship. Dive for cover as the gunship hovers outside the window and goes for a missile volley.

The gunship swings around the building and drops off reinforcements. Take cover and carve through the Blue Suns troopers until the gunship appears again. As soon as the troopers are out, the gunship lowers itself back to the window. Avoid missiles and keep burying shots into the hull. If you did not sabotage the gunship earlier, it can withstand a lot of hits. You will need to collect more thermal clips as needed, and don't stop blasting away until the gunship explodes. It may take several moves between the courtyard and the window to bring down the gunship, depending on whether or not you took out Cathka earlier in the mission.

Shotguns are surprisingly effective against the gunship armor—as long as you are right up against the window when firing.

TIP

After the Extraction

Defeating the gunship gives Joker enough clearance to get a shuttle down and extract Shepard, Garrus, and the team. With Dr. Chakwas's medical skills, Garrus is up and walking in no time back on the *Normandy*, but he's sporting some scars that will always serve as a reminder of the time he and Shepard took out three rival merc gangs on Omega—at once. Garrus has his own questions about Shepard's involvement with Cerberus, but since Shepard and Cerberus just dragged him out of Omega before he bled out, he is satisfied with Shepard's instincts.

> Be sure to make the rounds and talk to the crew, including Jacob and Miranda, after recruiting Garrus to the mission. Remember; it takes repeat conversations to foster romance with the crew, so be sure to keep coming back to them after missions to further the relationship.
>
> **NOTE**

Garrus takes up his station in the main battery on deck 3 of the *Normandy*. Stop by and talk to Garrus. Find out why he really ended up as Archangel. It's not a pleasant conversation—Garrus is carrying some heavy baggage. But he appreciates the talk nonetheless.

> Now that Garrus is part of the crew, a female Shepard can flirt with Garrus, but a full-fledged romance is not possible.
>
> **NOTE**

Hit up Shepard's private terminal for any incoming messages. There are several waiting. If you stopped that kid from joining up as a merc freelancer prior to the Archangel mission, look for a thank you note. The next message is from Cerberus.

> Special assignments like N7: Lost Operative are optional, but taking them not only increases your credits but results in valuable experience that helps you level up Shepard faster. Going up against the Collectors is no cakewalk, after all.
>
> **TIP**

> Did you grab that datapad near Jaroth at the Eclipse hangout? Near the first barricade? You can now take it to Aria back on Omega.
>
> **NOTE**

> You can also return to Omega now and undertake the special assignment The Patriarch.
>
> **TIP**

If you are still seeking recruits, direct the *Normandy* to your next stop. Garrus can now be a part of the away team.

Introduction

Training

Upgrades and Research

Archangel

Walkthrough

Special Assignments

Planetary Database

Appendix

SUBJECT ZERO

Of the recommended recruits put forward by the Illusive Man, the convict known as Jack is an intriguing option. Held in deep cryo on the Blue Suns–controlled prison ship *Purgatory*, Jack has a hard-core criminal record that includes some heinous violent crimes. However, Jack is also rumored to be the most powerful human biotic in existence. If Jack could be freed and convinced to use those powers to stop the Collectors, the convict would be a welcome addition to the team.

Spoils of War
- **Credits: 30,000**
- **Element Zero: 500**

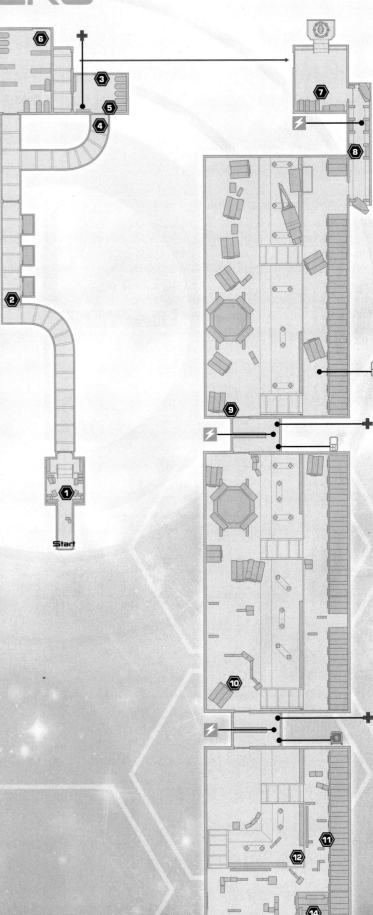

Start

LEGEND

1. **Warden Kuril (first encounter)**
2. **Prisoner Row (Prisoner 780, Prisoner 403)**
3. **Purgatory Security Controls**
4. **Prison Guard**
5. **Refined Element Zero**
6. **Outprocessing**
7. **YMIR Mech Corpse: Damage Protection**
8. **Dead Prison Guard**
9. **Shotgun**
10. **Dead Prison Guard**
11. **Generator Coupling #1**
12. **Generator Coupling #2**
13. **Generator Coupling #3**
14. **Warden Kuril (after freeing Jack)**
- **Spare Parts**
- **Wall Safe**
- **Medi-Gel**
- **Datapad**
- **Computer**
- **Power Cell**

Objective 1: Outprocessing

Converted from an ark ship designed to transport animals, the *Purgatory* is now a prison ship owned by the Blue Suns mercenary force. The ship's population, partially composed of political prisoners and prisoners of war, is officially listed at 4,350. However, the ship's population fluctuates; some reports have placed the actual prisoner count at over three times that amount when the ship is especially overcrowded. The *Purgatory* is a large vessel but not sizable enough to safely hold that many prisoners.

The Illusive Man has already arranged for Jack's release. When Shepard arrives at *Purgatory*, all that is left to do is wait for the Blue Suns that run the ship to bring the prisoner out of cryo and prep Jack for transfer. The Blue Suns guard waiting for Shepard and the team at the docking bay requests that they leave their weapons with him. Shepard refuses. Warden Kuril intervenes and decides to allow Shepard to enter the ship fully armed.

The Warden leads Shepard and the team into the ship, passing by cell block 2, where the Blue Suns keep the worst of the worst in deep cryo. Kuril explains that each prisoner cell is a pod that can be jettisoned into space with the press of a button, and he has not been shy about blasting a few into the ink to underline his authority on *Purgatory*. Shepard can also talk to the Warden about Jack and the costs of running the prison ship. Kuril has no kind words for Jack, but when describing the convict's penchant for violence, there is a degree of reverence in his voice.

Prisoner's Row

Follow the Warden's directions to Outprocessing. As you walk, you pass a few holding cells. Stop at the first one. A prisoner in the holding cell is being savagely beaten by a guard while another watches. This is a Paragon/Renegade moment. You can encourage the guards to keep on thrashing the prisoner, forcefully tell them to stop, or appeal to their better natures and convince them that the act is beneath them. Helping call off the beating earns Paragon points while turning a blind eye is a Renegade action.

Talk to Prisoner 780 in the next cell. He initially wants you to free him, but when he hears Jack is leaving with you, his desire for freedom ebbs. The prisoner tells you about his crime and life on the Purgatory.

Once you enter Outprocessing, the Warden springs his trap. Kuril has no intention of handing over Jack. He is going to keep the credits and imprison your team for a ransom. Such treachery should have been expected of the Blue Suns. When you refuse to go quietly, the Warden sends in a platoon of Blue Suns troopers and centurions.

Introduction

Training

Upgrades and Research

Subject Zero

Walkthrough

Special Assignments

Planetary Database

Appendix

Get to Cryo

The Outprocessing room quickly fills with Blue Suns. Use the benches in the room as cover for you and your squad and return fire. Hold them at the door as long as possible. The centurions have shields, so you must blast through those before using biotics to take them down. Since these are organic beings, incendiary ammo works well. Cryo ammo puts the Blue Suns into deep freeze for a few seconds, giving you time to advance and blast them without any return fire.

The Blue Suns also release FENRIS mechs into the room to stop you. Blast the galloping mechs before they get close enough to zap you with taser bite.

The corridor leading out of Outprocessing and into the cryo chamber is blocked by Blue Suns. Duck behind cover and blast the Blue Suns troopers and legionnaires as they storm the hall. They will look for cover themselves, so you may need to advance to flush the stragglers out of hiding.

The cryo technician in the next room is calling for reinforcements. Cut him down and then ransack the room for eezo and medi-gel.

All that is left to do now is unfreeze the cryo prisoners to free Jack. Other prisoners will escape, though.

Jack is not exactly what you expected. The most powerful human biotic in the galaxy is a small, lithe woman covered in tattoos from head to toe. Jack breaks the bonds that hold her in the cryo pod and stumbles forward just as three YMIR mechs close in to keep her contained. It doesn't take long for Jack to concentrate her biotic power on the closest YMIR. You need to get down there before her temper lets her not only rip up the YMIR but also escape the *Purgatory* for good.

MASS EFFECT

Objective 2: Find Jack

Chase

When you drop down into the cryo chamber, you discover the ruined shells of the three YMIR mechs. Scan the wreckage of the middle mech with your omni-tool to pick up Ablative VI. This damage protection tech adds 10 percent to your squad's shields, barriers, and armor. It's a useful find considering the gauntlet you must soon endure to chase down Jack as she makes her way to the exit.

There are human prisoners in the trench below the bridge. They are engaged with the Blue Suns but will not hesitate to turn on you. The YMIR mech is programmed to kill anything that is not Blue Suns, so while it may at first look like the YMIR is trained on the escaped prisoners, don't get too comfortable. Those guns will turn on you soon enough. There is a Blue Suns commando in the bay, too. Armed with a rocket launcher, it can cause real trouble from a distance. If you have a grenade launcher or sniper rifle, target the commando early.

> **TIP**
> Do not target the prisoners. Let them continue firing on the Blue Suns, effectively doubling your firepower until the prisoners are overwhelmed by the Blue Suns.

Follow the corridor past some downed Blue Suns (Jack's been through here, obviously) and pick up power cells that resupply heavy weapons.

The corridor empties into a huge bay that bears all the signs of Jack: fire, explosions, and wreckage. The Blue Suns are holding their ground in this room, firing back with everything they have. A YMIR mech joins the Blue Suns squad, unleashing gunfire as well as rockets. You can use the railing of the bridge overlooking the bay as cover or move down to the right of the bay and inch up behind crates.

Before moving through the open door on the far side of the bay, check the body of the prison guard off to the left. Scan his shotgun to pick up the Synchronized Pulsar upgrade, which increases shotgun damage.

Pick up the medi-gel and power cells in the hall behind the bay. The datapad of the nearby dead guard contains 4,500 credits if you can manage the hack.

Use heavy weapons to flush out the Blue Suns when they hide behind pillars, crates, and barricades.

Introduction

Training

Upgrades and Research

Subject Zero

Walkthrough

Special Assignments

Planetary Database

Appendix

Another bay, another squad of Blue Suns. These centurions seem to have the prisoner population under control, so they immediately turn their fire on you. Dive behind the crates and take out the first set of Blue Suns spotted in the trench. An explosive container rests on the bridge opposite you, right next to some additional Blue Suns troopers. Nail the container before the troopers stray too far from it. The blast is powerful enough to kill. Even if the troopers manage to avoid death, they will lose a lot of health.

You cannot pick off everybody from the crates near the door. You must enter the trench. There are several barricades in the trench to use for cover, but the Blue Suns have the same idea. Do not rush the trench. These are not krogan you are dealing with. The Blue Suns troopers will hang back and use cover. If you try to advance too quickly and get too far out in the open, the troopers will cut you down.

Move your squad up the trench with you. While you can easily help them out with Unity if they get into a tough spot, they cannot always return the favor.

TIP

As you move down the trench, another YMIR stomps into action. Duck from the rockets and return fire. If a squad member has Overload, use it on the mech to pop its circuits.

There is no shame in retreating back up the trench. Lure the Blue Suns under one of the bridges and then scramble above them for the vantage point.

TIP

When you can duck out of the trench to the right, advance from crate to crate. Never remain out in the open.

Snag 1,500 credits from the body of the dead prison guard at the far side of the bay, next to the catwalk bolted to the wall. Cross the bridge to the left and hack the PDA of another dead guard for 4,500 credits.

NOTE

When the bay is clear, pass through the far door. There is a hackable wall safe (3,000 credits), a medi-gel station, and a crate of power cells just around the corner.

Objective 3: Stop Warden Kuril

The Warden is furious that Shepard has made such a mess of his prison. While Kuril might not be able to contain Shepard now, he does plan to recapture Jack. Shepard and the team must take out Kuril as soon as possible before the Blue Suns can regroup and hunt Jack.

Take Out the Shields

The Warden's minions remain outside the shield bubble to defend the generators. Do not focus on the shield  generators to the exclusion of the Blue Suns. Shield generators do not shoot back. Once you have dropped enough Blue Suns to cause a break in the firefight, then focus fire on one of the towers.

Kuril takes few chances mounting his assault on you. The Warden hides behind a shield, which is powered by three generators. To disable the shield and put the Warden out of business, you must destroy the three generators. Look for the towers with crackling blue energy arcing out of their spires. The blue panel on each tower is the weak spot. Blast that panel to blow up the tower and weaken the shield. You must destroy all three generators before you can attack Kuril.

The Warden

As soon as the Warden is exposed, train your fire on him. Kuril is armed with an assault rifle and has a good shot, so always use cover while the Warden is firing. When there is a break in the assault, return fire. The Warden will duck behind a barricade, so try to catch the Warden before he disappears or right when he pops back up.

> The Warden has both shields and armor.

NOTE

The Warden has the upper hand by virtue of his perch, but sniper rifles or heavy weapons are great equalizers. If  any part of the Warden is exposed, target the spot with one of these weapons. The splash damage from a grenade launcher or missile launcher alone will shred Kuril's shields as well as his health.

Blue Suns legionnaires fill the room between you and the Warden. Take them out before sweeping to the left or right to target the towers.

Introduction

Training

Upgrades and Research

Subject Zero

Walkthrough

Special Assignments

Planetary Database

Appendix

Taking Jack

After the Warden falls, Shepard watches Jack sprint toward the docking bay. Jack is cornered by Blue Suns as she approaches the docking bay, which slows her down. After dispatching some of them with her biotic powers, she spies the Cerberus symbol on the side of the *Normandy*. This sends Jack into a fit. So distressed by the fact that Cerberus has come for her, she completely misses a Blue Suns merc sneaking up behind her.

Shepard drops the merc just before he can get a shot off on Jack. Although you just saved her life, Jack still seems mistrustful—you're Cerberus. Talk to Jack to solve the standoff. Eventually, Jack proposes a deal. Allow her to see the files Cerberus has on her and she will go with you. Shepard can either immediately agree or bluff and risk angering Jack later. However, letting Jack into Cerberus files certainly is not going to endear Shepard to Cerberus...

After Picking Up Jack

Jack wants that access right away. Shepard can either give it to her or make her wait until she's settled in. Either way, Jack takes up residence down in the lower level of deck 4, the engineering deck. Shepard should take a moment to go down and speak to Jack before heading off on the next mission.

> On the way down to deck 4, stop off for a quick visit with Chambers by the galaxy map to get her assessment of Jack's stability.
>
> **NOTE**

If Shepard allowed Jack to look at the files, the convict's stance softens. Down in engineering, Jack warns Shepard that Cerberus is into some pretty nasty stuff—and she's an expert on nasty stuff. Jack will go along with the mission for now, but she still plans to comb the data for incriminating evidence to use against Cerberus.

It comes to light that Jack hates Cerberus because Cerberus essentially made Jack what she is. Cerberus raised her in a research facility, but Jack escaped. Cerberus has been chasing her ever since.

The conversation also presents Shepard with the opportunity to get a little closer to Jack. Jack marvels at the power of the *Normandy* and suggests Shepard take it as a pirate vessel. Shepard can either defend the mission or ask Jack how she would help. Could this little flirtation be the start of something?

> It's possible for a male Shepard to have a fling with Jack, but this eliminates the possibility of a full romance with another crew member later.
>
>
> **CAUTION**

95

Introduction

Training

Upgrades and Research

Walkthrough

The Warlord Okeer

Special Assignments

Planetary Database

Appendix

THE WARLORD OKEER

The Illusive Man recommends that Shepard find Dr. Okeer. The krogan, also known as Warlord Okeer, is researching a cure for the genophage and has been in contact with the Collectors in hopes of trading for the technology needed to develop an antidote. This familiarity with the Collectors makes Okeer an ideal candidate for the crew. Shepard has experience with the krogan, despite not always seeing eye to eye with former crew member Wrex about the morality of genophage.

Should Shepard wish to recruit Okeer, head to the nearest mass relay and plot a course for Korlus.

Spoils of War

- **Credits: 40,000**
- **Platinum: 2,000**

Rana Thanoptis will only appear if you imported your character from *Mass Effect* and she survived those events.

NOTE

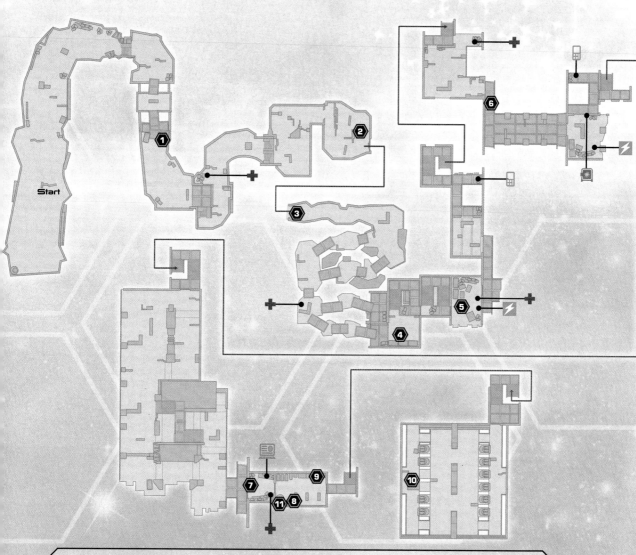

LEGEND

1. **Wounded Merc**
2. **Tank-Grown Krogan**
3. **Blue Suns Corpse ($2000)**
4. **Refined Platinum**
5. **Sniper Rifle**
6. **Blue Suns Corpse ($$$)**

7. **Rana Thanoptis**
8. **Warlord Okeer (Console on return trip)**
9. **Lab Terminal (Krogan Vitality)**
10. **Jedore (starting position)**
11. **Okeer's "son"**

- **Spare Parts**
- **Wall Safe**
- **Medi-Gel**
- **Datapad**
- **Computer**
- **Power Cell**

Objective 1: Infiltrate Compound

Dr. Okeer is currently working in a Blue Suns compound on wreckage-strewn Korlus. It's not known if Okeer is on Korlus by choice or by force. What is known is that the Blue Suns don't like unexpected visitors. The landing party should be prepared for combat.

The long road to the Blue Suns outpost is littered with derelict ships.

Observation Post

The post is the first point of contact and combat with the Blue Suns on Korlus. Use the barricades outside of the post for cover, and fire on the Blue Suns troopers that guard the door to the observation post.

The Blue Suns are trained in military tactics and will seek cover in a firefight. If this is your first encounter with the Blue Suns, be sure to check out tips and strategies for defeating the mercs in the "Training" chapter or from the Archangel mission description.

NOTE

You stumble upon a wounded Blue Suns merc just beyond the observation post. The merc's injuries are not as bad as he thinks. Use that to your advantage. When the merc starts to clam up during the interrogation, offer a medi-gel to loosen him up. He'll tell you that Okeer is in a lab engineering an army of krogan for Jedore, the leader of the Blue Suns. The problem with the army, though, is that most of the krogan Okeer creates are crazy. The Blue Suns use the mad krogan for live ammo target practice.

Blue Suns command radios the wounded merc, demanding a situation report. You can either convince the merc to give them the all-clear or force him to report that Shepard's squad is heading to another part of the base, sending security the wrong way. This choice results in Paragon or Renegade points.

If you shake the possibility of reinforcements, continue to question the merc about the whereabouts of Okeer and the lab's fortifications. The merc lets slip that the main defenses are big guns for ship attacks. There are not many defenses against commandos like your squad. You have the advantage if you move on the lab. You can tell the merc either to take a hike or that it's too risky to leave him alive before seeking out the lab. If you failed with your persuasion and the merc calls for reinforcements you can choose whether or not to kill him.

Objective 2: Find the Lab

Blue Suns Assault

It doesn't take long before you run into the next line of Blue Suns. When you see the giant RX painted on an abandoned hull, you'd better seek cover by the barricades. Blue Suns troopers are on the landing across the clearing.

Follow the path down into the trench. Several dead krogan lie face down in the dirt, victims of a recent round of target practice. Take cover at the barricade and look for a Blue Suns trooper on the bridge above the trench. Pick him off and then inch forward in the trench. More Blue Suns troopers are waiting for you to get a little closer to the back of the trench.

At least two Blue Suns troopers are at the end of the trench on the landing. Wait for them to show themselves and then take your shots.

> There is a medi-gel pack in the trench. It's off to the left, near the middle of the trench.
>
> **TIP**

Second Assault

The end of the trench feeds into another yard. A long landing on the opposite side of the wrecking yard is crawling with Blue Suns. In addition to Blue Suns troopers, look out for the Blue Suns heavy packing the rocket launcher. Use cover to avoiding getting plastered by a rocket.

More Blue Suns heavies are waiting for your squad farther down the yard.

Target Practice

The yard leads to a Blue Suns firing range, where the mercs have cornered a krogan. The krogan is peppering the ledge above him with shotgun blasts, leading the Blue Suns to duck and cover. Let the krogan keep the Blue Suns busy while you take shots from the relative safety of the back of the range.

> You may need to slip to the right side of the range to get a clean shot at the Blue Suns troopers hiding behind cover.
>
> **TIP**

Introduction · Training · Upgrades and Research · Walkthrough · The Warlord Okeer · Special Assignments · Planetary Database · Appendix

After the fighting subsides, approach the krogan. The krogan does not attack, recognizing that you are also fighting the Blue Suns mercenaries. Though his speech is not fully developed, the krogan is able to articulate some disturbing information about his short life. He's been alive for just seven days and is burdened with the need to kill.

The krogan explains that he feels the need to fight in his blood and bones. He recalls a voice he heard in the tank (these krogan are born fully grown out of a tank) that told him he was a failure. You may question the krogan about Jedore and the voice in the tank, which the krogan called "father" until he was rejected. Before leaving, the krogan tells you that the lab is beyond the "broken parts" and guarded by many of "you fleshy things." He opens a shortcut to the lab, but it's a narrow corridor—there's not a lot of room to plan evasive action should the situation go sideways.

Loot the Blue Suns corpse just inside the door to pick up 8,000 credits.

Gauntlet

Sure enough, as soon as you start down the path the krogan revealed, Blue Suns troopers step out to attack. There's nowhere to hide, so give the mercs everything you have to bring them down.

The barricades at the bottom of the slope are a good place to set up defenses against the incoming krogan berserkers, bred by Okeer. These mindless krogan warriors stomp through the paths carved in the wreckage. They are armed with shotguns and use devastating charge attacks to slam your squad. Keep the krogan at a distance with long-range attacks and biotics. Fall back if necessary. Do not engage the berserkers in close combat.

> If you whittle a krogan down to a sliver of health, finish the job. If you give the krogan any breathing room, it will regenerate health.
>
> **TIP**

> Do not use the yellow-rimmed crates for cover unless necessary. They are fragile and splinter after just one or two blasts from the berserkers.
>
> **CAUTION**

> Biotics are useful attacks against the berserkers, who do not have barriers or shields. Use the Push biotic attack to shove them off the walkways into the abyss.
>
> **TIP**

After dispatching the berserkers, follow the sounds of the Blue Suns as they regroup. Pick up the refined platinum from the crate on the far side of the walkways and then turn to the left to start ascending the lab tower. Okeer is at the very top, but there are many Blue Suns between you and him.

The Blue Suns don't let up until you move deeper into their tower. Heavies continue to launch rockets from great distances. This gives you time to take evasive action. Dive into cover so the rockets streak harmlessly overhead. Move up when it's safe and pick the heavies off as they reload. Do not stand up if there is a rocket airborne. A direct hit from a rocket is absolutely devastating.

Hack the door at the top of the first flight of stairs to proceed up the tower.

The next landing is a gold mine of pickups: medi-gel, power cells, and a sniper rifle that grants you the Scram Pulsar tech. It adds 10 percent to sniper rifle damage for the entire squad.

Hack the PDA on the ground where the Blue Suns heavies were positioned for 6,000 credits.

Just outside the treasure trove, several Blue Suns heavies are ready with rocket launchers. They volley rockets across the divide as soon as you open the door, so dive in and take immediate cover. Wait for the heavies to reload their launchers and then open fire from safety.

Continue up the tower and take cover when you hear the next Blue Suns squad. The squad is made up of heavies, centurions, legionnaires, and troopers. Watch out for both rockets and regular gunfire. Splitting the squad up here to flank the Blue Suns will keep the bad guys guessing, so don't be afraid to throw an order to a comrade to break away and advance alongside the enemies.

TIP

Pull the Blue Suns off their perches with biotics and drop them into the empty space between the two catwalks.

Introduction

Training

Upgrades and Research

Walkthrough
The Warlord Okeer

Special Assignments

Planetary Database

Appendix

Tear up the centurions as they round the corner to back up the heavies.

Stop when you reach the next door, and before going through, look for a nearby Blue Suns corpse. Hack its PDA to bank 4,000 credits.

Search the corpse of the Blue Suns merc near the centurions for 10,000 credits.

Last Stand

You can overhear the Blue Suns leader command that they fall back out of the labs (where the berserkers are made) and refocus their attack on Shepard's squad. Keep pressing into Blue Suns territory, putting down mercs as fast as you can. Since these are humans, incendiary and cryo ammo do extra damage to them.

Just beyond the door at the top of the stairs, the Blue Suns mount one last big counteroffensive. The mercenary gang calls in every man in the facility, from troopers to heavies. They spread across the area and take cover, forcing you to stay low and pick your targets. You can do more damage if you split your forces and cut paths into the Blue Suns territory.

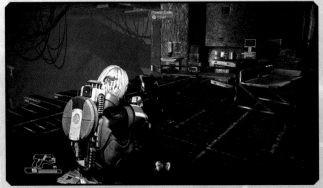

Keep an eye out for a crate of power cells and a wall safe. The wall safe has 4,000 credits in it.

Watch for Blue Suns on the high ground.

Blast the centurions on the bridge and then use it yourself to mop up the next batch of Blue Suns that attack.

The majority of the Blue Suns are down, but this battle isn't over yet. Pass through the door the Blue Suns were guarding to recover medi-gel and access a terminal containing 8,000 credits. Once you collect the goods, move through the next door to catch up with the good krogan doctor.

Okeer

Okeer has been waiting for you to finish with the mercs and come help him complete his experiment. Okeer does treat you with a mix of suspicion and respect. The krogan brings up Shepard's actions on the

commander's original mission as a Spectre, when it was discovered that Saren was working on a cure for the genophage. Okeer does not necessarily disagree with the outcome of that event. He believes it was necessary to stop Saren and that the krogan Saren wanted to mass produce would not have been real krogan. Okeer believes that his engineered krogan are superior to Saren's.

Okeer has been working hard on creating the perfect krogan, a flawless soldier. The rejects from his experiments were supposed to be used in Jedore's Blue Suns army, but the berserkers proved too difficult to train and contain. But Okeer has now completed his one perfected krogan and is ready to leave Korlus with his precious cargo in tow. Since Okeer has knowledge of the Collectors, Shepard is eager to accommodate this request.

Before Shepard can extract Okeer back to the *Normandy*, Jedore intervenes. The Blue Suns leader orders the release of a toxic gas into Okeer's lab. Okeer requests that you take out Jedore before she can poison the new krogan soldier. If you do this, Okeer will tell you everything he knows about the Collectors.

Objective 3: Fight Jedore

Jedore

The merc leader is in the warehouse below Okeer's lab. Jedore can be heard barking orders as you enter. Take cover behind the huge metal panels. Watch out for Jedore's YMIR mech, which is equipped with miniguns and a rocket launcher. Jedore also has a rocket launcher, so stay in cover as much as possible.

Split the attention of Jedore and the YMIR by splitting the squad.

TIP

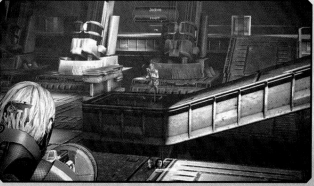

A sniper rifle or heavy weapons are your best bet against Jedore, especially if you want to fight from long range.

Jedore has both shields and armor. It will take a lot of direct hits or powerful splash damage to weaken her.

CAUTION

Introduction

Training

Upgrades and Research

Walkthrough
The Warlord Okeer

Special Assignments

Planetary Database

Appendix

Lure the YMIR between the metal plates on its side of the warehouse. Peg the arms as they stick out.

The longer Jedore lasts, the more berserkers she calls into the battle.

CAUTION

Return to Okeer

Once Jedore and the YMIR are defeated, EDI comes over the comm and warns you that the lab is flooded with toxins and that Okeer's life signs are failing. Hurry back to the lab before Okeer dies and his knowledge

of the Collectors is lost. As you close in, you hear emergency vents kicking in to flush the gas out of the lab. But is it too late?

Unfortunately, Okeer succumbed to the gas before you could finish off Jedore. However, the krogan recorded a message for you with his last breath. He admits that he doesn't know why the Collectors have been targeting humans but asks you to take care of his legacy, his perfect soldier.

The crowd comes to a consensus (some grudgingly): take Okeer's krogan. If the krogan is as strong as

Okeer suggested, then he could be a worthy ally in the fight against the Collectors. Shepard orders the *Normandy* to prep for an extraction.

Back on the *Normandy*

Jacob and Miranda are split on the value of the genetically engineered krogan joining the mission. Miranda worries he will be impossible to control and could do a great deal of damage in the confines of the *Normandy* because krogan are best in close-quarters combat. Shepard decides to place the krogan in the cargo hold until the decision is made to release the krogan or keep him permanently in stasis.

Following the meeting, make the rounds on *Normandy*, Stop in to visit with Jacob and Miranda. They become a

little more talkative as the mission goes on.

Many personal conversations between crew members of the *Normandy*, such as between Shepard and Miranda, are not tied to finishing a specific mission. That's why you should keep checking in with them. Over time, as the crew goes through hardships together, they open up. .

NOTE

The gun Shepard has been pointing at Grunt's gut the whole time greases the wheels of Grunt's loyalty, too.

After checking in on the crew, it's time to finally make the big choice about the krogan in the cargo hold down on Deck 4. Shepard is not required to open the tank. But the krogan could be such a great asset to the crew that it should be difficult for Shepard to resist. After a brief talk with EDI about the ramifications, Shepard opens the tank. The krogan emerges.

And sure enough, Miranda was right.

The krogan explodes out of the tank and slams Shepard into the back wall, holding the commander down with his massive forearm. The krogan gets right in Shepard's face. He does not attack. He assesses. He demands a name. The krogan speaks of Okeer clinically. Whereas the berserker on Korlus seemed to have an affinity for Okeer as some kind of father, this krogan finds Okeer's voice hollow.

The krogan remembers hearing the word "grunt," though. That's what he will call himself: Grunt. Grunt says he will follow Shepard if he can prove his strength against him. Otherwise, the krogan will snap Shepard in half right here. Shepard appeals to Grunt's inherent sense of pride by telling him he will only make the crew—the clan—stronger. And Grunt will have the chance to kill some worthy adversaries.

> Shepard can fail in taming the krogan. Shepard must be aggressive with the krogan so he will see the commander as a worthy leader. If the conversation gets too out of control, Shepard may have to shoot the krogan to get its attention. Shepard even has the option to put the krogan down. However, the krogan is a worthy addition to the crew—he is an excellent blunt force instrument to use in close-quarters combat situations. So unless Shepard is feeling particularly renegade, try to keep the krogan alive.

CAUTION

Got Your Recruits?

Once you have collected the first four recruits off of the Illusive Man's list (the team now has seven members, including Shepard), the next mission opens up: Horizon. You cannot move on in the fight against the Collectors until you have completed all four recruitment missions. Only then does the salarian Mordin Solus finish the countermeasures to thwart the Collector swarms; without the defenses, you don't stand a chance.

If you want to do any shopping back at Omega, now is a good time to return and purchase gear or tech you might not have been able to afford before. If you have not visited the Citadel yet, this is also a great opportunity to go see Shepard's old stomping grounds. Not only is there good shopping on the Citadel, but Shepard can also find out what has happened with the Council during the last two years. The Citadel and the Council have changed quite a bit, and Captain Anderson is just the person to help Shepard sort it all out.

Introduction

Training

Upgrades and Research

Walkthrough

The Warlord Okeer

Special Assignments

Planetary Database

Appendix

HORIZON

The Illusive Man sends Shepard the name of a human colony that the Collectors are about to strike: Horizon. Shepard must rush to Horizon and try to stop the Collectors from abducting the colonists—if the operation cannot be stopped, he must gather as much information about the Collectors as possible.

Horizon is located in the Terminus Systems. The world is lush and offers abundant fresh water, making it an ideal location for a human colony. The site was chosen for its economic potential, and within just eight years it has thrived. It would be a horrendous loss for humanity if the Collectors were able to abduct the colonists and spirit them away to the Reapers.

Spoils of War
- **Credits: 60,000**
- **Platinum: 2,000**

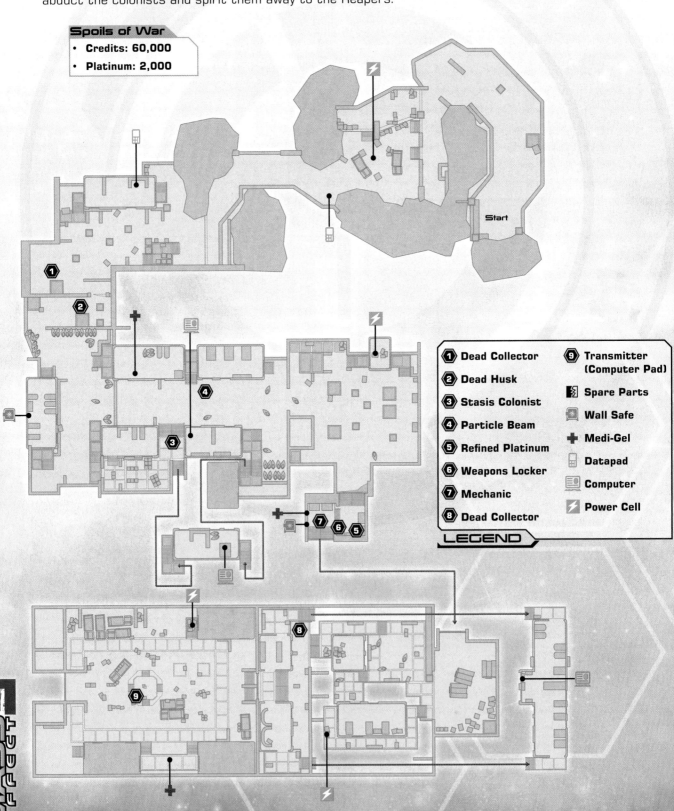

Start

LEGEND

1. Dead Collector
2. Dead Husk
3. Stasis Colonist
4. Particle Beam
5. Refined Platinum
6. Weapons Locker
7. Mechanic
8. Dead Collector
9. Transmitter (Computer Pad)

- Spare Parts
- Wall Safe
- Medi-Gel
- Datapad
- Computer
- Power Cell

Objective 1: Explore the Colony

The Collectors reach Horizon before Shepard. The Collector ship drills down to the planet surface, casting its shadow across the colony. The swarms spread out, delivering their paralytic toxin to the colonists. Prior to the invasion, an Alliance trooper was stationed on Horizon to get the massive defense guns that protect the colony online. However, the trooper's attention was diverted to communications as soon as the Collectors silenced the colony.

NOTE

The identity of the Alliance soldier on Horizon is determined by two factors: Shepard's gender and whether or not you imported a save file from the original game. If Shepard is male and Ashley Williams was killed, Kaidan Alenko is at the colony. Ashley is in the colony if Shepard is female and Kaidan was killed. If this is a new game, then the Alliance soldier is the opposite gender of Shepard.

Shepard lands on Horizon as the Collectors are in mid-operation. The commander and his squad must move quickly to head off the Collectors before the colonists are abducted and the Collector ship raises anchor and vanishes back into the cosmos.

Advance on Horizon

It doesn't take long before Shepard encounters the Collectors on the outskirts of the colony. Collector guardians and Collector drones are stationed by the crates near one of the giant turrets that should have protected Horizon from the invasion.

As the swarms freeze the colonists, the Collectors drop down to the surface and begin sweeping up their quarry. In the heart of the ship, Harbinger uses a special power to possess a Collector drone on the surface. Harbinger then directs the other nearby Collectors to seize the colonists.

Take on the Collectors, taking cover among the crates and dodging their attacks. The Collectors are fearless.  Although they will use cover, they are not exactly survivalists. Collectors will move on you and your squad and take risky shots if they think they can bring you down.

CAUTION

Be mindful of the fragile crates when looking for cover. Collector weapons shatter those crates in seconds.

Introduction

Training

Upgrades and Research

Horizon

Walkthrough

Special Assignments

Planetary Database

Appendix

Enemy Profile: The Collectors

Collector Drone

- **Classification: Minion**
- **Powers:** —
- **Defenses:** —
- **Weapons: Particle Beam**

Collector Guardian

- **Classification: Elite**
- **Powers: Hive Shield**
- **Defenses: Barrier**
- **Weapons: Heavy Particle Beam**

Collector Assassin

- **Classification: Elite**
- **Powers:** —
- **Defenses: Barrier**
- **Weapons: Particle Cannon**

The Collectors all look alike. They flutter down to the surface like flying ants and scan the landscape with their myriad eyes. But while the Collectors may seem identical, their battlefield behaviors are not. The Collector drones are just that: drones whose primary objective is to collect colonists—the Collectors' equivalent of cannon fodder. Without shielding , these Collectors fan out and attack with entry-level particle weapons. But entry-level for a Collector is still tough stuff for you. Particle weapons do incredible damage.

Collector guardians are one rank up from the drones. Guardians use a barrier to protect against damage, and their weapons are more powerful. Guardians earn their names from their ability to deploy hive shields. These power shields pop out and protect the Collectors from incoming fire. It takes several shots to destroy a hive shield. The Collector assassins are the nastiest of the three Collector classes. They attack with particle cannons that rip through all kinds of protection, such as armor and shields. If a Collector assassin has you in its sights, find cover immediately and do not come out unless you have the kill shot or the assassin is reloading.

Collector drones are susceptible to headshots, so look for a peeking drone and then blast its face off.

Pick up the power cells in the middle of the area to restock your heavy weapons.

Hack the datapad on the picnic table for 12,000 credits.

Follow the swarm's trail of destruction to the Collector ship, looming in the distance over the colony. As you move  deeper into the colony, Joker tries to radio you, but the Collectors are disabling communications. You are on your own until you drive the Collectors out.

> The arrival of a Collector is often preceded by the buzzing of its wings. You may also hear the clicks and hums of their language.

TIP

The Collectors advance on you through a small neighborhood. The Collectors come up the middle of the area, so either seek cover and take them head on or use the buildings on the right side to flank them. The windows provide great vantage points for snipers and other long-range attacks. You can typically get off a few shots before the Collectors reorient themselves and turn their fire on the windows. Flanking through the buildings is also a good way to neutralize the effectiveness of the hive shields. You can blast the Collectors from the sides instead of using rounds to shatter the shields.

Husks mingle with the Collectors in this assault. These are the same creatures you turned back on Eden Prime. The appearance of husks, weaponless drones that attack with brute force and numbers, confirms that the Collectors are indeed in league with the Reapers.

Enemy Profile: Husk

- **Classification: Minion**
- **Powers: —**
- **Defenses: —**
- **Weapons: Husk Smash**

Husks are humans that have been drained of their living essences and reduced to animated constructs. Husks do not use weapons. Instead, they rush and attack with husk smash. Alone, this attack doesn't do too much damage. If you're caught in a gaggle of husks, look out. Husk smashes from every direction will wear you down fast.

Hack the datapad in the building to the right for 5,400 credits.

Scan the dead Collector in the field with your omni-tool to acquire the Lattice Shunting tech upgrade.

The Husks

When you round the corner from the first big Collector attack, you locate a motionless husk. On Eden Prime, Shepard witnessed the geth impaling humans on spires to turn them into husks. This husk was already prepared, so the Collectors must have a supply of husks with them aboard the ship. Also, they're not turning Horizon's colonists into husks. Instead, they are taking the colonists alive. There is little time to waste, so push deeper into the colony to find the next batch of Collectors gathering up humans.

More Collectors

When you reach the pods stacked against the wall, prepare for another platoon of Collectors. You can sneak up on the Collectors by inching up to the corner overlooking the next courtyard. From here you can launch a surprise attack. Pick off one with a headshot or lob a heavy weapons shell into the Collectors.

As in the previous area, there are buildings you can use for cover. Flank the Collectors from the sides instead of taking them on directly. Winnow their numbers from the windows, taking shots at their heads and ducking down when they return fire with their particle weapons.

> Bypass the wall safe's lock in the building to the right of the Collector attack for 4,200 credits. There is medi-gel in the building on the left.

TIP

Introduction

Training

Upgrades and Research

Horizon

Walkthrough

Special Assignments

Planetary Database

Appendix

After the battle, move through the area until you reach the colonists stuck in stasis. Inspect the first pair of frozen colonists you find and then cross into the lawn to the left. There is a Collector particle beam leaning against one of the pods. Pick it up. It will be extremely useful against the new type of Collector you are about to encounter.

Use the stairs to enter an apartment above the lawn. Hack the computer on the bed for 3,600 credits.

Remember this perch. It is a great sniping spot for the upcoming battle, which is triggered by walking halfway across the lawn below.

TIP

Several Collectors swoop down to the lawn. In the ship, Harbinger watches the scene through the eyes of the troops in the field. Harbinger picks one of the assassins and takes control of it, just as Shepard witnessed when the colonists were abducted. Harbinger takes on all of the powers of the Collector it assumes, but makes it stronger. Harbinger is

also very clever about possessing Collectors that are close to death. When a near-death Collector is possessed, it is replenished with full armor and full barrier. As soon as the armor is destroyed, Harbinger leaves the Collector body.

Take cover and use the particle beam to rip through your foe's barrier and armor before it can attack.

Harbinger will keep possessing Collectors for as long as there are Collectors in the fight, so take down the Collectors as fast as possible. Leave no Collector with a sliver of health, lest Harbinger take possession of its body.

There can only be one possessed Collector at a time.

NOTE

It's easy for the particle beam to run dry, but more power cells are located in the small room at the back of the lawn.

Blast through the Collectors, using the building to flank from and the crates in the lawn as cover. When the fight is over, collect any thermal clips dropped in the grass and then investigate the locked door off to the right. Hack the door controls and open it to find a survivor as well as a weapons locker and 2,000 units of refined platinum.

Survivor

There is a lone survivor inside the small bunker. It's a mechanic who sought cover as soon as the swarm attack began. He is shocked to learn that the colony's assailants are Collectors. He always thought they were myths

to keep humans out of corners of the galaxy where they weren't wanted. The mechanic blames the Alliance for the attack. The colony was fine until the Alliance showed up, installed one of their representatives, and built the giant defense guns. The mechanic also thinks the Alliance was poking around Horizon for reasons other than installing defenses.

The mechanic complains that the guns don't even shoot straight. Calibrating the guns had been a major headache. The guns, though, could be your ticket to turning back the Collectors. If you can reach the main transmitter on the other side of the colony, you can access the targeting controls of the defense tower guns. The mechanic will stay behind. Load up at the weapons locker, take the medi-gel and platinum, and then move out.

Objective 2: Locate the Spaceport

Block 7

Look for Collectors by the stairs to your left when you step out of the mechanic's hideout and into the next block of the colony. They have not seen you yet. Don't linger. Raise your weapons and take the first shot. Make it count! As soon as that first shot rings out the Collector drones, guardians, and assassins will swarm the area.

aware of the assassins and possessed Collector. Don't take many risks here. Stick to cover and move up only when you can take and hold position.

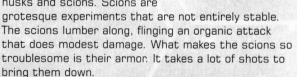

Enemy Profile: Scion

- **Classification: Minion**
- **Powers: —**
- **Defenses: Armor**
- **Weapons: Blast**

The Reapers have bolstered the Collectors' attack force with husks and scions. Scions are grotesque experiments that are not entirely stable. The scions lumber along, flinging an organic attack that does modest damage. What makes the scions so troublesome is their armor. It takes a lot of shots to bring them down.

The scene soon gets complicated. Harbinger possesses one of the Collectors and husks rush through the middle of the area. The throng of husks can be cut down with gunfire, although you must stay

Don't relent against this batch of Collectors. As soon as you take down one possessed Collector, Harbinger will have another Collector body picked out. Weed out any weak Collectors because there is a good chance one will be the next hijacked Collector. Harbinger's attacks are deadly. Just a few direct hits are enough to put Shepard down.

Scan the dead Collector farther up the stairs in the block to pick up the Hyper Amp. This tech increases damage from biotic attacks by **10 percent**.

Bypass the locked door on the opposite side of the block after you have eliminated the Collectors and scoured

the place for clips, power cells, credits, and tech scans. This door leads to the spaceport, where you can work on the targeting systems for the colony's defense towers.

Objective 3: Activate Tower

First Wave

The spaceport looks abandoned. The transmitter is on a raised platform in the middle of the area. However, the silence is soon broken by the moans of husks. Look to the left of the port. The stirring behind the railing is husks pulling themselves off the ground and getting ready to charge you. Target them before they get out from behind the railing and can surround you and your squad. There is medi-gel up there to collect once the husks are down.

Before long, more husks activate. They are joined by a scion that moves across the port like a tank, blasting anything in front of it. Though it moves slowly, it's difficult to bring it down. The scion seems to inhale ammo, which will make the rest of this battle harder.

Heavy weapons bring the husks down faster, but don't waste all of your ammo. En route to the spaceport, you'll find no shortage of enemies you should use heavy weapons ammo on.

There are power cells on the right side of the spaceport.

Investigate the Transmitter

After eliminating the first wave of husks and scions, you need to hack the computer terminal on the platform. The terminal puts you in contact with the *Normandy*. EDI is able to recalibrate the defense towers on Horizon, but it will take a little time to bring the towers fully online. While EDI is working on the towers, the Collectors will surely see the energy signals at the transmitter. They will realize what you are doing and launch an attack. Get ready for a serious Collector push-back. Reload all of your weapons and find some cover.

Defend the Tower

The Collectors drop down to the far side of the port behind the transmitter. Within seconds, Harbinger

possesses a Collector and the remainder of the Collectors spread out. The port is full of crates, so you have no shortage of places to hide. Use cover to rest and reload. In addition to Collectors, look for more husks and scions.

> Never forget that you have two teammates. Don't assume you have to do everything yourself. Move them around the field and use them to intercept enemies while you concentrate on your own targets.

NOTE

Move around the port. The Collectors are always on the lookout for you, and if you stay in one place, they will converge on your position. Flank Collectors by darting from crate to crate, getting the Collectors to either look around for you or get distracted by your squad mates. While a Collector trains its particle weapon on a friend, you can line up a punishing headshot.

Fueled by rage, Harbinger moves around. It tends to mount assaults rather than stick to cover.

If you spot a Collector guardian ducking behind a hive shield, flank and try sniping the foe from the side rather than shooting apart the shield.

As the battle rages, EDI keeps you abreast of the status of the recalibration. You must hold the port until the guns are fully online. The Collectors do not let up, moving on the port in waves. Just when you think you have stopped their assault, Harbinger possesses another Collector and the assassins take up defensive positions around the perimeter of the port.

Introduction

Training

Upgrades and Research

Horizon

Walkthrough

Special Assignments

Planetary Database

Appendix

The Praetorian

The Collectors soon realize that the guns are almost online, and so Harbinger sends in a praetorian, a monstrous entity that is the toughest monster you've fought yet. The praetorian drops in from the sky, ready to do what the Collectors could not: bring you down. The other Collectors fall back, leaving you to deal with the praetorian in a three-on-one fight. Despite those odds, it's still the praetorian that has the upper hand.

Enemy Profile: Praetorian

- **Classification: Boss**
- **Powers: Barrier, Death Choir**
- **Defenses: Armor**
- **Weapons: Twin Particle Beams**

The praetorian is a winged monster that wields twin particle beams. These beams cut through shields and armor. Direct hits seriously weaken defenses. Repeat strikes in rapid succession are deadly. The beams last for several seconds, so when the praetorian starts to charge up a shot (look for the gathering of purple energy near its base), find cover.

The only way to kill a praetorian is to destroy its armor. However, the praetorian is surrounded by an additional barrier that it's able to regenerate. To chip away at the armor, you must first expend a lot of ammo in depleting the regenerating barrier . Once the barrier has been dispelled, you only have a few seconds to fire on the praetorian's armor before the beast recharges the barrier to full strength.

Just before the praetorian recharges, it slams into the ground and unleashes its Death Choir attack. A purple barrier envelops the praetorian, rendering it temporarily invulnerable to attacks. The Death Choir attack grievously injures anybody close to the monster.

Keep moving during this battle. Do not let the praetorian draw a bead on you. Always have cover nearby. When you spy the particle beams charging up, slam into cover and dodge the incoming strike.

When the praetorian's barrier is down, capitalize on those few seconds before the creature crashes into the ground and uses Death Choir. Wait until a particle beam attack is finished and then pop out of cover. If you have heavy weapon ammo left, unload it and then back away before the Death Choir recharges.

The praetorian cannot be damaged while it is charging up its barrier.

The praetorian needs a few moments between particle beam attacks. Use those seconds to pop out of cover and pepper its underbelly with rounds.

Just as you neutralize the praetorian, the Collector ship leaves the colony. Half of the colonists have already been harvested by the Collectors and are aboard the vessel, but you struck a blow against the Collectors today. You killed many of them, dropped possessed Collectors, and took down a praetorian. The Collectors will not be able to ignore that.

Reunion

Once the Collector ship departs, the Alliance representative comes out of hiding. (For the sake of this meeting, let's just refer to the Alliance rep as Kaidan. If you are playing a male commander or if Kaidan was killed in the first *Mass Effect*, it would be Ashley striding across the port to greet you.) Kaidan is not exactly happy to see Shepard. He's upset that the commander has not been in contact in over two years. Nor is he pleased to hear that Shepard is involved with Cerberus.

Kaidan is hearing none of Shepard's rationale for falling in with Cerberus. Kaidan has too much history with Cerberus to believe they are acting nobly. He questions the commander's loyalty and refuses to join Shepard's crew. Kaidan storms off to file a report with the Alliance, leaving Shepard to call Joker for a lift back to the *Normandy*.

After the Mission

Shepard joins the Illusive Man via holo-conference. The Illusive Man is pleased that Shepard was able to fight the Collectors and interrupt their operations on Horizon. Shepard is not amused that the Illusive Man let slip to the Alliance that Shepard is working with Cerberus, thus souring a close past relationship. But the Illusive Man says he needed to do this to find out if the Collectors are just after humans or if they aretrying to get directly to Shepard. Attacking a colony where there is a former associate of Shepard makes it clear. The Collectors are after Shepard.

The Illusive Man says that he is devoting all of his resources to discovering a way to pass through the Omega 4 mass relay and take the fight into Collector territory. While he works on that part of the puzzle, Shepard must continue building a team. The Illusive Man gives Shepard three more dossiers on potential recruits: an assassin, a justicar, and a quarian.

During the meeting, the Illusive Man says that Shepard needs to make sure not only that the team is complete, but also that it is completely dedicated to the mission. Shepard needs to go to each member of the team and make sure they have no qualms about rushing headlong into a dire situation. They need to be focused. And that means cleaning up any loose ends in their lives. So in addition to the finding new recruits, Shepard should find time to also see how to best earn the absolute loyalty of the team.

As always, take the time to make the rounds on the *Normandy*, checking in with every crew member. Check in with Chambers for any updates, read the private terminal to see if any new special assignments are available, and launch research projects. If minerals are an issue, there is no better time than now to travel to distant worlds and mine resources to put into tech.

Introduction

Training

Upgrades and Research

Horizon

Walkthrough

Special Assignments

Planetary Database

Appendix

DOSSIERS, PART 2

The Illusive Man recommends that Shepard expand the team by adding more recruits. As before, the Illusive Man has prepared dossiers on potential squad members. There are three this time: a quarian, an assassin, and an asari justicar. Shepard is free to recruit them in any order, but without their talents, the mission cannot continue.

NOTE

You must recruit at least two of these three recruits to advance the story. Once you have a total of eight squad members (Jacob and Miranda count as the first two), the Illusive Man then informs you that you must work on the loyalty of each squad member.

The Engineer Map on next page

Tali has been located on the planet Haestrom, which was once a quarian colony established to observe the star Dholen. Dholen is an unstable star that threatens to prematurely go red dwarf. However, the quarians lost the planet to geth attack and it now serves as a geth outpost. The geth have built thousands of orbital platforms around Haestrom, but it is not known exactly how many geth exist on the planet.

The Citadel has issued strong warnings for all to avoid the planet, but a quarian research team has been dispatched to Haestrom to investigate quarian history on Haestrom. Shepard must somehow extract Tali from the planet before the geth tear apart her entire research team.

Objective 1: Look for Tali

As the Cerberus shuttle lands on the surface of Haestrom, EDI informs Shepard that Tali's last known location was the ancient quarian ruins close to the drop zone. This is an area of high geth activity, so the commander and squad should expect heavy resistance. And as if the geth weren't enough to deal with, Dholen has been flaring up. Shepard must avoid direct sunlight or else the magnetic disruptions will damage shields. Attacking the geth in the sunlight is just too risky.

Avoid the Sun

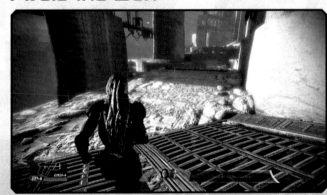

EDI was not exaggerating about the sunlight disrupting your shields. If you do slip out of the shade, your shields immediately start degrading, as noted by an on-screen note. If you stay out too long, the shields completely go down, leaving you exposed to attacks, so, make sure you run through the areas with no shadow, such as at the bottom of the ramp just next to the landing zone.

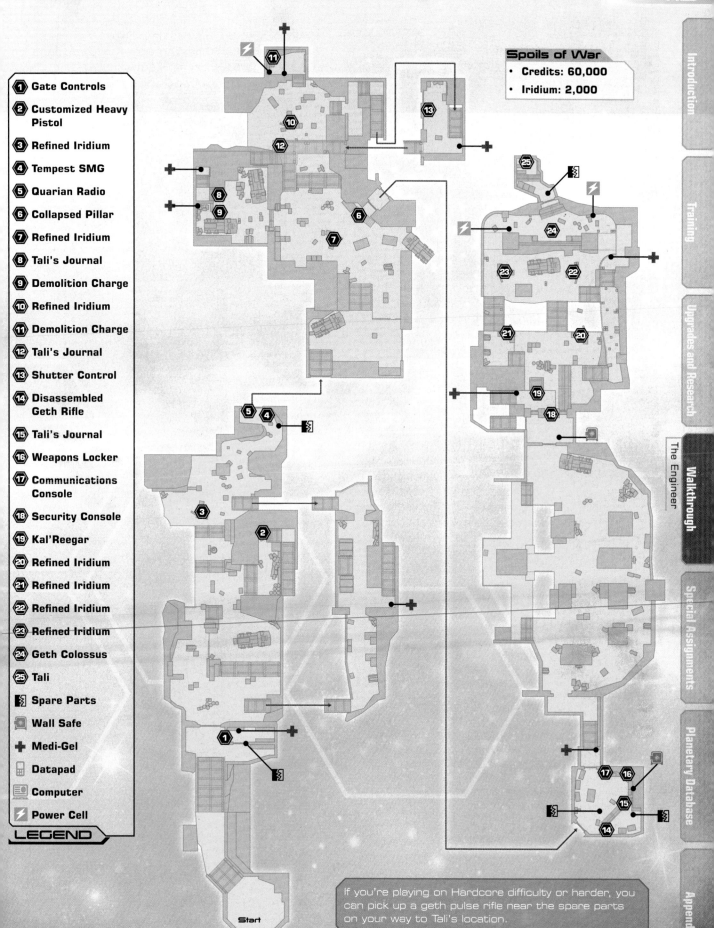

LEGEND

1. Gate Controls
2. Customized Heavy Pistol
3. Refined Iridium
4. Tempest SMG
5. Quarian Radio
6. Collapsed Pillar
7. Refined Iridium
8. Tali's Journal
9. Demolition Charge
10. Refined Iridium
11. Demolition Charge
12. Tali's Journal
13. Shutter Control
14. Disassembled Geth Rifle
15. Tali's Journal
16. Weapons Locker
17. Communications Console
18. Security Console
19. Kal'Reegar
20. Refined Iridium
21. Refined Iridium
22. Refined Iridium
23. Refined Iridium
24. Geth Colossus
25. Tali

- Spare Parts
- Wall Safe
- Medi-Gel
- Datapad
- Computer
- Power Cell

Spoils of War
- Credits: 60,000
- Iridium: 2,000

TIP

If you're playing on Hardcore difficulty or harder, you can pick up a geth pulse rifle near the spare parts on your way to Tali's location.

Start

Introduction

Training

Upgrades and Research

Walkthrough

The Engineer

Special Assignments

Planetary Database

Appendix

There is a locked gate at the bottom of the ramps. The controls for the gate are in a small room next to it, but so is a dead geth. A quarian left a recording unit that automatically plays when you get close: Tali must be found, as she has the data that the quarian expedition team was after. Grab the medi-gel from the nearby crate and scan the dead geth for 9,000 credits. Cerberus pays well for salvaged geth technology.

Within moments of walking through the gate, you are spotted by the geth. Ancient quarian architecture features a lot of large blocks and geometric shapes, which double as excellent cover. Dive behind a block and begin targeting the geth troopers that are fanning across the area. The geth seem unfazed by the sunlight, so they are allowed greater movement. Go for headshots to bring the geth down faster.

Enemy Profile: Geth Trooper

- **Classification: Minion**
- **Powers: Hive Fanaticism**
- **Defenses: Geth Shielding**
- **Weapons: Pulse Rifle**

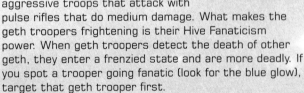

Geth troopers are the backbone of the geth. These minions are aggressive troops that attack with pulse rifles that do medium damage. What makes the geth troopers frightening is their Hive Fanaticism power. When geth troopers detect the death of other geth, they enter a frenzied state and are more deadly. If you spot a trooper going fanatic (look for the blue glow), target that geth trooper first.

Advance farther into the ruins to discover more geth activity. Use the taller blocks for cover from the sun,

darting to them for a quick shield repair. The geth are extremely hostile and aggressive. They move forward and stand their ground without using much cover. This is advantageous to you but also makes it easier to get pinned down.

The area ahead is bathed in sunlight, so move to the right and check out the shadowy alcove. There is some scannable tech at the base of a long ramp, but as you near it, geth troopers start filing down the ramp. Pick them off as they attempt to drop to your level. If you hide behind a block near the bottom of the stairs, you can control the influx of geth on the ramp. Once the geth have stopped coming down, scan the heavy pistol on the deceased quarian. It is a Titan Pulsar, which increases heavy pistol damage by 10 percent.

> **TIP**
> There is a medi-gel station at the top of the ramp.

You can use the area at the top of the ramp to flank the geth rocket troopers ahead or use the blocks back on the main floor.

Introduction

Training

Upgrades and Research

Walkthrough
The Engineer

Special Assignments

Planetary Database

Appendix

Enemy Profile: Geth Rocket Trooper

- **Classification: Minion**
- **Powers: —**
- **Defenses: Geth Shielding**
- **Weapons: Rocket Launcher**

Geth rocket troopers are technically weaker than regular geth troopers; they do not possess Hive Fanaticism. But their rocket launchers are incredibly accurate and powerful, so prioritize these geth early.

Scan the damaged geth hunter for an additional 9,000 credits.

One of the dead quarians in this shaded area has a new weapon: the Tempest submachine gun. It's an upgrade to the machine pistol.

TIP

After wiping out the rocket troopers from cover, run across the sunlight to pick up 400 units of refined iridium from the crate.

Fight in the Shade

A radio next to a dead quarian squawks. The quarian team leader, Kal'Reegar, is trying to reach his fallen comrade. Answer the radio to get a situation report from the squad leader. He and his team were there to investigate the quarian ruins, but the sun activity has prevented them from uploading their data back to their flotilla. The leader explains that there are a lot of geth in the ruins but that the geth dropship has not left to fetch reinforcements, nor is it able to transmit back to other geth ships.

Kal'Reegar says that the remnants of his team are hunkered down at a base camp across the nearby valley. He relays that Tali is with them and currently seeking shelter where she can hold down a chokepoint and keep the geth from reaching her. According to the squad leader, getting Tali and the data out safely is their top priority. It's yours now, too.

The area on the far side of the first soaked field is completely shaded, but don't expect easy passage. When you move to the large red door and start infiltrating the ruins to the right, more geth troopers attack. This is close-quarters combat, so go for headshots to end encounters as soon as possible, or use blunter weapons like the shotgun.

Objective 2: Explosive Charges

No sooner does your conversation with Kal'Reegar wind down than a geth dropship moves through the air and attacks. The ship blasts a giant column, dropping it directly in front of the door that would lead you to Tali. You must find two sets of demolition charges in the ruins (one in a bunker near the construction site and another in a small room on the lower level) to blow the column and keep pressing toward Tali.

Construction Yard

The geth turn up the heat when you drop down the ramp near the toppled pillar to find the demolition charges. Not only do more geth troopers attack your position, but a geth hunter also sweeps through the area, using its cloaking talent to make it hard to get a lock on it. Fortunately, the cloaking device does not obscure the geth's blue eye, giving you something to track as the hunter advances.

Enemy Profile: Geth Hunter

- **Classification: Elite**
- **Powers: Tactical Cloak**
- **Defenses: Geth Shielding**
- **Weapons: Geth Shotgun**

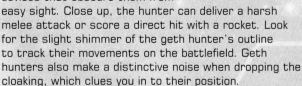

Geth hunters attempt to sneak up on their targets with cloaking devices that obscure them from easy sight. Close up, the hunter can deliver a harsh melee attack or score a direct hit with a rocket. Look for the slight shimmer of the geth hunter's outline to track their movements on the battlefield. Geth hunters also make a distinctive noise when dropping the cloaking, which clues you in to their position.

- **Classification: Elite**
- **Powers: —**
- **Defenses: Geth Shielding**
- **Weapons: Arc Thrower**

The geth destroyer is typically supported by geth troopers. They work in tandem, with troopers moving in to hold a target down so the destroyer can move in and finish it off with the close-range arc thrower, an energy-like flamethrower. The weapon is actually the destroyer's weak spot. A direct shot at the weapon causes it to go critical. The resulting explosion can ruin the destroyer.

More geth troopers move through the construction equipment. Use cover to hold your position, and pick off the geth before they get too close.

The first set of charges is in the bunker to the left of the construction site. Several geth troopers emerge from the bunker as you close in. The door is an easy hold. Position your squad members around the door and cut down any geth that try to make it out. The geth hunter is your top target. It does the most damage with its rifle, so do not let it get too close. Pick the geth hunter off first and then mop up the rest of the geth troopers.

The first charge is on a desk, next to a terminal. Pick up the charge and then step around the corner to grab some medi-gel from the medical station. Listen to Tali's message on the terminal. She is seeking a core sample from the ruins to get a timeline on the sun's degradation. It is deteriorating entirely too fast, and researching the sample should help determine what is happening to the sun of this former quarian planet.

Turnabout Is Fair Play

When you try to leave the bunker to locate the next set of charges, geth attack and attempt to pin you down at the door. But this geth force is augmented by a geth prime, which is a terrifying enemy unit. It advances without fear since it has the armor and shields to withstand a lot of incoming fire. Those defenses let the geth prime close the gap and get in close with enough health (and sometimes armor) left to do tremendous damage.

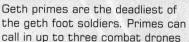
Enemy Profile: Geth Prime

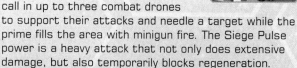

- **Classification: Sub-boss**
- **Powers: Drone Swarm, Siege Pulse**
- **Defenses: Geth Shielding**
- **Weapons: Minigun**

Geth primes are the deadliest of the geth foot soldiers. Primes can call in up to three combat drones to support their attacks and needle a target while the prime fills the area with minigun fire. The Siege Pulse power is a heavy attack that not only does extensive damage, but also temporarily blocks regeneration.

Shotguns at close range are good for bringing down a geth prime.

Pick up the 400 units of refined iridium in the crate just outside the door. It's much easier to spot coming out of the bunker.

After clearing the door, cross the open space and veer off to the right. A wide ramp leads down to a lower area, but you must fight back the geth trying to advance up it. The geth are led by a mighty geth destroyer. The geth destroyer coolly moves up the ramp, hammering you and your squad. Use cover to chip away at the geth destroyer's shields, and then finish it off before it reaches the top of the ramp.

Alternatively, you can use the bridge spanning the area and pick off the geth from above, but the bridge is largely baked in sunlight. The crates offer a little relief from the sun, but you will not be able to stay out of the sunlight and fire on the geth. A computer on the bridge contains another entry in Tali's journal. Apparently the Haestrom sun started deteriorating just 200 years ago, which is just too short of a period for a star to turn to a red giant.

NOTE

At the base of the ramp, hang a left and slip through the doorway. Walk up the long, narrow ramp inside the small room. Pick up the medi-gel from the station at the top.

Return to the main area and then slip through the door next to the fragile crate. There are power cells and another medi-gel station just inside this small area. The power cells are critical pickups because of the enormity of the enemy you must face at the end of this mission: a geth colossus. The second charge is next to the power cells box. Now that you have both charges, you can blow the column blocking the door.

On your way back to the column, grab the 400 units of refined iridium from the crate directly between the two small doors that led to the charges and the medi-gel.

TIP

While you were grabbing the second set of charges, the geth were regrouping. When you step back out, the geth have spread across the clearing and taken the bridge. Geth rocket troopers on the bridge rain shells from above. Use cover to dodge the rockets, and return fire while the geth are reloading. Inch across the clearing, moving from cover to cover, to push back the geth troopers and geth destroyer.

When the scene calms, move to the column and plant the charges. You have 10 seconds to fall back to a safe distance. When the column explodes, you can then explore deeper into the ruins in search of Tali and anybody that is left from her team. Geth activity heats up, so reload and keep your cool.

Objective 3: Contact Quarians

Now that you have destroyed the column and opened a route to Tali, go through the new door.

Dead Geth

The door opens, revealing the aftermath of a fight between quarians and geth. It was a bloodbath. The dead are everywhere, slumped over consoles and lying on the floor. Access Tali's journal on the terminal inside the room. As you listen to Tali speak of a time when quarians walked without head coverings, pick up all of the extras in the room. An ancient wall safe contains credits. Salvage the geth in the room for 6,000 credits. The geth near the terminal is worth 9,000 credits. The damaged geth in the center of the room is worth 12,000 credits. The disassembled geth rifle on the desk unlocks the Kinetic Pulsar upgrade, which increases assault rifle damage.

Playing on hardcore difficulty? Check the room for a geth pulse rifle, a special sniper rifle that is exceedingly lethal and accurate.

NOTE

After picking up all of the credits and treasure, access the communications console next to the locked door in the back of the room. This opens a line to Tali. Talk to Tali about her mission, and she will explain how to reach her. Tali is holed up inside an observatory, located through the door and across a field, where she is currently cornered by geth. Tali says there are some quarians left; they are firing on the geth outside Tali's position. Tali asks Shepard to help her and the remaining quarians get out alive.

Objective 4: Get to Tali

The First Batch

There are still a lot of geth surrounding Tali's position. When you move toward the field, you are spotted by geth recon drones. These hovering turrets are both annoying and deadly, mainly because they alert other nearby geth to your position. Blast the recon drones out of the air as soon as you see them.

Enemy Profile: Geth Recon Drones

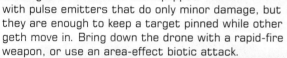

- **Classification: Minion**
- **Powers: Tactical Cloak**
- **Defenses: —**
- **Weapons: Pulse Emitter**

Geth recon drones are flying units that relay advance intel back to the other geth. The drones are equipped with pulse emitters that do only minor damage, but they are enough to keep a target pinned while other geth move in. Bring down the drone with a rapid-fire weapon, or use an area-effect biotic attack.

Don't keep your eyes up for too long, though. Geth troopers and a geth prime weave through the giant blocks to shred your squad. Drop into cover and target that geth prime first. The monster is the deadliest thing in the area, so bringing it down right away improves your chances of getting through the rest of the drones and troopers in one piece.

Just beyond the door is a medi-gel station, along with a wall safe containing 6,000 credits.

The Field

After opening the safe, activate the security controls console to raise the shutters overlooking the field Tali was referring to in her previous message. With the shutters open, you can see the full scale of the geth trying to reach Tali. Not only are several foot troopers working on the door to Tali's position, but there is a massive geth colossus dominating the field. You cannot rescue Tali without bringing down the geth colossus.

Beyond the shutters is the only surviving quarian besides Tali: Kal'Reegar. He is sitting next to the med kit with a medi-gel. Speak to Kal'Reegar. He explains that Tali is in a good spot since the observatory is heavily fortified, but unless the geth colossus is taken care of, she will soon be in trouble. Kal'Reegar has kept the colossus busy with rockets, but the other geth keep providing enough cover for the colossus to repair itself.

Kal'Reegar cannot move deeper into the battlefield since his suit has been compromised, but he does have a lot of information. There is a bridge on the right side of the field that would make a great sniper perch, but it is easy to get pinned down up there. The left side offers cover from the colossus, but the geth can easily track you. Running up the middle offers cover from the geth, but the colossus can always see you. There are no great options, only options that are not as bad as the others.

Introduction

Training

Upgrades and Research

The Engineer

Walkthrough

Special Assignments

Planetary Database

Appendix

Enemy Profile: Geth Colossus

- **Classification: Boss**
- **Powers: Shield Boost, Siege Pulse**
- **Defenses: Geth Shielding, Heavy Armor**
- **Weapons: Minigun**

The geth colossus instills much fear thanks to its size and powerful weapons. But the real reason to be terrified by the colossus is its ability to hunker down and regenerate its shields if given a moment's chance. When the colossus fully refreshes its shields, you must start all over in order to break through them to chip away at the colossus' armor. Heavy weapons like the missile launcher or Collector particle beam work best for taking down a colossus. If you run low on ammo, look for one crate of heavy weapon ammo on each side of the colossus.

If you have a sniper, the perch works well for picking off the geth. If you have heavy weapons, sneaking up on the geth from the left is good because you can unload on it without it seeing you until you're on its doorstep. If you have a strong squad with assault rifles and lots of medi-gel, taking the middle will offer cover and plenty of spots to fight back, but you will be under constant barrage.

Kal'Reegar offers to help by peppering the colossus with rockets. You can either accept his offer or tell him to stay down. After all, Tali did ask that you keep Kal'Reegar alive. However, that means sacrificing Kal'Reegar's rockets. It's your call, but know that losing Kal'Reegar to take down the colossus will earn you Renegade points.

Emphasizing your order for Kal'Reegar to stand down requires an interrupt.

No matter which route you take, you will face serious resistance. The geth hold their position extremely well. The colossus is hard to bring down from a distance, so instead worry about the geth in the field as you close in on the colossus.

> Watch out for the colossus to fire. When you spy the blue light on its head lighting up, it is about to unload an attack.

CAUTION

> The sunlight is still a problem on this battlefield. Take few risks with the sun. You need to maintain your shield integrity as much as possible. If the colossus catches you with disrupted shields, it will drop you.

CAUTION

There is refined iridium in crates scattered across the area terrorized by the colossus. To the left, you locate 200 units. There are another 200 units in the center of the field. The final 200 units are close to the ramp leading up to the bridge on the geth side of the field.

The geth colossus is huge. It will take a long time to bring it down without using heavy weapons,  since you must damage the shield and then chip away at the armor before it replenishes the shield. Fortunately, there is a crate of power cells on each side of the geth colossus.

When you are close to the geth colossus, it switches to a rapid-fire gun instead of relying only on its powerful single blasts.

The colossus can only target one of you at a time. Do not shy from using your squad as interference. If you send

one of your squad up one side of the field to draw the attention of the geth colossus, you can lay into it with heavy weapons without being fired upon.

> Geth troopers will try to defend the colossus. If they pin you down, the colossus will have a chance to repair itself.

CAUTION

The geth forces fall apart as soon as you bring down the colossus. Mop up any stragglers and then approach the door behind the colossus' former position to locate Tali.

Tali

Inside the observatory, Tali is working on one last download. Check the room for salvage opportunities before talking to Tali and ending the mission. The damaged geth just inside the door is worth 9,000 credits. After collecting the credits, speak to Tali.

Tali is quite grateful for Shepard's help. Without Shepard's arrival, her mission might have been an even bigger disaster. Discovering more about the degradation of the star above the former quarian colony was just too important to Tali, although she is beginning to wonder if the data was truly worth so many lives.

Tali is now able to go with Shepard. Kal'Reegar (if he is still alive) can upload the data to the quarian admirals while Tali joins Shepard on the *Normandy*.

Back on the *Normandy*

Cerberus has seen footage of Tali in combat situations and is pleased that she has agreed to join the mission. Tali is not entirely happy to be working with Cerberus considering that Cerberus has threatened the quarian fleet before. However, if Shepard is willing to trust Cerberus, then Tali is willing to set aside her differences with the organization for now. Tali then reports to her position on the engineering deck. Shepard can talk to her there.

As usual, speak to various crew members, such as Yeoman Chambers, and consider any new research projects available in the tech lab. Mordin always has something new he could be working on for the squad or the *Normandy*. If Tali was the first recruit from this batch, Shepard can immediately set out to find the next two recruits. They are both located on Illium.

.

ILLIUM

The garden world of Illium is an asari-controlled planet that serves primarily as an entrepôt between the Terminus Systems and the Asari Republic. Because Illium is considered a colony planet (despite having multiple advanced metro areas), Council laws are more relaxed. Here, asari and other races trade in goods without maximum safety considerations; they also traffic in sapients, which essentially amounts to indentured servitude.

LEGEND

1. *Normandy*
2. *Serrice Technology*
3. *Trading Floor*
4. *Eternity Bar*
5. *Shipping/Cargo*
6. *Seryna*
7. *Liara's Office*
8. *Tracking Office (to Samara)*
9. *Baria's Frontiers*
10. *Gateway Personal Defense*
11. *Memories of Illium*
12. *Taxi Stand*

NOTE

Two of the three recruitment missions take place on Illium, so use this hub guide for your attempts to get Samara and Thane on board the *Normandy*.

First Arrival

Shepard and the squad land at Nos Astra, one of the largest cities on Illium. Shepard is immediately greeted by an asari envoy. She cheerfully tells Shepard that she has been instructed to waive all docking and administrative fees for this and all future visits. The order comes from Liara T'Soni, the asari in Shepard's original crew. Liara has set up operations on Illium, reinventing herself as an information broker. Liara would like to see Shepard as soon as possible.

124

PRIMA Official Game Guide | primagames.com

MASS EFFECT 2

The envoy explains that Shepard should be wary of signing anything on Illium. This is a free-trade world with relaxed regulations. Anything is for sale here, including people. Shepard may recoil at the idea of slavery, but the envoy is quite matter-of-fact about the way it is administered on Illium. It is technically voluntary, although the contract is binding. While the envoy can recommend shopping, she cannot point Shepard toward individuals like Samara or Thane. Shepard will just have to find these people the old-fashioned way: with a little detective work.

There are three main sections to Nos Astra: the trading floor, the shipping plaza, and the transportation hub. There is shopping at the transportation hub, so if Shepard feels some credits burning a hole in a pocket, that and the main shopping district are good areas to visit.

Trading Floor

The first place you can explore is the trading floor, which features stores as well as a bar that is a good place to get information. The stairs to Liara's office are also in this district, near the door that leads down to transportation and shipping.

Serrice Technology

The asari merchant running Serrice Technology on the main floor specializes in tech. You can use either charm or intimidation tactics to wrangle a discount out of the asari. Once you have achieved this discount,

check out the kiosk for a full catalog of goods, such as the Hyper Amp module, which increases your current biotic damage by 10 percent. The merchant says she may have special items arriving soon, so be sure to check back later in your adventure to see what else this asari can get her blue fingers on.

Eternity Bar

Upstairs from the trading floor is the Eternity Bar. The bar is buzzing with activity. When you first breeze through the door, you can chat up a slave broker and a quarian to accept a special assignment (Indentured Service). There's a bachelor party near the bar. On the way to the bartender, you can eavesdrop on the conversation for a few laughs.

Introduction

Training

Upgrades and Research

Illium

Walkthrough

Special Assignments

Planetary Database

Appendix

The asari behind the bar is a matriarch. She ended up on Illium because her advice as a wise matriarch was not respected. At this bar, everybody listens to her. You can speak to the matriarch about her 1,000-year life and pick up some interesting stories about the matriarch's family. Her mother and father were involved in the Krogan Rebellions and Rachni Wars. Speaking to the bartender is entirely optional, but it's a good way to get some insight on the asari.

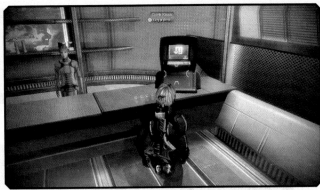

You can buy drinks from the bar kiosk. The liquor is good. The mystery drink, though, does a real number on your ability to walk in a straight line for a few moments.

Shipping Plaza

The shipping area between the two major parts of Nos Astra is small. The only feature here you can really interact with is the shipping counter. The asari at the desk is not helpful at all during your first visit. However, after you visit with Liara and get information on how to pursue Thane, the asari at the shipping desk loosens her lips and is the key to pursuing the potential recruit.

Transportation Hub

The transportation hub is the largest of the three districts. There is a taxi stand directly ahead of you when you first enter the district. You will use the taxi stand later when pursuing recruits. For now, explore the two arms of the hub on each side of the taxi queue. There is a special assignment here, too: Medical Scans. Talk to the colonist near the police station off to the right to get started on that if you like, or just do some shopping.

Baria Frontiers

Baria Frontiers is not a manned shop. It is a kiosk near the police station. The kiosk sells star charts for a number of clusters; the charts clear up blank areas on your galaxy map. These maps are completely optional; every cluster you must visit to defeat the Collectors appears on your galaxy map thanks to intel from the Illusive Man. However, if you want to complete all of the N7 special assignments, you must buy all four of the star charts at this kiosk.

Police Station

Right now, there is nothing to do at the police station. Officer Dara at the desk waves you away with a curt "move along" if you try to speak to her. When you get information from Liara about pursuing Samara, Dara has much more to offer.

Gateway Personal Defense

This weapons shop is on the left side of the transportation hub. There are several customers crowded around the kiosk. Browse the shop inventories for items like the Kinetic Pulsar upgrade, which increases assault rifle damage, or the Lattice Shunting, which extends Shepard's health. There is no shopkeeper to bargain with, so you are forced to pay retail.

Memories of Illium

Memories of Illium is a small terminal. The shopkeeper is nearby, but she is occupied with matters other than commerce right now. She is being courted by a krogan and is unsure of how to respond to his poetry. If you guide the asari through this small special assignment (Blue Rose of Illium), you earn a discount. Memories of Illium sells ship models and fish for the aquarium in Shepard's cabin.

Liara

Liara is your key to getting the two recruits needed from Illium. When you walk up the stairs leading to her office, stop by the receptionist's desk. Nyxeris is a good source of preliminary information about Liara, especially if this is your first time seeing Liara. After talking to Nyxeris, enter Liara's office.

Liara is in the middle of threatening a human when Shepard enters. Liara wraps up the conversation quickly when she realizes Shepard is in the office.

Sit with Liara and talk to her about the two recruits you are after. Liara says that Dara at the police station will be able to help you locate Samara, who has been tracked since arriving in Nos Astra. Liara is also aware of Thane. Her sources say he is on Illium to kill a corporate executive. Shepard can track down Thane by starting at the shipping desk.

Liara is unable to join Shepard's crew. She is currently too embroiled in some intrigue on Illium and has many debts to pay. Shepard can accept a special assignment (The Observer) from Liara at this point.

NOTE

THE JUSTICAR

Justicars are an ancient sect of asari warriors. Of the Asari Republic's forces, the justicars are the most powerful and the most deadly. Tangling with a justicar is a losing proposition, which is why the Illusive Man has recommended Shepard convince the justicar to join the crew to fight the Collectors. Samara, the justicar, is located on Illium. This poses a potential problem for Shepard since justicars are required by oath to bring down anybody breaking asari law, and are permitted to use lethal force. Since just about everybody on Illium is skirting the law in one way or another, the body count could get high if the justicar indeed follows through on her duty.

After speaking to Liara about Samara, report to Officer Dara at the police office for directions on where to find Samara.

Objective 1: Talk to Locals

Pitne For

When you arrive at the spaceport, you catch a snippet of dialog between an asari detective and a volus dealer named Pitne For. The detective tells the volus he cannot leave Illium until the murder of his business partner is solved. Pitne protests and says the asari detective should look at the mercenary gangs that the police are unable to contain on Nos Astra.

Spoils of War
- **Credits: 60,000**
- **Platinum: 2,000**

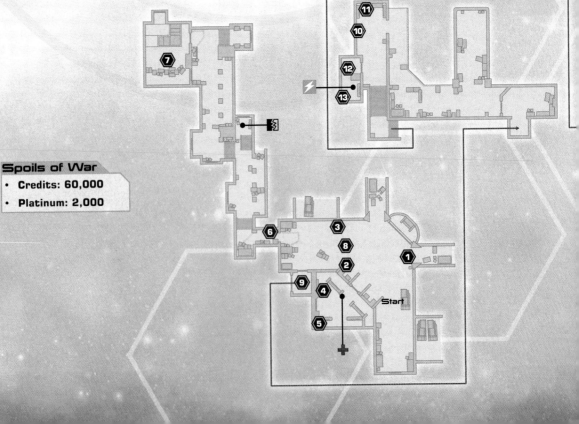

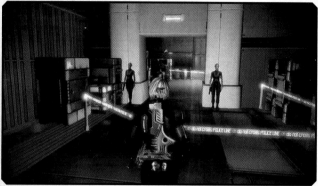

Talk to the locals, since the scene of the murder is sealed off and you cannot enter. Start with Pitne For, the volus. Pitne is quite intent on getting off of Illium before the justicar causes an incident. Pitne says that Samara is in the alley where his business partner was killed. Pitne thinks Eclipse mercs killed him, but there are reasons to suspect the volus himself.

Detective Anaya

After speaking to Pitne, you need to find the detective working on the murder: Anaya. The asari is in the police station. Anaya hopes that you have no intention of causing trouble on Illium. She has enough on her hands with the murder and the presence of the justicar, Samara. Ask her about Samara to gather additional information. Anaya wants the justicar out before the situation gets even more complicated and is willing to grant you access to the crime scene in order to help you recruit her. The sooner Samara is gone, the faster Anaya can quietly wrap up this case. However, you must be mindful of the Eclipse mercenaries, which are indeed in control of most of the port's alleys.

Speak to Anaya, who instructs the asari guards to let Shepard access the crime scene.

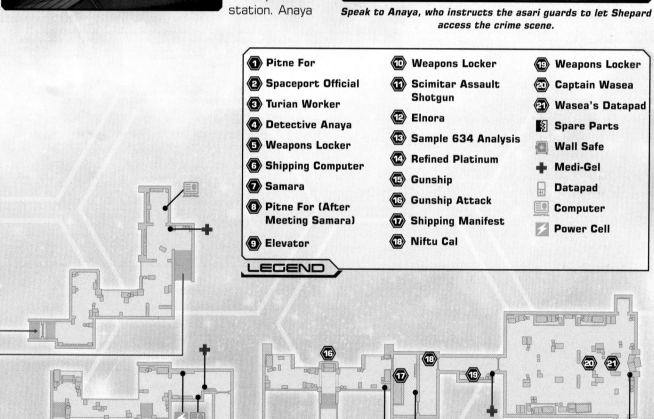

LEGEND

1. Pitne For
2. Spaceport Official
3. Turian Worker
4. Detective Anaya
5. Weapons Locker
6. Shipping Computer
7. Samara
8. Pitne For (After Meeting Samara)
9. Elevator
10. Weapons Locker
11. Scimitar Assault Shotgun
12. Elnora
13. Sample 634 Analysis
14. Refined Platinum
15. Gunship
16. Gunship Attack
17. Shipping Manifest
18. Niftu Cal
19. Weapons Locker
20. Captain Wasea
21. Wasea's Datapad

- Spare Parts
- Wall Safe
- Medi-Gel
- Datapad
- Computer
- Power Cell

Objective 2: Visit Crime Scene

Upon entering the crime scene, turn and download a message on a nearby shipping terminal. This shipping information is related to an optional special assignment (Stolen Goods Found). As soon as you have the shipping data, continue down the alley to push into Eclipse territory.

Salvage the circuit boards near the shipping terminal for 6,000 credits.

First Eclipse Sightings

It does not take long before you uncover the first signs of the Eclipse gang in the back alleys of the spaceport.

There are LOKI mechs, an Eclipse vanguard, and a Sisterhood initiate in the alley ahead. They attack as soon as they detect your presence. The LOKI mechs are the easy targets. It is the Sisterhood initiate that gives you trouble, so after dropping the easy mechs, go after her. After dropping the Eclipse thugs, pass through the door at the end of the alley to get your first glimpse of Samara.

> It's possible to snipe one of these hostiles from a distance, before they notice Shepard's presence. This begins the fight earlier, but also allows you a head start on taking out your enemies.
>
> **TIP**

Enemy Profile: Sisterhood Initiate

- **Classification: Minion**
- **Powers: —**
- **Defenses: —**
- **Weapons: Assault Rifle**

Sisterhood initiates are would-be Eclipse assassins that have yet to make their bones with the merc group. As such, they are eager to notch a kill—and that kill is you. Sisterhood initiates do not have any special armor, so you can use biotic and tech attacks on them right away.

Samara is questioning an Eclipse vanguard that is suddenly without her backup. (Samara dispatched them with ease.) Samara is asking the vanguard where she "sent her." The Eclipse vanguard refuses to give up the information. Samara throws her out of a window and then floats down to continue the interrogation. When the vanguard refuses to spill the name of the ship the justicar wants, Samara breaks her neck.

Samara then turns her attentions to you. You can either assure the justicar that you are a friend or tell her that she shouldn't be killing the wounded, even if they are Eclipse thugs. Samara informs you of the Justicar Code. You ask Samara to help you take down the Collectors. Samara is interested in joining your fight; she respects the Collectors as a worthy foe. But she is currently hunting a fugitive and must finish her mission before she can help.

Detective Anaya joins the conversation. She tries to convince Samara to leave with you, but the Justicar Code prevents it. However, the Code does require Samara to stand down for a single day at the request of a police officer. After that, if Anaya continues to detain Samara, she will just kill her and then resume her investigation. There is a solution: If you can discover the name of the ship the justicar wants, then Samara will not have to kill Anaya and she will join you.

Objective 3: Question Pitne For

When you return to the port after Anaya takes Samara into custody, you must continue the justicar's investigation.

Pitne explains that he has recently smuggled an illegal substance onto Illium that boosts biotic powers but is also toxic. Prolonged exposure to the dust is lethal. Pitne left that part out of his original story, which had the Eclipse mercenaries hunting him. Pitne agrees that if you help keep the mercs off of him, he will help you break into the Eclipse base, where you will find the name of the ship. The volus provides a passcard that lets you access the elevator to the Eclipse base, which is located in a wall adjoining the police station, down the same wing as the crime scene.

The first stop: Pitne For. Approach the volus near the police tape and question him about why the mercs are after him. Don't take Pitne's stalling for an answer. Demand that he work with you to help solve the murder—and hopefully find the name of that ship in the process. The volus relents and agrees to help you.

Objective 4: Attack Eclipse Hideout

Ride the elevator into the Eclipse base of operations. As soon as you walk around the corner at the top of the ride, the Eclipse are all over you. While you're battling the mercenaries , clouds of red dust explode into the air whenever the rectangular canisters get shot; this must be the substance Pitne mentioned. While the effects of the dust do boost your biotic powers, they are toxic. An on-screen meter reflects the current toxicity level in your blood. If that meter fills, you will collapse.

The Eclipse thugs use LOKI mechs as cannon fodder.

Dust Clouds

An Eclipse vanguard greets you as you enter the base. The vanguard is not alone. She tries to retreat into the base to seek cover and return your attacks. Keep on top of her while avoiding the clouds of toxin. Your enemies will use these clouds as cover. They will also blast open canisters to make traveling through the base more difficult, effectively making some routes riskier than others.

Eclipse vanguards and Sisterhood initiates are your main foes in this base. The Eclipse fighters are not military trained, but they are versed in cover tactics. Watch the Eclipse seek cover and then find some yourself. Engage in firefights, taking shots at your foes when they reload or stand to move to a new cover spot.

Introduction

Training

Upgrades and Research

The Justicar

Walkthrough

Special Assignments

Planetary Database

Appendix

Sisterhood initiates can be brought down faster with headshots.

Fight through the enemies until you reach the far side of the shipping bay. There is a small room to explore. Look for the shotgun on the desk. It's a Scimitar assault shotgun—a new weapon. It is a potential upgrade to your current shotgun and a great find (Grunt is likely to approve). You can use the nearby weapons locker to change your weapon loadout and give the new shotgun to any squad member proficient in close-quarters combat.

Come Out

When you pass through the door at the top of the stairs, you spot a pistol on the ground. It's near a barricade—a perfect spot for an Eclipse merc to hide until you get too close. An asari Eclipse, Elnora, stands up. The asari can be reasoned with, but if you use the Renegade interrupt, you can drop the Eclipse thug before she has a chance to try any funny business.

> A quick trigger finger is the mark of a Renegade. However, if you let Elnora go peacefully, you earn some Paragon points. Just be ready to learn that Elnora was lying to you about her involvement with the Eclipse.
>
> **NOTE**

> Take the crate of power cells next to the Eclipse merc.
>
> **TIP**

More Mercs

When you pass through the door at the top of the nearby stairs, more Eclipse mercs attack. They are joined by

LOKI mechs. Sisterhood initiates are trouble, as they use cover quite well, ducking down just as you open fire or unleash a biotic attack. But the Eclipse vanguards, with the barriers, should almost always be your priority targets. Vanguards are tough to take down.

Look for another Eclipse vanguard on the far side of the room, near a long staircase leading up.

Just beyond the Vanguard is a medi-gel station, along with a hackable terminal worth 6,000 credits. After scooping up the treasures, use the stairs.

At the top of the stairs, the Eclipse mercs offer more resistance. In addition to LOKI mechs and Eclipse vanguards, an

Eclipse heavy provides rocket support. Use cover to avoid the incoming rockets, and return fire through the red mist.

> Asari Eclipse vanguards are different from human ones—they carry assault shotguns that make them deadly at close range.
>
> **NOTE**

Continue fighting through the enemies to reach another small waystation with medi-gel and an Eclipse

terminal. The terminal can be hacked for 12,000 credits. That's a lot of cash, so be careful with the hack. Use the stairs to locate another Eclipse vanguard patrol. These vanguards are just an appetizer. Around the corner, you must face down multiple Eclipse thugs and mechs.

There are two Eclipse heavies around the gunship area, so watch out for rockets streaming through the air. Fortunately, there are lots of crates to use as cover around the gunship port. After taking down the heavies, push through the Sisterhood initiates. (Don't be afraid to use melee attacks on them—they go down fast.)

Behind the gunship port, locate a small terminal and a crate of power cells to replenish heavy weapon ammo. Listen to the message. It's Elnora, a new Eclipse merc boasting of earning her stripes by killing Pitne For's partner—at close range (she's actually the Eclipse merc you encountered earlier whose pistol was on the floor). Take the message as evidence, loot the medi-gel station, and then follow the doors.

Several LOKI mechs patrol the next corridor. Blast them from cover, but be sure not to hide behind fragile crates for too long.

The gunship you saw docked earlier is now fully operational and buzzing the area in search of you. Use heavy weapons to lower the gunship's armor and bring it down. There is a crate of power cells on the bay to replenish stocks. Stick behind cover and launch shell after shell at the gunship. If you do not have a heavy weapon, then pepper the gunship with whatever weapon you do have.

The gunship sweeps low and slow overhead. This gives you plenty of time to make accurate shots, but it also means the gunship can return fire with equal accuracy.

As you weaken the gunship, the Eclipse mercs send in more mechs. FENRIS mechs gallop across the bay, hunting you. Watch out for their taser bite attack. If you get zapped by the taser bite while the gunship is zooming overhead, you are a perfect target.

After the battle is won, take the medi-gel from the station on the wall next to the locked door. You must bypass the lock to continue your Eclipse hunt and get to the bottom of this investigation.

Pick up the shipping manifest on the other side of the door. The manifest of toxic drugs is proof that Pitne For is indeed a criminal. This manifest will be useful later and potentially a source of great profit.

> **TIP**
> Hack the Eclipse terminal on the opposite wall from the manifest for 12,000 credits.

Introduction

Training

Upgrades and Research

The Justicar

Walkthrough

Special Assignments

Planetary Database

Appendix

Niftu Cal

Continue down the corridor until you spy the rotund little backside of a volus named Niftu Cal. He's trying to get some munchies out of a vending machine. The little volus is on quite a trip, drugged up to the point where he thinks he's the galaxy's greatest biotic.

Question the funny little fellow about his connections to Pitne For. Niftu says he used to work for Pitne before becoming a biotic superstar. But now he is looking for the asari leader of the Eclipse band on Nos Astra, Wasea. This little volus may have the right idea, but he's too delusional to do anything but get himself killed. You can use a Paragon interrupt to knock Niftu over so he takes a short nap while you go in and take care of Wasea. If you allow Niftu to wander off to his doom, you pick up Renegade points.

> Just before going into Wasea's chamber, check your loadout at the weapons locker and raid the medi-gel station.
>
> **NOTE**

Captain Wasea

Wasea has problems. She's got a justicar on her tail thanks to sapient smuggling, and now Shepard has tracked her down, killing many of her minions in the process. Wasea would like to turn this day around, so she fires up her biotic power and launches into an attack.

> Wasea uses Push to knock over multiple toxic canisters, filling whole sections of the room with the poisonous dust.
>
> **CAUTION**

Wasea is a powerful biotic and uses Barrier to protect herself from attacks. She can replenish Barrier.

Wasea does not enter this battle alone. She is flanked by Eclipse heavies and Sisterhood initiates. These warriors know to use the dust clouds as cover. You need to use your squad members to juggle these extra enemies while you concentrate your attack on Wasea.

Wasea uses biotic attacks like Charge and Push.

Watch out for toxic canisters thrown through the air by Wasea or the Sisterhood initiates.

Once Wasea and her thugs have been taken care of, it's time to loot the room. Hit up the terminal behind Wasea's desk for 6,000 credits. Then, take Wasea's datapad from her desk. The datapad contains the name of the ship Samara is looking for: AML *Demeter*. This is the lead the justicar was looking for. You should head back to the spaceport's police station now and deliver all of this evidence to the asari detective, Anaya.

At the Spaceport

Inside the police station, present Samara with the evidence from Wasea's datapad. With the name of the ship, Samara can continue her pursuit. However, there is a certain matter of the Justicar Code that places Samara in a strange spot. Now that she has agreed to follow your orders, they will take precedence over the Justicar Code. But that doesn't mean Samara won't offer her opinion when she deems it warranted. The justicar agrees to meet you aboard the *Normandy*.

When you leave Wasea's room, you instantly return to the spaceport. Pitne For is waiting for you just outside the police station. Pitne wastes little time asking if you happened to find a shipping manifest. Pitne presents you with a choice. You can either hand over the manifest to Pitne for profit or give it to the detective for the cause of good (this is part of the special assignment Smuggling Evidence). If you don't mind picking up some Renegade points, give the manifest to Pitne. For Paragon points, give it to the detective.

You can then discuss the case of the murdered volus with Anaya. The justicar vouches for the evidence. The case is then closed, as the asari killer was taken out during the mission. This ends the Samara recruitment mission—she is now a member of the *Normandy* crew.

Back at the *Normandy*

Cerberus welcomes the recruitment of Samara. She will be a powerful ally in the fight against the Collectors. Samara takes up residence in the observatory so that she can look out on the stars. It's time to

make the rounds again, making sure to stop by to see Chambers, next to the galaxy map, for a brief update (and a little optional flirting). See what new projects are available in the tech lab. And then be sure to stop by the observatory to speak to Samara. The justicar is not terribly willing to talk about her previous mission but is more amenable to subjects like taking on the Collectors.

If you still have recruitment missions to undertake, you can pursue those now. Remember; you need at least two of the three recruits to have a crew worthy of battling the Collectors. However, there is zero harm in getting all three recruits—it will increase your options for away teams, and improve your chances of beating the game.

NOTE

Introduction

Training

Upgrades and Research

The Justicar

Walkthrough

Special Assignments

Planetary Database

Appendix

THE ASSASSIN

There is a second potential recruit on Illium: Thane Krios. According to the Illusive Man's dossier on Thane, he is an expert marksman and sniper trained from childhood to be an assassin. Thane is also skilled at infiltration, making him particularly deadly. Thane's skills as an assassin are sought across the galaxy, but he has slowed his pace in recent years. Thane's sniping expertise and his quick-kill biotic specialties would make him an excellent asset to the team. But to recruit Thane, Shepard must intercept the drell on his current assignment, before he can slip away again.

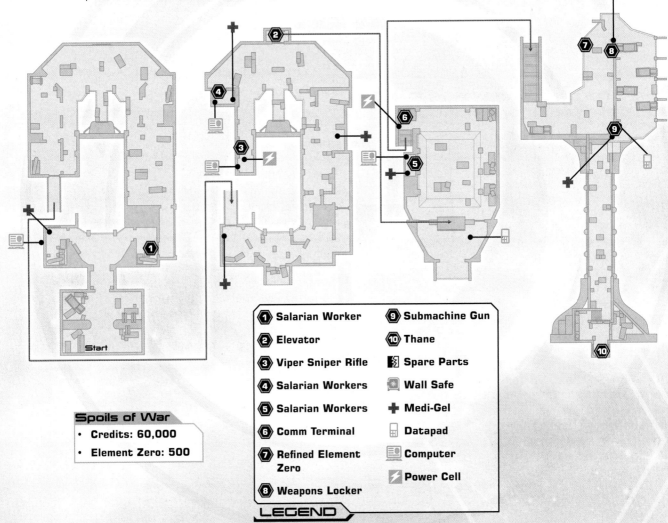

LEGEND

1	Salarian Worker	9	Submachine Gun
2	Elevator	10	Thane
3	Viper Sniper Rifle		Spare Parts
4	Salarian Workers		Wall Safe
5	Salarian Workers		Medi-Gel
6	Comm Terminal		Datapad
7	Refined Element Zero		Computer
8	Weapons Locker		Power Cell

Spoils of War
- **Credits: 60,000**
- **Element Zero: 500**

Objective 1: Find Thane

Shepard cannot just land on Illium and immediately seek Thane. The assassin is not just walking around. Shepard must get a lead on the drell from Nos Astra's resident information broker, Liara.

Talk to Seryna

As soon as you speak to Liara about Thane in her office, you can then report to the shipping department in the midsection of Nos Astra. There, speak to Seryna, the asari at the desk facing toward you. Seryna has no desire to speak of Thane in public, so she motions you to follow her away from the shipping desk and to a quiet corner.

Seryna has a lead on Thane's current whereabouts. While in the employ of Nassana Dantius, a ruthless asari, Seryna was contacted by Thane for information. Nassana recently fired Seryna, who could have given Thane bad intel on Nassana but instead told him exactly where to find Nassana as well as what opposition to expect. Nassana is in business with Eclipse, so the Dantius Towers will be crawling with mercenary thugs and dangerous mechs.

According to Seryna, Thane is working his way toward the penthouse of tower one. That is where he will strike. You must get there as soon as possible before he kills his target and slips away.

Seryna says she can help you get close to the towers. She hopes that you do not stop Thane. If anything, you will serve as a distraction for the Eclipse mercs, allowing Thane to cross from tower two (still under construction) to tower one. When you are ready to leave, accept Seryna's offer of a ride.

The Eclipse thugs in the towers fight alongside hostile mechs. When selecting your squad, consider that you need to take down targets with shields as well as inorganic enemies.

NOTE

As Seryna drives you to the towers, she gives you a plan of action. You must infiltrate tower two and then use a sky bridge to access tower one. She warns you that as you close in on the penthouse, the Eclipse presence will increase.

Glossary

Drell: The drell are a race of reptilian beings that hail from the planet Rakhana. Due to environmental disasters and war on their homeworld, many drell were forced to flee. They currently serve the hanar, the race that assisted with the exodus of the 375,000 drell that escaped Rakhana before complete collapse of the planet.

Hanar: The hanar are a jellyfish-like Citadel race with a reputation for politeness and reserved personalities. The hanar have a face name that they share with colleagues and a soul name that is kept only for close friends and relatives.

Objective 2: Climb the Tower

The second you arrive at the towers, you witness a bloodbath. LOKI mechs are cutting down fleeing salarian workers. It's a good indication of the threat you will find inside the towers, as well as a hint that you may find some salarian survivors inside. All survivors offer assistance in some form, so locate every innocent.

Mech Attack

Two FENRIS mechs crash through the giant window at the bottom of tower two. Cut down the FENRIS mechs as they cross the clearing, aiming for their optics for maximum damage. Get them before they move too close, because when you disable a FENRIS mech with

a headshot, it explodes. The explosion can cause splash damage. After dropping the FENRIS mechs, concentrate on the LOKI mechs pulling up the rear of the welcome party.

Neither FENRIS nor LOKI mechs have any shields, so they can be affected with biotics like Pull or Slam.

TIP

Veer to the right as you approach the base of the tower to find one of the salarians attacked at the onset of the mission. The salarian is a night worker and has no idea why Nassana unleashed the mechs on a murderous spree against her own employees. To get additional information out of the salarian, consider using the Paragon interrupt to give the worker one of your medi-gels. However, even if you keep the medi-gel to yourself, the salarian still tells you that you must take the service elevator up the tower to the bridge.

Introduction

Training

Upgrades and Research

The Assassin

Walkthrough

Special Assignments

Planetary Database

Appendix

A door opens behind the salarian, but before looking for the elevator, cross to the other side of the tower base to find a medi-gel station and a hackable safe with 4,800 credits.

Fight to the Elevator

Just beyond the salarian is a long corridor. As you walk down it, you hear chatter from Eclipse mercs. They are nearby, so reload and get ready for battle. When you enter the room with the Eclipse troops, you are initially greeted by mechs. Clip the mechs with gunfire as they approach, or fling them around the room with biotics. The Eclipse troopers are a little more trouble than the mechs because they actively seek cover.

> **TIP**
> Incendiary ammo works against the mercs, but cryo ammo is more versatile. It affects both merc and machine.

Eclipse troopers and vanguards attack in the next room. If you have a powerful biotic on the squad, use Pull to yank them over the giant hole in the floor.

> **TIP**
> Because the tower is under construction, there is no shortage of crates and pallets of building materials to use as cover. Remember that you can slide into cover when you near it, which is a good way to pop off a shot or two and then hide when your target returns the favor.

Additional mechs and Eclipse thugs are moving into the area. Meet them head on, dismantling the mechs as they march toward you. The Eclipse vanguards and troopers hang back and let the mechs occupy your attention while they shoot at you from afar. Try to quickly drop those mechs with clean headshots, and then turn your attention on the Eclipse fighters. Look out for the Eclipse vanguards—they have barriers, which complicates the use of biotics. Watch their status bars; as soon as you see the barriers go down, hit them with a biotic or rush in and finish the job close up with a stronger weapon, such as a shotgun.

> **TIP**
> Have a tech-oriented squad member like Tali? Use Combat Drone to release a distraction into the room. While the mercs turn their guns on the drone, you can take advantage of their exposed flanks.

The Eclipse thugs were guarding a door that leads up to the next floor.

When you reach the top of the ramp, pick up the two medi-gels and thermal clips while eavesdropping on Nassana ordering her hired Eclipse guns to head off Thane. Nassana knows an assassin is there. Her mercs do not last long against Thane, as single shots silence their voices.

More LOKI mechs and Eclipse mercs storm the area at the top of the ramp. There is a huge opening to the left that is great for tossing enemies over via biotics. Otherwise, move across the room using cover. Dive from crate to crate, taking the room back from the enemy. As the spaces between walls narrow, a close-quarters weapon like the shotgun becomes useful. The Eclipse troopers and LOKI mechs do not have the armor to withstand many shotgun blasts.

In larger rooms like this, close the gap with biotics such as Pull or Charge. If biotics are limited, stick to longer-range weapons like the assault rifle. At least special rounds do not lose any potency over distance.

Move up through the building site, collecting medi-gel as you claim Eclipse territory. Listen for chatter from the mercs or clicks from the mechs to tell how far away the next batch is from your current position. The mechs are always more manageable than the mercs, even if there are more of them. Whereas the LOKI will just march toward you with guns outstretched, a human Eclipse vanguard will hang back and wait until you are occupied before unleashing a biotic attack.

Don't be too eager to pile the squad into the elevator once you clear away the Eclipse opposition. Pass the elevator, moving toward the left. There is a corridor on the far side of the room, next to a door that requires a bypass. Hit the corridor first to hack the "secure" terminal for 4,200 credits and to pick up the Viper sniper rifle. This weapon will serve Garrus quite well. Plus, Thane can also use it once he has been recruited. Unfortunately, even if you do have Garrus with you on this mission, there is no weapons locker nearby to make the potential upgrade. There is, however, one on the roof of the tower.

After claiming the spoils of the battle, bypass the locked door. The small room holds salarian survivors. They are happy to see somebody who isn't with Eclipse holding a gun. Speak to the salarians to find out that Thane locked them in the small room for their own protection. When the salarians leave, you can access a medi-gel crate and a terminal. Extract the 3,000 credits from the terminal—no hack required.

Introduction

Training

Upgrades and Research

The Assassin

Walkthrough

Special Assignments

Planetary Database

Appendix

The Elevator

When you call the elevator, don't just stand in front of the door and wait for the car to drop down. Immediately seek cover. (Try to steer clear of any explosive containers on the floor, though.) Eclipse mercs pour out of the elevator as soon as it reaches your floor.

The elevator deposits a krogan bounty hunter and two Eclipse engineers on your floor. Look out for combat drones from the engineers. They are needling menaces. But the real target is the krogan. Prioritize the bounty hunter, but do not get headstrong about standing your ground. The krogan has shields and barriers, so it can withstand a lot of hits. It uses that resilience to get close enough to use the krogan rush attack. Fall back to a safe distance and unload gun attacks on the bounty hunter. Only after its shields are down can you hope to use any biotics to finish the job.

Top Floor

Ride the elevator to the bridge level of tower two. When you step out, you discover an Eclipse mercenary communicating with other teams. The merc is too engrossed in his conversation to notice you until it's too late. You have him surrounded. Interrogate the mercenary about Thane's position, backing him up to the large window. You can use a Renegade interrupt to kill the merc by pushing him out of the window, but the noise will just bring nearby Eclipse thugs into the room to investigate. You'll have another fight on your hands.

You can avoid the fight by not taking the Renegade interrupt and just threatening the mercenary with tough questions. The mercenary tells you that you must cross the bridge to find Nassana (and Thane). If you choose to let the merc go at this point, you earn Paragon points. The merc does not alert his comrades as he leaves.

Pick up the datapad next to the elevator to unlock the Salarian Family Data special assignment.

Objective 3: Find the Bridge Mercenaries

The hall next to the elevator leads to a giant chamber. You can hear more radio chatter between Nassana and the Eclipse troops as you enter. Stay quiet to get several paces into the room and scope out the scene. There are Eclipse mercs in the back, dormant mechs to the left and right. You can get the drop on either one, but the mechs are closer and easier to dispatch with early shots.

> **TIP**
> Stay clear of the explosive crates in the room, but always monitor the proximity of the enemy to them. Use these crates as bombs to deliver devastating damage.

The Eclipse vanguard in the room is your toughest rival. Get rid of her first and then mop up the troopers and remaining mechs.

There is a communications console at the rear of the room next to a crate of power cells. Nassana barks orders into the comm, demanding a report. Give her one.

There is a locked door on the main floor of this room. Bypass the security measures to free more trapped salarians. You are greeted with a pistol. The salarian holding it is scared. A Renegade interrupt lets you drop the salarian just for even pointing a gun at you, but if you wait it out, the salarian will lower his weapon. The salarians inside the room explain that the merc threatening the salarians was killed before their very eyes. It's more evidence of Thane. After letting the salarians go, you can claim a medi-gel and hack the PDA on the dead merc for 6,000 credits.

Follow the ramp near the communications console to the tower exterior—and another battle.

The Exterior

The bridge is indeed heavily guarded. Eclipse mercenaries (including vanguards) and LOKI mechs patrol the bridge. They attack immediately. The bridge offers a benefit to biotics with Pull or Charge. You can knock enemies off the bridge. (If you use Charge, just line up the targets so their backs are to the empty space.) By now, the mechs are no problem. The vanguards, though, are especially aggressive. Take cover from their Warp attacks and chisel their barriers until they are exposed. Since they are organics, incendiary ammo will do additional damage.

Introduction

Training

Upgrades and Research

The Assassin

Walkthrough

Special Assignments

Planetary Database

Appendix

If you drop a vanguard's barrier, go for the kill. Otherwise, you risk them recharging the barrier.

CAUTION

There is a crate of 500 units of element zero on the edge of the bridge. Don't go for it until the battle is over, though.

Before stepping to the outer edge of tower two, use the weapons locker to make any gear changes, such as using the sniper rifle recovered earlier. You can pick up a medi-gel from the box near the weapons locker, too. After your squad is all set, it's time to move across the bridge and close in on Nassana.

An entire Eclipse patrol waits for you. The troopers, commandos, and vanguards open fire upon your arrival. Use

cover right away to avoid the incoming volley, and train your fire on the explosives crate to the right. Light it up to kill two foes and better the odds. Because the troopers have no extra protection and the commandos only have armor, you can use some biotics on them. The vanguards have much higher resistance, so you must pick them apart as you move across the exterior.

Enemy Profile: Eclipse Commando

- **Classification: Sub-Boss**
- **Powers: Warp**
- **Defenses: Armor, Barrier**
- **Weapons: Combat Shotgun**

Eclipse commandos are the most elite of the Eclipse thugs, able to flank and use cover. Their combat shotguns are deadly at close range, but keeping your distance is not without danger. Commandos can use Warp to rock you back. Dismantle the commando's barrier and armor as fast as you can so you can counter with biotic and tech attacks of your own. A submachine gun is great for chipping away both of the commando's defenses.

Just before the bridge, loot the corpse of a fallen merc. Take the medi-gel and scan the submachine gun for a tech upgrade: Microfield Pulsar. Submachine guns now do extra damage. Finally, hack the PDA to claim 12,000 credits.

The more you upgrade the submachine gun, the better the weapon is for taking apart shields and barriers, thanks to its high rate of fire.

TIP

Use the wind whipping across the bridge to your benefit. Lift enemies with Pull and let them blow away into the night.

TIP

The vanguards on the bridge are flanked by LOKI mechs and Eclipse troopers. Biotics can launch the

mechs and troopers off the bridge with Pull, Charge, or Warp. If you lack these biotics, you must deal with the Eclipse more conventionally. Move across the bridge, crate to crate, for cover. Take the bridge by inches, pushing the enemy back until you reach the far side of the bridge.

Introduction

Training

Upgrades and Research

The Assassin

Walkthrough

Special Assignments

Planetary Database

Appendix

When you reach the far side, two rocket drones on the top floor open fire. You must stick to cover to avoid rocket attacks. Snipers or soldiers can bring down the drones, but if you get below them, the drones can no longer target you. Of course, more Eclipse thugs rush out to prevent you from moving out of the drones' field of fire. Keep in cover as you advance on the mercs.

> **CAUTION**
>
> The rocket drones have shields, so you cannot just lift them out of their perches.

An Eclipse commando blocks the door into tower one. Commandos love close-range combat—not only can they use a shotgun more effectively, but they can pepper you with Warp strikes without much delay. Use cover to guard against these attacks, and lay into the commando with whatever you have. You do not need your weapons inside tower one, so if you have any heavy weapon ammo left, use it on the commando to finish the fight.

Nassana

Inside the tower one penthouse, Nassana awaits her fate. She assumes that Shepard is the assassin that has been stalking her. Shepard keeps Nassana talking, unwittingly allowing time for Thane to infiltrate the room. Before Nassana truly realizes that Shepard is not there to kill her, it's too late. Thane has slipped behind her and taken out the last of her Eclipse guards.

Thane wastes little time fulfilling his contract. The drell assassin pulls Nassana close and buries a bullet in her gut. As she slumps over her console, Thane crosses her arms over her chest and says a prayer. Now that Nassana is dead, Shepard can ask the assassin to join the team and pursue the Collectors. Thane agrees to the mission and reports for duty on the *Normandy*.

Back on the *Normandy*

Following the recruitment of Thane, there is some consternation over having a mercenary join the mission. Shepard is willing to give Thane the benefit of the doubt because he is not asking for any sort of payment. There is a deeper reason he is offering his services. Go to the life support chamber on deck 3 so Shepard can discuss Thane's reasons for joining the crew. Much of it has to do with his own condition; he is dying from Kepral's Syndrome but expects to live as long as the mission needs. It will be a good final assignment for him. Thane seems troubled by what he has done with his life, and saving humanity from the Collectors will help the drell put his soul at rest.

> **NOTE**
>
> Once Thane joins the crew, a female Shepard can pursue a romantic relationship with him.

COLLECTOR SHIP

As soon as Shepard finishes recruiting the four new squad members, the Illusive Man has news for the commander: he has located a disabled Collector ship. The Collector ship was damaged in a battle with a turian cruiser. The turians were completely wiped out. The Illusive Man needs Shepard to race to the vessel and look for any hard data on a potential means for reaching the Collector homeworld. All systems on the Collector ship seem to be offline, but that doesn't necessarily mean there will not be any resistance. Shepard needs to get in and out before the ship is reactivated. Hopefully, EDI can use the data Shepard finds to discover a way to take the fight to the Collectors.

Spoils of War
- Credits: **75,000**
- Element Zero: **500**

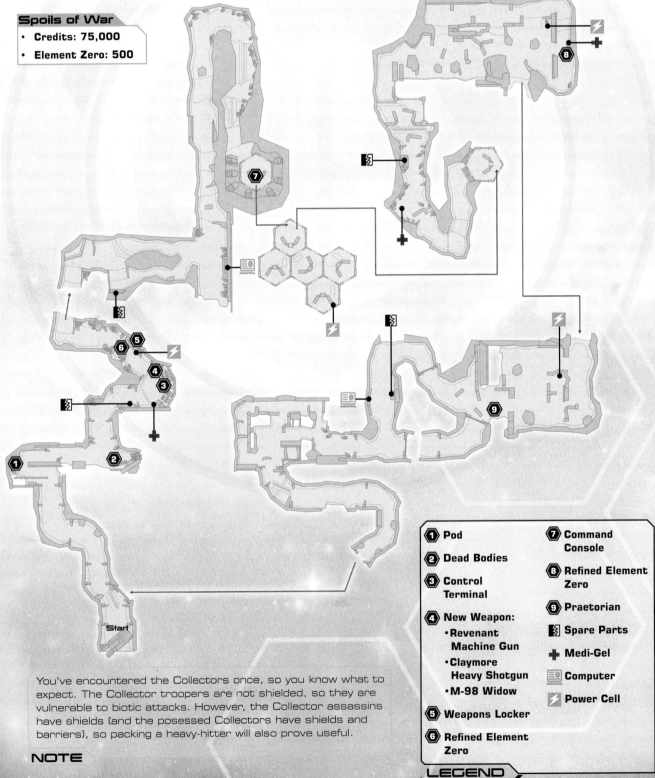

NOTE

You've encountered the Collectors once, so you know what to expect. The Collector troopers are not shielded, so they are vulnerable to biotic attacks. However, the Collector assassins have shields (and the posessed Collectors have shields and barriers), so packing a heavy-hitter will also prove useful.

LEGEND

1. Pod
2. Dead Bodies
3. Control Terminal
4. New Weapon:
   - Revenant Machine Gun
   - Claymore Heavy Shotgun
   - M-98 Widow
5. Weapons Locker
6. Refined Element Zero
7. Command Console
8. Refined Element Zero
9. Praetorian

⚡ Spare Parts
✚ Medi-Gel
🖥 Computer
⚡ Power Cell

First Arrival

Joker pulls the *Normandy* alongside the Collector ship. Shepard and the squad take a small shuttle over to the vessel and dock. The inside of the Collector ship looks like a giant insect hive. Right now, the scene is quiet. But that won't last long, so Shepard and the squad need to be ready for anything.

Objective 1: Investigate Collector Ship

Within seconds of docking, EDI reports that it has located an uplink within the Collector ship. Shepard needs to reach that uplink and establish a connection to the AI.

Looking Around

After leaving the shuttle, follow the corridor into the depths of the Collector ship. As you walk, EDI reports that she has scanned the ship and determined that this is the same vessel that destroyed the original *Normandy* and almost killed you two years ago. As you walk, you find an empty pod.

A few steps beyond, you discover the answer: a stack of bodies. Inspect the bodies to discover that the Collectors are somehow using humans for an experiment. These dead bodies are apparently from a batch of test subjects that did not fit the needed profile.

> Want a few easy Paragon points? Lament that death might be a better fate than a Collector experiment.
>
> **TIP**

Farther down the corridor, you locate another series of pods. These are hooked up to machines. After picking up the medi-gel from the nearby crate, investigate the pods. The control terminal next to one of the pods allows you to download an immediate upgrade. Depending on your class, you have different options. For example, a vanguard may have the option to download the ability to use assault rifles or sniper rifles.

> Consider this selection carefully. You may even want to save before making the choice in case you determine that your chosen upgrade does not necessarily fit your plan of action. If you have not found or researched many assault rifle damage upgrades, taking on the assault rifle skill might not help much. Of course, you can always change that after acquiring the use of the assault rifle.
>
> **NOTE**

Just beyond the pods is heavy weapon ammo, a weapons locker for changing your loadout, and a crate of 250 units of element zero.

Introduction

Training

Upgrades and Research

Collector Ship

Walkthrough

Special Assignments

Planetary Database

Appendix

Continue down the path through the Collector ship. When the ceiling rises, look up. There are hundreds of pods built into tunnels that spider into the depths of the ship. A little farther down the route, you locate some salvageable Collector technology. Scan it with the omni-tool to bank 15,000 credits.

Keep moving through the ship. Just as the corridor takes a sharp turn to the left and begins to climb, there is a scannable terminal that gives up a damage protection upgrade: Ablative VI.

The passage leads to the heart of the Collector ship. The hollow is lined with thousands upon thousands of pods. There are enough pods in here for the Collectors to harvest every human in the Terminus Systems. If multiple vessels like this move toward Citadel space, it would be possible for the Collectors to steal away every human being on Earth.

The path through the hollow ends at a hexagonal platform. There is a green panel at the center of the platform: That's the uplink. Activate the panel to establish a link with EDI. EDI immediately starts downloading data from the Collectors. However, activating the panel also raises the platform into the hollow, placing you and the squad in plain sight. Within seconds, company arrives.

Collector Assault

There are several walls on the platform. Use one for cover and make sure your weapons are fully loaded.

More hexagonal platforms are moving fast through the hollow, with multiple Collectors on board. When those platforms dock with yours, you will be boarded. Be ready to repel.

The closest platform deposits Collector drones and a Collector guardian right on your doorstep.

The second platform carries a scion. The scion is a brute, but it doesn't move very fast. Concentrate on the Collectors right in front of you. Take down the drones as soon as possible because Harbinger is about to possess one of the Collectors on the platform. If you destroy the other two Collectors, you limit Harbinger's options for possessing another Collector when you take this one down.

> Do not leave Collectors with slivers of health. Put them completely down. Otherwise, you risk Harbinger possessing them, which not only powers up their weapons but effectively translates that little bit of health into full shields and armor.

CAUTION

Unless you went for the scion earlier, concentrate your fire on the monster when no more platforms move down the hollow. Take out the scion to end this battle in the heart of the Collector ship.

It doesn't take long for reinforcements to arrive after you take apart the Collectors on the first platform. Another batch of drones moves into place, docking with your platform. You have a few moments to tear apart the drones before Harbinger possesses one of them. As before, try to limit Harbinger's ability to possess other Collectors by taking them down. The platforms are floating above the hollow, so you can also use Pull or Charge to knock the Collectors off the platforms and out of the battle.

> In between taking down the incoming Collectors, turn some of your fire on the scion.
>
> **TIP**

> Listen for a high-pitched whine. That is the sound of another platform moving into position. When you hear it, expect reinforcements within seconds.
>
> **NOTE**

Expect at least one possessed Collector per platform. Unless you board the new platform right away, the possessed Collector will not move in close. While there is some distance between you and the possessed Collector, clean out the other Collectors. Direct your squad to target the Collectors so they do not train their fire only on the possessed Collector. Collector guardians are part of the reinforcements and will put up hive shields to block your shots, but you can angle biotic attacks around the shields if you get far enough to the side.

> Out of heavy weapon ammo? There is a crate of power cells on the platform with the scion.
>
> **TIP**

When the battle subsides, return to the panel that linked the Collector ship to EDI. This moves the platform through the remainder of the hollow and deposits it back on the ground. You can now continue pressing through the ship's corridors, taking out Collectors as you attempt to find a way back to the shuttle.

Collector Packs

As you move off the platform, EDI offers directions. Follow her directions into a room with medi-gel. There is a ramp leading away from the medi-gel to a chamber with more Collectors. On the way, scan the Collector technology on the left side of the corridor for 7,500 credits.

When you reach the bottom of the ramp, Collector drones move into position. One of these drones will soon become a possessed Collector—there is no way to kill them all fast enough to avoid it. So, instead of just opening fire on any target, sweep through the Collectors and put them down one at a time. Since the drones have no shields or armor, use biotics as well as gunfire to wound them.

Introduction

Training

Upgrades and Research

Collector Ship

Walkthrough

Special Assignments

Planetary Database

Appendix

Stick behind cover when the possessed Collector appears. This foe's heavy weapon is devastating, so duck incoming rounds and return fire only when it is safe to stick your head back up.

The path leads to another clearing. The buzzing of Collector wings fills the air within moments of your arrival. If you are fast, you can shoot the Collector drones and Collector guardians before they land. Select one of them and finish it off before moving on to your next target.

The guardians set up hive shields as soon as they land.

NOTE

You can take on the Collectors in this room directly, but there is a route to the left that offers sniping points as well as the means to get behind the Collectors in the room. Move up the ramp to the left. There may be Collectors moving along the route, but if there is a possessed Collector on the main floor, you will not encounter one on this upper route. The high ground is advantageous. Not only can you see incoming Collectors, but also you can

get the drop on the Collectors on the main floor with biotic attacks. There is no way for them to avoid the effects of attacks like Pull or Slam unless the Collector seeks cover behind a pillar.

There are power cells at the bottom of the ramp on the far side of the upper route. Medi-gel and 250 units of element zero are nearby.

TIP

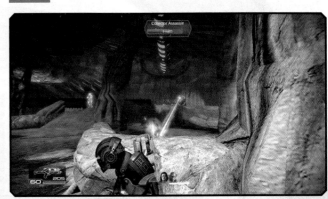

Watch out for the Collector assassin in the room, too. The possessed Collector is your toughest target, but the assassin's particle beam will rip through your shields within seconds.

After finishing off the Collectors in this area, drop down the ledge to keep moving back toward the shuttle.

Praetorian

EDI comes over the comm. The AI has located a door and will force it open as long as it can to give you a shortcut back toward the shuttle. However, the door is on the far side of a chamber that hosts a praetorian. The monster drifts down from the ceiling as you approach. Lock and load because the praetorian will do everything in its power to drain your ammo stocks and keep you from escaping the ship.

The praetorian behaves exactly like the one you took down at Horizon. The praetorian hovers in the air, tracking you with its glowing eyes. Its main weapons are twin particle beams that tear through shielding and armor. You must use cover to avoid getting stripped of your protection. When you see those eyes light up, duck down because the beams are about to rip through the air.

Stay back from the praetorian. If it gets too close it will slam into the ground and unleash its Death Choir attack. This attack regenerates its shields, which extends the battle. It is practically unavoidable because the praetorian will move toward you, but keep your distance whenever possible to minimize the number of times the monster refreshes its shields.

While the praetorian keeps your eyes on the ceiling, husks rush the room. Push them back; otherwise they will surround you.

Return to high ground to finish off the praetorian. From above, you can lay into the beast while your squad on the ground concentrates their fire on incoming Collectors or any remaining husks. When the praetorian's shields are down, unload everything you have into it to destroy the armor and finish it off.

Collector drones also infiltrate the room. Use biotics to attack them, saving any heavy weapon ammo for the praetorian.

After destroying the praetorian, move through the door EDI opened and follow the tube down another corridor. Scan the Collector technology to pocket 7,500 credits. Scan the terminal directly across from the technology (under the tube) to discover a Multicore Amplifier, which increases tech damage.

Introduction

Training

Upgrades and Research

Collector Ship

Walkthrough

Special Assignments

Planetary Database

Appendix

Final Attack

Pass through the door on the far end of the corridor. This leads to another room full of Collectors, but this is the last batch of them you must fight before exiting the Collector ship. There are several pods just inside the door. Use one for cover when the Collectors arrive. Expect at least one Collector drone and one Collector assassin right away. Whichever one of the pair you do not take down is likely to turn into a possessed Collector. Because the drone is the weakest, destroy it first.

Enemy Profile: Abomination

- **Classification: Minion**
- **Powers: Death Blast**
- **Defenses: —**
- **Weapons: —**

Abominations are unstable husks that rush you like regular husks, but when they get in close, they initiate a death blast explosive attack. Abominations also explode when their health is drained; this can be used like a bomb to destroy other enemies. (It can also injure you and your teammates.)

Collector guardians hide behind hive shields, but you can either blast through them or launch biotic attacks around them.

Move along the top of the room to work over the remainder of the Collectors in the area. From up here, you can launch attacks on the posessed Collector in the room as well as press through the rest of the Collector drones. Before you can leave the room, though, you must defeat a scion stationed by the exit. Keep back to avoid its blasts.

Before you can leave the Collector ship, you must survive one last wave of husks. Just a couple husks round the corner at the end of the corridor at first, but soon the floodgates open. More than a dozen husks rush down the corridor. Pick off the first few but fall back as the horde grows. If you have biotics at your disposal, use them on the husks because they do not have any shields. (Charge is perfect for closing the gap between you and the husks.)

Board the shuttle just beyond the husks. The shuttle immediately takes off just as the Collector ship comes back online. The shuttle docks just in time for Joker to take evasive maneuvers and avoid the Collector ship's incoming attack. Joker engages the FTL drive and rockets away from the Collector ship. When you are at a safe distance, it's time to check in with the Illusive Man. He'd better have some answers.

The Illusive Man

Shepard confronts the Illusive Man in the communications room. Shepard is furious—the Illusive Man marched the crew right into a trap just to gather data on the Collectors. Although Shepard is angry, there is no arguing that the mission was a huge success. The data reveals that the Collectors and Reapers are using a system of IFFs (Identify Friend or Foe) to pass through special relays, such as the Omega 4 relay. Shepard must acquire an IFF.

Following the meeting with the Illusive Man, Shepard explains Cerberus's actions to the crew. Not everybody is in agreement with being treated like bait. But there is a consensus that the Collector ship mission was a success. During the meeting, EDI reveals that by following the course of Collector ships through the relays, it has discovered the location of the Collector homeworld: the center of the galaxy. A swirling vortex of exploding suns and black holes, the center of the galaxy cannot support a life-sustaining planet.

Fortunately, Cerberus scientists have located a derelict Reaper ship. The Illusive Man believes that Shepard can extract that Reaper ship's IFF and use it to pass through the Omega 4 relay. However, the team is just not ready to go after it. The Illusive Man recommends that Shepard finish off any outstanding recruitment missions as well as solidify the loyalty and determination of the crew. Passing through the Omega 4 relay threatens to be a one-way trip. The crew needs to be at peace with such a daunting prospect.

Considering what the Reapers are capable of— building the Citadel and the mass relays—it is not impossible

to suggest that the Reapers have created a safe zone inside the center of the galaxy for the Collectors. If such a safe zone exists, the Normandy should be able to slide into it and attack the Collector homeworld.

Introduction

Training

Upgrades and Research

Collector Ship

Walkthrough

Special Assignments

Planetary Database

Appendix

LOYALTY

Passing through the Omega 4 relay and taking the fight to the Collectors is considered a suicide mission, even by the Illusive Man. And so the Illusive Man advises helping the crew dedicate themselves to this one-way ticket by seeking closure in their lives. Each team member has some unfinished business in the galaxy that they would like to attend to before rushing headlong at the Collectors. Tying up a loose thread will command absolute loyalty. Loyalty results in unlocking a brand-new power for the team member.

At first, only one of the loyalty missions is open: Jacob's. However, as you complete these missions, more become available. For example, after Jacob's loyalty mission is complete, Miranda's loyalty mission is opened. Here is the order in which the loyalty missions are unlocked:

1. Jacob
2. Miranda
3. Jack
4. Mordin
5. Grunt
6. Garrus
7. Samara
8. Tali
9. Thane
10. Legion

NOTE

This list details the order in which the loyalty missions will appear if all characters are recruited. If you don't recruit Samara until later in the game, for instance, Tali's loyalty mission will appear before the justicar's.

To initiate a loyalty mission, you must speak to the team member aboard the *Normandy* first. Yeoman Kelly Chambers will always tell you when one of the team members wishes to speak to you, but you can also consult the available list of missions to see if a new one is open. Go to that team member's station on the *Normandy* and listen to their story. You do not have to complete the mission just because you spoke to them. You can set aside the mission and move on to other activities.

When you go on one of these missions (with the exception of Samara's loyalty mission), you are required to take the squad member that requests the assistance. When going on Jacob's loyalty mission, for example, you can only select one other squad member because Jacob is automatically on the squad. So, consider the specialties of the required squad member when selecting the second. If you are going on Miranda's loyalty mission, you may wish to balance her biotics with a strong weapons expert like Garrus or Grunt. You can trigger Samara's loyalty mission on Omega even if she isn't in your squad; she'll show up at the right times!

NOTE

These missions are not entirely optional, although not all of them need to be completed for the next step in the mission to become available. Five non-critical missions must be completed for the next step to open up: Collector Ship. The five missions can be loyalty missions or special assignments brought to your attention via your private terminal.

CAUTION

Spoiler alert: Completing a team member's loyalty mission increases the chances that they will not meet an *unfortunate* end during the final mission. You can also help your team's chances by upgrading the *Normandy*. Start looking into this now, searching the galaxy for the necessary minerals to fuel the research projects that upgrade the ship's shields, armor, and guns.

JACOB: THE GIFT OF GREATNESS

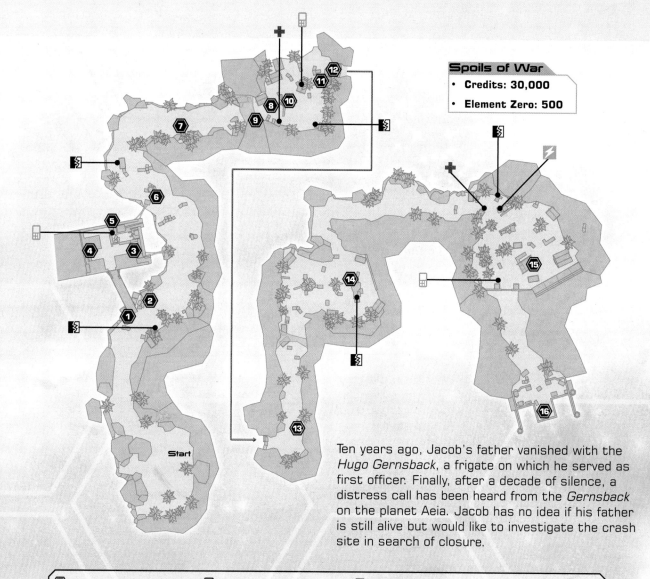

Spoils of War
- Credits: 30,000
- Element Zero: 500

Start

Ten years ago, Jacob's father vanished with the *Hugo Gernsback*, a frigate on which he served as first officer. Finally, after a decade of silence, a distress call has been heard from the *Gernsback* on the planet Aeia. Jacob has no idea if his father is still alive but would like to investigate the crash site in search of closure.

1 Partial Officer's Log		**6** Survivor encounter		**11** Doctor		**16** Ronald Taylor
2 Activated Beacon VI		**7** Stripped Mech		**12** Inactive Mech		Spare Parts
3 Doctor's Log		**8** Survivors		**13** Dead Bodies		Medi-Gel
4 Partial Crew Log		**9** Food Stores		**14** Heavy Pistol		Datapad
5 Partial Crew Log		**10** Statue		**15** Refined Element Zero		Power Cell

LEGEND

Objective 1: Travel to Aeia

After speaking to Jacob, you must travel to the planet 2175 Aeia. Scan the planet surface in search of the distress beacon. When you discover the beacon, launch a probe to the surface. Once the location of the crash site has been confirmed, you can then land the shuttle on the surface and begin the mission.

Before landing, though, you should mine the planet. Aeia is a garden world, so you will find valuable element zero deposits as well as other minerals on the surface. These minerals are useful for research projects back at Mordin's lab on the *Normandy*.

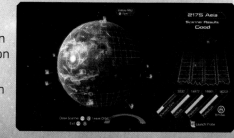

Vertical tab labels (right margin): Introduction · Training · Upgrades and Research · Walkthrough · Jacob: The Gift of Greatness · Special Assignments · Planetary Database · Appendix

Crash Site

Upon landing, start walking toward the wreckage of the *Gernsback*. It's impossible to miss. The trail along the beach is lined with parts from the frigate. It's been stripped and salvaged. There are some spare parts on the right side of the trail toward the crash site, near the actual distress beacon. Salvage the spare parts for credits.

You should also listen to the partial log directly across from the spare parts. It's an upsetting message. It sounds as if something horrible was done to the ship's crew during the time between the crash and the activation of the beacon. You'd better check out the distress beacon a little farther up the beach to start piecing together what happened here.

The beacon message says the distress call was purposefully paused by acting captain Ronald Taylor, Jacob's father. Question the beacon about the status of the crew. More disturbing circumstances of the crash and subsequent actions of the crew are revealed when the beacon relays information about the food given to the crew and the resulting neural decay. It seems that digesting local flora causes memory degradation as well as disrupted functionality.

Objective 2: Find Ronald Taylor

Survivor Sighting

As you walk along the wreckage trail, one of the survivors pops out from behind some crates. She is happy to finally see a rescue team, but she warns that the hunters will not allow you to assist. She seems to be suffering from the effects of neural decay.

As she speaks to you about the leader's machines and the splitting of the tribe between those that wish to follow and those that question the leader's authority, another survivor rises from behind some more crates. He is one of the hunters. He aims at the woman speaking to you. You have a Paragon interrupt opportunity here to get her out of the way before the man fires a lethal shot.

The feral hunters take cover behind the crates and engage you. You should duck behind the crates, too, and return fire when the hunters rise up and start to fire. The hunters have no armor. You can pick them off easily with well-placed headshots or biotic attacks. Throw or Slam them to clear the beach and continue your investigation.

Scan the spare parts near the hunters' position for credits. Pick up dropped clips to keep your weapons firing, too.

NOTE

There is a stripped mech on the beach. Scan it to learn more about the aggression of the hunters.

Camp

Continue moving along the beach trail to locate the survivor base camp. The survivors at this camp are not hostile to you. More intriguing, though, is that the camp is occupied only by women. Approach the camp to speak to some of the survivors and continue piecing together the mystery of the *Gernsback* wreck. Several of the women recoil from Jacob, seeing his father in his face. They claim his father, the leader, forced them to eat the food that caused decay.

Inspect the campsite for spare parts and medi-gel. Check out the food stores to see the rot that is decaying the crew members' minds.

Scan the PDA in camp to pick up some credits.

TIP

When you walk to the far side of camp, the women dive for the ground. LOKI mechs are entering the camp. Take

cover and hammer the mechs, aiming for the heads to take them down as fast as you can. Since the LOKI have no armor, you can also freely use biotics on them. The LOKI are not much of a threat since you have eliminated so many of them already.

Just beyond the mechs is a doctor. She cowers from you at first. But when she sees that despite Jacob having

his father's face he fights the machines, she opens up. The doctor hands Jacob a datapad. The datapad reveals that the crew thought the deployment of the beacon was taking too long. Jacob's father split the crew from the officers, taking refuge in the ship and hoarding the unspoiled food for himself and his trusted circle. The mechs were used to keep the crew in line and force them to eat the ruined food.

It gets worse. Jacob looks at the casualty list and sees that within a year all of the male crew were either killed

or banished. The women were then assigned to the male officers. Once the beacon was repaired, the male officers were then killed, and all of the women were reassigned to Jacob's father. Jacob is now determined more than ever to find his father and press him for an explanation of how things went so sideways after the crash of the *Gernsback*.

Objective 3: Confront Taylor

Mech Attack

After reading the datapad, hack the wrecked mech against the crates. This initiates a self-destruct

mechanism. Fall back so you are not injured in the explosion. The blast clears the crates from the trail, opening a path farther down the beach. As you walk, Jacob's father makes an announcement over the PA system in camp. He claims he has been waiting for your arrival, held captive by a crew that went insane.

When you spy the blue tower in the distance, reload your weapons. More LOKI mechs are marching toward you, ready for a firefight. Give it to them. Duck into cover and pop the mechs in their heads to short them out right away. Direct Jacob to use his biotic attacks, such as Pull, on the mechs. While the mechs fly through the air, you can shoot them down.

Keep advancing through the second camp. Mech reinforcements fill the place of the dropped LOKI. Duck behind the crates to pick off the next batch of mechs. Keep using Jacob's biotics to lift the mechs off their feet. If your second squad member has any biotics, deploy those too. Keep aiming for the mechs' heads to drop them right away. Move up through the camp, zipping from crate to crate, and clear out the LOKI.

Scan the heavy pistol against the crates on the far side of camp to pick up the Titan Pulsar upgrade, which gives you extra damage when using heavy pistols.

The spare parts near the heavy pistol upgrade are worth credits.

NOTE

Jacob's biotics are extremely useful against the mechs, since they have no shields or barriers. If he is not using Pull as much as you would like on his own, give him orders to do so via the Power Wheel.

Continue along the beach until you spot another mech patrol under a canopy. Use the crates in the middle of the sand as cover and launch attacks on the mechs.

Close in on the mechs under the canopy. Jacob's father sends out another distress call, telling you that you must fight the mechs and guards in order to rescue him. It only infuriates Jacob. As you wreck the mechs, pick up the power cells and medi-gel under the canopy. There are spare parts on the left side of the path to bank, too.

Ronald's "Guards"

Jacob's father is guarded by brainwashed survivors and a YMIR mech. The human guards do not have any shielding, but they are armed well. They duck behind some cover in the center of the area while the YMIR stakes the perimeter. Fortunately, you have plenty of cover options, too. Dive behind crates and ship wreckage to avoid the YMIR's rockets and minigun. During lulls in the YMIR's assault, return fire with a heavy weapon.

The YMIR is a more immediate threat than the human guards. Direct your squad to bring it down first.

The guards do have shields, so until you break those, Jacob cannot use most of his biotics. Circle the guards and deplete their shields with gunfire. Since these are organic targets, incendiary ammo is quite useful for doing extended damage with each landed shot.

After clearing out the YMIR and guards, scavenge the site for a crate of element zero and a PDA loaded with credits.

Open the door behind the guardpost to locate Jacob's father. He stands alone at the beach. He is no threat, so you can lower your weapons.

Ronald Taylor

You turn to the beach, giving Jacob the opportunity to confront his father without your interference.

Ronald claims that he has been waiting for a rescue team like yours to arrive, but Jacob is having none of it. He questions his father about the dead crew and Ronald feigns helplessness. At first Ronald does not recognize Jacob, but when Shepard points out that Jacob is Ronald's son, Ronald takes back some of his lies. He tries to convince you that what he did was actually beneficial for the crew.

Jacob's father seems to understand that some of what happened was wrong, which is why he delayed deploying the beacon. He knew that what happened with the food stocks and assigning the women to officers would look bad. You can decide how to end this encounter, whether with a harder edge or a softer touch. Either way, Jacob has the answers he needed about his father. They just weren't the ones he wanted.

Back on the *Normandy*, Jacob speaks with the Illusive Man about the situation. Jacob wants to know how and why this beacon information got to him. Was the Illusive Man just toying with Jacob, waiting until now to let slip the situation with the *Gernsback*? It turns out that the person responsible for forwarding the beacon to Jacob was actually Miranda. She recalled that Jacob always wanted closure with his father, and so she decided now was the right time to alert Jacob to the *Gernsback* wreck. Regardless of whether Miranda did this to help or hurt him, Jacob is just relieved to have it behind him. He is now 100 percent loyal to the mission, and his Barrier power is unlocked.

Introduction

Training

Upgrades and Research

Walkthrough

Jacob: The Gift of Greatness

Special Assignments

Planetary Database

Appendix

MIRANDA: THE PRODIGAL

Miranda acts cool and collected on the surface, but she is just as complex and as human as the next person. Much of her personality results from her relationship with her father, who intended her to be not just his daughter, but his legacy. She was created with the best genetics available to be smart, to be beautiful, and to be ruthless. Miranda fled when she discovered the truth about her father.

Miranda has a twin sister, Oriana, who was once part of her father's web. Miranda took her away from him so she would not be hurt. Her sister is living on Illium, but Miranda has learned that her father now knows where she is located. Miranda wants you to help her get her twin safely off of Illium and out of her father's clutches.

> Miranda is a biotic. The majority of the targets you fight in this mission are human and only some are shielded. If you have biotics, you may want to rely on a weapons expert for your third squad member. If you are a soldier, though, bringing along another biotic could prove useful in sweeping your enemies off their feet.
>
> **NOTE**

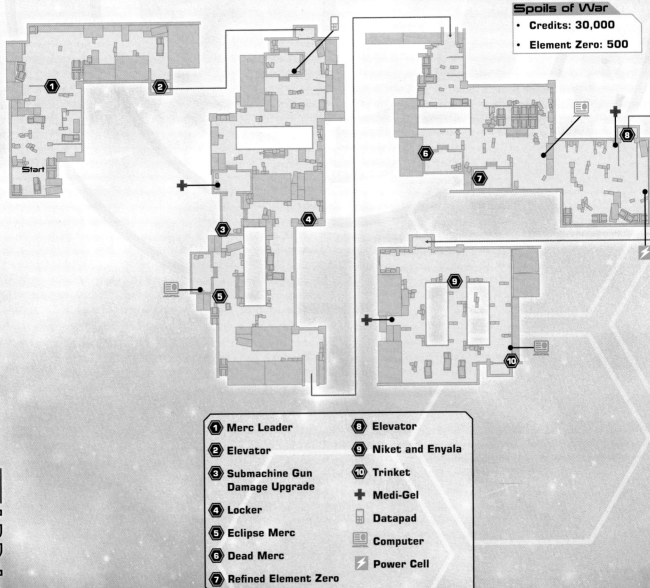

Spoils of War
- **Credits: 30,000**
- **Element Zero: 500**

LEGEND

1. Merc Leader
2. Elevator
3. Submachine Gun Damage Upgrade
4. Locker
5. Eclipse Merc
6. Dead Merc
7. Refined Element Zero
8. Elevator
9. Niket and Enyala
10. Trinket
➕ Medi-Gel
📱 Datapad
💻 Computer
⚡ Power Cell

Objective 1: Speak to Lanteia

After docking on Illium, report to the Eternity Bar. Miranda's contact, Lanteia, is waiting for you in a small room in the back of the bar. She says that Miranda's father has hired Eclipse mercs to collect Oriana. Lanteia also says that Niket, Miranda's confidant, is also on Illium. Niket has offered to escort Oriana off the planet. Miranda hatches a plan to run interference against the Eclipse mercs so Niket can get Oriana to safety.

Naturally, you are not pleased about how this mission is getting more complicated by the minute. However, Miranda needs your help, so it's off to the shipping area near Nos Astra to help Niket and Oriana get safe passage out of the city.

> After the conversation in the Eternity Bar, you automatically go to the shipping area.
> **NOTE**

Objective 2: Find Niket

Welcome Wagon

As you approach the shipping area via a small shuttle, Eclipse gunships spirit ahead and drop off mercenaries. The mercs turn their guns on you. When the merc leader sees that Miranda is in the shuttle, he demands that his crew hold their fire, but the shuttle has already been damaged. It crashes.

When you get out, the Eclipse leader comes forward and tells you that Captain Enyala of Eclipse is moving in on Oriana. As for Niket, don't count on him helping you out. The merc refuses to elaborate on that point. Instead, he warns you just to back off and let Enyala take Miranda's sister. While he's threatening you, you have a chance to start the fight to your advantage.

A Renegade interrupt will get you close enough to the merc leader to snap his neck while Shepard drops an explosive crate on the merc's men. It's a dirty opening play, but it makes the battle with the merc go a lot smoother. Otherwise, you must drop into cover and engage in a protracted firefight with the full Eclipse force, which includes troopers, heavies, and engineers.

The Eclipse troopers are easy targets since they have no armor. Biotics, either from you or Miranda, make short work of them. The engineers and heavies require more work. The engineers can send out combat drones to draw your fire away from them. Pick off the drones quickly and then train your weapons back on the mercs.

Introduction | Training | Upgrades and Research | Miranda: The Prodigal | Walkthrough | Special Assignments | Planetary Database | Appendix

After breaking through shields, use biotics to mop up the Eclipse thugs.

Move through the shipping containers to locate another Eclipse patrol. The patrol is initially made up of troopers, which have no shields. Take these down quickly with gunfire and biotics. When the troopers are on their backs, call the elevator. You locate one of the Eclipse radios. While Miranda scans it to figure out how many Eclipse thugs are waiting at the top of that elevator, she explains the entire situation with her sister.

Oriana is Miranda's twin, but only genetically. Oriana is much younger than Miranda. Her father grew Oriana  when Miranda was a teenager. Oriana was to be a replacement for Miranda. Miranda explains that while she is the older sister, she is not the first child their father created. She is just the first child her father kept. It's a chilling proposition. As you take the elevator, Miranda assures you that Niket is on the up-and-up.

Shipping Yard

The elevator drops you off at a shipping yard. Miranda warns that the shipping yard is full of moving belts and containers. Not only will it be harder to pick targets, but the shipping yard will be full of hazardous materials. Watch what you shoot. But be on the lookout to use those explosive containers on your enemies. Just outside the elevator, dart into an open shipping container to find a PDA. Hack it for credits and then move on to the first conveyor belt.

The Eclipse mercs swarm the opposite side of the first conveyor belt. The crew is made up of troopers and engineers.  Look for the engineers to hang back, using their shields as cover while popping out to release combat drones. These drones float around the belt and move into your territory. Try to shoot them as they cross the belt, because if they get too close, they can quickly close in and zap you.

There are explosive containers on the opposite side of the conveyor belt. You can either shoot them or use Overload (this is one of Miranda's powers) to make them explode and damage the enemy. Biotics will also lift troopers or unshielded engineers into the air, making them helpless targets.

Introduction

Training

Upgrades and Research

Walkthrough
Miranda: The Prodigal

Special Assignments

Planetary Database

Appendix

Remember that headshots are particularly effective against organic targets like the troopers.

After dropping the last of the mercs in this area, cross to the other side of the belt and investigate the large cargo container with the open door. There is medi-gel inside. On the nearby desk, scan the submachine gun to get a Microfield Pulsar. This upgrades submachine gun damage for the entire squad. Leave the container and follow the path toward the next conveyor belt. Another batch of Eclipse thugs is waiting for you.

> Open the lockers on the way to the second belt for some credits.
>
> **TIP**

Conveyor Belt

More Eclipse troopers and engineers swarm the next conveyor belt. Use the crates as cover—the mercs certainly do. Pick off the explosive containers through the space between the crates, either with bullets or with Overload. Try to catch the Eclipse thugs in the explosions and weaken their shields.

Look out for combat drones to flit around the belt and sneak up on you. Pop them before they get too close.

Pull Eclipse mercs into the void beneath the conveyor belt to dispatch them.

The Eclipse enemies will attempt to move around the left side of the belt and close in on your position. Cut them off.

Use the crates as cover to stop troopers and possibly a heavy from crossing into your territory. Duck to avoid incoming fire, and chisel away any shields before popping out and using a biotic to finish the job. Alternatively, you can rely on weapons to eliminate the rest of the mercs in this area. Remember to go for headshots whenever possible. When the Eclipse thugs take cover, they often leave a part of their heads exposed. Zero in on that and open fire to drop them much faster than if you plugged them in the arm or torso.

CAUTION

After the battle, hack the terminal inside the cargo container for credits, and scan the dead Eclipse thug outside for a Microscanner upgrade. This allows you to carry more medi-gel.

Moving Parts

Watch out for Eclipse troopers and heavies as you move between the containers on the way to the next conveyor belt. The patrol around the next belt is composed of Eclipse troopers, engineers, and heavies—but also look out for LOKI mechs that draw your fire away from more dangerous targets. Yank those without shields off their feet and finish them off with weapon fire as they float away. When you get close to the belt and the rest of the Eclipse patrol erupts from the container behind it, use the explosive containers as bombs against them.

Watch the ceiling above the belt. A pulley moves an explosive crate over the Eclipse fighters. Shoot the crate as it swoops over your targets. The crate falls and explodes on the mercs.

A walkway beneath the belt connects the two sides of the area. Look out for combat drones to slip through

this walkway and sneak up on you. As the battle progresses, the Eclipse thugs will also attempt to use this walkway. There are crates on your side of the walkway, so duck into cover and pick them off if they attempt to make the cross.

Don't ignore the stopping power of a shotgun. Although you must get close to make it truly effective, a shotgun will drop an unshielded target with just one or two hits. And it is quite powerful against shields, too.

TIP

There's a crate of eezo in the next shipping container.

Crack the secure terminal against these containers for more credits.

As you approach the next encounter, EDI says that the Eclipse thugs are locking down the elevators to slow your progress. EDI will override the locks, but in the meantime, you need to deal with the mercs filing into the area. There are several explosive containers you can pop to blast your foes. Use these to thin the herd.

Continue keeping an eye on combat drones from the engineers. However, as pesky as those engineers are, your real targets in this wave of Eclipse are the vanguards. These mercs have biotic powers like Miranda and will use them to knock you around. When you see an incoming warp field, dive into cover to keep from being rocked back on your heels and vulnerable to incoming fire. The vanguards use Barrier to block your attacks, so you must cut through that before you can really damage them.

There is medi-gel near the elevator and a box of power cells in the rear. As you collect these things, you hear Enyala on the radio. She says that Niket is in position and ready to move the family into an Eclipse transport. Miranda cannot believe what she is hearing.

Inside the elevator, Miranda starts coming to grips with Niket's betrayal.

Dock 94

When Miranda steps out of the elevator, she sees Niket. And he's with Enyala. Niket has indeed sold Miranda out, but not for money. He sees Miranda's kidnapping of Oriana as something less noble than a rescue—he sees it as revenge against her father. However, out of sympathy for Miranda, Niket has kept the exact location of Oriana secret from her father. He wanted to handle this peacefully.

Miranda realizes this makes Niket the only loose end. She raises her pistol to shoot him. You can use a Paragon interrupt to keep her from killing Niket. However, Niket's fate is sealed either way. If Miranda doesn't shoot Niket, then Enyala does. She's doing this to get paid. She doesn't have time to deal with Niket and Miranda's back-and-forth.

Introduction

Training

Upgrades and Research

Walkthrough

Miranda: The Prodigal

Special Assignments

Planetary Database

Appendix

Objective 3: Kill Enyala

Miranda knocks Enyala back with Warp but does not kill her. Enyala calls in backup. Several Eclipse mercs spread across the area. You must eliminate Enyala to end this mission, but the other mercs are masterful at interfering with that task. There are troopers, engineers, and vanguards in Enyala's personal entourage.

Look for an explosive container on a pulley above the battlefield. Shoot it down so it drops on some mercs.

Push through Enyala's crew. The troopers are the easy kills. Without shields, they can be battered with biotics or dropped with headshots. The vanguards need a lot more attention because they have barriers to protect them from attacks. Using Overload to break through barriers and shields is useful.

Enyala is a tough kill. She is protected with both a barrier and armor, so you have a lot to chew through in order to do real damage to her. Enyala is armed with a shotgun, which does great harm at close range. Try to dismantle her barrier from a distance. Heavy weapons do a lot to cleave through her protection.

If you have biotics like Pull or Charge, you can toss Enyala as soon as she's down only to health. While she's floating away, pepper her with shots to make sure she isn't coming back.

Once Enyala is down and her mercs have been cleared out, look for a locket on a crate next to the elevator door. Pick this up to start a small special assignment on Illium (Lost Locket Found). Inside the elevator, Miranda laments that she allowed a mission to get personal. Back at Nos Astra, Miranda catches a brief glimpse of Oriana with her new family. Depending on Shepard's conversation with her, Miranda either talks to her or decides against saying anything to her, lest she draw any more unnecessary attention to her sister. This ends the mission. Miranda is now loyal to the team and has unlocked the powerful Slam biotic, which lets her lift an enemy into the air and then immediately smash it into the ground.

JACK: SUBJECT ZERO

How did Jack end up becoming one of the most powerful human biotics in the galaxy? When Jack was a child, she was abducted and placed in a special Cerberus facility. There, she was tested on for years. Tortured. Abused. All in the name of science. Cerberus scientists believed that by inflicting enough pain to move the pain threshold, they could discover a way to make a human more susceptible to gaining biotic powers.

After combing through Cerberus files, Jack has learned the exact location of the Cerberus facility: the planet Pragia. She wants to put some of these haunting memories out of her mind and thinks that destroying the facility is just the therapy she needs. Plot a course for Pragia to fulfill Jack's request.

As the shuttle nears the Cerberus base, EDI picks up multiple thermal readings. This is supposed to be an abandoned base. Jack starts getting cold feet as the shuttle closes in on the base but steels herself when the shuttle lands. She just wants to get in there, plant the bomb, and get out.

Jack is a hardcore biotic, so you may wish to complement her skills with a weapons expert since the Cerberus base is full of things to shoot at.

NOTE

Spoils of War
- Credits: 30,000
- Element Zero: 500

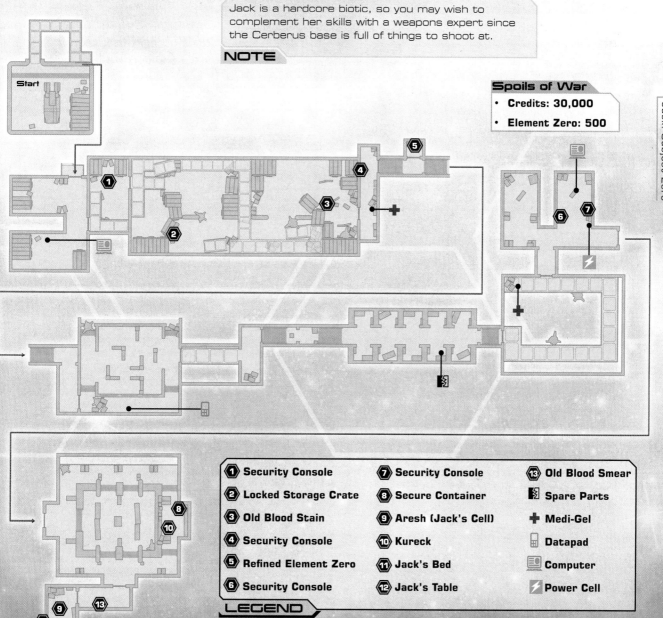

LEGEND

1. Security Console
2. Locked Storage Crate
3. Old Blood Stain
4. Security Console
5. Refined Element Zero
6. Security Console
7. Security Console
8. Secure Container
9. Aresh (Jack's Cell)
10. Kureck
11. Jack's Bed
12. Jack's Table
13. Old Blood Smear
- Spare Parts
- Medi-Gel
- Datapad
- Computer
- Power Cell

Objective 1: Enter Facility

Security Logs

After the squad disembarks from the shuttle, you must find the entrance of the Cerberus base. The door is down the stairs from the landing zone. The inside of the base is quiet. Nature has taken its course on the abandoned base, breaking it down as plants slowly reclaim the area. Inside the base, look for a door on the left wall that leads deeper into the facility.

Hack the secure terminal in the small room on the far side of the door to bank some credits.

At the bottom of the next staircase, you discover a security log. When you play it, you start to get a better picture of what was happening at this facility. Apparently, the Illusive Man wanted a report on what was happening at the facility, but the experiments were being obscured from Cerberus. It seems the scientists at the facility had gone rogue and were doing things not approved by the Illusive Man.

Pass through the door next to the security log to enter a courtyard. Jack recognizes the courtyard. As she tells you about her childhood at the base, search the courtyard for a crate. Hack the lock on the crate to recover some credits. Then move through the door on the far side of the courtyard to re-enter the base. In the next hallway, pick up a medi-gel from the crate just inside the door.

The security log at the end of the hallway reveals that something in the facility went terribly wrong. The subjects at the facility were going wild. The guards were instructed to protect Jack at all costs.

Deeper in the facility, you discover dead varren. These are fresh kills, too. Somebody—or something—is in this facility with you.

Introduction

Training

Upgrades and Research

Jack: Subject Zero

Walkthrough

Special Assignments

Planetary Database

Appendix

Bypass the door next to the varren to pick up a crate of element zero.

TIP

Blood Pack

When you step through the door at the bottom of the stairs, you encounter Blood Pack mercs. What are they doing here? The patrol is led by a Blood Pack warrior. The warrior is flanked by troopers. All of these brutes can regenerate their health, so when you start working on one target, be sure to put it down so it does not slink off, heal, and come back with a vengeance.

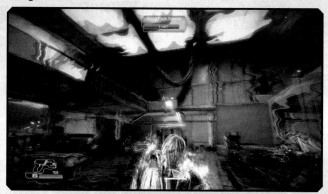

Use biotics (yours or Jack's) to nail the trooper on the ledge above the courtyard.

You cannot access the part of the courtyard off to the left, but the Blood Pack has. At least two troopers pop  up from the windows and rain down bullets. Take shots at their heads when they stand up to fire on you, or arc biotic attacks into the windows to lift them into view.

Hack the PDA in the corridor on the right side of the courtyard to pick up additional credits.

Moving Deeper

After clearing out the Blood Pack thugs from the courtyard, bypass the locked door and cross a narrow bridge to enter the next section of the facility. More Blood Pack troopers wait for you on a catwalk above the next set of stairs. They hide behind the wall and pop up to take shots at you. Use the crates in front of the stairs as cover and fire back at the troopers. Use Jack's biotics to arc over the wall and attack the troopers.

In the hall at the bottom of the stairs, be ready for oncoming varren. Target the varren as they rush you. Jack's  biotics are useful to stop the varren in their tracks. After shooting down the varren, check out the small rooms off of the hall for some spare parts to salvage.

Pick up the medi-gel on the catwalk next to the door on the far side of the hallway.

NOTE

The door leads to two small labs. The lab to the right contains security logs. Watch them to learn just how awful the experiments at this facility truly were. The Cerberus scientists were injecting, freezing, and torturing other children to determine which test procedures were safe enough to use on Jack. Jack refuses to believe that anybody at the facility had it worse than she did.

Hack the research console at the chair to receive the Hyper Amp upgrade. It increases the damage caused by biotic attacks.

More Blood Pack

In the next room, you discover the rest of the Blood Pack, led by a krogan, Kureck. They are at the facility to salvage whatever they can find but are sorely disappointed by what was left at the base. You catch Kureck by surprise, but the krogan directs his pack into battle right away. The Blood Pack troopers, warriors, and pyros in the room fan out.

Shoot the tanks on the Blood Pack pyros to turn them into walking time bombs. Use zoom to get the shot just right.

Unleash biotic attacks on the unprotected troopers.

The second toughest Blood Pack enemy in the room is the warrior. If the krogan gets close enough, it

will charge you. If you have heavy weapons, drop the warrior immediately with a few well-placed shots. If you lack heavy weapons, you must at least shoot through the armor before ripping into it with biotics.

Kureck is serious trouble. The krogan not only has armor like a Blood Pack warrior, but he also has a barrier. You cannot use biotics on Kureck right away thanks to these defenses. Instead, you must pick away at those defenses with heavy weapons or repeated fire. Kureck will also charge at you if he gets too close, so move around the room to keep him at a safe distance.

> Kureck can use the Warp biotic attack against you.
>
> **CAUTION**

If you can lift Kureck into the air with Pull or Slam, he's much easier to finish off.

> There are credits in the secure container behind Kureck's post.
>
> **TIP**

Objective 3: Find Jack's Cell

Bad Memories

Jack's cell is just beyond the Blood Pack room. When you step through the door, you hear somebody else in the room. You give whoever it is a chance to come out peacefully. It's a former test subject named Aresh. He came back to pick up the pieces of his childhood and eventually restart the facility. Aresh wants to complete the research that was started on him. He refuses to believe that it was all for nothing.

Jack wants to kill Aresh for even suggesting reopening the facility. It's up to you to stop her (or not). After the situation with Aresh has been resolved, you can look around the room with Jack. Inspect the window, the table, the bed, and the blood stain in the hall. Jack has a story attached to each of them. After listening to Jack close this old wound, tell Jack that it's time to leave.

The shuttle takes off, leaving the facility in the distance. Jack fidgets with the detonator, unsure what to do. Ultimately, she makes the decision to wipe her tortured childhood off the face of Pragia. As the shuttle rises to dock with the *Normandy*, a mushroom cloud rises from the jungle. Jack is now loyal to the team and has unlocked the Warp Ammo power.

Back on the *Normandy*, you discover Jack and Miranda locked in a biotic struggle in Miranda's office. You tell both of them to knock it off. Jack is furious with Miranda for denying that Cerberus was behind the experiments at Pragia. You get between the two of them. If your Paragon or Renegade score is high enough, you can resolve this situation without alienating either crew member. However, if you do not have the left dialog options available, you must make a tough choice right now. If you side with Miranda, you lose any chance of friendship (or more) with Jack. She shuts you out. Taking Jack's side turns Miranda cold. While this decision may close down social avenues with either crew member, you can still use them on missions.

> **NOTE**
>
> Unless you can max out your Paragon or Renegade score before the final mission, you cannot gain the loyalty of both of these crew members. If you manage to get a high enough morality score on either end of the pendulum, you can make up with the offended crew member.

Introduction

Training

Upgrades and Research

Walkthrough

Jack: Subject Zero

Special Assignments

Planetary Database

Appendix

MORDIN AND GRUNT: TUCHANKA

Two of the loyalty missions take place on the krogan world of Tuchanka, located in the Krogan DMZ. Use the hub guide of Tuchanka for visiting the planet. When you are ready to undertake the loyalty missions, skip to the strategy sections for Mordin and Grunt after the city guide.

Tuchanka

The krogan homeworld of Tuchanka bears the scars of war. Where once mighty forests stood and cities rose, now only ash and ruins remain. After the krogan almost destroyed Tuchanka and their own race in a nuclear civil war, the salarians relocated them to a toxin-free planet so they could rebuild their population and fight effectively in the Rachni Wars. However, a krogan population explosion ensued, and the krogan began to rise up and threaten the rest of the galaxy. Salarian scientists developed a genophage that controlled the krogan birthrate, causing the race to almost collapse but still retain some stability. The genophage is one of the galaxy's great morality questions. The krogan had the strength and numbers to conquer the galaxy. But was the genophage really closer to genocide?

Tuchanka has become partially hospitable only within the last few centuries. Krogan clans have returned to Tuchanka to assert their dominance over the planet, making it one of the most violent places in the galaxy.

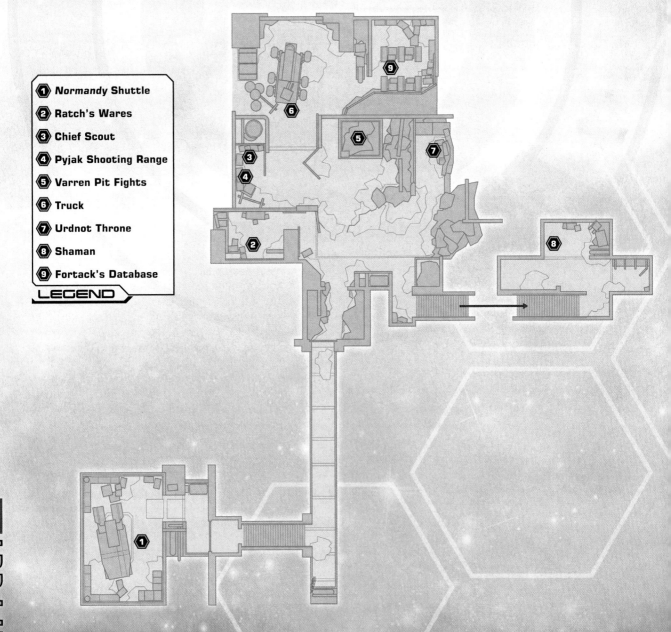

LEGEND

1. *Normandy* **Shuttle**
2. **Ratch's Wares**
3. **Chief Scout**
4. **Pyjak Shooting Range**
5. **Varren Pit Fights**
6. **Truck**
7. **Urdnot Throne**
8. **Shaman**
9. **Fortack's Database**

City Guide

Landing Zone

When you first arrive at Tuchanka, you see a small crowd of krogan near which you can make small talk with a Blood Pack recruiter. If you completed the Blue Rose of Illium assignment with the Paragon interrupt, you can also listen in on Charr, a krogan repeating love poetry to a woman,. When you try to enter the city, a krogan captain stops you and demands that you speak with the clan leader. While not essential to do right away, speaking with the clan leader is necessary to gather more information on the clan structures of the krogan.

Ratch's Wares

There is not much shopping in Tuchanka. The only proper store kiosk is just inside the city, although there is a science terminal you can purchase significant upgrades from deeper in Tuchanka. The store is run by Ratch, a krogan with a surprisingly welcoming attitude toward non-krogan. Credits speak louder than loyalty.

Ratch does not offer a discount like other retailers. Instead of charming or intimidating him to shave a few credits off his prices, you must instead complete a small task for him. When you return, Ratch offers the discount on his wares, such as Stabilizing Gauntlets that increase shield strength or a Microfusion Array that increases heavy weapon ammo capacity.

Ratch has a pet varren with him named Urz. The varren has been domesticated. You can actually pet it. If you buy some pyjak meat from Ratch's terminal after the hunt, feed it to the varren. The varren will then follow you around Tuchanka. Making Urz your pet isn't just a nice thing to do; you can win extra credits from the varren pit fights using Urz.

Killing Pyjaks

Want a discount at Ratch's shop? Then you need to hunt pyjaks, little beasts that annoy the krogan. Report to the gun range in the center of Tuchanka and step up to the left gun battery. This begins the game. There are four waves of pyjaks. You must shoot all of the pyjaks in each wave without running out of ammunition, which is noted on the right side of the screen. There is a catch to this range, though. There are two guns, one mounted on each side of the range. They alternate. The pyjaks run through a field of old tires, and if you try to blast a pyjak with a gun on the opposite side of the range, you risk hitting only tires.

Try to get in a rhythm with the pyjaks. Aim ahead of the pyjaks so the shot lands right on top of the pyjak as it runs, although there is a blast radius that allows a little wiggle room. Don't let them get too far down the field by waiting for them to enter the clearings among the tires or else they may scurry away.

Introduction

Training

Upgrades and Research

Walkthrough

Tuchanka

Special Assignments

Planetary Database

Appendix

Varren Pit Fighting

The krogan love to wager credits over varren fights. Use the terminal next to the pit to place a bet on the next varren fight. Pick your varren and then watch the fight. The bet is 100 credits. If your varren wins, you pocket 500 credits. There is no surefire way to tell which varren will win, so choose the varren that you like best and hope for victory.

Fortack's Database

The krogan scientist Fortack is busy inside his lab next to the giant truck. Although Fortack will not interact with you, you can shop his database of weapon upgrades. There are excellent damage upgrades in this shop, but they are very expensive and there is no opportunity for a discount. However, since the upgrades are so powerful and many research projects require certain levels of upgrades, spend your credits here. The investment in arms is well worth the lighter pocket.

Pop the pyjak standing in the corner for laughs.

Clan Chief Urdnot Wreav

If you imported your character from *Mass Effect* and Urdnot Wrex survived, Wrex will be the clan leader that Shepard speaks with throughout the following section.

NOTE

Speak to clan leader Wreav for the official welcome to Tuchanka. Wreav speaks to you about your victory against Saren as well as your decision regarding the genophage cure Saren was seeking. Wreav is also the leader of Urdnot Wrex's clan, the krogan in your original team. Wreav is flanked by Uvenk, an envoy from a rival clan.

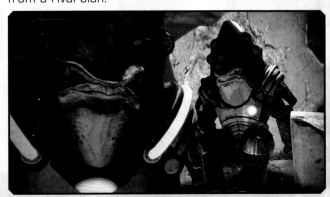

Uvenk is decidedly less friendly than Wreav and speaks openly of a day when his clan will usurp clan Urdnot.

If you have come to Tuchanka for Mordin's loyalty mission, ask Wreav about the salarian the Blood Pack merc carried through here. Wreav has little regard for mercenaries. He refers you instead to his chief scout, who was recently surveying Blood Pack operations.

There is a krogan shaman upstairs from the main entrance. The shaman will not speak to you on your visit to Tuchanka unless you are pursuing Grunt's loyalty mission.

NOTE

MORDIN: OLD BLOOD

Mordin was a scientist working on the krogan genophage project. After discovering that krogan population levels were rising following the initial deployment, Mordin was called back to help develop a modified genophage that would stabilize the krogan birthrate, making only one of every thousand krogan pregnancies viable.

Mordin has grappled with the morality of his participation in the genophage for years. But the news that Maelon, Mordin's former assistant and protégé, has been captured by Blood Pack mercenaries on Tuchanka spurs the salarian into action. If a krogan clan has captured a scientist that worked on the genophage, the assumption is that the krogan are seeking a new avenue for a cure. Mordin wants to travel to Tuchanka to rescue Maelon.

Once on Tuchanka, speak with the chief scout by the pyjak shooting range. The krogan will tell you of a missing scout sent to investigate the Weyrloc clan.

> Mordin is a tech expert, so his defenses are quite able. He is not a strong weapon user, so if you are a biotic player, bring along a strong soldier.
>
> **NOTE**

Walkthrough

Mordin: Old Blood

Spoils of War
- **Credits: 30,000**
- **Iridium: 2,000**

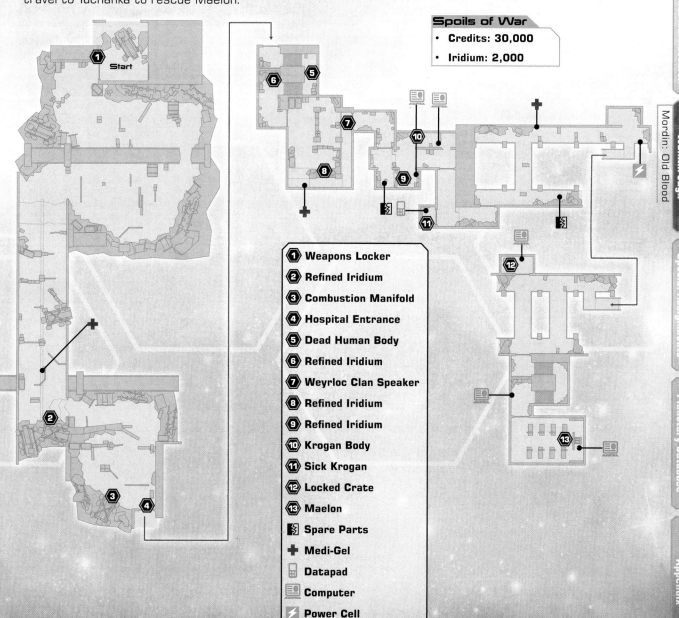

Start

LEGEND

1. Weapons Locker
2. Refined Iridium
3. Combustion Manifold
4. Hospital Entrance
5. Dead Human Body
6. Refined Iridium
7. Weyrloc Clan Speaker
8. Refined Iridium
9. Refined Iridium
10. Krogan Body
11. Sick Krogan
12. Locked Crate
13. Maelon
- Spare Parts
- Medi-Gel
- Datapad
- Computer
- Power Cell

Objective 1: Talk to Scout

When you first arrive in Tuchanka for Mordin's loyalty mission, speak to the clan leader. Wreav directs you to his chief scout over at the gun range. The chief scout is well aware of Maelon's situation: He sent a scout to check out what the Blood Pack mercenaries were doing with the salarian on Tuchanka, but that scout has gone missing. The scout tells you to take a truck out to clan Weyrloc's base (it's in a hospital) to check on the salarian yourself.

Before taking the truck, speak to the mechanic working on one of the land rovers. The mechanic needs a combustion manifold. If you agree to look for one, this adds a special assignment to your log. The combustion manifold is found near the Weyrloc base.

When you are ready to go, speak to the chief scout and tell him you want to take the truck. Load up and drive the truck out of the city, closing in on the Weyrloc base. The truck stops at a wall. There is a weapons locker in front of the wall where you can change your loadout. The base is crawling with Blood Pack mercs, so be sure you arm your squad with the best weapons you have in your arsenal.

Objective 2: Find Weyrloc Base

Klixen

Your first battle is not with Blood Pack. Klixen scurry out from behind rubble to greet you. Keep back from the klixen. Not only do they try to spit fiery venom at you, but when you kill them, they explode. Since the klixen do not have armor, use biotics like Pull or Throw on them. While the klixen are tumbling through the air, they cannot fire on you.

When you pass through the narrow opening in the wall, another klixen attacks. It's joined by varren. Fall back and cut them off at the chokepoint.

Enemy Profile: Klixen

- **Classification: Elite**
- **Powers: Death Blast**
- **Defenses: —**
- **Weapons: Fire Spit**

Klixen are dangerous creatures without any sense of fear or self-preservation. They often travel in packs. Klixen skitter right at their targets, lobbing gobs of burning spit at them. The don't have armor, so it is easy to battle a klixen, but make sure you don't do it at close range. When the klixen's saliva is exposed to air, it reacts violently. The explosion can cause serious damage.

Blood Pack

Don't advance too far into the next area after taking down the klixen and varren. Blood Pack boom-squads are hiding behind a barricade on the far side of the area. Duck behind the concrete barricade near the narrow opening to hide from rocket attacks. The boom-squads linger out of cover for a few seconds before and after launching a rocket, giving you plenty of chances to return fire.

Introduction

Training

Upgrades and Research

Walkthrough

Mordin: Old Blood

Special Assignments

Planetary Database

Appendix

> **TIP**
>
> Arc a biotic attack around the barricade to sweep the boom-squad off their feet. They have no armor or shields to protect them from biotics.

Blood Pack troopers wait for you at the top of the ramp beyond the boom-squad. Use the barricades for cover as you advance along the road. The troopers have no armor either, making them vulnerable to most biotic attacks. Go for headshots whenever possible to do extra damage. A Blood Pack warrior on the far side of the road comes out of hiding only after you take down several of the troopers. The warrior is armored, but you have enough distance between you and it to pick apart the protection before it becomes a real threat.

> **TIP**
>
> Blood Pack thugs are vorcha and krogan. Use incendiary ammo to do additional damage and prevent the Blood Pack from using their regenerative powers.

More varren gallop down the road at you. They close the distance fast, so toss them aside with biotics if possible.

> **NOTE**
>
> There is medi-gel and a crate of refined iridium at the far end of the road.

Blood Pack pyros at the far end of the road wait behind cover for you to get close and then pop out to blaze you with flame-throwers. Fall back and target their tanks.

When you reach the hospital exterior, more Blood Pack thugs fall in line to defend the base. Stay back and plug

the troopers you see when first approaching the door. When the first few are down, ease into the area to reveal the remainder of the patrol. These troopers have no armor, so you can drop them with headshots or biotic attacks.

> **TIP**
>
> Looking for the combustion manifold for the krogan mechanic? It's located on the overturned truck next to the hospital.

Objective 3: Enter the Hospital

Clan Weyrloc

The hospital is quiet. There is a human body at the bottom of the stairs just inside the entry. Inspect the body to discover that somebody is using humans as test subjects to locate a genophage cure. The genetic makeup of humans is so diverse that they make excellent test subjects when seeking cures or trying out new chemical/biological weapons. Continue down the stairs to probe deeper into the base and locate a crate of refined iridium.

In the next room, the speaker for clan Weyrloc addresses you from the opposite side of the room. The krogan tells you that you should be dead already, but the clan leader has instead decided you should be allowed to flee and spread word of the rise of clan Weyrloc. The speaker talks too much, though, revealing that the salarian scientist they kidnapped is working on the genophage cure. Weyrloc in tandem with the Blood Pack will expand and take to the stars to spread krogan dominance.

While the speaker boasts, you have a Renegade interrupt opportunity. You will have to fight these krogan no matter what, but if you take the interrupt, you shoot the gas tank beneath the speaker. The explosion eliminates the krogan you would have had to fight in this battle, but you take on Renegade points.

No matter how the battle begins, you need to take cover as soon as the krogan attack. The krogan are armored, but the Blood Pack troopers that join them are not. As soon as the troopers file down the stairs, clean

them out with headshots and biotics. The krogan are tougher targets. They try to get in close and charge you. Sidestep the charge attack and then chip their armor away. If you have a biotic on the squad, you can fling unarmored krogan into the air to render them helpless.

After the battle ends, scour the room to pick up more iridium and a medi-gel.

Hospital

Go through the door behind the krogan clan speaker to locate the medical bays of the hospital. There are no enemies inside. Search the rooms to find spare parts you can salvage for credits, more iridium, and computer terminals. Look at the files at the terminals to learn more about Maelon's role in the Weyrloc genophage project.

Speak to Mordin about the genophage while looking at terminal files.

In another room, you locate the body of a rare female krogan. The krogan allowed herself to be experimented on in order to find a cure for the genophage. This particular sight deeply affects Mordin. Talk to him about the ramifi-

cations of the genophage. The body moves Mordin to question his previous assumptions about the genophage, even seeking rationale (and comfort) in spirituality. This is a new side of Mordin and one that greatly humanizes the salarian.

> Your dialog choices in this conversation earn you either Paragon or Renegade points depending on how sympathetic you are to Mordin.

NOTE

> Hack the research terminal near the krogan body to earn the Microfiber Weave upgrade. It increases Grunt's health.

TIP

At the end of the hall leading away from the medical labs, you can either open a door to your immediate

right or continue down a corridor to the left. Open the door to the right to discover the Urdnot scout. The krogan has been experimented on and his spirit is broken. He wishes to remain at the base and die. You can either let him sit there and rot or encourage him to return to his clan as a warrior. Tell the krogan that the genophage project is only to help clan Weyrloc multiply, not all krogan. If you have enough charm or intimidation, you can rouse that krogan to his feet and send him on his way. This results in Paragon or Renegade points, depending on your actions.

> Finding this scout ties into the Missing Scout special assignment from the chief scout back in the city.

NOTE

Blood Pack

The next area is heavily guarded. EDI warns you that there are a lot of explosive containers, but Mordin

sees them as potential bombs. Use them to shatter krogan armor. When you first enter, the Blood Pack mercs do not see you. Target the troopers across the courtyard to get their attention. After you drop one of the troopers, the courtyard fills with Blood Pack. The opening in the center of the courtyard is perfect for dropping enemies into via biotic attacks.

Let the Blood Pack troops cross the bridge in the center of the courtyard. Shoot the explosive crate to send them flying.

> Salvage the circuit boards on your side of the courtyard for credits before crossing to the opposite side to pick up medi-gel and trigger the next wave of enemies.

NOTE

Varren precede the Blood Pack foes. The varren sprint through the courtyard. Fall back and cut down

the varren before they overwhelm you. Then, concentrate on the Blood Pack warriors filtering through the door on the far end of the courtyard. You can use explosive crates along the walkway as bombs to weaken the krogan.

> Watch out for your squad members. If they move too close to an explosive crate, order them to a new location so they are not caught in a blast.

CAUTION

Pick up the power cells near the stairs and then drop to the lower level to confront more Blood Pack forces. Warriors rush toward you. Use heavy weapons to keep them at bay.

Introduction
Training
Upgrades and Research
Mordin: Old Blood
Walkthrough
Special Assignments
Planetary Database
Appendix

TIP

Don't neglect Mordin's tech powers, like Incinerate. It's quite effective against Blood Pack scum.

Look out for more varren to rush the lower courtyard. Take them down before they cross the central bridge.

Multiple Blood Pack warriors follow behind the varren, but the real target is Weyrloc clan leader Guld. Guld is a battle-ready krogan, decked out in a barrier as well as armor. You cannot hammer him with biotics until these defenses have been lowered. Heavy weapons will shatter the barrier and the armor, but it will take a lot of hits to make Guld vulnerable.

Don't ignore the warriors, although it is useful to let your squad mates concentrate on them while you tackle Guld.

Guld is armed with a combat shotgun and tries to get close to effectively use it. There is no shame in

falling back. You want to keep Guld at medium range so he cannot charge or hit you with the full force of his shotgun. Keep wearing him down with heavy weapons. If heavy weapons run dry, use everything else to keep picking apart his armor until he is left with only his health. Once Guld is exposed, biotics will keep the krogan off his feet while you finish him off.

TIP

The biotic attack Charge is useful against tough targets like Guld. You can knock him down and then unload an entire clip in him as he struggles to his feet.

NOTE

Before going downstairs to find Maelon, open the door that Guld stormed through. Hack the locked crate inside to bank some credits.

Hack the research terminal at the bottom of the stairs to pick up another Micro-fusion Array upgrade, which increases heavy weapon ammo capacity.

Maelon

When you reach the bottom of the hospital, you find Maelon busily working on a cure for the genophage.

He is not being held against his will to do so, either; Maelon is willingly trying to help cure the genophage out of guilt for his previous involvement. He justifies his methods—live test subjects—as just more blood on already bloody hands. Maelon does not see a galaxy with controlled krogan populations as any less violent than it is now with batarian piracy, rogue Spectres, and Geth attacks.

It's up to Mordin to deal with this situation, but you can influence him. When Mordin raises his weapon

to Maelon, you can use a Paragon interrupt to stop him. If you do, you can then convince him to let Maelon go. However, he leaves all his data. You can either opt to destroy it all or keep it. Keeping the data is a Renegade option, while ruining it is a Paragon choice. Once the choice has been made, this mission ends. Mordin is now loyal to the team, and his Neural Shock power is unlocked.

NOTE

Before leaving the lab, hack the terminal in the back of the room for credits.

GRUNT: RITE OF PASSAGE

Grunt is having serious problems down in the cargo hold. Something is happening to him, something he cannot explain. He just feels…violent. Grunt believes the answers for what ails him are located on Tuchanka. Chart a course to the krogan homeworld and take Grunt before the Urdnot clan leader to discover what Grunt needs to get his mind back on the mission.

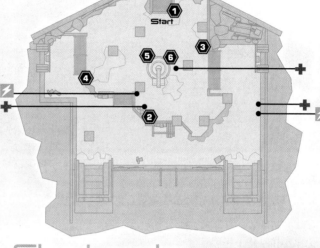

Start

Spoils of War

- **Credits: 30,000**
- **Platinum: 2,000**

LEGEND

- **1** Keystone
- **2** Refined Platinum
- **3** Urdnot Corpse
- **4** Urdnot Corpse
- **5** Urdnot Corpse
- **6** Urdnot Corpse
- **7** Uvenk
- **8** Urdnot Corpse
- **9** Urdnot Corpse
- **Spare Parts**
- **Medi-Gel**
- **Power Cell**

Objective 1: Talk to Clan Leader

> You might speak to Wrex, not Wreav, during this encounter if you imported your character from *Mass Effect* and Wrex survived.

> Uvenk keeps talking trash about Grunt. You have a Renegade interrupt that shuts his mouth. If you use it, the shaman takes an immediate liking to you.

NOTE

Once back on Tuchanka, report to clan leader Wreav in the center of the city. Ask Wreav about Grunt's problem. The clan leader only needs to look into the young krogan's eyes to diagnose the problem: He is a juvenile not trained in the ways of the krogan by a proper clan. When you explain to Wreav that Grunt was tank-bred by Okeer, the rival clan leader Uvenk dismisses Grunt as not worthy to even walk on Tuchanka.

Upstairs, Uvenk is already speaking to the shaman in hopes of keeping Grunt from taking the Rite of Passage, but the shaman believes Grunt should be allowed his chance as long as Wreav gives his permission. The shaman says that Grunt needs his krantt—his allies—to join him in this battle.

NOTE

Wreav, on the other hand, thinks Grunt has potential and should undertake the krogan Rite of Passage so that he may become an adult krogan and be tied to a clan. In order to begin the Rite of Passage, you must speak to the shaman upstairs.

Once you accept the Rite of Passage from the shaman, you are automatically transported out to an arena. A keystone in the middle of the arena releases several waves of creatures to challenge you. You must defeat each wave in order to survive the Rite and make Grunt a loyal member of the team.

Objective 2: Survive

Each time you press the keystone, another wave of creatures enters the arena. There are multiple medi-gel crates in the arena, as well as clips and heavy weapon ammo boxes. Do not burn through these right away—especially the medi-gel and the heavy weapon ammo. Save that ammo for the third wave of the rite—you will need it. You should also pick up the crate of refined platinum sometime during the trials.

First Wave: Varren

Because the arena is limited on space, the varren have an advantage. They move much faster than you and are able to corner you effectively, especially when they pair up. Never stop moving when fighting the varren. If you stop, the varren will converge on you. Use close-quarters weapons to blast the varren in half, and rely on biotics to fling them around like rag dolls. If you have cryo or incendiary ammo, use it. Freezing or burning the varren makes them easier to manage.

After the action subsides, salvage the turbine parts to collect extra credits. When you are ready for the next wave, activate the keystone again.

Second Wave: Klixen

The second wave of the rite begins with a giant creature flying overhead. It drops klixen into the arena. Because klixen explode when killed, you need to keep your distance from these creatures while hunting them. Klixen also spit fire at you when you get too close. Use longer-range weapons to manage the klixen, and don't shy away from biotic attacks. Even if the biotic attack does not destroy the klixen, toppling it with something like Charge at least keeps it from following you. You can fall back and safely finish it off outside the blast radius.

Third Wave: Thresher Maw

The goal of the final wave of the Rite of Passage is to survive a thresher maw attack. If you can live through five minutes of a thresher maw attack, you complete the Rite. The thresher maw is a massive insect-like creature that bursts out of the ground and attacks with a venom strike. You cannot survive many direct hits from this attack. The thresher maw can move around the outskirts of the arena, so you cannot just camp behind a pillar.

While the trial can be finished by just surviving the thresher maw's attacks, you can actually bring it down. Use heavy weapons to target the thresher maw when it bursts out of the ground. Wait for its venom to pass and then step out. Deliver a few good shells or blasts to its flat head and then seek cover again. Refill your heavy weapon with the power cells littered around the arena—this is why you didn't want to use them in the early parts of the Rite.

Uvenk

After seeing you survive (or defeat) the thresher maw, Uvenk greets you at the arena. He respects Grunt's strength and believes he can tip the balance of the clans on Tuchanka. But Grunt sees through Uvenk, knowing Uvenk only wants Grunt as a trophy. And Grunt is nobody's trophy.

Uvenk is flanked by multiple krogan warriors. They have the same strengths and weapons as Blood Pack warriors. You must strip them of their armor in order to finish them off with headshots or biotics. Uvenk hangs in the rear of the battlefield, hoping his warriors will soften you up for the kill. Push through the warriors so they do not attack you when you try to bring down Uvenk.

Scan the Urdnot corpses in the battlefield to pick up some credits.

Surround Uvenk with your squad so he cannot easily pick a target. Uvenk will desperately attempt to choose one of you to charge, so stay back and let him fret. Use special ammo like cryo or incendiary to do extra damage to Uvenk. Once you drop his barrier and armor, you can finish him off with biotics or close-quarter attacks with shotguns.

As soon as Uvenk falls, the shaman arrives in the arena to congratulate you. Grunt is welcomed into the Urdnot clan, but he chooses you as his battle-master. It's an honor. Grunt is now loyal to the squad, and his Fortification power is unlocked.

Introduction

Training

Upgrades and Research

Walkthrough

Grunt: Rite of Passage

Special Assignments

Planetary Database

Appendix

GARRUS: EYE FOR AN EYE

Garrus has some unfinished business on the Citadel he would like to see to before you head for the Omega 4 relay. The turian has located his former partner from Omega, Sidonis, who betrayed his team and got a lot of good men killed. Sidonis is currently keeping company with Fade, a forger who specializes in making people disappear. Garrus wants his revenge. Travel to the Citadel and seek out this Fade to discover Sidonis's hiding place and give Garrus the peace of mind he needs to be 100 percent committed to the mission.

Spoils of War
- **Credits: 30,000**
- **Iridium: 2,000**

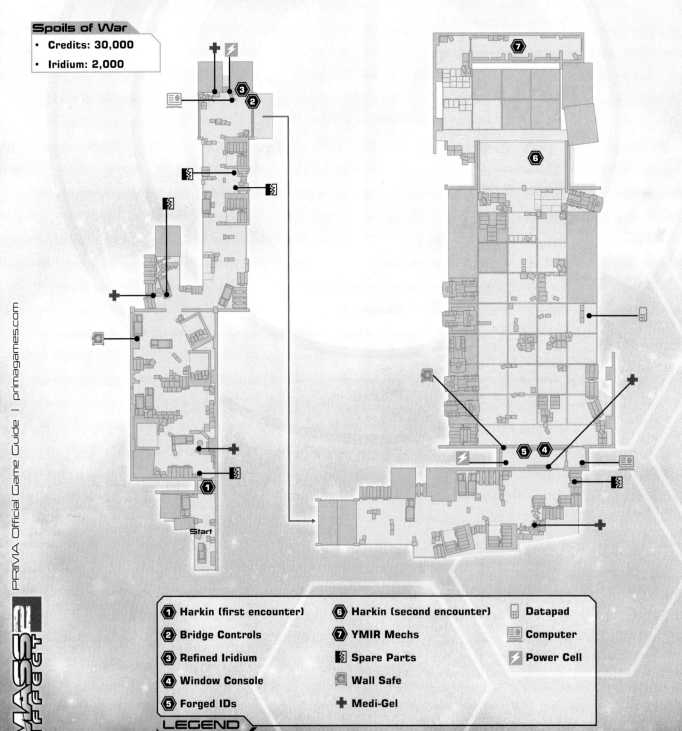

Start

LEGEND

1	Harkin (first encounter)	6	Harkin (second encounter)		Datapad
2	Bridge Controls	7	YMIR Mechs		Computer
3	Refined Iridium		Spare Parts		Power Cell
4	Window Console		Wall Safe		
5	Forged IDs		Medi-Gel		

Objective 1: Find Fade

When you reach the Citadel, you need to locate Fade in a warehouse near the Neon Markets in Zakera Ward. If this is your first visit to the Citadel, be sure to check out the "Citadel" chapter for a tour guide.

Fade

Fade is located at the entrance to the shipping warehouses on level 26 of the Zakera Ward. The volus steps out to greet you when you enter the warehouse at the bottom of the stairs. The volus is flanked by some krogan warriors. When Fade refuses to help you find Sidonis, you can use a Renegade interrupt to take down the krogan and convince Fade to see things your way. If not, you must battle the krogan guards. After you take down the guards, the volus is quick to confess that he actually is not Fade. Fade is down in the warehouse district, working out of the old pre-fab foundry.

The volus warns you that Fade is surrounded by Blue Suns. It turns out that Fade is actually Harkin, a former C-Sec officer that Garrus used to work with in the old days before the Saren strike. To reach the warehouse district now, head to a Rapid Transit terminal and select the desired destination.

When you arrive at the warehouse, you immediately run into Harkin. He is surprised to see you—both of you. Harkin orders his Blue Suns mercs to attack and keep you busy while he flees.

Objective 2: Confront Harkin

Blue Suns

Harkin leaves just a handful of Blue Suns troopers behind at the gates of the warehouse to hold you back. The troopers are easy targets. Using the crates for cover, duck from the troopers as they fire on you. When they reload, pop up and return fire. The troopers have no armor, so biotics are useful.

Inside the warehouse office, check the trash for scrap to salvage for credits and a medi-gel.

LOKI mechs attack from a nearby cargo container as well as the crate-lined path away from the office. Follow the path to push through a second wave of LOKI mechs as well as a couple of Blue Suns troopers. Use the crates as cover. The mechs and troopers keep coming, but without any armor, they are pushovers. (Don't expect this to last...)

Make sure the coast is clear before attempting to crack the wall safe in the warehouse. If you are attacked while hacking the safe, you cannot try again.

CAUTION

Pick up medi-gel and salvage spare parts next to the giant hole in the floor.

TIP

Introduction · Training · Upgrades and Research · Garrus: Eye For an Eye · Walkthrough · Special Assignments · Planetary Database · Appendix

Methodically move through the shipping containers on the right side of the hole in the floor. There are multiple LOKI mechs and Blue Suns troopers hiding among the crates. Look for LOKI mechs in open containers. The mechs are dormant until you close in, but if you rush the containers before the mechs unfold into active positions, you can cut them down before they fire a single shot. The troopers, of course, are already active and on the hunt. They work in groups, so try to thin their numbers right away with biotics or sniper fire from a distance.

> Use the explosive containers along the path as bombs.
>
> **TIP**

> Check the sides of the route for spare parts and circuit boards you can salvage for credits.
>
> **NOTE**

When you near the end of the path through the containers, Blue Suns legionnaires step out.

Collect medi-gel, heavy weapon ammo, and iridium at the far end of the shipping containers. Hack the computer next to the iridium for credits.

Bridge Control

Use the control panel near the iridium to lower a bridge, and start moving up the opposite side of the shipping containers. You have a long line of sight, so use it to snipe any targets early. You need to clear out lesser targets like troopers so you can concentrate on the two main enemies along this path: a Blue Suns commando and a YMIR mech.

Unload your heavy weapon into the YMIR mech. The path between the shipping containers is narrow, which is advantageous for the mech. Its miniguns and rockets are hard to dodge in close quarters.

> While you zero in on the YMIR, direct your squad to attack the commando—or vice versa. You need to work over these enemies together since both are powerful.
>
> **TIP**

The door beyond the YMIR mech leads to Harkin's office. There is a wall safe to hack inside as well as heavy weapon ammo to collect. Swipe the forged IDs off the desk to start a special assignment within the Citadel: Found Forged ID. After collecting all of the goods, open the windows. You take a peek at Harkin. He's cornered. Harkin is prepping a small army of LOKI and YMIR mechs to stop you from reaching him on the far side of the next area.

Talk to Garrus about the plan to bring down Harkin. After the conversation, open the door and hack the terminal for a sniper rifle damage upgrade before making a big push toward Harkin.

Harkin

As you enter the next area, EDI informs you that there are YMIR mechs hanging from cranes overhead near Harkin's hiding spot on the far side of the room. Beware of Harkin's intention to drop them on you as you close. The LOKI mechs are easy kills as you move across the room. When you reach the raised platforms, clamber between the crates to locate a datapad (loaded with credits), and then make a play for Harkin.

The two YMIR mechs that guard Harkin roar to life as you close in. Stick to the platforms loaded with crates to battle these mechs. You need the cover to protect yourself and your squad from the miniguns and rockets. The YMIRs are slow, so you have plenty of time to dismantle one of them from a distance before they both cross the open area of the room. However, once one of the YMIRs reaches the crates, you need to switch positions. Let the mech get caught up in the crates—it is not easy for the YMIR to maneuver among the boxes. In the open area, you can zigzag to avoid any incoming attacks while the mech is all tripped up.

After you destroy the mechs, the platforms in front of Harkin move. A small patrol of LOKI mechs starts moving down the platforms. Blast them as you climb up to Harkin's position.

When you reach Harkin, you easily take him into custody. Harkin is not forthcoming with Sidonis's location, but a little convincing with a boot on his neck loosens his lips. Harkin agrees to call Sidonis and arrange a meeting with one of Harkin's agents, giving Garrus a perfect opportunity to ambush him. You need to meet Sidonis at the Orbital Lounge. You have a Paragon interrupt when Garrus raises his weapon to shoot Harkin. If you take it, Garrus will only bash Harkin on the way out of the office and you bank some Paragon points.

Sidonis

Before going to meet Sidonis at the lounge, you share a transport with just Garrus. Garrus is angry and he's planning a revenge kill. You can attempt to talk him down a little, but Garrus is pretty intent on getting his revenge. Garrus's plan is to have you meet Sidonis out front of the lounge. Garrus will then snipe Sidonis while you have him distracted.

You now have a choice. When speaking to Sidonis, you can either step aside and let Garrus make the hit, or you can purposefully block Garrus's shot and warn Sidonis that he's a heartbeat away from death. If you decide to block Garrus, use the Paragon interrupt to keep Sidonis from walking away and right into Garrus's line of fire. If you speak to Sidonis long enough, you learn that Sidonis feels nothing but regret for his betrayal. Once Sidonis confesses his involvement with the death of Garrus's team, you have one last chance to step aside and let Garrus kill him. However, if you talk Garrus out of it, you earn a wealth of Paragon points. Either way, completing this mission earns Garrus's loyalty and unlocks his Armor-Piercing Ammo power.

Introduction

Training

Upgrades and Research

Walkthrough

Garrus: Eye For an Eye

Special Assignments

Planetary Database

Appendix

TALI: TREASON

Tali has just received a message from the quarian Migrant Fleet. She has been accused of treason against the Fleet. Tali has been called before the quarian Admiralty Board to stand for her alleged crimes—although Tali is not exactly aware of the charges. She needs to report to the flotilla to stand trial and defend her name. The sentence for treason is exile, and treasonous quarians are stripped of their names and forbidden from ever stepping foot on a quarian ship again. To help Tali, you must travel to the Migrant Fleet's current location in Raheel-Leyya in the Valhalla Threshold.

PRIMA Official Game Guide | primagames.com

Spoils of War
- **Credits:** 30,000
- **Palladium:** 2,000

LEGEND
1. Shala'Raan (first meeting)
2. Conclave
3. Shala'Raan (second meeting)
4. Admiral Gerrel
5. Admiral Koris
6. Veetor'Nara
7. Kal'Reegar
8. Admiral Xen
9. Shuttle Guard
10. Quarian Log
11. Repair Drone
12. Quarian Log
13. Quarian Log
14. Refined Palladium
15. Wall Console
16. Quarian Log
17. Dead Quarian
18. Model Flotilla Ship
19. Quarian Console
- Wall Safe
- Medi-Gel
- Datapad
- Computer
- Power Cell

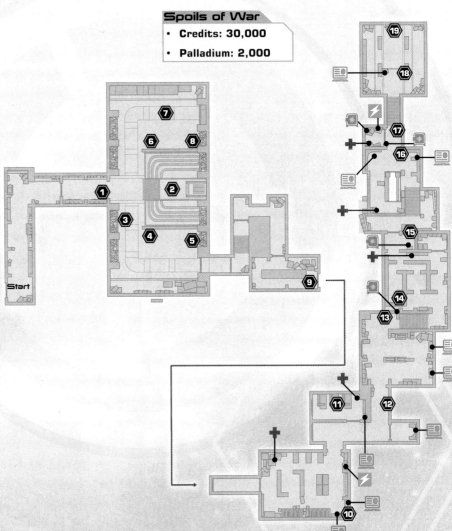

Objective 1: Go to Hearing

A quarian patrol led by Captain Kar'Danna greets you when you step off the *Normandy* and on to the quarian flotilla. The charges are finally revealed to Tali: She is accused of bringing active geth aboard the Fleet as part of a secret project. Tali denies the charges. She sent only inactive geth pieces back to her father, who was working on a project to develop an anti-geth weapon. Tali is told she must remain aboard the ship until the trial takes place.

If Legion is part of your squad on this mission, Captain Kar'Danna confronts you. It's possible to convince the quarians to allow Legion on board, but Shepard will face nothing but mistrust and hostility from the quarians in the geth's presence.

CAUTION

Tali meets Shala'Raan as you approach the hearing hall. She is Tali's aunt. She reveals that Tali has been stripped of her quarian fleet identity already and given a new name in accordance with her allegiance to the

Normandy. Losing her name is a great disgrace. Shala'Raan says that Tali will be represented by Shepard in the trial. Shepard will speak for her defense.

As soon as the trial begins, you discover this is not going to go well for Tali. The board that will pass judgment is mixed in their sympathies for Tali. The charge of bringing active geth onto a Fleet ship is serious. Tali counters that all of the geth pieces she sent back for research were harmless, but she is then asked to explain why the science vessel her father was serving on, the *Alarei*, was recently taken over by geth.

The board has considered destroying the *Alarei,* but you offer to help Tali retake the ship in an effort to clear Tali's name. The board agrees with your proposal. A shuttle will take you to the ship.

Before going to the shuttle, talk to the quarians at the conclave to learn more about quarian politics and the maneuvering that went into the trial.

Objective: Retake the *Alarei*

Geth Attack

As soon as you set foot on the *Alarei*, geth troopers attack. Duck into cover to avoid their shots, and return fire when the shooting pauses. A geth hunter enters the room and deploys combat drones to complicate the battle. Target the hunter and stay on it so it cannot use its cloak to sneak up on you. Direct everybody to bring down the hunter and then mop up the remainder of the troopers once the brute is on its back.

> **TIP**
>
> Make sure you expand points to upgrade Tali's talents, such as Combat Drone and AI Hacking. Those are powerful against geth.

Pick up medi-gel and heavy weapon ammo before moving on to the next lab. Hack the laptops to bank some credits.

> **NOTE**

Open the door next to the orange windows. There is not only medi-gel inside, but also a repair drone. Inspect the drone with Tali. She tells you about how she has been regularly sending geth parts back to her father. He was looking for evidence of new technology the geth had created beyond what the quarians built. Before leaving the small lab, hack the terminal for more credits.

Hack the monitor in the corridor next to the small lab to recover Cyclonic Particles. This upgrade improves geth shielding.

Introduction

Training

Upgrades and Research

Tali: Treason

Walkthrough

Special Assignments

Planetary Database

Appendix

In the next lab, look for a rampaging hunter. Take cover to hide from the hunter's blaster and then pop out to take shots at the shielded geth. Direct your squad to target the hunter to pick apart its shields. When the hunter is exposed, use any available biotics to throw the hunter around and eventually bring it to its knees. Hack the laptops and wall safe in the room for credits before moving up the stairs to the next lab.

Geth troopers filter into the lab as you enter. Duck down and cut through the troopers with return fire. Watch out for the troopers to go fanatical when they see you cut down one of their brethren. When a geth uses fanaticism, it gains shields, which prevent you from effectively using biotics on them. Geth hunters also storm the room. Let your squad mates concentrate on the hunters while you clean out the troopers, then work with them to finish off the hunters. After removing the geth, take the palladium and medi-gel off the counters and hack the safe just outside the door on the far wall.

Let Tali examine a monitor near the wall safe to learn more about her father's experiments on geth systems. It seems he may have been constructing geth and then using them as live subjects. Appeal to Tali's honor to earn Paragon points, or agree with the need to crush the geth by any means necessary for Renegade points.

The next set of stairs leads down into a geth stronghold. Geth hunters and troopers are waiting for you with guns pointed up the stairs. Use the crates at the top of the stairs as cover when raining bullets down on the geth. Try to keep the geth from coming up the stairs. It is much easier to cut down a trooper on the steps, though, than a hunter, since they have shields.

> Geth are not affected by incendiary ammo, but cryo ammo certainly slows them down. If you freeze a geth hunter, for example, you can then slam it into the ground and shatter it.
>
> **TIP**

After thinning the geth, fight your way down the stairs to clear out the remaining troopers on the lower floor.

> Hack the computers on the bottom floor to bank some credits. Pick up the nearby medi-gel.
>
> **TIP**

In the next hall, inspect the quarian corpse with Tali. It's her father. Tali is wracked with guilt and sadness. You can use a Paragon interrupt to comfort her. A final recording from Tali's father says a console deeper in the lab must be disabled to prevent the geth from accessing the geth network.

Open the door next to the body to locate medi-gel, power cells, and wall safes stocked with credits.

Objective 3: Disable Geth Console

Geth Console

When you enter the bright lab at the top of the steps beyond Tali's father, you spot a small platoon of inactive geth. You know they will not stay that way for long. Before stepping too far into the lab, stop at the desks to pick up a model flotilla ship (for the wall in your private quarters on the *Normandy*) and hack a computer for credits. After collecting the stuff, proceed into the lab to target the geth against the far wall, including a deadly geth prime.

Bring down the prime with heavy weapons while it is distracted by another member of your squad.

After wiping out the geth in the lab, use the console against the back wall to shut down any remaining geth elsewhere on the *Alarei*. Watch a video log of Tali's father discussing the assembly of live geth for research. His team had been using the geth parts she sent back for these experiments. It is an admission of guilt

that would clear Tali's name, but she is reluctant to use this evidence and damage her father's legacy.

The Trial

You and Tali stride into the conclave to announce that the *Alarei* has been retaken. But that's not enough for the board. Tali's loyalty is not what's in question right now—it's her judgment. You can now either give the board the evidence against Tali's father (breaking her heart but clearing her name) or deny the existence of any wrongdoing by her father, leaving Tali to take the blame.

If you turn over the evidence against Tali's father, you fail the loyalty mission.

CAUTION

If you have enough charm or intimidation, you can push back against the board for even questioning Tali's judgment. For defending her honor, Tali is loyal to you and her Energy Drain tech is unlocked, which helps drain enemy barriers.

For saving Tali's neck, you are given a Multicore Amplifier that increases tech power damage. Before returning to the *Normandy*, you can speak to the quarians in the conclave chamber. If you sent Veetor home with Tali on Freedom's Progress, you can also speak with him on the ship.

NOTE

Introduction · Training · Upgrades and Research · Walkthrough · Tali: Treason · Special Assignments · Planetary Database · Appendix

SAMARA: THE ARDAT-YAKSHI

Samara eventually opens up to you about the fugitive she was hunting on Illium—it is her daughter, Morinth. Morinth suffers from a rare genetic disorder that classifies her as an Ardat-Yakshi. She is able to destroy her partner's mind during sex. Samara finally has a lead on her location: Omega. The justicar needs to find Morinth and end her career as a serial killer.

Once you return to Omega, go see Aria in Afterlife. Aria is not surprised to hear there is an Ardat-Yakshi on the planet. There have been reports of bodies and minds drained in ways only the Ardat-Yakshi are capable of. Aria tells you that Morinth's last victim was a young human woman who lived in the tenements near Afterlife. You should start your hunt for Morinth there.

Spoils of War
- **Credits: 30,000**
- **Iridium: 2,000**

Use the Omega map on page 63 to help you find your way around during this mission.

NOTE

Objective 1: Go to Apartment

Diana

Approach the entrance to the slums where you once sought Mordin. Instead of entering the slums, though, turn left and duck inside a door to meet Diana, the victim's mother. Diana is convinced that her daughter, Nef, was murdered. Agree with her and tell her that you are looking for her killer. Diana offers some help: She gives you a general description of Morinth and explains how she lured her daughter into a world of sex and drugs. Diana lets you inspect Nef's room for any clues as to where she met Morinth.

Sympathize with Diana to earn Paragon points. If you are going Renegade, be cold.

TIP

You need to look through Nef's room for clues and to learn the password for the VIP section of Omega. Check

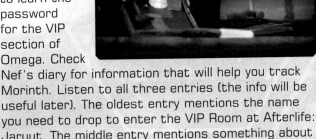

Nef's diary for information that will help you track Morinth. Listen to all three entries (the info will be useful later). The oldest entry mentions the name you need to drop to enter the VIP Room at Afterlife: Jaruut. The middle entry mentions something about dancing with Morinth and using Hallex, a drug. The newest entry says Morinth was taking Nef to her apartment. Samara is not surprised by Nef's diary—Morinth preys on creative people.

You also need to check the note in Nef's room. Nef mentions an elcor artist named Forta. That is a crucial clue for this mission.

NOTE

Samara recommends that this operation cannot just be a simple assault—Morinth will run if she spots Samara. You must lure Morinth out. Samara is convinced Morinth will be drawn to you; you have a spark that few do, and Morinth would love to be the one to extinguish it.

Objective 2: Go to VIP Room

Name-Dropper

Report to the bouncer outside the Afterlife VIP Room. Drop the name Jaruut to enter the club. Inside the VIP Room, Samara tells you that you must find Morinth and pique her curiosity. You must use courage. Hurt somebody in defense (she likes aggression, but won't be impressed if you pick a fight) or show skill working a crowd to get her attention. To convince Morinth to take you home, you must excite her with talk of violence and vigor. Do not show meekness or modesty. Above all, remember Nef's clues. Morinth likes dancing while on the drug Hallex. She likes the elcor sculptor Forta's work.

On your way into the club, somebody asks you for tickets to a concert by Expel 10. Apparently, an asari told him it was her favorite band and he wants to take her. Ask about the band. They are a sensory band. Their music worms its way into you. Remember this—it is a critical piece of information about Morinth.

Walk around the club, speaking to different patrons. Start with Horftin. He needs to help a friend who's an investigative reporter. Drop a password (in the right order) to her that lets her know she's in serious trouble and needs to bug out of the bar: terminal eternity. Help her out, but don't be too nice about it.

Vertin the turian is planning some muggings. If you have enough intimidation, you can get in his face and tell him that there will be no more muggings tonight. There is no way to charm your way out of this situation. Paying the turian off is an option, but it is far too meek to get Morinth's attention.

Speak to the bartender. If you have enough Paragon points to unlock the charm interaction in this conversation, you can convince the bartender to treat everybody to a drink. That will help prove to Morinth that you know how to work a crowd.

Morinth

Completing any of the above events with charm or intimidation attracts Morinth's attention. She slinks up to you and says you are the most interesting person in the bar. She invites you to her private booth. Morinth wastes little time probing you. Speak to Morinth about art, music, and travel—do not bring up family or the justicars. When talking about Morinth's preferred subjects, rely on your advance intel. When talking music, mention the band Expel 10. Claim that you enjoy Hallex. Discussing art? Mention Forta. When talking about vids, let slip that you enjoy the violent ones. Pretty soon, Morinth is convinced that you should be hers tonight. When she starts asking about power, don't shy away. Draw Morinth in by claiming that power is its own reward.

Objective 3: Distract Morinth

The Apartment

Morinth leads you back to her apartment. Keep Morinth interested while Samara closes in on the apartment and prepares to strike down her own daughter. Walk around the apartment and admire Morinth's belongings, like the sculpture of a krogan, a chess set, a pill bottle, or the sword on the wall.

> **TIP**
> Scan the assault rifle on Morinth's wall to pick up the Kinetic Pulsar upgrade, which improves assault rifle damage.

Morinth and Samara clash. There is little you can do but watch them fight. Samara is resolute in bringing her daughter to justice. Morinth tries to convince you to let her take Samara's place on the *Normandy*. You break Morinth's concentration, allowing Samara to get the upper hand. Samara executes her daughter. Samara has no desire to talk about what has happened, but she is now loyal to you. Her loyalty unlocks the Dominate power, which twists the minds of enemies to make them attack their friends..

Morinth cannot take it anymore. She closes in on you, ready to take you. Morinth asks you to look into her eyes. Tell her you want her. Tell her you would kill for her. Fortunately, before Morinth consumes you, Samara breaks into the apartment. She confronts her daughter, determined to stop her killing spree.

Morinth

If you have a high Renegade rating, you can force an incredible turn of events at the end of Samara's loyalty mission. You can actually allow Morinth to kill Samara and assume Samara's identity on your crew. Morinth is a powerful biotic, just like Samara. Morinth also has access to the Dominate biotic attack.

- **Weapon Training:** Assault Rifle, Heavy Pistol
- **Powers:** Pull, Throw, Dominate

How does having Morinth on your team change the story? Not at all. It just alters the personal dynamic of the team. Allowing Samara to be killed is a serious Renegade action that will go a long way toward solidifying your position as a ruthless leader.

Morinth Powers

Power	Description	Evolution 1	Evolution 1 Description	Evolution 2	Evolution 2 Description	Tip
Ardat-Yakshi	Boosts Morinth's combat skills, weapon damage, and health. Improves her power recharge time.	Erdua-Yakshi	Morinth's considerable stamina further increases her health and reduces the recharge time of her powers.	Malian-Yakshi	Morinth's consumption of lives further increases her health as well as her weapon damage.	Want to turn Morinth into a killing machine? Take the Malian Yakshi evolution
Dominate	Brainwash an organic enemy, forcing him or her to attack allies.	Enhanced Dominate	Your domination's duration is vastly increased against a single target.	Group Dominate	Your mastery of the mind is so complete you can affect multiple organics near one target point.	Morinth is the only team member with this power.

THANE: SINS OF THE FATHER

Spoils of War
- **Credits: 30,000**

Thane's losing fight with disease has him mulling over his life's mistakes. His greatest regret is the way he left things with his son, Kolyat. Thane was already a distant father, working off-world as an assassin, but after Kolyat's mother died, Thane placed the boy in the care of aunts and uncles and immersed himself in his work. He has not seen his son in many years.

> Use the Citadel map on page 59 to help you find your way around during this mission.
>
> **NOTE**

Thane has kept track of his son, though. And now Thane is sad to learn that his son has taken up the mantle of his father: He has become an assassin. Kolyat is on the Citadel right now, about to go on a hit. Thane worries that Kolyat is trading on his father's name for work and is getting in over his head. The drell wants you to go to the Citadel with him and stop his son from making the same mistakes as his father.

Objective 1: Investigate

This is not a combat mission. Instead, you must follow Kolyat's tracks on the Citadel in hopes of discovering his assignment and stopping him before he pulls the trigger. The first stop in your mission is the C-Sec office on Zakera Ward to see Captain Bailey.

Speak to Bailey

At the C-Sec office, Bailey helpfully dives into his files to look for any signs of drell on the ward. Sure enough, he finds news of a drell speaking to Mouse, a petty criminal. Mouse is not the person who assigned the hit to Kolyat, but he is a good lead for finding out who did. After talking to Bailey about Mouse, you must seek him out upstairs.

Speak to Mouse

Sure enough, Mouse is located on level 28 of the ward. He is standing near Rodam Expeditions. Approach Mouse and speak to him about Thane's son. He is surprised to see both you and Thane. Thane knows Mouse—he was a former contact for him on the Citadel. Mouse clams up, but you have a Renegade interrupt that forces him to speak up faster. You can also try a charm later in the conversation, to get the same information. Mouse agrees to let slip a name: Elias Kelham.

Return to Bailey

Drop the name Elias Kelham on Bailey's desk. Bailey is not too happy to hear that name. They have something of

an arrangement: Elias donates to C-Sec and Bailey gives him a little space. Bailey agrees to have Elias brought in. Bailey will have his men place Elias in a small interrogation room while making himself scarce. As Elias is brought in, word comes that the crook's lawyer is already en route to C-Sec. You have to work fast to get the needed information about Kolyat.

> You and Thane play the good cop/bad cop routine. You get to choose which one of you is the good cop.
>
> **NOTE**

Elias demands to see his lawyer right away and refuses to speak about the hit. If you choose to be the bad cop, you get a handful of Renegade interrupt opportunities to make him sing. If you are the good cop, you can use Paragon interrupts to offset Thane's ruthlessness. You do not have to take every interrupt, but it will accelerate the interrogation and get you the information you require to save Kolyat. The target is Joram, a turian politician running on an anti-human platform of cleaning up the Zakera Ward. That would put the squeeze on Elias's bank account.

Speak to Bailey about Joram. Joram may be running to clean up the streets, but he is mixed up in race politics—anti-human politics. Bailey calls a patrol car for you and Thane to get to the 800 blocks and stop Kolyat from assassinating Joram.

Objective 2: Tracking Joram

Once you reach the 800 blocks, Thane comes up with a plan to protect Joram and track his son. While Thane finds dark corners to hide in on the main floor of the block, you must sneak through the catwalks above to give the drell constant updates on Joram's position. Keep the turian in your sights and report in often so Thane can keep up on the main floor but not be seen. If you fail to report in and the turian disappears, Thane loses his son forever, and you fail this loyalty mission.

Catwalks

You begin the next segment of the mission in the catwalks above the 800 block. You can hear Joram spouting his anti-human propaganda below. While listening in, be sure to hack the datapad on the nearby desk for a Titan Pulsar upgrade, which increases heavy pistol damage. Watch Joram move through the ward. His krogan bodyguard is easy to track.

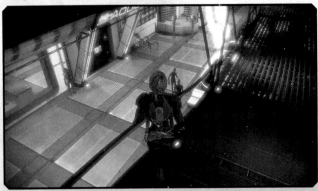

Keep moving along the catwalks. Thane is in constant contact. If you let Joram get too far ahead, Thane gets a little panicky. Consistently update Thane to keep the operation moving smoothly.

In the catwalks, you discover a human scout. You can use a Renegade interrupt to knock him out or you can talk to him, which eats up time.

If you kept up, you see Kolyat make his move on Joram. You call out, alerting Joram. Kolyat opens fire and shoots the krogan bodyguard while Joram runs. Kolyat pursues Joram and corners him in a dark room. Thane catches up to Kolyat before he pulls the trigger and kills the turian. Bailey and C-Sec are right behind him.

You must end this standoff peacefully to help Thane. There is a Paragon interrupt that makes you fire a shot right past Kolyat's head, distracting him so you can move in and knock the gun out of his hand. Once he's been disarmed, you try to facilitate the reunion between Thane and Kolyat. It is not an easy one—Kolyat holds a long grudge against his father.

Thane tells Kolyat that the reason he disappeared following his mother's death was that he was hunting the assassins who killed her. She was killed to hurt Thane, and he wanted to exact revenge. He eventually got it, but it took much longer than anticipated. When he returned, Kolyat was much older. Kolyat softens a little. Bailey intervenes and orders C-Sec to take Thane and Kolyat back to the station. They are to be given a private room for talking and as much time as they need. Resolving this matter makes Thane loyal to the team and unlocks his Shredder Ammo power.

DERELICT REAPER

Cerberus scientists have located a derelict Reaper ship in the Thorne system of Hawking ETA; the Reaper is believed to be over 37 million years old. The vessel is in orbit of the brown dwarf Mnemosyne. There is no outward sign of life on the ship, but energy signatures indicate a mass effect shield that keeps it from falling into the star. The science team that discovered the Reaper has ceased communications.

Shepard and the squad must infiltrate the Reaper ship and take the IFF so the *Normandy* can pass through the Omega 4 relay. Without it, the Collectors will continue to operate unhindered from their homeworld, able to continue striking human colonies without warning and without recourse.

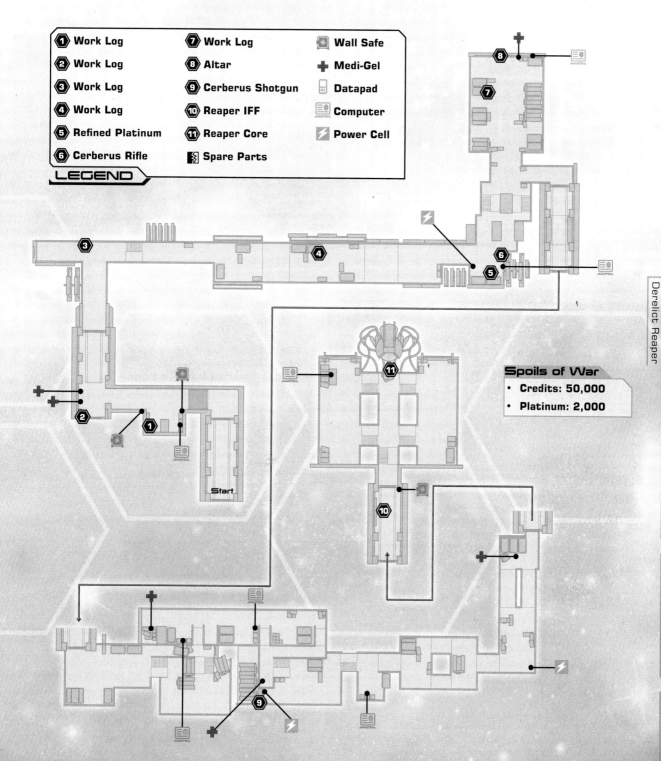

LEGEND

① Work Log	⑦ Work Log		Wall Safe
② Work Log	⑧ Altar	✚	Medi-Gel
③ Work Log	⑨ Cerberus Shotgun		Datapad
④ Work Log	⑩ Reaper IFF		Computer
⑤ Refined Platinum	⑪ Reaper Core		Power Cell
⑥ Cerberus Rifle	§ Spare Parts		

Spoils of War

- Credits: 50,000
- Platinum: 2,000

Start

Introduction · Training · Upgrades and Research · Walkthrough · Derelict Reaper · Special Assignments · Planetary Database · Appendix

Objective 1: Investigate Collector Ship

When Joker nears the Reaper, the crew discovers a second ship alongside of it. The profile fits a geth ship. It is not transmitting at all, but it gives an indication of why the science team stopped reporting in.

No Sign of Life

You and the squad disembark the *Normandy*, stepping into the science ship. There is blood on the walls. This is not necessarily a sign of the geth, which have been generally bloodless killers in previous attacks on human settlements and ships. Now you must explore the ship not just for the IFF, but for any sign of life.

There are two wall safes and a secure terminal down the hall to the left of the air lock. One of the wall safes and the terminal offer 2,000 credits. The other wall safe has 4,000 credits inside of it.

Activate one of the terminals to see a message from a Cerberus scientist. The effects of Reaper indoctrination have already begun to set in, unsettling the scientists.

At the end of the hallway, next to a medi-gel station, is another Cerberus terminal. Play the message. The team had begun taking samples of the Reaper. The scientists studying the samples from the Reaper were starting to act differently, just staring at the samples for hours on end, claiming to be "listening" to them.

When you pass through the door next to the medi-gel station, the entire ship shudders. It seems the Reaper might not have been as dead as originally thought. According to Joker, the Reaper has just put up kinetic barriers blocking the rest of the team on the *Normandy* from entering the science vessel or the Reaper. In order to get off the Reaper, you must shut down the generators that are keeping the Reaper alive.

EDI pinpoints the location of the core thanks to the energy spike from raising the barriers. There is a catch, though: Taking down the core will also shut down the mass field that has kept the Reaper from falling out of orbit. After destroying the core, the squad will not have very long to escape before they are doomed along with the Reaper.

Objective 2: Escape the Wreck

The door leads into the Reaper. Only a few steps of human technology remain. Once you step off the Cerberus bridge, you are completely enveloped by the Reaper. The signs of massacred human beings on the bridge are discomforting, to say the least. But there is no turning back now.

Seeking the Core

Before leaving the bridge and stepping all the way into the Reaper, watch the video log on the bridge terminal. Two Cerberus scientists are discussing their marriages. But something is wrong. Each believes himself to be married to the same woman. They both remember the same stockings. Why are they sharing memories?

As you work your way down to the bridge, you see the first stirrings of life: husks. Several husks pull themselves

up to the bridge and rush you. Quickly assign your squad to target the husks, and then unload your first clip, too. Stand your ground and try to keep the husks from reaching you on the upper level of the bridge. Since the husks have no armor or shields, biotics are effective for pushing them back. Pull can fling them off the bridge, and the recoil from Charge or Warp will also push them out of the way.

> Use the explosive containers on the bridge as bombs. When the husks near the containers, shoot them. There are explosive containers farther back on the bridge (closer to that first terminal with the shared memory log), so don't be afraid to fall back and let the husks swarm near the bombs.

TIP

Another video log on the bridge plays disturbing video. A scientist thinks he sees a gray shape moving out of a wall panel, but it vanishes when he looks directly at it.

As you near the corner of the Cerberus ship's bridge, more husks move into position. However, they are shot by an unseen assailant. The husks collapse and the shooting stops. You need to find the shooter—it could be a Cerberus survivor.

There is a good trove of pickups at the end of the bridge. There are not only clips and power cells, but also a crate of refined platinum and a Cerberus sniper rifle. When you scan the rifle, you receive the Scram Pulsar, which upgrades sniper rifle damage for the entire squad. Hack the terminal to pocket 3,500 credits.

Farther down the bridge, you encounter another pack of husks. Abominations mingle with the husks. Blast the abominations when they are surrounded by husks so that the resulting explosion damages them. You should also use the giant explosive

crate in the center of the area as a makeshift bomb, waiting until the husks swarm around it to detonate it. The explosion is powerful enough to rip apart any husk standing right next to the crate.

Introduction

Training

Upgrades and Research

Walkthrough Derelict Reaper

Special Assignments

Planetary Database

Appendix

If a husk gets close, knock it back with a melee attack and then finish it off with your weapon.

Before long, the husks and abominations are joined by a scion. The lumbering scion does not rush you. Instead, it lingers toward the back of the platform and releases its blast attack. The scion does not seem aware of the explosive crates on the bridge and often walks right next to them. Use the explosions to weaken the scion's considerable armor before you have to get close to finish it off.

When the scene calms, collect the clips around the bridge. Pick up the medi-gel near the terminals and then hack one to recover Lattice Shunting, a health booster. Before leaving the area (you need to bypass the locked door to the right), play the video log on one of the terminals. The scientists were truly starting to crack under the mental effects of the Reaper, calling it a god.

Fear the Reaper

Moving through the door allows you access to the actual Reaper, not just the outside area where the

Cerberus ship was docked. However, soon you see yourself through a scoped weapon. Something has you in its sights. But instead of shooting you, it snipes the husks sneaking up on you. Who is this unexpected ally on the Reaper?

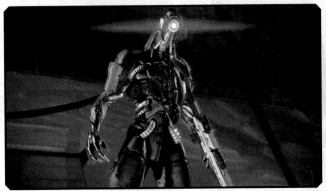

It's a geth.

Astonishingly, the geth sniper calls to Shepard by name, then slinks away. Soon, more husks arrive.

The husks pull themselves up from the depths of the ship. Shoot them as they clamber onto the platform. You have space behind you to fall back so the husks don't get too close, but make sure you do not back yourself completely into a corner. Mix up gunplay with biotics to eliminate the husks.

Charge is a great biotic attack to use against husks. The impact is strong enough to shatter their weak, unarmored bodies. Slam is also quite effective against husks.

More husks and abominations pull themselves up on the platforms. Shoot the abominations so that their explosions damage the husks.

As the husk raid subsides, a scion enters the picture. The lumbering monster moves toward you, fearless. Back off. If you have heavy weapons, use them to break down the scion's armor. Biotics are not necessarily effective against the scion right away, so hold off on using them. Instead, concentrate on keeping your distance and making shots count.

Move up the ramps to find clips, medi-gel, and a terminal. Hack the terminal for 3,000 credits.

There is another terminal farther down the bridge worth 3,500 credits.

When you drop back down to the main level of the ship, more husks and abominations rise from the floor below. Stay back and open fire as the husks gather themselves up. Unload on the explosive crate and explosive container on the platform. The explosions should tear apart a few of the husks and seriously weaken those nearby. As you clear out the husks, another scion shambles down the steps. Empty a few clips into the scion before it has a chance to unleash its attack.

> Incendiary ammo and cryo ammo are very effective on the husks.
> **TIP**

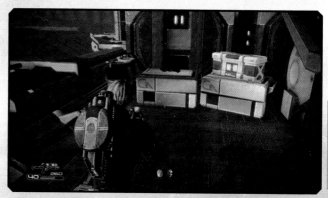

If you need more heavy weapon ammo for the scion, open the power cells crate behind you. There is a Cerberus shotgun to scan, too, which increases shotgun damage.

Hack the terminal at the top of the steps the scion used for 3,500 credits.

Introduction

Training

Upgrades and Research

Derelict Reaper

Walkthrough

Special Assignments

Planetary Database

Appendix

Walk down the ramp to the next area of the ship, but only to trigger the next husk wave. Pull back as the husks crawl into view, and then target them from a distance. The explosive containers on the floor are great crowd control, but you may wish to save them for the pair of incoming scions.

After collecting the power cells where the bridge turns to the left, look for more husks.

> Have Shockwave? Use it on the husks to knock them to the floor.
>
> **TIP**

More scions shuffle into the fray. Back away from the scions and let them move close to the explosive containers. The splash damage from these containers weakens the scions' armor, but you will need to use heavy weapons or your strongest normal weapon (the weapon with the most upgrades) to finish them off.

As soon as the last two scions are down, pick up the medi-gel from the crate at the end of the platform and bypass the locked door. It leads to a short corridor with a wall safe (2,500 credits) and a terminal.

The terminal reveals that the Cerberus team did indeed recover the IFF. Go through the next door to locate the Reaper core so you can get off this derelict before it's too late.

The Core

Inside the core chamber, the geth sniper is busy accessing the core and shooting husks that attempt to stop it. The geth is taken down just as you arrive, but not before using the terminal in front of the core to lower a barrier between you and it. You must now destroy the core in the center of the room. The core has a revolving shield on it. When the crackling core is revealed, you can unload on it. But when the shield moves across the front, you are far better served taking down the dozens of husks swarming the chamber.

A hackable laptop is to the left of the core, guarded by an abomination and some husks. The laptop is worth 1,000 credits. Don't go for it, though, until you have cleared the area. Otherwise, you risk having the hack disrupted and losing the credits.

The husks in this room use their numbers to overwhelm your squad. You cannot stay in one place for very long or the

husks will surround you. Move around the room, constantly putting distance between you and the horde, and pick them off until you eliminate them all.

Keep an eye on the core at all times. When the shield lifts, shoot the core. If you have any remaining heavy weapon ammo, drop it into the core to do maximum damage. However, any weapon will work here. Even the heavy pistol will damage the core—and if you have upgraded the weapon multiple times, you may be surprised by how much damage it (or any upgraded weapon) does.

When the core is almost destroyed, concentrate all of your fire on it. Let your squad keep the husks busy while you move around the floor and hammer the remainder of the core. No matter how many husks are in the room, as soon as the core has been destroyed, the battle ends.

The Escape

As soon as the core is ruined, the entire Reaper starts to shake. The mass field is failing. Your squad gathers around the geth that helped you earlier. Something was different about this geth. It spoke. It acknowledged you by name. No geth has been known to interact with a human before, much less save one. You take the geth back to the *Normandy*; you'll decide what to do with it later.

Outside, Joker brings the *Normandy* close. He opens the air lock. You throw the geth into the air lock while your squad holds off the last of the husks. Then, you jump, sailing through the warped gravity field. Joker pulls the *Normandy* away from the Reaper just as the derelict falls into the brown dwarf. It implodes as it reaches crush depth. You now have the IFF and a mysterious geth.

Back on the *Normandy*

The crew collects in the communications room to discuss the geth aboard the ship. It has been stored near EDI's AI core for now. Miranda is pleased with the discovery. She thinks that Cerberus could learn a lot by studying this advanced geth. Jacob dissents; he's been on the wrong end of geth attacks too many times to put his mistrust aside, no matter how unique this geth seemed back on the Reaper. You can choose whether to leave the geth dormant or activate and interrogate it.

> With great tech abilities like AI Hacking and Combat Drone, the geth would make an excellent addition to the team. If you activate the geth and complete its loyalty mission, though, a potential rift could develop between you and Tali. She is furious that there's a geth on board, and even holds the geth at gunpoint. If you have a high enough Paragon or Renegade rating, you can defuse this situation without alienating either crew member. However, without the charm or intimidate dialog options, you must make a choice between them. If you choose the geth over Tali, this shuts down a relationship with her.

NOTE

EDI comes over the comm and says that she has discovered how to integrate the IFF with the *Normandy*, but she advises caution. It is Reaper technology. You have a choice. You can either turn it on right away or allow EDI to further investigate the IFF, and she will tell you when it is ready to go online.

At this point, you can continue the main mission or complete any additional recruitment or loyalty missions. If you brought the geth aboard and want to test it, now is also a good time to go to EDI's core and switch on the geth.

Introduction

Training

Upgrades and Research

Derelict Reaper

Walkthrough

Special Assignments

Planetary Database

Appendix

NORMANDY ATTACKED/ LEGION

The Reaper IFF

Just as Shepard decides to go on the next mission, EDI says that it is time to test out the Reaper IFF. Joker recommends that Shepard and the squad use the shuttle for the mission; by the time they get back, he and EDI will have the IFF fully integrated with the *Normandy*. Shepard agrees and departs the *Normandy* with a squad.

However, something goes dreadfully wrong when the IFF is brought online. EDI discovers that the IFF has begun broadcasting the exact location of the *Normandy* to the Collectors. A massive Collector ship comes out of warp right on top of the *Normandy*. A virus emitted from the IFF has fully disabled the ship's defenses. The *Normandy* is helpless against the incoming Collector attack. EDI tells Joker that it is possible to save the *Normandy*, but he must get out of that pilot's chair and physically help her flush the virus from the system.

Save the *Normandy*

The crew of the *Normandy* prepares to be boarded. EDI implores Joker to give the AI control of the ship. Joker is skeptical as he knows of too many bad results when AI assumes complete control of anything. EDI says it can initiate countermeasures if Joker unlocks its sealed databases by hand. Joker must go into the depths of *Normandy* and access EDI's AI core.

However, Joker must avoid using any of the main corridors. The Collectors have boarded and are already wreaking havoc on the crew. The stasis swarms are freezing the crew, and the Collectors are dragging them off. If Joker follows the emergency floor lighting, EDI will lead him to a small maintenance tunnel in the science lab that will deposit him at EDI's core.

No Joke

Sure enough, EDI's emergency lighting leads to the secret tunnel. Follow the lighting away from the bridge and into the CIC. The crew is trying to hold back a praetorian that has broken through into the CIC. As the crew opens fire on the praetorian, duck through the door to the tech lab.

Inside the tech lab, look for the maintenance shaft to deck 3 at the back of the room. There is another praetorian attacking the *Normandy*'s drive core, but it cannot break through the window into the lab. Crawl down the ladder to reach deck 3, the crew deck. One of the crew tells you that the crew deck is

crawling with Collectors. He will try to cover you so you can reach the AI core in the medical lab. Follow the lighting on the floor. The crew member doesn't last long against the Collectors. When you pass the elevator, a scion is dragging another *Normandy* crew member away. You're almost to the medical lab.

Move through the medical lab and into the AI core room. Access the terminal inside the core to give EDI control over the *Normandy*. Next, EDI requests that you go to the engineering deck and reactivate the primary drive. This requires another dive into the maintenance tunnels.

Follow the lights on the floor to pass through engineering and reach the main drive. As you walk, EDI explains the plan to save the ship. Just as the drive comes back online, EDI will open the air locks and eject the Collectors when the ship enters warp. This will not injure the crew as they are already gone. The Collectors have taken them all.

Access the terminal in front of the core to bring the drive back up. When the drive is functional, EDI ejects the Collectors and enters warp, blasting away from the Collector ship. When the ship is a safe distance away, EDI sends a message out to Shepard's shuttle and informs the commander of the dire situation on the *Normandy*.

Shepard's Back

Shepard and the squad return to the *Normandy*. Miranda berates Joker for losing the entire crew and almost the ship, but EDI informs her that it was not Joker's fault. Nobody saw the bad code in the IFF. Fortunately, EDI and Joker have completely flushed any remnants of it from the system. The *Normandy* is no longer transmitting its position to the Reapers.

Joker says that with the IFF now online, the *Normandy* can pass through the Omega 4 relay. Shepard can now go  straight for the relay, continue any outstanding recruitment missions, or fulfill any loyalty requests from the crew. Joker's work on EDI's core also unlocked some new conversation options with EDI.

If you make the decision to activate the geth, it joins the crew. The geth's loyalty mission—A House Divided—is optional. However, the first part of the walkthrough section does deal with the conversation following the geth activation and the acquisition of its name, Legion.

NOTE

Legion: A House Divided (see map on next page)

Once in the AI core, Shepard can awaken the geth salvaged from the derelict Reaper. The reactivated geth speaks to Shepard, though EDI erected a field between the two to keep the geth contained in the event it turns hostile. Because the geth are a collective, it constantly refers to itself as "we," despite it currently being cut off from the rest of the geth. As part of this newfound individuality, the geth is given a name by EDI: Legion, in reference to the famous Biblical verse, "My name is Legion, for we are many."

The existence of the heretics implies that there is a greater degree of free will to the geth programming than originally thought. If the geth were truly a collective, then majority rule would have prevented any alliance with Saren. The use of the word "heretic" also has religious implications. The geth recognize a basic philosophy or set of core beliefs that the actions of the minority betrayed.

NOTE

The discovery of the heretic geth completely upends all previous assumptions about the geth. The geth and most of the Citadel species actually have a common goal: survival. This has far-reaching potential. Shepard agrees to have Legion join the crew. Together they will fight the Reapers.

Legion explains that there is a growing schism between the heretics and the mainstream geth. The heretics are a small portion of the geth. The majority of the geth have largely kept to themselves (Legion says that the geth believe all intelligent life should command its own destiny) while the heretics are those that have lashed out against humanity. The schism occurred when some of the geth were assigned to study the Reapers, which the geth called the Old Machines. The geth heretics decided to worship the Old Machines and agreed to help them create a new future for the geth. The remainder of the geth oppose the Reapers because they understand that the geth and the Reapers, while both machines, are not the same. The geth fall outside the Reapers' plans for continued dominance.

But first, Legion wishes for Shepard to go to the Heretic Station, which is just beyond the Perseus Veil and in geth space. Legion says that the heretics have developed a geth virus that will be spread with the help of the Reapers. This virus will "convert" the rest of the geth to the programming of the heretics. The IFF is already online, so this is an optional mission right now. However, resolving the geth heretic situation could have major repercussions in the galaxy in addition to solidifying Legion's loyalty to the team.

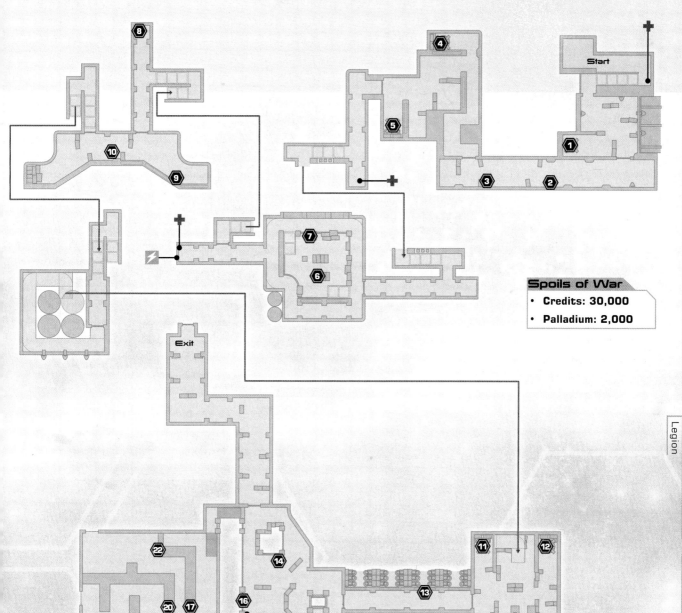

Spoils of War
- Credits: 30,000
- Palladium: 2,000

LEGEND

1. Geth Hub
2. Inactive Rocket Drone
3. Inactive Rocket Drone
4. Geth Hub
5. Geth Hub
6. Inactive Rocket Drone
7. Inactive Rocket Drone
8. Refined Palladium
9. Geth Terminal
10. Inactive Rocket Drone
11. Geth Hub
12. Geth Hub
13. Geth Servers
14. Inactive Rocket Drone
15. Inactive Rocket Drone
16. Geth Terminal
17. Inactive Rocket Drone
18. Inactive Rocket Drone
19. Inactive Rocket Drone
20. Inactive Rocket Drone
21. Inactive Rocket Drone
22. Inactive Rocket Drone
➕ Medi-Gel
⚡ Power Cell

Objective 1: Infiltrate Heretic Station

When you arrive on the Heretic Station, you learn that the heretic virus is now complete and could be relayed to the non-heretic geth at any point. Legion says there are now two options. The virus could be repurposed to program the heretics to shed their allegiance to the Reapers and "think" like the rest of the collective. Or, the station could simply be destroyed, taking the virus and all heretics on board with it. The choice will be yours if you can reach the main core of the station.

> Don't forget to allocate Legion's squad points when you start this mission. Legion has some excellent skills, such as AI Hacking, which lets it reprogram heretics to attack their own kind, and Combat Drone, which releases a small battle robot to help with the fight.

TIP

Legion has deployed data noise to the programming aboard the Heretic Station. The geth programming will busy itself to scrub the noise from the system, thus allowing you to move through the ship undetected. However, there are more conventional alarm systems in place.

Look for green bands along the floor—these are data streams. Avoid stepping on them. If you step on one of the bands, the geth along the band will activate and attack.

Silent Infiltration

Unfortunately, the only way out of the first room in the Heretic Station requires you to step over a data stream to reach the door. Before doing so, look to the right of the door. Three geth are hooked into a geth hub: two geth troopers and one geth hunter. You can get the drop on these geth by attacking first. However, as soon as a single shot hits one of the geth, all three activate. Make that first shot count, for instance by unloading your heavy weapon into the back of the geth hunter.

After eliminating the geth hooked up to a hub, destroy the hub. Salvage the hub to earn 3,000 credits. Use this technique throughout the Heretic Station.

Legion explains how the geth hubs work. They are mobile platforms separate from the geth network. Normally, attacking one geth would filter out to all others. Take this moment to further question Legion about the heretics and the shared geth experience. Legion explains how all geth see the same thing with the same eyes, but their perception is what makes them different. That perception is then uploaded into the collective software.

The geth are machines, so don't bother using incendiary ammo or attacks in this station. Stick to cryo and shredder ammo.

CAUTION

In the next room, Legion points out some inactive rocket drones. You can assume control of these drones, but the drones will only "fight" for you for a few seconds before self-destructing. So, make sure to activate the drones when the battle is just about to start. Otherwise, the drones will self-destruct before the first geth shows its head.

However, if you open the door at the end of the hall, a geth hunter steps out. Draw the geth hunter into the corridor with the drones so they will attack with their rockets, shattering the hunter's shields.

The next room is lined with data streams. These streams lead to two geth hubs. The streams are not linked. The stream closest to the door leads to a geth hub to your left (just as you enter). The data stream across the room (it starts along the wall on the right) hooks into a geth hub against the far wall. In a firefight, it will be easy to accidentally step on the second data stream and wake all of the geth in the room.

Because of the low gravity in the station, using biotics to throw the geth around is effective.

Use Legion's AI Hacking power to turn the geth against each other. Depending on how much you advance the skill, the hack can last up to a few seconds. You can use the hacked geth to attack its brethren, then finish it off when its back is turned. After all, that geth will turn its gun on you when the hack wears off.

TIP

Tear apart the geth in the room with a mixture of gunplay and biotics. When the coast is clear, sweep the room and salvage the hubs for credits.

When you move into the next corridor, take cover and attack the geth troopers. If you destroy one, expect the other to use its fanaticism to raise shields and become a tougher target. There is medi-gel at the end of the corridor. After collecting it, head up the ramps to the right.

More geth troopers occupy the corridor at the top of the ramps.

Introduction

Training

Upgrades and Research

Legion

Walkthrough

Special Assignments

Planetary Database

Appendix

Crucible

The next chamber is silent. There are multiple rocket drones on top of walls. Wait to activate these drones until you step far enough into the room to activate the geth guards. Geth hunters fan across the room, fearlessly marching toward you with guns outstretched. Once the geth show themselves, use the drones.

Stay along the edges of the room. The drones will pepper the geth hunters with rockets. Pound the geth from above with guns until the shields go down, and then direct biotic attacks at them.

Not all geth hunters move through the center of the room. Look for at least one geth hunter to track you along the outer edge.

The rocket drones will not attack you, but if you are close enough to a geth hunter when the drone strikes, you risk getting hit with splash damage.

CAUTION

At the conclusion of the battle, sweep the room to pick up clips. Leave through the door on the opposite side of the room from the one you came through. There are power cells and a medi-gel at the corner in the hall. Collect them and then use the ramps to drop farther into Heretic Station.

When you reach the bottom of the ramps, turn away from the door to collect a crate of refined palladium. There are 2,000 units inside.

We've Been Spotted

More geth lurk just beyond the door at the bottom of the ramp. When you step inside, a geth hunter initiates a cloak and two geth troopers flank. There is cover immediately inside the door, but you should also hack the rocket drone so it hammers the geth. Once the geth are down, turn around and hack the geth terminal along the window bay. The terminal unlocks the Cyclonic Particles upgrade, which increases geth shield strength—fortunately, just for the geth in your squad.

After dropping the geth, exit the room and ease down the ramps. The next room is lined with data streams, so watch your step. Follow the data streams to the bottom of this chamber. When you reach the locked door, look to the left and the right. There are twin geth hubs, each with two geth hunters and a geth trooper. Stepping on the data stream wakes them, but so does a shot. The two hubs are linked, so firing on one alerts the other. Pick a target and then unload. Get a few free shots in before the geth move on your position.

The geth hunters are tough, but do not ignore the geth troopers at their expense. If one of your squad destroys a geth trooper while you are not looking, you may turn around to find a fanatic on your back.

If you have biotics at your disposal, use them whenever you eliminate the shields of any of the geth. Slam, for example, will finish off a trooper.

In such close quarters, the geth hunters will not rely on their cloaking. It's hard to hide in such a narrow area

and make it effective. Instead, these hunters are rather brutish—getting right up in your face. If you have special ammo like cryo, use it to defeat the hunters. Cryo ammo will freeze a geth. The frozen geth then lifts off the ground. Keep firing and you can shatter the frozen geth, finishing it off no matter how much health it had left.

> Don't forget to salvage those geth hubs. Easy credits!
> **TIP**

Eliminating all of the geth in the room unlocks the door. Exit and walk alongside the geth servers. Ask Legion about the servers. Legion explains that these are not like the hubs. These servers contain the programming for thousands upon thousands of geth and a portion of the accumulated heretic memories. As Legion looks at the servers, it discovers that the heretics have truly broken ranks with the rest of the geth. The heretics have been spying on the rest of the geth. This implies that the heretics have disconnected part of their programming from the collective. That is a new development for geth, which normally share everything with the collective.

Objective 3: Defend the Core

When you leave the server window, you locate the main terminal, which will allow Legion to either rewrite the heretic code or initiate the station's destruction. No matter which you choose, you still have to delete the virus from the system. Legion says he can do that, but it will take time. While the virus is being purged, all geth on the station will become aware. They will attack, filing into this room to stop you. You must hold the room until the virus has been scrubbed.

Fortunately, there are several rocket drones in the room that you can hack when the geth do attack. Wait until the geth enter and get close enough to the drones to use them.

Wave after Wave

The geth come through the room below the terminal. You can move down into the chamber. Only the geth can come up those ramps and attack you on the upper floor. However, you do have a good view of the lower floor and can get off some great shots on the geth. Be sure to use the rocket drones to soften up the first and second waves of geth that storm into the room.

The first wave is just geth troopers. These are not difficult to manage. However, wave two adds geth rocket troopers to the mix. These geth are much deadlier, thanks to their rocket launchers. When you see these spreading across the lower floor, target them first. Weaken them so that when they do reach the upper floor, you can finish them off before they strike with their rockets.

There is a single medi-gel next to the geth terminal.

TIP

The third wave of heretics is made up of geth hunters and geth troopers. These hunters quickly weave through the servers on the bottom floor and

take to the ramps. Deliver what damage you can from above and then fall back to repel the geth hunters as they come up the ramps. The geth troopers use the distraction of the hunters to fan out. Move from one target to the next, clearing them out systematically instead of just shooting at anything that moves.

Surviving this onslaught is not easy. You need to keep up your own shields by diving into cover whenever you see that you are running low. Let those shields regenerate before trying anything too brave.

NOTE

Once the battle ends, Legion returns to the terminal. It is now time to make the choice. You can either use the rewritten virus to reprogram the heretics or destroy all of them aboard the Heretic Station. Neither path is without risk. If you choose to rewrite the heretics, they will shed the allegiance to the Reapers, but their experiences will join the collective. That has potential for being trouble down the line. If you destroy the station, just know that though this is the central station, there are other heretics out there. They will not leave this attack unanswered. Neither result is an immediate problem—it's just something to think about before telling Legion what to do.

Rewriting the code and saving the heretics results in Paragon points. Destroying the station is a major Renegade action.

NOTE

Either way, you are going to need to do some running. If you opt for the destruction, you need to flee the

station before it blows up. If you rewrite the virus, you need to escape before a powerful EMP rips through the station as the new code is broadcast. You have three minutes to exit the station.

Escape the Station

When you initiate the move on the servers, the countdown begins. You must rush through the station and return to the *Normandy* before the countdown ends. The path through the station is clearly marked and easy to navigate, but it is not without threat. Geth attack as you rush through the station. Geth troopers, for example, are just outside the door to the server room.

Keep moving! A geth prime around the next corner will slow you down. If you have any heavy weapon

ammo left, use it to rip through the geth prime's shields and armor. The geth prime is a real monster and will not budge (unless you budge it with biotics after lowering its defenses).

The geth prime releases combat drones to slow you down.

After defeating the geth prime, make a break for the door at the end of the corridor. This leads directly to the *Normandy*. Joker pulls away from the Heretic Station just in time. Legion is now loyal to the team, and his Geth Shielding power is unlocked.

Back on the *Normandy*

After the Heretic Station has been dealt with, Shepard must deal with a more immediate geth problem aboard the ship. Tali has found out that a geth is on board and is furious. She has Legion at point-blank range in the AI core. She discovered Legion uploading information about the quarian flotilla to the geth collective. Legion says that just as the quarians are working to protect themselves from the geth, the geth must also be free to do the same. Shepard has multiple choices for ending this stand-off.

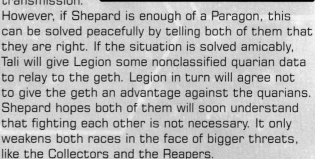

Shepard can either tell Tali to stand down, which sorely disappoints her, or tell Legion to cease the transmission. However, if Shepard is enough of a Paragon, this can be solved peacefully by telling both of them that they are right. If the situation is solved amicably, Tali will give Legion some nonclassified quarian data to relay to the geth. Legion in turn will agree not to give the geth an advantage against the quarians. Shepard hopes both of them will soon understand that fighting each other is not necessary. It only weakens both races in the face of bigger threats, like the Collectors and the Reapers.

> If this was the final loyalty mission, then you are ready for the Omega 4 relay. If you have outstanding loyalty missions, you can undertake those now to unlock extra powers. The battle on the other side of the Omega 4 relay is the toughest yet. Consider making additional upgrades. If you need minerals, use this opportunity to go on mining excursions across the galaxy to excavate the needed elements. Once you are ready, plot a course for the Omega 4 relay.

NOTE

ENDGAME

Omega 4 Relay

The team is complete. The IFF is online. The *Normandy* and her crew are ready to pass through the Omega 4 relay and take the fight to the Collectors. In the last thousand years, no ship has ever passed through the Omega 4 relay and returned. The *Normandy* might not be the first to survive, but there is no other course of action left. The Collectors, powered by their Reaper alliance, will continue to attack humanity until their ends are met. The only way to learn their reason for targeting humanity is to travel through the Omega 4 relay.

As soon as Shepard charts a course for the Omega 4 relay, Joker says it will take approximately two hours for the *Normandy* to arrive. During these hours, Shepard and the crew must make final preparations for the journey. That includes fulfilling any last wishes, since there is a very good chance that this is a one-way ticket.

Before Shepard passes through the relay, the commander has one last hologram conference with the Illusive Man. The Illusive Man is sorry to not have more intelligence on what is just beyond the relay, but he wants to express his gratitude for all you have done so far and what you are risking to go through with this mission.

The IFF allows the *Normandy* to pass through the Omega 4 relay. Immediately on the other side of the relay, the *Normandy* encounters a minefield of debris. Joker decelerates as best as he can to avoid slamming into any of the ghost ships and wrecks floating through space. EDI pinpoints the location of the Collector base amid the field of debris. But as the *Normandy* approaches the base, the Collector's first line of defense springs into action. Small orbs called oculi tail the *Normandy*, blasting it with laser fire.

> **NOTE**
>
>
>
> If you have pursued a romance with any of the squad members, now is when that relationship is consummated. For example, if you played as a male Shepard and were extra friendly to Miranda, always taking her side in arguments (such as when she and Jack were fighting), Miranda will surprise you at the CIC once you give Joker orders to head for the relay.

Hull Breach

An oculus slams into the *Normandy*, tearing through the shields. You must rush to the cargo hold and destroy this interloper. Select your squad and weapon loadout. The action then automatically moves to the cargo hold.

Debris Field

The debris field batters the *Normandy*. You may lose squad members during the pounding this ship takes en route to the Collector station, depending on whether or not you made any upgrades to the *Normandy*. There are three possible upgrades detailed in the "Upgrades and Research Projects" chapter. For every upgrade you did not make, you will lose one team member. Your squad choices affect who is lost. For example, when the drive core is hit, the resulting explosion may vaporize Tali if you did not select her for the squad to fight the oculus. However, if you do choose Tali for the squad, Legion might be destroyed when the drive core fails.

The oculus twists and turns inside the hold, cutting through everything in its path with its powerful red laser. The laser is its only weapon, but it slices through shields and armor within seconds. You must move from cover to cover to avoid getting caught by the beam. The oculus does not have a barrier or any health; you just need to cut through its thick armor to defeat it.

> You can damage the oculus at any time. You do not need to look for a weak point. Just point and shoot.

NOTE

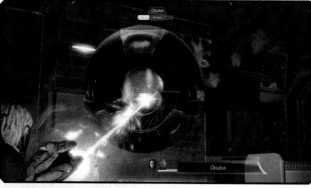

The easiest way to bring down the oculus is with heavy weapons. There are multiple crates of heavy weapon ammo around the hold, as well as medi-gel near the rear of the hold.

> Many crates in the hold are fragile. Seek cover behind sturdy objects like pillars.

CAUTION

The oculus darts around the hold, sometimes buzzing out of the room for a few seconds before cutting back inside.

When the oculus departs, use those few seconds to collect spare ammo and medi-gel. Since the oculus is only armored, you are better off using weapons to finish it off; biotic attacks do very little to the oculus.

Another oculus breaks through the hull and moves into the cargo hold. This oculus is just like the first one—all armor and one killer laser. Track the oculus through the cargo hold, ducking behind heavy objects to avoid incoming laser blasts.

> Watch out for explosive containers in the hold. They are on the ground, so if one blows, it will injure only you and the squad, not the oculus.

CAUTION

Introduction

Training

Upgrades and Research

Omega 4 Relay

Walkthrough

Special Assignments

Planetary Database

Appendix

Crash Landing

When the *Normandy* finally clears the debris field, you have a straight shot at the Collector base. A Collector ship flies out of the base, revealing just how massive the Collector home truly is. The Collector ship, which absolutely dwarfs the *Normandy*, is tiny compared to the base. The Collector ship opens fire on the *Normandy*. The ship is hit. If the shields were not upgraded, another team member is killed in the explosion.

Joker moves the *Normandy* into an attack position and rushes the Collector ship as it fires. The *Normandy* delivers a deadly blow at the heart of the Collector ship. When the Collector ship explodes, the force knocks the *Normandy*'s mass effect field generators offline. The *Normandy* is on a collision course with the Collector base. EDI advises everybody to brace for impact. The *Normandy* crashes into the Collector station. EDI says it will take a while for the ship to be in flying shape again. It is time for you to lead your squad into the Collector station and end their reign of terror on the human colonies.

> **CAUTION**
> If you did not upgrade the *Normandy*'s armor, you lose another team member during the crash landing.

Collector Station (see map on next page)

The Collector station on the other side of the Omega 4 relay is a monster. Because no ship has ever successfully made it through the Omega 4 relay, the Collectors do not have much of a defense system in place. After the *Normandy* crashes into the station, the Collectors themselves must take up arms to defend their base.

Prior to departing the *Normandy*, you must come up with a plan of attack. EDI is able to project a schematic scan of the Collector station. The station's weak spot is found at the main control center. The location of the *Normandy* crew and any remaining colonists is in the central chamber. There is no easy way to access the crew. It is determined that the team must split up. Two squads will keep the Collectors busy, increasing the chances of you getting through to the crew in time.

At this point, you must make some critical decisions about the makeup of your squad. You may have already lost some team members. When you select squad members for special assignments inside the Collector station, you take them out of rotation for the overall mission. First, you must select which squad member will infiltrate the locked doors that divide you from the crew. A tech specialist is needed for this assignment. Your likely choices are Mordin, Garrus, Jacob, and Legion.

After selecting the specialist to infiltrate the locked doors, you must then choose who will lead the second fire team. Miranda volunteers, but the choice is ultimately yours. You will meet up with the second fire team in the central chamber. Make your choice based on the available team members that you have established absolute loyalty with.

Once the roles have been assigned, it's time to head out. You can choose whether or not to give a speech to the team before leaving the *Normandy*. If you decide to offer a small speech, you have the choice of making it a rousing call to victory or a hard-edged demand for revenge and punishment.

This is a total **spoiler alert**, so if you do not want to know the fate of some of the team members, stop reading this note right now. The tech specialist you choose to unlock the door will die unless you have won their loyalty. The level and skills of the specialist are not a factor in their success. So, while placing a loyal team member in the tube will take their upgraded skills and powers out of circulation for part of the mission, at least you can do so with the knowledge they will not perish, unlike a team member whose loyalty was not won.

NOTE

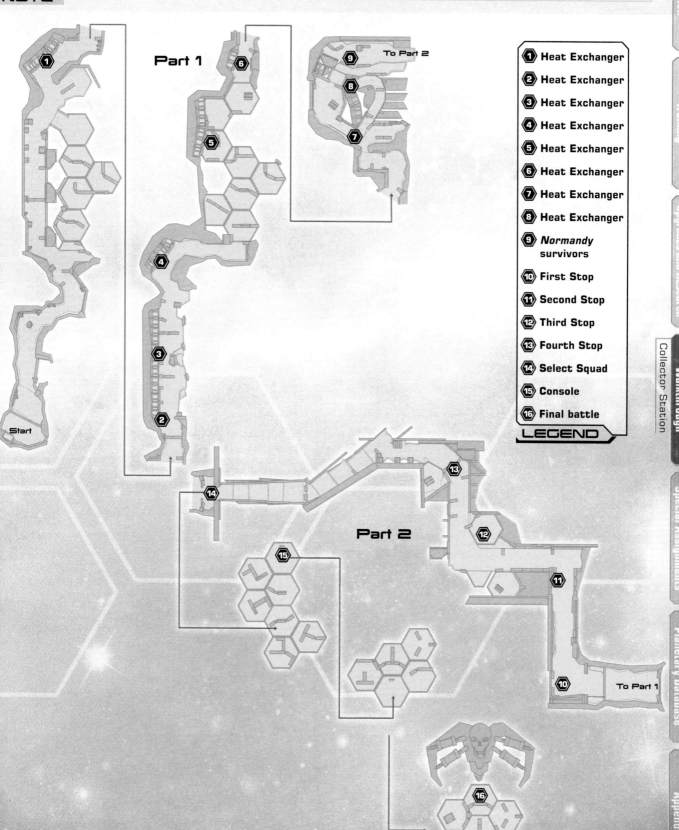

Part 1

To Part 2

Part 2

Start

LEGEND

1. Heat Exchanger
2. Heat Exchanger
3. Heat Exchanger
4. Heat Exchanger
5. Heat Exchanger
6. Heat Exchanger
7. Heat Exchanger
8. Heat Exchanger
9. *Normandy* survivors
10. First Stop
11. Second Stop
12. Third Stop
13. Fourth Stop
14. Select Squad
15. Console
16. Final battle

To Part 1

Introduction

Training

Upgrades and Research

Walkthrough
Collector Station

Special Assignments

Planetary Database

Appendix

Objective 1: Open Valves

The Collector station is quiet at first, but you know that the Collectors are on their way. The specialist selected to move through the tunnels will need your constant help throughout the first portion of this mission. You must balance assisting the specialist with pushing back against the Collectors charged with driving you out of the station.

First Contact

As you enter the station, the specialist in the tunnel reports that it is quite hot. There are no hostiles in the tubes, but the rising temperature will be a real problem. You need to open a series of eight valves along the tube of the specialist to survive. If the specialist dies, the mission ends in failure.

It doesn't take long before you meet your first batch of Collectors. The drones spread out across a hexagonal platform, just like those you found in the Collector ship. Target the drones with weapons, but mix in biotic attacks. Powers like Pull and Slam seriously injure the unshielded drones, softening them up so you can finish them off with bullets.

Watch for reinforcements. If you push forward (or use a passage to the left to flank), you can pick them off as they fly down to the surface. Biotic attacks work on the flying Collectors.

After the first batch of Collectors, you locate the first panel that opens a valve in the tube. Activating the panel opens

the locked door in the tube, allowing the specialist to progress. However, all locked doors in the rest of the tube need to be opened within a time limit. If you leave your specialist at a door for too long, they perish. Use the on-screen timer and the specialist's vitality meter to keep tabs on the situation.

> The Collectors will try to slow you down. However, you do not have to kill every Collector around a panel to activate it.

NOTE

As you reach the second valve, more Collectors arrive. Cut them down before Harbinger can possess any of them. If the specialist gets in trouble, you must rush past the possessed Collector and access the panel to keep the specialist alive.

The third valve is also guarded by Collectors. If you're fast, you can yank the Collectors out of the air with biotics before they land and attack. When dealing with a possessed Collector, though, you must rely on gunplay and disruptive biotics like Overload and Warp. Follow the tube to reach the fourth valve, which is unguarded. The specialist continues down the tube as you work your way to the fifth valve control panel.

The fifth control panel is across a busy field of Collectors. The Collectors flutter down from the ceiling to take up their attack positions. Wound as many as you can as they fly down, and then mop up the rest on

the floor. You must advance while attacking. You cannot just hold the line when the Collectors first attack. Your specialist cannot last for the entire battle with the Collectors. You must rush up and hit the panel. Then, turn back and shoot the Collectors from behind as you move toward the sixth panel, which is right beneath the tube on the far side of the chamber.

*Before reaching the seventh valve, you must slash through a small **Collector** patrol. Hammer the drones with available biotics and then finish them off with weapons.*

In the next chamber, you encounter more than just Collector drones. There are Collector assassins that unleash particle beam attacks, along with Collector guardians. Use Overload to break down their shields (if you have access to that biotic power). You cannot use other practical attack biotics like Slam and Pull while these beasts still have their shields up. Watch for Harbinger to possess one of the group right away. If you can juggle the possessed Collector with the rest of the squad, target as many of the remaining Collectors as possible as you fight toward the next panel. Deny Harbinger another vessel to possess.

> Use Charge to quickly cross the distances between the panels. Target a Collector near a panel. The biotic power slams you into the Collector and deposits you right next to the panel.
>
> **TIP**

You do not need to clear out every Collector in the chamber. As long as you access the eighth panel, this part of

the mission ends in success. Your squad survives the first Collector battery and you meet up with the second fire team.

The teams find the *Normandy* survivors. They are in pods linked up to giant tubes that stretch up into the

ceiling. The team races to break the crew and colonists out of the pods, but the Collectors activate the pods. One of the survivors is liquefied before your very eyes. Frantically, the team breaks open the rest of the pods and pulls the crew to safety.

Among the survivors is Dr. Chakwas. She informs you that the Collectors have been processing humans down

into a paste, which is sent via the tubes to another part of the station. The path to the heart of the station is thick with swarms. There are too many for Mordin's countermeasures. You need an alternative plan. A biotic could produce a force field that grants safe passage. However, this biotic would be unable to fight while erecting the barrier. You must select a biotic from your squad. When you choose a team to join you on the way to the center of the station, that biotic will not be an option.

Chakwas and the survivors are in no condition to fight. Fortunately, Joker and EDI have repaired enough of the

Normandy to pick them up. You have another choice to make. You can either send the survivors on their own to reach the *Normandy* or send them with one of your squad as a guard. The decision results in Paragon or Renegade points and the removal of one more team member. Whoever is sent with the survivors cannot be used again for the rest of this mission.

Introduction

Training

Upgrades and Research

Walkthrough — Collector Station

Special Assignments

Planetary Database

Appendix

Objective 2: Escort Biotic Specialist

After the survivors leave to find the *Normandy*, you must continue through the ship and discover where those tubes of human genetic material are going. That's the location you must reach to also destroy the station. Moving through the swarms is slow. Your biotic cannot run while holding up such a powerful barrier. It drains them physically, slowing them down. You must move methodically with the biotic, staying within the barrier.

Under the Dome

Follow your biotic along the path to the center of the station. The biotic does a good job keeping the swarms back, but there isn't much they can do about the incoming Collectors. When you hear the heads-up about Collectors, look to the skies. Blast the Collectors as they attempt to land. Use biotic attacks to push them to the ground or fling them aside.

The biotic has to stop. While the biotic rests, you can attack the Collectors. The Collectors fire upon you from the left, down in a clearing. You have the height advantage, though, which makes it easier to pop off headshots and arc biotic attacks over the barricades below that the Collectors use as cover. There will be a possessed Collector among them (possibly more if you do not eliminate the other potential vessels). It stays back at first, giving you ample time to duck its attacks. Return fire and cut through its barrier and armor.

> **TIP**
>
> Overload disrupts the possessed Collector's barrier. It is one of the few effective biotic attacks on this enemy.

When the Collectors are down, tell your biotic it is time to move. As the squad inches down a ramp, you spy movement on the floor. Husks and abominations pull themselves up to the surface on the platform and rush the biotic barrier. Shooting the abominations makes them explode, which is a good way to keep the husks back. You should never step outside the barrier to attack. You need to target the husks from afar. If any do breach the barrier, push them back with a melee attack and then finish them off with guns.

Your biotic takes refuge behind a pillar when a new wave of Collectors begins to attack. Look across the

area to the right at the incoming Collectors. A possessed Collector immediately appears among them. Collector guardians erect hive shields to block your attack. Since you are restricted to the barrier, it is difficult to flank the shields. Instead, either shoot through them or move as far as possible to either side of the barrier and arc a biotic attack around the hive shields.

As always, you should try to deny Harbinger additional bodies to possess. Watch out for the possessed Collector to make its way right to the edge of the barrier and fire inside of it. The possessed Collector may also step inside of the barrier, which is serious trouble. It is hard to fight it at close range, but a shotgun is the best weapon to use in this instance.

Move Out

Your biotic takes you deeper into the ship until the arrival of more husks and abominations. These creatures are joined by a scion. The scion stays back, allowing you to concentrate on the husks. Cut down the abominations before they breach the barrier so their explosions do not affect your squad. The husks are also a problem if they get inside, because their melee attacks bump you around. You do not have a lot of room to fall back inside the barrier, so try to avoid any close-quarter combat with the husks.

Though the scion lingers outside the barrier, it still attacks. Take cover from its blasts and return fire. A heavy weapon will cut down the scion faster, allowing you to get moving again.

As your biotic inches forward, look out for husks to attack from the left.

Your biotic begins to seriously struggle as you near the door to the center of the station. The biotic slows down as you work your way down a long ramp. Shoot the additional husks that attempt to breach the barrier as your biotic stumbles forward. You just need to reach the bottom of the ramp to make it into the central chamber and discover the mystery at the heart of the Collector station.

Once at the bottom, your biotic uses a last bit of power to fling the force field at the Collectors closing ranks behind you. The doors slam shut behind you, cutting off the Collectors. The second team comes in over the comm. They are pinned down at another door leading to the same room. You force open the door and allow the fire team inside.

> There is a chance the leader of the second fire team is shot down just as the doors close.

NOTE

The Collectors are building outside the doors. It will not take them very long to breach one of the doors and attack. Miranda suggests that you lead a squad to the heart of the station while the rest stay back and cover the door. That should buy you enough time to reach the station's center and initiate its destruction. You must select two squad members to go with you. This will be your squad until the end of the mission, so choose carefully. You are about to fight many Collectors with different armor and shields as well as an enemy that is too large to move with biotics. Select teammates that either reinforce your preferred play style, such as Garrus and Grunt if you are a soldier class commander, or fill holes in a rounded team strategy. If you are a strong biotic, for example, you may want to bring some effective soldiers. There are no synthetic enemies from here on out, so tech-oriented skills like AI Hacking have zero use—but a tech with Overload, like Miranda, is great against shielded Collectors

219

Introduction

Training

Upgrades and Research

Walkthrough

Collector Station

Special Assignments

Planetary Database

Appendix

Objective 3: Reach Station Center

Cross the Platforms

After leaving the rest of the team behind, you climb on to one of the Collectors' hexagonal platforms. Within moments, another platform glides through the air to join yours. Reload and take cover. The incoming platform is loaded with Collector drones. Look up and pepper the drones with available biotic attacks, softening them for the kill.

The next platform harbors Collector guardians and drones. Hit the drones with biotics as the platform is locked into place. The guardians will likely hunker down behind hive shields. You have more room to maneuver than you did inside the barrier, so veer left or right to flank the guardian. If you cannot get a clean shot, try to arc a biotic attack behind the shield or use something like Slam. If these are not options, direct fire will crack the hive shield and expose the Collector guardian beneath.

When you hear the whine of the third platform, look for the glow of a possessed Collector. Don't bother shooting it as it moves into position. Instead, take down the other Collectors on the platform. Then, train your weapons on the lone possessed Collector. If you have any heavy weapon ammo, use it to bring down the possessed Collector quickly.

New platforms snap into place only once you have destroyed the Collectors on the current platform.

NOTE

Two platforms sail toward you next. These platforms carry not only a possessed Collector, but also Collector guardians and a Collector assassin. Within seconds of docking, the possessed Collector moves on you while the assassin opens fire with its particle cannon. Taking it down will result in another as long as there are other Collectors on the platform. Keep the possessed Collector busy with your squad mates while you tear through the other Collectors first. You must break through their shields before you can effectively use some biotics like Pull, so use cover to get close and pound them with gunfire until they are exposed and vulnerable.

The final platform glides toward you carrying abominations and two scions. The abominations are easy targets from a distance. You can use either guns or biotics to pop them. The scions are much tougher. They are heavily armored and will drain your weapons. Heavy weapons will drop the scions sooner. Keep back so the scions cannot injure you with their blasts. Once the second scion falls, you can access a terminal on the scion's platform and fly into the heart of the Collector station.

Objective 4: Destroy the Reaper

As you fly toward the center of the station, EDI comes over the comm. She has determined that the tubes are feeding into a large structure that emits both organic and machine energy signatures. The structure is actually a new Reaper. But the Collectors are not building just any Reaper. They are constructing the first human Reaper.

EDI scans the Reaper for information. It seems that the Reapers are built by other species and often take on the form of the organic life harvested to create the new Reaper. This is why the Reaper Sovereign looks different than this new Reaper. Sovereign was built to look like the species that created it. The Collectors have used tens of thousands of humans to build this Reaper-human larva. EDI calculates that the Collectors will need many times that to finish it.

EDI suggests a plan of action. Four large tubes feed the human genetic material into the Reaper. These tubes also support the massive structure. If you can destroy the four tubes, the Reaper will fall. The tubes are armored, so you must wait for the shielding on the tubes to lift as the genetic material is pumped into the Reaper-human larva.

Feeding Tubes

The Collectors do not let you have free rein with their creation. When you attempt to target the feeding tubes, more Collectors rush in to protect it. Platforms lock with yours, dropping off Collectors from drones to assassins. Harbinger regularly possesses these Collectors, making them more powerful foes. Listen for the whine of an incoming platform and then use your weapons and biotics to pick off the easiest targets before the platform docks.

Always keep an eye on the tubes. However, if you are not looking, one of your squad mates will always tell you when the tubes are exposed. You only have a couple of moments to fire on the tubes, but they are fragile. A few shots is all it takes to shatter the tube.

If you are fast, you can actually destroy two feeding tubes in a single cycle. Use a heavy weapon or a larger rifle and strafe across the surface of two tubes next to each other.

TIP

After you destroy a tube, another Collector platform moves into position.

Introduction

Training

Upgrades and Research

Collector Station

Walkthrough

Special Assignments

Planetary Database

Appendix

While many Collectors will remain on their platform, the possessed Collectors often move into your space.

Juggle the incoming Collectors with firing on the tubes. Any time there is a slight lull in the battle, look up to the feeding tubes and take aim. Then quickly take evasive action, seeking cover against the next batch of incoming Collectors. When you wreck the fourth tube, the Reaper collapses and falls into the depths of the Collector station.

You call in for a report from the rest of the team. They are still holding the door but need extraction. Joker and EDI have fixed the Normandy and can take off soon. Direct the rest of the team back to the ship. You need to stay a few more minutes and prep the annihilation of this station.

The Choice

EDI patches through a signal from the Illusive Man. Appearing in holographic form, the Illusive Man congratulates you for making it this far. But when you tell him that you are just about ready to destroy the station, he says he has a better idea. Instead of blowing up the station, he suggests using a timed radiation pulse that will kill all of the Collectors on the station but leave the machinery intact. The Illusive Man wants to save the base and the technology to build a Reaper. He says it will only help humanity's fight against the Reapers as well as smooth the path for human dominance in the galaxy. You must now choose to either follow the Illusive Man's plans to keep the base or go through with blowing it up.

> Choosing to destroy the base results in Paragon points. Saving it gives you a wealth of Renegade points.
>
> **NOTE**

Human Reaper

No matter what you choose, the human Reaper pulls itself out of the heart of the station. The mechanical monster rises above the platform and starts to charge up an attack from either the cannon in its mouth or its chest. The Reaper-human larva's attack is a sustained blast that starts out as a slow-moving energy sphere. The sphere floats toward you, tracking your movements. When it has a lock on your position, the sphere explodes into a giant beam of burning energy. If you're caught in it, your shields fry and you lose health. You must duck behind cover to avoid the incoming attack.

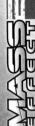

PRIMA Official Game Guide | primagames.com

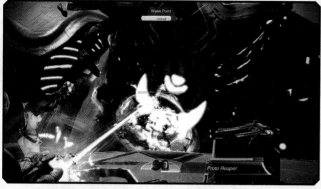

Aim into the energy vortex swirling around the cannon to do extra damage to the Reaper.

Look out for the appearance of possessed Collectors once you have the Reaper under half of its original health.

CAUTION

Don't get too close to the edge of the platform. The Reaper will slash at you with its giant unfinished hand—lots of sharp edges.

TIP

Catch a possessed Collector between you and the Reaper's energy attack to fry the Collector with the blast.

The Collectors take a last stand to protect the Reaper. More platforms with Collector drones and guardians slide up to your position and unload their deadly cargo. Attack the Collectors with biotics since they do little good against the Reaper, but do not ignore the giant monster for long. Quickly dispatch the Collectors and then turn your weapons back on the Reaper.

The Reaper's energy blast is devastating. Fortunately, you have ample warning of an impending shot. When the whooshing sound of the Reaper's vortex stops, you have a few seconds to hide.

Empty your heavy weapons into the Reaper to do the most damage to it.

Your heavy weapons will not last forever. You must switch to conventional weapons to eventually destroy the  Reaper. Anything works. Even a shotgun at medium range will do some damage to the Reaper, so don't turn up your nose at any weapon. Just keep plugging the Reaper with whatever you have and push away the Collectors with biotics. Eventually, you will break the Reaper's armor and deliver the killing blow.

The Reaper collapses into the center of the station again, but this time it's not getting back up. The Reaper pulls the platforms down with it as it falls, threatening to bring you with it. You barely escape with your squad, making a run for the *Normandy*.

After you bury the dead and make one last transmission to the Illusive Man, Joker hands you a small datapad. There's something on there that draws your eyes to the stars.

As you run for the *Normandy*, Harbinger works to save the station. It taunts you, saying that this small victory means nothing, that your species has overreached. But Harbinger soon finds itself without a direct link to the Reapers. The Reapers, disappointed by today's failure, abandon the Collectors. Harbinger is left alone in its final moments before the blast rips through the station, killing all of the Collectors. The *Normandy* pulls back through the Omega 4 relay, escaping certain doom.

And the stars look back.

After the credits roll, you resume control of the *Normandy*. The crew members that survived the mission through the Omega 4 relay are back on board the ship. You can now complete any outstanding special assignments, go on mining missions, or just crisscross the galaxy.

NOTE

SPECIAL ASSIGNMENTS

Stopping the Collectors from helping the Reapers destroy humanity is your primary mission. However, that doesn't mean you cannot take on extra assignments while zooming across the galaxy. Accepting special assignments is beneficial for a number of reasons. Not only do you earn additional experience that's critical for helping you raise your squad levels and master powers, but you also earn bonuses like morality points and valuable minerals.

There are two kinds of assignments to take: city assignments and N7 assignments. City assignments are small jobs that you pick up and complete while visiting the hub worlds, such as Omega or Illium. These are easy tasks that require minimal effort but help build Paragon and Renegade points, as well as earn credits and experience. N7 assignments are actual missions, not unlike those that you undertake as part of your drive against the Collectors. When you accept or seek out an N7 mission, you visit a planet and drop into a dangerous situation. N7 assignments are worth more experience and credits than the smaller jobs you take in the cities, but don't let that steer you away from the city assignments.

CITY ASSIGNMENTS

You receive many assignments while visiting the *Normandy* or hub worlds like the Citadel, Omega, and Illium. Most of these assignments are received simply by talking to people, but a handful begin when you pick up an object, such as the lost locket. Most of these assignments involve you fetching an item or clearing up a misunderstanding. The rewards for completing these assignments are experience points and, depending on how you handle the task, morality points. If you seek an amiable solution for all parties, for example, you earn Paragon points. Just getting the job done typically results in Renegade points.

Each assignment listing includes when the assignment is available upon visiting the location. You will visit some locations multiple times, such as Illium, where two loyalty missions take place, but not every assignment will be available right away. Certain assignments might not open up until a subsequent visit, so pay attention to your timing as well as to your location. The originator of the assignment is also detailed so you can go straight to the source of the task.

Normandy

Serrice Ice Brandy

Available: Immediately

Assignment Started By: Dr. Chakwas

Reward: 40 XP, +1 medi-gel capacity

Dr. Chakwas served with you on the original *Normandy*. When that ship was destroyed by the Collectors, the doctor lost a bottle of Serrice Ice Brandy. She had been saving the bottle for a special occasion. She laments its loss, but you can rectify the situation for her the first time you visit the Citadel or Omega.

Go to the small bar on the right side of Afterlife's main floor and purchase a bottle of brandy.

When you return to the *Normandy*, give the bottle to Dr. Chakwas. She is ecstatic to have the replacement.

You can even sit with the good doctor and share it, drinking toasts to the fallen and to new hopes. Just know that Serrice Ice Brandy is hard stuff. After getting sloshed with Chakwas, you will stumble around the *Normandy* for the next few minutes, unable to see straight. No harm is done, though.

FBA Couplings

Available: Immediately

Assignment Started By: Engineer Donnelly

Reward: 40 XP

Engineer Donnelly down on the engineering deck of the *Normandy* is doing a fine job of keeping the vessel in top shape. However, if engineering had some FBA Couplings, they could run maintenance tests much faster. Offer to find the FBA Couplings.

Introduction

Training

Upgrades and Research

Walkthrough

Special Assignments

Planetary Database

Appendix

The FBA Couplings are on sale down at Kenn's Salvage on Omega.

Take the couplings back to Donnelly on the *Normandy*. The engineers happily accept them. This boosts your relationship with the engineers. They will invite you to play cards with them. You can either feign being no good or go for the throat in the game. You win money if you go to either extreme, but your tactics affect what kind of morality points you receive, too.

Special Ingredients

Available: Immediately

Assignment Started By: Sergeant Gardner

Reward: 40 XP

Sergeant Gardner is behind the counter in the *Normandy*'s mess hall. Speak to the cook about his needs. Gardner wishes he had better provisions to give the crew since it is likely that many of them will meet their end on this voyage. Gardner mentions that there are great provisions on sale at the Citadel. The next time you visit the Citadel, go to the cafe on the 27th floor of Zakera Ward and buy the requested provisions. Take them back to Gardner to complete the assignment.

Omega

Struggling Quarian

Available: Immediately

Assignment Started By: Kenn

Reward: 40 XP

Kenn is a young quarian on the bottom of the Omega marketplace. He runs a small salvage shop, trying to eke out a

living since he was robbed of his credits not long after coming to Omega. He is not having an easy go of it. Harrot, the elcor running an emporium on the main floor of the market, has muscled Kenn into selling his goods at excessively high prices. You can help Kenn either by speaking to Harrot about his treatment of the quarian or by giving Kenn 1,000 credits so he can buy a ticket off Omega.

NOTE

If you help Kenn, you get a discount at his shop.

Do not fear Harrot. The elcor will listen to reason—and by reason, we really mean intimidation or charm.

Batarian Bartender

Available: Immediately

Assignment Started By: Batarian Bartender

Reward: 40 XP

This assignment was detailed in the Omega city walkthrough as an example of how special assignments work in a hub world. So, here's the short version: Visit the lower level of Afterlife and order a drink from the batarian bartender. The batarian hates humans, so he poisons you. You pass out. When you come to, an Omega resident tells you what happened. You can now return to the bartender and either threaten him to make him drink his own poison or make a fuss so other patrons hear.

If you make some noise about the bartender serving poisoned drinks, a turian inserts himself into

the situation—and then inserts a bullet into the batarian. Whenever you visit the lower level bar after this assignment, you're greeted by a friendly salarian bartender and drinks are on the house.

Missing Assistant

Available: The Professor

Assignment Started By: Mordin

Reward: 40 XP

When you finally reach Mordin's clinic and try to recruit him, the salarian scientist tells you he will only join you after the plague in the slums has been cured. Before you leave the clinic to place the cure in the air circulation systems of the slums, Mordin mentions that his assistant, Daniel, has been gone into the slums for too long. Mordin is worried about him.

Follow the directions in the walkthrough to find Daniel. Daniel is being held up by some ill-tempered

batarians. You can decide how this encounter ends. Either peacefully allow the batarians to leave or blast them. If you free Daniel, he returns to the clinic. You can see him there later when you finish the recruitment mission.

> This assignment is part of The Professor, Mordin's recruitment mission on Omega, despite its appearance in the special assignments section of your journal. Daniel's exact location is detailed in the mission walkthrough.
>
> **NOTE**

The Patriarch

Available: After Archangel or The Professor

Assignment Started By: Grizz in Afterlife

Rewards: 40 XP, Data on N7 mission

This assignment is first offered after you complete either the Archangel or Professor recruitment mission. Pay a visit to Grizz in Afterlife. Grizz tells you about the Patriarch, a krogan warlord who ran Omega before Aria showed up. Apparently the Patriarch is being threatened by some Blood Pack thugs. Aria doesn't necessarily want the Patriarch hurt, but she cannot be seen showing a soft spot for anybody on Omega. Grizz asks if you would go speak to the Patriarch and tell him to make himself scarce for a while.

The Patriarch is downstairs, in a small room just off the lower level of Afterlife. Speak to the Patriarch about the threats. You can listen to the krogan tell the story of how he fought Aria for control of Omega and ultimately lost. But the bottom line is, you need to tell the Patriarch to scram if he wants to live. The Patriarch sees the threat as an opportunity, though. Maybe he should stick around to make things hard for Aria. You can either underline the point and get the Patriarch to leave, tell him that you'll take care of the Blood Pack for him, or convince him to go out in a blaze of glory by fighting the Blood Pack and die a happy krogan.

If you agree to take out the Blood Pack threat for the Patriarch, essentially becoming his phantom krantt, step through the door leading outside of the lower level of Afterlife. Confront the krogan Blood Pack warriors that have been sent to kill the Patriarch. This situation ends with two dead krogan.

> If you kill the Blood Pack thugs for the Patriarch, Aria receives the news of an empowered Patriarch with little joy. If the Patriarch leaves, she is much happier.
>
> **NOTE**

Deliver Datapad

Available: Archangel

Assignment Started By: Locating Datapad

Rewards: 40 XP, Data on N7 mission

While undertaking the Archangel recruitment assignment, look for a datapad on a table near the first barricade where you speak to Jaroth of the Eclipse mercs. The datapad reveals that the mercs have Aria in their sights. Return the datapad to Aria after the mission. Aria is furious that the information slipped past her intelligence gatherers but is grateful you caught it.

Ish

Available: After Archangel and the Professor

Assignment Started By: Ish

Rewards: 3,375 Credits (for both shipments), 40 XP

Introduction

Training

Upgrades and Research

Walkthrough

Special Assignments

Planetary Database

Appendix

Ish is a salarian merchant who stands just outside the apartment entrance in the main area of Omega. Ish has a special request. He needs you to bring two shipments back to him on Omega. If you agree to help him, he will pay you. One of the shipments is on the Citadel, just outside Saronis Applications. The second is on Illium, up in the Eternity Bar. Gather both shipments and bring them back for the reward.

> **TIP**
>
> You can also either warn or threaten Ish to give up his wicked ways for morality points.

Illium

The Observer

Available: Immediately

Assignment Started By: Liara

Rewards: 2,000 Credits, 80 XP

When you visit Liara on Illium, you catch up on old times and learn about her life following her time on the *Normandy*. Liara has become an information broker on Illium. Liara is currently investigating the Observer, an agent of the Shadow Broker. She needs to shore up her business and assert her dominance on Illium. You can help, but this is dirty work. You will earn Renegade points for helping Liara with this assignment, especially the back half of it.

The first thing Liara needs you to do is locate a series of security terminals in the transportation area of Nos Astra. You need to hack the terminal and then quickly find the terminal tethered to it. The tethered terminal has sensitive data that Liara needs. You must locate the tethered terminal within one minute or else it will go offline. The tethered terminals are very close to the security terminals. Here are the security terminal locations:

- To the right of the door into the transportation hub
- To the left of the weapons kiosk
- Behind the weapons kiosk

After you complete this part of the task, Liara tells you how much she appreciates your help. There is more you can do for her, but you need to check back in with her later. If you did this assignment when you first arrived in Illium, check back with Liara after completing whichever recruitment mission you chose first. If you waited until after both recruitment missions to help Liara, come back after you have completed any other mission.

When you return to Liara, she needs you to help her determine the identity of the Observer. Liara has assassins on call, ready to strike. To help Liara, you must go to the trading floor of Nos Astra and hack five terminals to get snippets of data. The snippets help you determine which of five potential targets is the Observer. After finding the data, call Liara and tell her who to kill. Here are the terminal locations:

- Eternity Bar
- To the left of the upgrades kiosk
- Near the base of Liara's stairs
- To the right of the upgrades kiosk
- Near the entrance to the trading floor

If you tell Liara the correct identity of the Observer based on the data, she has the threat neutralized and is grateful for your help. If you tell her the wrong target, you essentially have blood on your hands.

> **NOTE**
>
> The correct answer is: none of the above. The data points to somebody other than Liara's suspects. It's actually her secretary!

Indentured Service

Available: Immediately

Assignment Started By: Quarian in Eternity Bar

Rewards: 40 XP, 2,000 Credits

When you first visit the Eternity Bar on Illium, listen in to the conversation between the asari and the quarian just inside the entrance. There is a serious problem with the quarian's indentured servitude contract—the asari from Synthetic Insights who was going to buy it is not interested. You must now convince either the asari slaver or the Synthetic Insights rep (also in the bar) to fix the situation. You can either twist the slaver's arm to let the quarian go or appeal to the Synthetic Insights rep's desire for some good PR.

Tell the rep that buying a quarian slave and freeing her would look good (though slavery is legal on Illium, it is still seen as barbaric by the Citadel). She goes for it. The quarian is freed from servitude.

> You can also toss aside the plight of the quarian and earn Renegade points.

NOTE

Medical Scans

Available: Immediately

Assignment Started By: Colonist in Transportation Hub

Reward: 40 XP

A colonist refugee recognizes you when you walk by—she was at Feros when you rescued it during the mission to stop Saren. The colonist has a new problem now. She has signed up for a contract on Illium and is now part of a medical test program that is bordering on cruel. The colonist asks you to speak with the Baria representation to clear up the situation.

Talk to the Baria rep. The asari is rough around the edges. If you just speak to her and appeal to her good side, she

buckles and cancels the tests. Go tell the colonist she is free from her contract. You can also choose to go Renegade and not help the colonist at all, siding with the asari.

Blue Rose of Illium

Available: Immediately

Assignment Started By: Asari Next to Memories of Illium

Rewards: 40 XP, Store Discount

When you visit Memories of Illium in Nos Astra, the asari shopkeeper tells you she is having a real personal dilemma. The krogan several feet away reading awful poetry is her ex-boyfriend. He wants her back, but she thinks the krogan is only interested in her for the sake of having kids. You can do one of two things: tell the asari either to trust her boyfriend's words (resulting in Paragon points) or to ditch him (which results in Renegade points). Either way, you get a discount at the shop for helping her with this problem.

Stolen Goods Found

Available: The Justicar

Assignment Started By: Finding Stolen Goods Report

Rewards: 40 XP, 2,000 Credits

After convincing the detective into letting you look at the crime scene in the Justicar recruitment mission, check the terminal behind the two asari officers. There is a manifest that hints at somebody stealing from an entity on Illium called Thrax. You can either release the data or keep it hidden. Thrax is actually a criminal, so if you choose to release the data, you end up helping him. Thrax's associate contacts you the next time you visit Illium to tell you how much "Mr. Thrax" appreciates your effort. The Renegade points you receive should tell you whether or not helping Thrax was a good idea.

Smuggling Evidence

Available: The Justicar

Assignment Started By: Finding Shipping Manifest

Rewards: 40 XP, 4,200 Credits

Follow the Justicar mission walkthrough to locate the shipping manifest. It proves that Pitne For, the volus at the spaceport, is indeed a criminal. Now, after returning from the mission you have a choice to make. You can either give the manifest to Pitne For for credits and Renegade points or give it to Detective Anaya for credits and Paragon points. The choice is yours.

Introduction

Training

Upgrades and Research

Walkthrough

Special Assignments

Planetary Database

Appendix

Pitne For would really like it if you just slipped him the manifest. It's a lucrative transaction, but it also boosts your reputation as a Renegade.

Datapad Recovered

Available: The Assassin

Assignment Started By: Finding Datapad Near Elevator

Rewards: 40 XP, 1,500 Credits

While recruiting Thane on Illium, keep an eye out for a datapad that is of interest to somebody back in Nos Astra. Follow the directions in the mission walkthrough to locate the datapad. When you return to Illium, seek out the talkative salarian in the shipping area of Nos Astra for the reward.

Give the datapad to the salarian in the shipping section of Nos Astra—the one that's always gabbing on his phone.

Lost Locket Found

Available: The Prodigal

Assignment Started By: Finding Locket

Rewards: 40 XP, 500 Credits

When you fight your way to the end of the shipping yard in Miranda's loyalty mission, The Prodigal, look for a locket on a crate next to the exit door. This locket belongs to an asari back on Nos Astra. The asari is near the entrance to the trading floor. The asari is so happy to have it back.

Tuchanka

Killing Pyjaks

Available: Immediately

Assignment Started By: Ratch

Rewards: 40 XP, Store Discount

Shopkeeper Ratch is willing to offer you a discount to his kiosk, but only if you help with the local pyjak problem. The vermin are getting into the food stocks on Tuchanka. Use the shooting range next to the chief scout and follow the strategies outlined in the Tuchanka walkthrough section. If you complete four waves of pyjak shooting, Ratch gives you a discount at his shop.

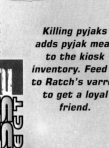

Killing pyjaks adds pyjak meat to the kiosk inventory. Feed it to Ratch's varren to get a loyal friend.

Combustion Manifold

Available: Immediately

Assignment Started By: Mechanic

Reward: 40 XP

When you first arrive in Tuchanka, visit the mechanic working on the giant truck. The mechanic needs a combustion manifold to make the necessary repairs to the truck. He could make a new one, but that would take days. If you offer to find one for him, the mechanic tells you that you might find one outside of the city. The combustion manifold the mechanic needs is found during Mordin's loyalty mission, Old Blood.

Before entering the hospital, swipe the combustion manifold from the overturned truck. After finishing the mission, return to the mechanic and give him the manifold. Assignment complete.

Missing Scout

Available: Old Blood

Assignment Started By: Chief Scout

Reward: 40 XP

In order to head out to the Clan Weyrloc base, you must talk to the chief scout for clan Urdnot, who is next to the pyjak shooting range. The chief scout mentions that he recently sent a scout out to Weyrloc territory to investigate the news of a salarian scientist in the clan's custody. However, that scout has since gone missing.

Follow the Old Blood walkthrough to locate the missing scout. The scout sits in a cell, alone and dejected. Get that krogan off his feet through harassment. Convince him to go back to the city, which takes a little tough love. The missing scout roars to life and escapes the Weyrloc base, completing the assignment.

Citadel

Captain Bailey

Available: Immediately

Assignment Started By: C-Sec Officer at Zakera Ward Entrance

Reward: None

When you first attempt to enter Zakera Ward on the Citadel, the C-Sec officer stops you. The scan he runs matches up with a profile for a dead person. The C-Sec officer obviously sees that you are not dead and refers you to Captain Bailey just beyond the door. Speak to Bailey about upgrading your status to living. The old C-Sec captain is happy to oblige for the former Spectre who saved the Citadel.

Krogan Sushi

Available: Immediately

Assignment Started By: Walking Next to Krogan

Reward: 40 XP

Walk slowly by the two krogan on level 27 of Zakera Ward. You overhear one of them, Kargesh, talking about the rumor that fish exist in the lakes on the Presidium. Though you do not engage with the krogan right now, you do pick up this assignment. You need to get hard proof of whether or not there are fish in the waters of the Presidium.

Visit the Dark Star bar and talk to the grounds-keeper. He says there are no fish up on the Presidium.

You now have a choice. You can either tell the krogan the truth about the fish, which makes him sad (but rewards you with Paragon points), or lie to him. To pull off the lie, you need to buy a fish from Citadel Souvenirs. Give the fish to Kargesh and tell him it was from the Presidium. The krogan cannot believe his eyes. He happily accepts the fish. You made a krogan's day, and the lie results in Renegade points.

Crime in Progress

Available: Immediately

Assignment Started By: Talking to Quarian, Volus, and C-Sec Officer on Level 28

Rewards: 40 XP, 3,000 Credits

A C-Sec officer is trying to sort through a problem between a quarian and a volus. The volus accuses the quarian of stealing his credit chit, but the quarian says she did no such thing. The C-Sec officer is leaning toward believing the volus, primarily out of his own prejudices. Interject and offer to solve the assumed crime.

Introduction

Training

Upgrades and Research

Walkthrough

Special Assignments

Planetary Database

Appendix

Return to the C-Sec officer. Tell the volus that his chit is at the shop. The volus seems disappointed that he can no longer harass the quarian. The C-Sec officer even tells the quarian that he's going to cite her for vagrancy. If you want some Paragon points, get in their faces and tell them they should be ashamed of themselves. They both shuffle away upset but duly chastened.

Speak to the merchant of Saronis Applications. The volus left his chit at the shop.

N7 ASSIGNMENTS

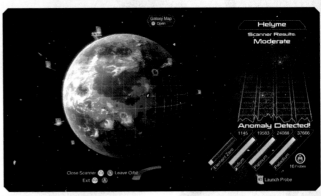

Use your scanner to seek out anomalies on the surface of planets. Follow the white arrow on the scanner to the exact spot of the signal. When you drop a probe on a signal source, you can then land your shuttle.

N7 assignments are much more involved than those you take on in the hub worlds. These assignments send you crisscrossing the galaxy in search of trouble spots that require your attention. These missions play out much like main story missions. You go to a world, select an away team, and then fight your way toward the goal. When the mission is complete, you earn experience, credits, and any minerals you find along the way.

There are two ways to find N7 assignments. A handful of the assignments are brought to your attention via your private terminal. These messages give you the general parameters of the assignment and tell you where to start looking. However, most of the N7 missions must be found by scanning planets. Now, you could scan the planets one by one in search of all of the N7 missions. But why not just use our list of all N7 assignments to cut short the detective work?

Not all of the missions are available right away. Several of the N7 assignments are chained together. Completing one opens the lead to another. It is also important to open up as many clusters on your galaxy map as possible to find all of the N7 assignments. To open up all of the clusters, you must first buy all four star charts from Illium— these place the Minos Wasteland, Hades Nexus, Pylos Nebula, and Shrike Abyssal on your galaxy map. Without these charts, you cannot see the clusters. Some clusters are only revealed after finishing up an assignment in a chain, too.

> Check the strategies for each assignment before determining your away team. For example, if you know you are about to face down geth on Canalus, you may wish to bring an engineer if you are not one yourself.
>
> **TIP**

Use this table to track all of the N7 assignments. The table includes the location of the assignment as well as how the assignment is discovered. If the assignment is just found via a scan, then go straight to the planet and scan it. Assignments received only via your private terminal are noted. Assignments that are links in a chain are marked as "After" with the name of the planet involved in the previously required N7 assignment.

> Don't skip mining trips just because you know where to find all of the N7 missions. You need to mine minerals if you want to complete the majority of the upgrade research projects offered in Mordin's lab aboard the *Normandy*.
>
>

Cluster	System	Planet	Mission Name	Found/Scan?
Caleston Rift	Solveig	Sinmara	Endangered Research Station	Scan
Caleston Rift	Talava	Taitus	Mining the Canyon	Scan
Crescent Nebula	Lusarn	Tarith	Blood Pack Communications Relay	Complete Patriarch and Deliver Datapad assignments for Aria
Crescent Nebula	Zelene	Helyme	Captured Mining Facility	Scan
Eagle Nebula	Amun	Neith	Wrecked Merchant Freighter	Scan
Eagle Nebula	Strabo	Jarrahe Station	Abandoned Research Station	After Neith
Hades Nexus	Sheol	Gei Hinnom	Quarian Crash Site	Email or scan
Hourglass Nebula	Faryar	Daratar	Eclipse Smuggling Depot	Scan
Hourglass Nebula	Ploitari	Zanethu	Estevanico	Scan
Minos Wasteland	Fortis	Aequitas	Abandoned Mine	Scan
Omega Nebula	Arinlarkan	MSV Strontium Mule	MSV Strontium Mule	After Joab
Omega Nebula	Fathar	Lorek	Lost Operative	Email
Pylos Nebula	Dirada	Canalus	Anomalous Weather Detected	Scan
Pylos Nebula	Nariph	MSV Broken Arrow	Imminent Ship Crash	Email
Rosetta Nebula	Enoch	Joab	Archeological Dig Site	Scan
The Shrike Abyssal	Xe Cha	Zada Ban	Blood Pack Base	After Tarith
Sigurd's Cradle	Decoris	Sanctum	Blue Suns Base	After MSV Strontium Mule
Sigurd's Cradle	Skepsis	Franklin	Javelin Launch	Email
Titan Nebula	Haskins	Capek	Hahne-Kedar Facility	After Jarrahe Station

These three missions are email alerts via your private terminal.

NOTE

N7: Lost Operative

A Cerberus operative has gone missing and is believed to be a prisoner in an Eclipse base on Lorek. The operative has sensitive data that would be harmful to Cerberus if it found its ways into Eclipse or Alliance hands.

Location: Lorek

Rewards: 125 XP, 2,000 Platinum, 7,500 Credits

Rescue Operative

When you arrive on the tropical planet Lorek, the shuttle drops you off directly outside a potential Eclipse base of operations. Pick up the refined platinum from the crate near the landing zone and then enter the base via the door to the right.

This is no potential Eclipse base. The base is crawling with mercs. The main room of the base is quickly overrun by troopers and vanguards. Immediately take cover behind the crates or on either side of the door and

systematically cut down the mercs. The first push comes through the door in the back of the room, so primarily target that area right now. Use biotics or tech attacks to soften the mercs.

Since these are organic targets, cryo, incendiary, or shredder ammo is especially useful.

TIP

After cutting down the first batch of Eclipse foes, inch your way into the room. More mercs stream down the right side of the room.

After cleaning out the main room of the base, venture into the back room to empty a wall safe with 3,750 credits and pick up a medi-gel. Once you have the credits and medi-gel access the terminal that controls the holding cells. Bypass the security on the terminal to unlock the door on the left side of the room, which leads to the prisoner.

Unlocking the cells triggers the next wave of Eclipse mercs. Troopers file into the room from the back corner. Dive behind a crate or use a pillar for cover and shoot the mercs before they can get too far into the room. You need to hold them back. When the flow thins, push into that half of the room, but watch the still-closed door against the left wall.

When you near the door two Eclipse thugs pop through it: a vanguard and the leader of the Eclipse at this base, Morl. Morl is a powerful engineer. Not only does he have Barrier as well as armor to protect him, but he will also deploy combat drones to keep you busy while the troopers attempt to spread into the room and flank.

Morl will keep refreshing his barrier if you do not take him down with an unwavering series of attacks. Direct the entire squad to target him so that when his barrier falls, his armor goes next and eventually his health.

Use the door in the back corner of the room to locate another crate of platinum.

TIP

Use the door Morl came through to locate the Cerberus prisoner. The door is easily bypassed by hacking through the symbols. The prisoner, sadly, has died. The data extracted from his interrogation is on the computer in the back of the room. Take the data. You can now upload the data to Cerberus, keep it for yourself, or send it to the Alliance. If you send it to Cerberus, you receive a slight credits bonus.

N7: Imminent Ship Crash

The derelict MSV *Broken Arrow* is in a decaying orbit over the planet Jonus. The ship is loaded with munitions. If it is allowed to crash, the explosive impact is likely to destroy a human settlement. Restore the engines to keep the ship from crashing—but beware of geth aboard the vessel.

Location: MSV *Broken Arrow*

Rewards: 125 XP, 2,000 Iridium, 7,500 Credits

Reactivate Engines

When you board the MSV *Broken Arrow*, the clock starts ticking. You have just six minutes to restore engine power before the ship's decayed orbit can no longer be saved. You must hack the security on the door to enter the control room. Hacking does not stop the timer—you must hurry so as not to waste too much time just looking at symbols. Fighting the geth inside the ship will consume enough of the clock as it is.

Right away, geth troopers attack. Stick to the door for cover and target the geth inside. If you have an engineer, use AI Hacking to turn the geth against each other. Otherwise, stick to gunplay and biotics to take down the troopers. Once the geth are down, access the console on the right side of the room to unlock the engine room.

There is a medi-gel on the left wall of this room, just inside the door. A crate of iridium is farther up along the wall.

TIP

As soon as you enter the engine room, look to the left. There are two catwalks above the engine room. The geth take up attack positions here. And they do not stop. Troopers, snipers, rocket troopers—they just keep filing onto the catwalks to rain rounds and shells down on you while you attempt to restart the engines. Fight your way into the room by returning fire, but soon you need to turn your attention to the engines.

> **TIP**
> Focus your squad mates on the geth to provide cover while you access the engines.

> **NOTE**
> Pick up the crate of iridium on the floor of the engine room. Scan the room to spot it.

There are two power couplings on the main floor of the engine room that you must turn back on. This is not as easy as flipping a switch. You must hold your omni-tool over the control panel until the meter fills. If you are shot while accessing the panels, the process is interrupted. You must start over.

Got biotics? Use them to rip the geth right off their perches.

> **TIP**
> Position your squad mates on the stairs so they are not firing up at the geth. If they can fire at them directly, they have greater accuracy.

After activating both couplings, climb the stairs to the top of the engine room and access the engine control panel. Hack the panel to restart the engines and stop the ship from crashing into the planet below. Even if there are still geth firing at you, starting up the engines is enough to end this mission in victory.

N7: Quarian Crash Site

A quarian ship has crashed on the surface of Gei Hinnom. Scanners show multiple life signs, although it is difficult to discern the profile of potential survivors from any local wildlife. Investigate the crash site for any survivors and keep them safe until a shuttle can be sent down to extract them.

Location: Gei Hinnom

Rewards: 125 XP, 2,000 Palladium, 7,500 Credits

> **TIP**
> Gei Hinnom is especially rich with element zero. Scan the equator to find several wealthy deposits.

Search for Survivors

When you first land on Gei Hinnom, the scene is quiet. A campsite implies there are indeed survivors of the crash.

Check the campsite for personal logs to determine what happened and pick up some medi-gel. Also, scoop up a crate of palladium between the tents on the right side of the camp.

After cleaning out the camp, follow the narrow path between the rocks to locate the survivors.

Introduction

Training

Upgrades and Research

Walkthrough

Special Assignments

Planetary Database

Appendix

The path opens up into a clearing. The survivors were ravaged by varren. The quarians took down several varren, but the varren also got most of the survivors. Only one remains. Stabilize the survivor and then protect her from packs of incoming varren until a pickup shuttle arrives in just a few minutes.

> The clearing is littered with explosive containers you can use to blow up varren.
>
> **TIP**

The varren are ruthless. They move into the clearing and close the distance fast. Some varren will attack you and your squad while others go for the helpless quarian. If the quarian is killed, the mission ends in failure. Protect the quarian by killing as many varren as you can from a distance.

> It's difficult to kill varren up close with a medium-range weapon like an assault rifle. Use shotguns.
>
> **CAUTION**

> Bring along a biotic who can lift the varren into the air and cast them aside like playthings.
>
> **TIP**

> Use incendiary ammo to hit the varren with extra burn damage, or freeze them in their tracks with cryo ammo.
>
> **TIP**

> The next two missions are chained together.
>
> **NOTE**

N7: Blood Pack Communications Relay

The Blood Pack mercenaries run a mining operation on Tarith that also hosts a communications relay. Disable the communications tower to disrupt Blood Pack operations in the system.

Location: Tarith

Rewards: 125 XP, 2,000 Platinum, 7,500 Credits

Disable Relay

The atmosphere of Tarith is thick, making it hard to see very far. The outline of the communications relay is faintly visible in the distance, but the trail through the rocks to the tower is not as easy to discern. Follow the beacons along the trail to locate the base of the tower. Each time you activate one of the beacons, it fires a beam of energy to the next beacon. This effectively creates a path for you to follow through the rock maze.

> The communications relay disrupts your own radar.
>
> **TIP**

Watch out for klixen using the thick fog as cover. Keep your distance and open fire on them.

The beacon beams lead you to the tower, but veer off the path to locate raw deposits of platinum.

Look back at the beacon path to see how far you've come.

PRIMA Official Game Guide | primagames.com

When you finally reach the base of the relay, look out for Blood Pack enemies. The Blood Pack is led by Salamul, a krogan who is a capable biotic. He uses Barrier to protect himself from your attacks and unleashes Warp throughout the battle. Salamul is brave and rushes you while his Blood Pack thugs fire rockets at you from the rear. Salamul is tough enough to handle on his own, so take

out the rocket troopers in the rear of the clearing so you can concentrate on the krogan without worrying about a rocket in the back of the head.

When Salamul and his minions are down, hack the terminal at the base of the tower to shut it down. This should make it tough for the Blood Pack to coordinate its operations for a while.

N7: Blood Pack Base

The Blood Pack has a weapons manufacturing plant on the planet Zada Ban. Taking this facility offline would further disrupt Blood Pack operations in this system.

Location: Zada Ban

Rewards: 125 XP, 2,000 Palladium, 7,500 Credits

Destroy Weapons Plant

Upon landing on Zada Ban, check out the datapads to gather intel on the Blood Pack in this area as well as to seek out a crate of palladium on the far side of a rock bridge that overlooks the plant.

When you drop down into the plant, the Blood Pack forces attack. Troopers take cover behind rocks on the ledge directly across from you. Additional Blood Pack fighters, such as Blood Pack boom-squads, spread out in the tunnel below. Use the explosive containers to blast the mercs.

Move down the metal ramps to close in on the plant and take the fight deeper into Blood Pack territory.

You must cross another rock bridge to access the plant. Several mercs attempt to stop you on the bridge. Seek cover from them with the crates. Look out for the mercs on the ledge above the bridge, too. A boom-squad up there drops rockets on you. If you have a biotic attack you can arc, like Pull, try to grab the enemies off the ledge.

When you reach the actual weapons plant on the far side of the bridge (and through the door), you must target the containment cells at the bottom of the giant tanks to destroy the facility. However, the Blood Pack isn't about to let you waltz in and ruin the plant without a fight. Led by Kalusk, a krogan, the Blood Pack fighters attack from all sides. Kalusk, though, is your main problem. The krogan has both shields and armor, so it takes a lot of shots to bring him down.

After dropping Kalusk and blasting all four containment cells, you need to get out of there. Exit through the door that led into the plant to complete the assignment.

TIP

Pick up crates of palladium as you inch toward the weapons plant.

NOTE

The next three missions are chained together.

Introduction

Training

Upgrades and Research

Walkthrough

Special Assignments

Planetary Database

Appendix

N7: Archeological Dig Site

Scans of Joab reveal that an archeological dig site that has uncovered Prothean remains is under siege by Blue Suns mercenaries. The Blue Suns must be stopped so that Prothean technology does not fall into dangerous hands.

You cannot take this assignment until you have revealed the Rosetta Nebula by accepting Jacob's loyalty mission.

NOTE

Location: Joab

Rewards: 150 XP, 500 Element Zero, 7,500 Credits

Retrieve Artifact

Unfortunately, the shuttle landing draws the attention of a Blue Suns scout. As you drop down to the surface, the merc runs inside the ruins to alert the rest of the group. When you start to spread across the clearing in front of the entrance (direct your squad to set up a crossfire from various rocks), the Blue Suns erupt from the mine. The mercs are led by a Blue Suns legionnaire. His shields make it difficult to effectively use most biotic and tech attacks. The troopers that flank him, though, are easy prey.

Pick up the crates of element zero from the clearing before moving into the mine.

Keep moving your squad around the rocks to prevent the mercs from coming up with a cohesive strategy. If they must choose between multiple targets, you can then easily catch their exposed flank.

Inside the mine, use the crates as cover against the Blue Suns. As before, spread your squad across the mine so the Blue Suns do not concentrate their fire on a single spot. Reinforcements arrive via two doors. The first is on

the main floor, off to the left. The second is at the top of the ramp on the back wall of the chamber. Pick off the reinforcements just as they enter the chamber so they cannot dig into cover themselves.

While fanning out across the chamber, watch out for the explosive containers. The Blue Suns will shoot them if you stand too close.

CAUTION

Following the battle, loot the room for credits (in the personal lockers) and a medi-gel.

NOTE

The door at the top of the large chamber leads to a smaller room with more crates and walkways to use as cover. More Blue Suns spring into action. They are tougher than the first wave of mercs, including a commando with both shields and armor. Use the upper landing of the room to spray bullets on the mercs below. If you take the high ground, the mercs cannot effectively use cover.

The Blue Suns are led by Lieutenant Locke. Locke has shields, so if you have any heavy weapon ammo, use it to blast through them and expose him.

There is a crate of element zero in this smaller room. It's just below the landing in the center of the chamber.

TIP

A datapad in the room reveals that an artifact has already been taken offworld on the MSV *Strontium Mule*. Enter the next room, though, to locate a Prothean ruin. Watch the video log on the ruin to see footage of a Reaper attacking a planet and wiping it off the face of the cosmos. This concludes the assignment.

N7: MSV *Strontium Mule*

The MSV *Strontium Mule* has gone silent—the crew will not answer any hails despite repeated attempts. Scans, however, reveal that the ship is making transmissions using a known Blue Suns encryption key. Board the ship via an emergency hatch in the cargo hold and stop the Blue Suns.

Location: MSV *Strontium Mule*

Rewards: 150 XP, 2,000 Iridium, 7,500 Credits

Recapture Derelict Ship

Upon entering the cargo hold of the vessel, take cover because the Blue Suns will flow through the door on the opposite side of the room within seconds. The Blue Suns crew includes troopers, legionnaires, and heavies, so watch out for rocket fire to streak through the air. There are explosive crates on the main floor, so be mindful about using those for cover. They make a tempting trap for the Blue Suns, but if you can keep them pinned at the door by spreading out across the room and focusing all fire on their origin point, you are much better off.

Climb the ramps in the next room to locate a small Blue Suns patrol.

Access the security console at the top of the ramps to unlock the doors in this room. There are three doors. Each winds around to another room of the ship that contains even more Blue Suns. Use the corridors to flank the Blue Suns. If you place a squad member inside each corridor, you can attack the Blue Suns from multiple angles and keep them guessing.

Follow the corridor to the right of the MCS-77 sign to locate another security console. This unlocks the door to the bridge.

The bridge is the last stand for the Blue Suns thugs on the *Strontium Mule*. The mercs are led by Captain Vorhess, a tough merc with shields. However, even more dangerous is his bodyguard, who dons armor and has a shield up. Slam into cover and direct your squad to spread across the bridge. Take out the troopers first since they have no armor or shields. Removing their guns from the battle early will let you concentrate on Vorhess and his guard.

239
Introduction
Training
Upgrades and Research
Walkthrough
Special Assignments
Planetary Database
Appendix

Do not engage Captain Vorhess or the bodyguard at close range. The guard has a powerful shotgun, so just stick to your cover and lay into the mercs with medium-range weapons, such as assault rifles or submachine guns (the latter are very effective for chipping through shields). When you expose either Vorhess or the guard, use biotics or tech attacks to finish them off.

Vorhess is able to engage his FENRIS mechs before dying. Turn around and face the bridge door to cut down the galloping mechs before they enter the bridge.

After checking the captain's log for the code to access the cargo, push through the Blue Suns that fell in behind you in the hold. These mercs are led by Sergeant Boortis. They set up an ambush at the end of the corridor that you will not break through without taking heavy fire. Use the doorway of the bridge as cover and fire on the mercs from safety. The mercs will expose themselves for brief moments, giving you ample chances to take your shots. This is not a clocked assignment, so take your time.

The Prothean cargo is on the far side of the ship, through the corridor marked EP-8. Pick up the iridium in the smaller hold and then grab the cargo to end the mission.

After returning to the *Normandy*, check your private terminal for a new message. Cerberus has discovered the location of the base where the MSV *Strontium Mule* was ambushed. It's in the Sigurd's Cradle cluster, which is now placed on your galaxy map.

NOTE

N7: Blue Suns Base

The Blue Suns are using a false distress signal from their base on Sanctum to lure ships into an ambush. The distress signal must be disabled before any more vessels fall into the same trap as the MSV *Strontium Mule*.

Location: Sanctum

Rewards: 150 XP, 2,000 Iridium, 7,500 Credits

Disable False Distress Signal

Just as at the mine entrance in the first mission of this chain, the Blue Suns find themselves in a fortified position. You must push into their territory. Surround the door to their base by spreading the squad

across the clearing and ducking behind the rocks for cover. When the mercs explode from the front door to attack, your multiple positions prevent them from becoming a unified fighting force. With their attentions split, it is easier to pick them off.

There is a crate of iridium to the left of the base door.

NOTE

Inside the base, you have the advantage of high ground. The mercs, including a powerful commando, must come up to meet you. Use cover at the top of the room to rain fire down on the mercs as they attempt to wind up

the ramps and take your position. As before, split the squad to cover all ramps. Keep an eye on your teammates, though. If the mercs try to strong-arm one particular ramp, you will need to help out.

Check out the living quarters at the bottom of the room (off to the right) to locate a wall safe stuffed with credits.

Next, move into the mess hall. A mining accident has left a gaping hole in the wall of the mess hall. The Blue Suns use

that mine to enter the hall and launch their attack. There is ample cover in the mess hall, so stake out positions and train your fire on the Blue Suns that emerge from the mine.

Explore the mine, picking up additional crates of iridium.

The mine leads to a transportation hub. When you enter the room, the Blue Suns activate two YMIR mechs. Though there is a lot of cover to use in the room (watch out for explosive crates), handling two YMIR mechs

is not an easy job. Fall back from the YMIR mechs and seek cover, popping out to attack once their miniguns have temporarily fallen silent. Aim for the heads—those are the mechs' weak spots. If you have any heavy weapon ammo, use it to break through the mechs' shields and armor.

Miranda is useful on this assignment because her Overload weakens the YMIR mechs' shields.

TIP

There is a medi-gel on the small raised platform on the left side of the room. Shoot through the fragile crate blocking the ramp to retrieve it.

TIP

After the two YMIR mechs are down, the Blue Suns have no choice but to attack to keep you from retaking

their base. The final merc band is led by Captain Narom. He is the prime target, but do not ignore the troopers that flank him. They may be weak, but if you let one get too close, they can ravage your shields with submachine gun fire.

Empty the wall safe in the wall of the transportation hub.

TIP

When the battle is won, bypass the security on the locked door in the back of the room. Overload the distress beacon inside the room to put an end to the Blue Suns' dastardly plot.

The next three missions are chained together.

NOTE

N7: Wrecked Merchant Freighter

Scans of the planet Neith reveal the wreckage of a merchant freighter. The crash was catastrophic; no survivors are apparent. However, the scans also show movement at the crash site. Investigate the crash to determine what happened and to discover the source of movement at the crash site.

Location: Neith

Rewards: 125 XP, 2,000 Platinum, 7,500 Credits

Investigate Crash

The site of the crash is littered with debris. Scour the site for damaged mech parts you can salvage for credits and crates of platinum. Pick up all of the platinum and mech parts now because a sandstorm is coming in that will soon make it difficult to see.

When you finally reach the shipwreck, pick up the crate of power cells to restock your heavy weapon. Inspect the security report to read about the mechs aboard the freighter activating on their own and taking the ship. In the battle, the ship crashed on Neith. Deactivate the distress beacon at the wreckage and then head back to the shuttle.

When you shut off the distress beacon, you finally see signs of movement at the crash site as indicated by initial scans. LOKI mechs are converging on your position. You must rush to the shuttle to escape the mech attack. However, as you press back toward the shuttle drop zone, the sandstorm begins to ravage the site. The closer you get to the shuttle, the more limited visibility becomes. Plow through as many mechs as necessary to reach the shuttle. You will not destroy them all—they just keep coming. You just need to reach the shuttle.

Cryo ammo freezes the mechs in their tracks.

TIP

As you close in on your shuttle, a YMIR mech stomps out of the storm. You must take down this mech to reach the shuttle. Slam into cover and spread your squad out to attack the YMIR from multiple angles. After dropping the YMIR mech, get to the shuttle and return to the *Normandy*.

N7: Abandoned Research Station

The shipwreck was determined to be the MSV *Corsica*, a merchant freighter. The ship's last reported location was the Jarrahe Station. Investigate the station to discover what caused the mechs on the freighter to malfunction and attack the crew.

Location: Jarrahe Station

Rewards: 125 XP, 2,000 Iridium, 7,500 Credits

Escape Jarrahe Station

The Jarrahe Station is a ghost ship. The entire crew is dead, killed without mercy. The station's intelligence is on red alert and is protecting itself from intruders. You must somehow thwart the intelligence and get off the station.

Methodically explore the station to discover crates of iridium. Pick up datapads and access terminals to learn more about the crew's final hours.

You cannot shut down the station without opening the locks to the intelligence core. You must press deeper into the station. Start by checking out the living quarters. The controls for power in the living quarters are in the very back. They unlock a series of computers on a nearby table. Access the central computer to hear the message: five doors enabled.

Unlocking the door next to the console lets you enter the barracks. Open the lockers to recover credits.

Return to the power control room and move into the research lab. There is iridium in the research lab. Use the console to restore power to the lab and then check out the reflective armor prototyping facility on the floor below.

There are four terminals at the desk overlooking the facility. These terminals adjust the position of the armor plating panels. Each time you adjust a plate, an electrical beam arcs through the facility. Adjust the plates to bounce the beam across the facility and blast the computer in the back. You must turn the second plate so the beam moves between the two plates without any reflection to solve the puzzle. Blasting open the computer in the back of the facility unlocks engineering.

Now, move to engineering from the central power room. The corridor through engineering is lined with pipes leaking intermittent blasts of plasma. These plasma blasts are dangerous. If caught in a blast, you lose shields and health. Your squad can get in real trouble in here, so order them to stay back, then dart through the plasma on your own. The lock for the intelligence core is in the very back of engineering.

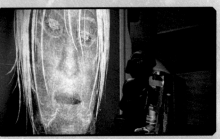

Return to the central hub and unlock the doors leading to the ship's intelligence core. Once inside, shut down the mainframe to end the VI's reign of terror. When you return to the *Normandy*, check your private terminal for a message that leads to the final assignment in this series: Hahne-Kedar Facility.

Introduction

Training

Upgrades and Research

Walkthrough

Special Assignments

Planetary Database

Appendix

N7: Hahne-Kedar Facility

Data mined from the station's intelligence in the previous assignment reveals that a virus caused the malfunction. The source of the virus is the Hahne-Kedar Facility on the planet Capek. This is a mech factory. The facility must be shut down before it can ship any more infected mechs that turn on humans.

Location: Capek

Rewards: 125 XP, 500 Element Zero, 7,500 Credits

Shut Down Factory

The Hahne-Kedar facility sits eerily silent on the surface of Capek. When you approach the entrance to the factory, fan out so you can efficiently take down the small army of FENRIS and LOKI mechs that race through the front door as you draw near. Blast the mechs and then slip inside the factory.

There are several dead bodies inside. The mechs were infected by a systemwide virus and destroyed each other. Grab the medi-gel from the nearby counter, empty the wall safe, and access the terminal. The terminal contains several messages about the emergency situation at the factory and the mech malfunctions.

Ease onto the factory floor, picking up a crate of element zero.

More FENRIS mechs attack as you move deeper into the factory. They are quickly joined by LOKI mechs. Catch the LOKI mechs near the ramp leading down to the lower factory floor. Use the ramp as a bottleneck to hold the mechs down so they cannot spread out across the upper floor.

> Cryo ammo freezes the mechs in their tracks.
>
> **TIP**

Weave through the labyrinth of crates on the factory floor, hunting LOKI mechs. Look for heavy weapon ammo crates. Though you do not have to face down a YMIR mech in this battle, heavy weapons clear out entire platoons of LOKI mechs with relative ease. Blast through the mechs as they mill through the crates and boxes. Use the crates as cover to guard against the mech attacks.

When you reach the rear of the factory, pass through the door. Grab the crate of element zero on the bottom floor of this room and then climb the ramps to reach the control panel that shuts down the factory. Hack the console. When you complete the hack, the production line grinds to a halt, stopping the mech menace.

> The next eight missions are discovered only by scanning planets.
>
> **NOTE**

N7: Endangered Research Station

The magnetic shielding that protects the human colony on Sinmara is failing. If the shielding goes offline, the entire colony below is vulnerable to its sun's solar flares. Save the colony by reactivating the shields.

Location: Sinmara

Rewards: 125 XP, 2,000 Palladium, 7,500 Credits

Activate Magnetic Shield

There are no enemies in this assignment, so you perform this mission without any squad mates.

After landing on the shield platform, approach the station control terminal and lower the doors up to the main platform. The system must be turned on in a specific order by powering up components in the correct order to effectively jump-start the shields.

The control switch in the center of the platform is the key to the system. Every time you access the switch, you redirect power to one of the three systems that make up the shield. First, access the switch

to run power to the shield generator, which is on your right. Turn on the shield generator. Because the shield is not up, you must engage the coolant system so it does not overheat.

The coolant system is to the left. Access the control switch to power up the cooling system. Once the coolant system has been activated, return to the switch and direct power to the shield controls. Hack the console to reactivate the shields and save the colony.

The mission ends following the activation of the shields, so make sure you pick up the crate of palladium on the landing platform first.

N7: Mining the Canyon

Surface scans of Taitus detect a YMIR mech with an unknown registration. The mech was being used in a mining operation but appears to be disabled. If the mech is reactivated and allowed to complete its mining program, it reveals large quantities of valuable minerals.

Location: Taitus

Rewards: 125 XP, 2,000 Platinum, 7,500 Credits

Activate Mech

There is a disabled YMIR mech near the landing zone. The datapad next to it reveals that the YMIR was abandoned by its owner after he was unable to repair the mech. Pick up the energy pack near the mech and place it on the mech's back. This powers up the mech, but only for a limited time.

The mech stomps through the canyon, blasting its way through rocks with its guns and missiles. Stay behind the mech and follow it, placing batteries whenever it powers down.

Introduction

Training

Upgrades and Research

Walkthrough

Special Assignments

Planetary Database

Appendix

Beware of varren lurking around the mech's batteries.

At the end of the mech's run, it reveals a rich vein of platinum. Recover the ore to end the assignment.

N7: Captured Mining Facility

Eclipse mercenaries have taken control of the Eldfell-Ashland Energy Corporation mining facility on Helyme. The mercenaries recently cut the facility's distress beacon.

Location: Helyme

Rewards: 125 XP, 4,000 Palladium, 15,000 Credits

Investigate Eclipse Presence

The shuttle lands just outside the facility. There are no Eclipse mercs waiting for you at the landing zone, but when you approach the facility exterior, the mercs leap into action. Use the door to the facility as cover and blast your way through the throng of troopers and vanguards to access the interior.

Hack the locked door inside the facility to recover palladium. There is an additional crate inside the main facility.

Inside the facility, the Eclipse band puts up a show of force. Vanguards and troopers dig into cover behind walls and crates to hold you at the door. Push your way into the facility interior by breaking their ranks. Go for the easy targets first, like troopers. Thinning their numbers makes the Eclipse foes more manageable.

Watch out for Eclipse heavies on the upper platform inside the facility. They attack with rockets.

You must fight your way to the mainframe computer on the upper platform of the facility. Hack the mainframe to access some encrypted data. You must then hold the facility from Eclipse reinforcements while the data is decrypted. The reinforcements are led by Captain Vorleon, who is flanked by additional troopers and vanguards. Use heavy weapons to pick off Vorleon's allies and then drop the captain himself. Once the captain is down, the data finishes decrypting and the mission ends.

> Vorleon can replenish his shields if left alone. Once you start in on the merc, finish him off. Do not allow him to retreat and hide.
>
> **CAUTION**

N7: Eclipse Smuggling Depot

Eclipse mercenaries have abandoned their smuggling depot on Daratar and left behind a trio of YMIR mechs to scuttle the stolen goods rather than let them fall into enemy hands. Cerberus would like the cargo, so destroy the heavy mechs before they can eliminate the crates of goods.

Location: Daratar

Rewards: 125 XP, 180 Credits per Crate

Destroy YMIR Mechs

The depot is directly next to the landing zone. When you enter the depot, the three YMIR mechs activate and begin their demolition duty. There are 20 crates at the depot. The mechs pound them with miniguns and rockets, destroying them at a rate of about one every 30 seconds. The more crates that remain at the end of the assignment, the more credits you earn from Cerberus.

Take down the YMIR mechs as fast as you can so you can pocket the maximum amount of credits. Bring a heavy weapon like missiles or a grenade launcher to do the most damage to the mechs. However, even more useful is a squad mate with Overload, such as Miranda. Overload breaks through the YMIR mech shields, allowing you to bring them down faster.

> There is a crate of heavy weapon ammo against the rock wall of the depot, but you need to get through the YMIRs to reach it.
>
> **TIP**

N7: Estevanico

The freighter MSV *Estevanico* was lost one year ago in the Ploitari system. Surface scans of the planet Zanethu reveal the presence of a giant shipwreck. The wreck bears signatures of the lost merchant freighter. A search of the wreck will confirm whether or not it is indeed the lost freighter as well as what brought it down.

Location: Zanethu

Rewards: 125 XP, 2,000 Iridium, 7,500 Credits

Investigate Wreckage

Shoot the panel of loose tiles to create a bridge below.

The wreck is indeed the *Estevanico*. It slammed into the side of a cliff. When the shuttle drops you off on the wreck, EDI warns you that disturbing the site too much could send all of it crashing into the canyon below. You must find a safe route through the wreckage to the ship's mainframe, which is miraculously still online.

Follow the giant structural supports into the heart of the wreckage, collecting the crates of iridium as you move. The ship shudders and shakes with greater frequency and intensity as you move farther away from the cliff and toward the red mainframe computer.

Introduction

Training

Upgrades and Research

Walkthrough

Special Assignments

Planetary Database

Appendix

Access the mainframe to gather intel on the final hour of the freighter. When the data download finishes, the shuttle picks you up. You jump aboard just as the wreck breaks away from the cliff and tumbles into the ravine below.

N7: Abandoned Mine

The mining facility on Aequitas has gone silent. Something has either chased away the miners or killed them. Investigate the site to determine what happened here and see if you can possibly stop it from spreading.

Location: Aequitas

Rewards: 125 XP, 2,000 Iridium, 7,500 Credits

Investigate Mine

Enter the mine. The husks you discover immediately answer the question about what happened to the miners. Find out what turned these miners into husks and destroy it.

Scan the tunnel for crates of iridium. Watch out for husks that swarm the crates, as they tend to swarm the moment you go for the iridium.

Watch the ceilings! Husks sometimes fall from the tunnel ceiling. If you run into an area without looking, you may find a husk right in your lap.

CAUTION

The mine tunnel is crowded with husks. The narrow passages are advantageous because they let you funnel the husks right into your waiting guns. You can create chokepoints with your squad members, holding a line that the husks mindlessly stumble right into. When getting ready to reload, use a biotic or tech attack to busy the husks for the few seconds you cannot fire.

Abominations make great walking bombs as long as you set them off when they are next to husks and not a squad member.

Bypass the security on the lockers inside the mine to pick up credits.

TIP

When the tunnel opens up into a large chamber with a vaulted ceiling, EDI comes over the comm. She has picked up the signature of a large alien device. EDI posits that the alien technology is what turned the miners into husks. Destroy the device to stop the husks. The only problem is that until you do manage to wreck the alien device, the husks will keep pouring into the area. They drop from the ceilings. They crawl out of the shadows. They pull themselves out of the cracks in the walls. The husks attack from all angles.

> **CAUTION**
> If you get cornered by the husks, they can beat you down. Use melee attacks to push them back and carve a path out of the horde.

> **TIP**
> Use a shotgun as crowd control in close quarters like this. A point-blank blast cleaves a husk in half.

Grab the heavy weapon ammo from the crate on the bridge above the chamber. Use heavy weapons to drop husks on the way to the artifact in the very back of the chamber.

There are two bombs in the room with the alien device that is turning miners into husks. Destroy each bomb to bring down the device. Shoot the bombs from a distance so you are not injured in the blasts. If you have access to Overload (through you or a squad member), use it to detonate the bombs from a safe distance. The mission ends when the second bomb goes off.

N7: Anomalous Weather Detected

Sensors detect anomalous weather patterns on Canalus. Scans also reveal significant geth activity. Investigate the site of the geth activity to determine whether or not the two incidents are related.

> **TIP**
> Since you fight geth on this mission, a squad member with AI Hacking is ideal.

Location: Canalus
Rewards: 125 XP, 2,000 Palladium, 7,500 Credits

Disable Climate Change Device

Explore the small rock alcoves leading away from the main path (marked by flares) to locate raw minerals.

The geth have developed a climate-altering device and are testing it on Canalus. When you land on the surface, you are enveloped by a thick fog that severely limits visibility. Though you may struggle to see through the haze, the geth do not have such problems and quickly target you as you press through a maze of rocks en route to the climate device. Follow the flares—and the geth shootouts—to locate the device.

The geth use the mists to hide from you, so you must rely on your HUD to single out targets. When you do spot a target, use appropriate measures to bring it down. A trooper, for example, can be ripped apart with gunfire or a good biotic attack. Shielded geth, however, need to have their shields either disabled via a tech attack or just ruined via gunplay.

Beware the geth hunters in the mist—their cloaking devices make them even harder to spot.

Once you fight your way through the geth, access the terminal at the base of the device to shut it down. The climate on Canalus will soon clear up. And Cerberus is quite happy to now have that technology in its hands.

N7: Javelin Launch

Batarians have seized control of an Alliance base on Franklin. The base is armed with Javelin Mk. II missiles to be used to defend the nearby human colony. A recent scan reveals that the batarians have launched two missiles. To save the colony, the team must storm the base and seize control of the missiles, destroying them before they reach their targets.

Location: Franklin

Rewards: 125 XP, 2,000 Palladium, 7,500 Credits

Stop Javelin Missiles

You have just five minutes to stop the missiles before they strike the colony. When you enter the base, a small patrol of batarians attacks right away. The batarians do not put up much of a fight—in fact, it's almost as if they were there only to slow you down. Just use the crates as cover and blast the batarians. None of them have armor or shields, so they are easy targets.

Fight through the next room of batarians. The door to the missile launch room is on the floor below, easily accessed via the ramps. However, the batarians will shoot you to keep you from completing the hack on the

door. You need to clear out at least the majority of the batarians before attempting it. Cross the room and drop the batarians with gunfire and biotic attacks. Pick up the palladium crates as you winnow the batarian herd.

The console to stop the missiles is on the far side of the room. There are only a small handful of batarians in this room, but the commander at the panel puts up a real challenge. He is equipped with shields and will replenish them unless you finish him off in one continuous attack. You cannot stop the missiles until the commander is dead. If you try to access the console and hack the missiles, the commander will thwart your hack by shooting you.

There is a wall safe with 3,750 credits to the right of the missile control panel. Hacking the security, though, does eat into your five-minute clock.

When you finally hack the missile controls, you are presented with a terrible choice: There is not enough time to stop both missiles. You must pick one. Do you destroy the missile heading for the colony, saving the people but rendering the spaceport useless to the Alliance? Or do you allow the missile streaking toward the colony to deliver its deadly payload, killing innocents but preserving the facility for Alliance expansion? If you are going for Paragon, save the colonists. If you want to keep building your Renegade rating, then let the missile obliterate the colonists while saving the spaceport.

PLANETARY DATABASE

Thanks to the discovery of the mass relays, humans have been able to explore a great deal of the galaxy and map much of its celestial contents. As a result of such expanded horizons, new minerals have been discovered and harvested. These new minerals are critical for the development of upgrades via research projects..

EXPLORERS OF THE 24TH CENTURY

The crew of the *Normandy* can scout out mineral deposits on planets in many of the galaxy's clusters. Since time is of the essence for Shepard in the fight against the Reapers, knowing exactly where to look for the different minerals will make upgrading technology and researching new projects much easier.

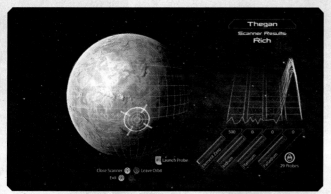

- Every planet has a random number of low-value deposits. These minerals will barely show up on your scanners. Pursue these minor deposits at your own discretion. Often, they will not be worth the cost of the probe.

- While there are general rules and assumptions for mineral distribution, do not assume every planet of the same type will give up the same minerals. Read the description of each planet before mining to see if the planet has any special properties that might affect your mining operation.

Mining for minerals on planets is not an exact science, though. You will not always find the same amount of mineral on one type of planet. Nor will it be in the same area. So, use these tips in conjunction with the planetary database to get the most out of your mining trips:

- Expect to find approximately 15 deposit sites on the planet surface.

- Look for sites that offer multiple minerals. You double the effectiveness of your probe if you drop one on a site that straddles two or more elements.

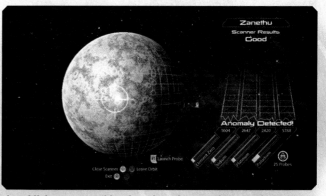

In addition to searching for minerals, you also use the scanner to seek out anomalies that indicate a potential special assignment.

Completing certain research projects will improve the efficiency of your exploration and mining operations. Talk to Miranda in her office to unlock the Argus Scanner Array research project; completing the project will increase the speed of your planetary scanners. Talk to Samara to unlock the Helios Thruster Tech research project; once completed, the *Normandy*'s fuel cell capacity increases by 50%, requiring fewer fueling stops while you explore the galaxies.

TIP

Planet Types

There are nine different planet types: brown dwarf, desert, garden, ice giant, Jovian, Pegasid, post-garden, ocean/ice, and rock. These planet categories offer blanket assessments of what to expect when mining.

Element zero (eezo) is found only on planets that have been previously inhabited.

TIP

Introduction

Training

Upgrades and Research

Walkthrough

Special Assignments

Planetary Database

Appendix

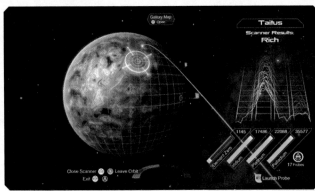

Each planet has a set quantity of minerals to harvest. The mineral content of a planet is measured in this database as **richness**. There are five levels of richness: rich, good, moderate, poor, and depleted. Though you should at least orbit depleted planets to add them to your personal database, don't waste the probes on mining them. Instead, concentrate first on "rich" and "good" planets, which provide the largest bounties. Since minerals and element zero are such important (and precious) commodities, in addition to noting the overall richness of the planet, these charts also measure the amount of each mineral and element zero. Ratings are rich, moderate, poor, and none.

> **TIP**
> You cannot complete all of the upgrade projects with the element zero found on missions. You must mine for element zero, too.

Brown Dwarf

- Frequency: Rare
- Examples: Osalri, Urdak
- Element Zero: None
- Iridium: 30%
- Palladium: 40%
- Platinum: 30%

Brown dwarfs are gas giants that almost had enough mass to become small stars but never quite started the final combustion process. However, as a result of their mass, brown dwarfs do have some luminosity. The minerals on a brown dwarf are typically spread out along the bands of the planet, so look there when mining.

Desert

- Frequency: Very Common
- Examples: Laena, Bovis Tor
- Element Zero: None
- Iridium: 20%
- Palladium: 60%
- Platinum: 20%

These arid planets are high-density, usually with a reddish-brown surface. Incredibly hot and dry, desert planets are not known for sustaining life. They are rich in minerals, but those deposits are spread out across the surface in small clusters.

Garden

- Frequency: Rare
- Example: Earth, Sanctum, Talis Fia
- Element Zero: Poor
- Iridium: 15%
- Palladium: 25%
- Platinum: 60%

Life-sustaining garden planets are rare in the galaxy. These worlds have a mixture of ocean and land and support both plant and animal life. Garden planets are one of the few planet types where you can expect to find element zero—look to the continents. The other minerals should be looked for in mountainous areas.

Ice Giant

- Frequency: Common
- Examples: Neptune, Tula, Alkonost
- Element Zero: None
- Iridium: 20%
- Palladium: 30%
- Platinum: 50%

These enormous ice planets are also gas giants but have an atmosphere composed of water vapor, ammonia, and methane. Minerals on a giant ice are concentrated in smallish clusters. Look for noticeable features, such as massive storms, for the location of rich deposits.

Jovian

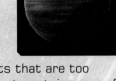

- Frequency: Common
- Examples: Bast, Nephros
- Element Zero: None
- Iridium: 30%
- Palladium: 30%
- Platinum: 40%

Giant Jovians are gaseous planets that are too small to have become stars but yet contain many of the required elements, like concentrated amounts of hydrogen and helium. As on brown dwarfs, the minerals on a giant Jovian are spread out across the colorful bands.

Pegasid

- Frequency: Rare
- Example: Rescel, Jontan
- Element zero: None
- Iridium: 30%
- Palladium: 40%
- Platinum: 30%

Giant Pegasids are similar to Jovian giants but are locked in close orbit with their parent stars. The orbit causes a tidal lock, meaning that there is a "hot pole" that faces the star and a "cold pole" that faces deep space (and is incredibly dark). Giant Pegasids have hurricane winds that move from the

hot pole to the cold pole. These poles are where you should expect to find the richest deposits, which is quite different from other planets, which typically see their deposits along the equator or in the horizontal bands.

Post-Garden

- Frequency: Rare
- Example: Helyme, Etamis
- Element Zero: Rich
- Iridium: 30%
- Palladium: 40%
- Platinum: 40%

Post-garden worlds are reminders of the dreadful power of the Reapers. These planets were once rich with life but are now husks with ruined cities and discolored landscapes. Element zero is highly concentrated on post-garden planets as a result of fallen civilizations. The remaining minerals are spread out across the equator with occasional deposits elsewhere.

Ocean/Ice

- Frequency: Common
- Example: Anedia, Maisuth
- Element Zero: None
- Iridium: 15%
- Palladium: 15%
- Platinum: 70%

These planets are high-density, with strong metallic cores surrounded by frozen oceans. Ocean/ice planets can support some life, but do not expect to find element zero on them. Instead, look for the mineral deposits in small clusters.

Rock

- Frequency: Very Common
- Examples: Moon (Luna), Gregas, Quarem
- Element Zero: None
- Iridium: 60%
- Palladium: 20%
- Platinum: 20%

Rock planets are typically small with little to no atmosphere and no native life whatsoever. When mining a rock planet, look to the impact craters for the richest deposits.

PLANETS BY CLUSTERS

As you explore the galaxy, you will encounter dozens upon dozens of alien worlds. Some will be lifeless balls of rock, good only for mining operations. Others will be busy hives of activity, such as the repurposed asteroid Omega, which is now an off-world den of unsavory pursuits.

All planets have been categorized by cluster. Within each cluster, there are potentially multiple planetary systems. Systems containing a fuel depot are marked with an ✶. Each planet is then listed by name with the planet type, richness of minerals, and a description of the planet. Planets with landing sites are listed in **bold**.

> Keep track of what you have excavated so you do not waste time (or credits) on a tapped source.
>
> **NOTE**

Caleston Rift

Aysur						
Planet	**World Type**	**Richness**	**Element Zero**	**Iridium**	**Platinum**	**Palladium**
Agnin	Rock	Rich	None	Rich	Moderate	Moderate

Description: A hothouse planet, Agnin has scorching clouds of methane and sulfur dioxide that give the planet a pale green color in visible light. The SO2 from volcanic activity rains down as sulfuric acid in the upper atmosphere, but this is boiled away before the liquid ever reaches the surface. Agnin's harsh environment has prevented exploration by anything except probes. Orbital Distance: 0.7 AU; Orbital Period: 0.6 Earth Years; Radius: 4,834 Km; Day Length: 61.1 Earth Hours; Atmospheric Pressure: 86.87 Earth Atmospheres; Surface Temperature: 684 Celsius; Surface Gravity: 0.5 G.

Alformus	Giant Jovian	Moderate	None	Poor	Moderate	Moderate

Description: A hydrogen-helium gas giant, Alformus had its helium-3 refueling stations destroyed in an attack by Grow Zero, an anti-population terrorist group that wanted no more immigration to Arvuna. A consortium of Arvuna-based corporations is currently rebuilding the stations. ALLIANCE ADVISORY: Alformus is not considered vital to the stability of the Aysur system. Civilians working on the helium-3 platforms should not expect Alliance military intervention in case of kidnapping or other violence. Orbital Distance: 10.1 AU; Orbital Period: 32.2 Earth Years; Radius: 67,626 Km; Day Length: 8.8 Earth Hours; Atmospheric Pressure: 1.81 Earth Atmospheres.

Introduction
Training
Upgrades and Research
Walkthrough
Special Assignments
Planetary Database
Appendix

Aysur (continued)

Planet	World Type	Richness	Element Zero	Iridium	Platinum	Palladium
Arvuna	Ocean/Ice	Rich	Moderate	Poor	Rich	Moderate

Description: With oceans covering 90 percent of Arvuna's surface, this moon of Dranen is classified as a water world. Besides its prodigious sea life, Arvuna is also home to avian and mammal-like life forms on its islands. None are currently considered sapient. Arvuna is home to thriving human colonies, though indigenous diseases and venomous pests similar to a horsefly cause high mortality rates. TRAVEL ADVISORY: Kidnapping for ransom is the number one violent crime on this planet. Please use all available security options when traveling to Arvuna. Population: 348,785,500; Colony Founded: 2160 CE; Capital: Asa; Orbital Distance: 2.5 AU; Orbital Period: 4.0 Earth Years (Aysur) 66 days (Dranen); Radius: 6,448 Km; Day Length: 29.2 Earth Hours; Atmospheric Pressure: 1.45 Earth Atmospheres; Surface Temperature: -11 Celsius (mean), 25 Celsius (equator); Surface Gravity: 1.1 G.

Dranen	Giant Jovian	Moderate	None	Poor	Poor	Poor

Description: A sizable hydrogen-nitrogen gas giant just on the far side of its pale yellow star's "frost line," Dranen is known for its spectacular storms. At least three persistent observable "spots"—actually cyclonic and anticyclonic storms—have lasted for over 544 years, significantly longer than Jupiter's Great Red Spot. The largest of these spots, the Ishna, has consistently held a diameter over three times that of Earth. Dranen has 44 moons. Two of them are of special interest to the Citadel Committee on Habitable Worlds. The first, Arvuna, is a life-bearing world that has already been colonized. The second, Alahya, is slowly being terraformed into an ammonia-based world for volus populations. Orbital Distance: 2.5 AU; Orbital Period: 4.0 Earth Years; Radius: 72,021 Km; Day Length: 17.1 Earth Hours; Atmospheric Pressure: 1.94 Earth Atmospheres.

Shasu	Rock	Rich	None	Rich	Moderate	Moderate

Description: Shasu is a dwarf planet that is believed to have been ejected from Agnin during a giant impact with another planet-sized body. At the time, Agnin had a magma ocean covering much of its surface, and the liquid rock sprayed into space, where it coalesced and cooled over millions of years. The theory is that during this cooling Shasu first orbited Agnin but was eventually pulled from that orbit by the gravity wells of other planets, primarily Dranen. Today Shasu is relatively temperate, with a light hydrogen-helium atmosphere attracting spacers who use its atmosphere to refuel. Its crust composition is similar to that of Agnin, as is evident in its high sulfur content. Orbital Distance: 1.4 AU; Orbital Period: 1.7 Earth Years; Radius: 1,454 Km; Day Length: 37.4 Earth Hours; Atmospheric Pressure: 0.34 Earth Atmospheres; Surface Temperature: 23 Celsius; Surface Gravity: 0.1 G.

Shir	Rock	Rich	None	Rich	Moderate	Rich

Description: A remote rock planet capped in ice, Shir has been exploited by Arvunan corporations for its minerals. Home to gold ore, which is used in spaceship shielding as well as jewelry, and to cobalt deposits used in high-tensile alloys, Shir shows no signs of being exhausted anytime soon. A light gravity helps keep the planetary exportation process cheap. Orbital Distance: 20.0 AU; Orbital Period: 89.7 Earth Years; Radius: 4,900 Km; Day Length: 31.0 Earth Hours; Atmospheric Pressure: Trace; Surface Temperature: -185 Celsius; Surface Gravity: 0.7 G.

Tamgauta	Desert	Good	None	Poor	Moderate	Rich

Description: The outermost planet of the Aysur system, Tamgauta is remote and largely unexplored. Its carbon dioxide atmosphere has long since frozen into fields of dry ice. Orbital Distance: 42.2 AU; Orbital Period: 275.1 Earth Years; Radius: 3,354 Km; Day Length: 64.8 Earth Hours; Atmospheric Pressure: Trace; Surface Temperature: -216 Celsius; Surface Gravity: 0.2 G.

Balor *

Planet	World Type	Richness	Element Zero	Iridium	Platinum	Palladium
Bres	Rock	Rich	None	Poor	Rich	Moderate

Description: A member of the Fomor Belt, Bres is a dwarf planet with no atmosphere. It is, however, rich in lithium, which is integral to the heat sinks of starships and hand-held weapons. A large robo-mining operation from Caleston can be found here. Orbital Distance: 2.9 AU; Orbital Period: 4.9 Earth Years; Radius: 975 Km; Day Length: 23.3 Earth Hours; Atmospheric Pressure: None; Surface Temperature: -146 Celsius.

Caleston	Desert	Rich	Moderate	Poor	Rich	Moderate

Description: The hostile moon Caleston is the largest satellite of the gas giant Cernunnos. An ancient asteroid strike deposited major loads of element zero within the molten sulfur mantle. Eldfell-Ashland Energy's mining operations have made it the largest source of starship drive core material in the Attican Traverse. Caleston is wracked with volcanism due to tidal stresses from Cernunnos. Because of the weak solar output, plant-like life on Caleston is not carbon-based and photosynthetic but silicon-based and thermosynthetic, requiring heat rather than sunlight to power its chemical reactions. These organisms flourish in volcanic vents and during solar flares when Balor can double or triple in luminosity. Sadly, sapient habitation is not possible here and Caleston's biodiversity is considered "threatened" by the Citadel Council Committee on Habitable Worlds. Population: 1,802,705,000; Colony Founded: 1975 CE; Capital: Syneu; Orbital Distance: 0.07 AU (orbits Cernunnos); Orbital Period: 21.5 Earth Hours (around Cernunnos); Radius: 6,600 Km; Day Length: 21.5 Earth Hours; Atmospheric Pressure: 0.9 Earth Atmospheres; Surface Temperature: 30 Celsius; Surface Gravity: 1.2 G.

Cernunnos	Giant Jovian	Moderate	None	Poor	Rich	Moderate

Description: Cernunnos is a sizable gas giant with a hydrogen-nitrogen atmosphere. It is believed to be an extrasolar capture due to its close stellar location. In a rare phenomenon it is near enough to its red dwarf star to be within the life zone, though its massive size prevents the tidal lock that usually occurs at such a range. While nothing could survive on the surface of a planet with such crushing gravity, Cernunnos's moon, Caleston, is habitable. Cernunnos is skimmed for its abundant hydrogen, and refineries on Caleston process it into a metastable metallic form for use as starship fuel. Orbital Distance: 0.07 AU; Orbital Period: 31 Earth Days; Radius: 49,231 Km; Day Length: 17.0 Earth Hours; Atmospheric Pressure: 0.86 Earth Atmospheres.

Elatha	Rock	Rich	None	Poor	Rich	Moderate

Description: A tiny rock planet, Elatha is noted for its frigid temperatures and crushing nitrogen and krypton atmosphere. Lying out beyond the Fomor Belt, it has little to recommend it. Orbital Distance: 5.5 AU; Orbital Period: 23.6 Earth Years; Radius: 1,812 Km; Day Length: 57.3 Earth Hours; Atmospheric Pressure: 43.34 Earth Atmospheres; Surface Temperature: -72 Celsius; Surface Gravity: 0.1 G.

Balor (continued)

Planet	World Type	Richness	Element Zero	Iridium	Platinum	Palladium
Partholon	Ocean/Ice	Rich	None	Poor	Rich	Moderate

Description: A large planet composed of ice surrounding a rocky core, Partholon retains trace gases of nitrogen and carbon monoxide. Its crushing gravity makes for an inhospitable stay and makes most mining unfeasible. However, its orbit's proximity to the mass relay in the system means space travelers will for the next few years use it for a gravitational slingshot to add speed on their way to and from Caleston. Orbital Distance: 11.2 AU; Orbital Period: 68.6 Earth Years; Radius: 11,921 Km; Day Length: 28.2 Earth Hours; Atmospheric Pressure: Trace; Surface Temperature: -236 Celsius; Surface Gravity: 6.6 G.

Solveig

Planet	World Type	Richness	Element Zero	Iridium	Platinum	Palladium
Sinmara	Rock	Good	None	Rich	Moderate	Moderate

Description: Surtur's moon Sinmara has been used for many generations to monitor its parent star Solveig. It has no atmosphere to interfere with solar observational equipment, which is critical at this juncture; the star recently showed signs of erupting prematurely into a red giant. In preparation for the day when the critical warning goes out the extranet channel from Sinmara's research station is given top priority throughout the comm buoys in the system. The chances of such a signal being received over the sun's magnetic interference at that time is low, but relegating it to a lower channel proved politically untenable. Colony Founded: 2044 CE; Population: 135; Largest Habitat: Trundholm.

Surtur	Desert	Rich	None	Poor	Poor	Rich

Description: Surtur is a small but dense desert planet close to its parent star. All but traces of its nitrogen-carbon monoxide atmosphere have burned away, leaving it cooler than similar planets in other systems. Robo-mining has proved lucrative as it has developed significant deposits of beryllium and palladium. Orbital Distance: 0.7 AU; Orbital Period: 0.6 Earth Years; Radius: 4,433 Km; Day Length: 65.0 Earth Hours; Atmospheric Pressure: Trace; Surface Temperature: 126 Celsius; Surface Gravity: 0.8 G.

Thrivaldi	Giant Jovian	Poor	None	Poor	Moderate	Poor

Description: The refueling stations of hydrogen-helium gas giant Thrivaldi provide helium-3 for commercial spacecraft visiting the system. It has nine known moons and many smaller bodies in its rings. TRAVEL ADVISORY: Recent attacks by pirates have targeted Thrivaldi's refueling stations. Authorities list the perpetrators as "at large." Travel is not recommended. Orbital Distance: 1.5 AU; Orbital Period: 1.8 Earth Years; Radius: 35,957 Km; Day Length: 11.0 Earth Hours.

Talava

Planet	World Type	Richness	Element Zero	Iridium	Platinum	Palladium
Aitarus	Rock	Moderate	None	Rich	Poor	Poor

Description: A large rock planet orbiting an F-class star, Aitarus is pummeled by radiation, heavy gravity, and tectonic activity. Its crust is mostly silicates and of little value. Travel is not advised. Orbital Distance: 0.5 AU; Orbital Period: 0.3 Earth Years; Radius: 8,945 Km; Day Length: 65.1 Earth Hours; Atmospheric Pressure: Trace Surface Temperature: 549 Celsius; Surface Gravity: 2.8 G.

Kaushus	Rock	Good	None	Rich	Moderate	Moderate

Description: Home to the spectacular Infinity Caldera, Kaushus is a young planet with extreme tectonic and volcanic activity. It has nine supervolcanoes that can throw out at least 1,000 cubic kilometers of dense rock equivalents each, and Kaushus's activity has put its atmosphere in a state of shroud. It will likely suffer from global dimming for at least the next 10 years. Though much of the surface is no more dangerous than many other inner-ring planets, this extreme tectonic activity has given Kaushus a bad reputation and discouraged all resource exploitation. Orbital Distance: 1.2 AU; Orbital Period: 1.0 Earth Years; Radius: 6,212 Km; Day Length: 42.6 Earth Hours; Atmospheric Pressure: Trace; Surface Temperature: 249 Celsius; Surface Gravity: 1.0.

Maitrum	Rock	Rich	None	Rich	Poor	Poor

Description: A small hot rock with few resources, Maitrum is used by the turian armed forces for its maximum security prison and interrogation centers. The temperatures are high enough to prevent any escape without an environmental suit but low enough that construction of additional buildings will not be hindered. Over 500,000 prisoners are detained on Maitrum, only a handful of which have ever managed even a temporary escape. A small supply economy and prefab habitats support the prison staff who usually work only for two-year tours of duty before they are rotated out to less stressful positions. Orbital Distance: 2.8 AU; Orbital Period: 3.6 Earth Years; Radius: 4,642 Km; Atmospheric Pressure: Trace; Surface Temperature: 74 Celsius; Surface Gravity: 0.4 G.

Taitus	Desert	Rich	None	Poor	Moderate	Rich

Description: A desert of whitish potassium salts and reddish iron oxides, Taitus is far enough away from its parent star to have a tolerable surface temperature. Though it has only a trace atmosphere of carbon dioxide and oxygen it is still hospitable enough for criminals in the Terminus Systems to use it as a staging base. Turian patrols sometimes fly through the area looking to pre-empt jailbreak attempts on Maitrum's prisons. TRAVEL ADVISORY: Unregistered starships have been spotted in the vicinity of Taitus. Civilian travel is not recommended. Orbital Distance: 4.0 AU; Orbital Period: 6.1 Earth Years; Radius: 6,045 Km; Day Length: 22.2 Earth Hours; Atmospheric Pressure: Trace; Surface Temperature: -1 Celsius; Surface Gravity: 0.9 G.

Introduction
Training
Upgrades and Research
Walkthrough
Special Assignments
Planetary Database
Appendix

Crescent Nebula

Lusarn						
Planet	**World Type**	**Richness**	**Element Zero**	**Iridium**	**Platinum**	**Palladium**
Doriae	Desert	Good	None	Poor	Moderate	Rich

Description: Doriae is a large hot world with a poisonous atmosphere of acidic nitrogen oxides. While the planet is too close to Lusarn for this to condense and fall as rain it makes the environment too hostile for forms of life more sophisticated than bacteria to evolve. Orbital Distance: 2.48 AU; Orbital Period: 3.0 Earth Years; Radius: 8,700 Km; Day Length: 63 Earth Hours; Atmospheric Pressure: 1.17 Earth Atmospheres; Surface Temperature: 204 Celsius; Surface Gravity: 1.2 G.

Euntanta	Desert	Rich	None	Poor	Moderate	Rich

Description: Euntanta is remarkably close to Earth. Its orbital distance is similar, and while slightly larger its reduced density yields similar mass, atmospheric pressure, and gravity. There the similarities end, for Lusarn is a hot class F star emitting over eight times the energy of Sol. Euntanta is a parched wasteland, its water long since boiled away into its nitrogen-carbon dioxide atmosphere. A handful of mining outposts dot the hellishly hot surface. The crews remain in underground bunkers, sending remotely controlled machines out at night to do surface work and load cargo for shipment. Population: 230; Orbital Distance: 1.04 AU; Orbital Period: 0.3 Earth Years; Radius: 7,740 Km; Day Length: 24.2 Earth Hours; Atmospheric Pressure: 0.98 Earth Atmospheres; Surface Temperature: 415 Celsius; Surface Gravity: 1.0 G.

Jontan	Giant Pegasid	Good	None	Moderate	Moderate	Moderate

Description: Jontan is a fairly standard close-orbiting Pegasid gas giant orbiting the star Lusarn at high velocity and heated to temperatures of over 1,000 degrees. Analysis of its orbit has revealed a core of heavy elements with a mass double that of the planet's hydrogen-helium atmosphere. Orbital Distance: 0.2 AU; Orbital Period: 25 Earth Days; Radius: 67,428 Km; Day Length: 25 Earth Days.

Tarith	Garden	Rich	Rich	Poor	Rich	Moderate

Description: Tarith is broadly Earth-like with a fatal flaw; it has a relatively high amount of chlorine in its atmosphere, which is the reason for the greenish haze that becomes apparent when looking at the horizon. Chlorine has become a vital component in Tarith's plant life; as a defense mechanism against native herbivores, many species evolved the ability to release clouds of toxic chlorine when disturbed. This gas is heavier than the atmospheric oxygen and tends to settle in low places. While avoidable, this has placed Tarith near the bottom of the lists for colonization. There are intermittent signals originating in the heart of a large chlorine swamp. They appear to be coded, though it is not impossible that they are garbled distress signals from a downed civilian ship. Orbital Distance: 7.8 AU; Orbital Period: 16.7 Earth Years; Radius: 5,677 Km; Day Length: 27.7 Earth Hours; Atmospheric Pressure: 0.84 Earth Atmospheres; Surface Temperature: 21 Celsius; Surface Gravity: 0.87 G.

Xetic	Giant Ice	Moderate	None	Poor	Moderate	Poor

Description: A common methane-ammonia gas giant, Xetic is best known for the infamous Kal'thor Camp. Established on the ice moon of Gesis, Kal'thor was a Blue Suns hostile environment training facility run by a cadre of former batarian Special Intervention Unit operators. In 2168 a cluster-wide scandal broke out when it was revealed that the mortality rate of recruits sent to the camp might be as high as 18 percent. Investigation by asari authorities based on Illium uncovered group graves around the facility containing the remains of several hundred recruits dating back two decades. The camp was immediately closed and the remains sent back to their worlds of origin. An inquest by the Blue Suns found the batarian commandos had used harsh training methods but ones that were consistent with their own training to join the SIU. The batarians were exonerated, though Kal'thor was shut down and they were reassigned to other units. As the Crescent Nebula is beyond the sphere of Council law no civil charges could be filed against the Blue Suns. Orbital Distance: 15.6 AU; Orbital Period: 47.4 Earth Years; Radius: 30,054 Km; Day Length: 13.7 Earth Hours.

Ondeste						
Planet	**World Type**	**Richness**	**Element Zero**	**Iridium**	**Platinum**	**Palladium**
Acaeria	Ocean/Ice	Rich	None	Moderate	Rich	Moderate

Description: Though nearly the size of Earth, Acaeria contains only 28 percent of its mass. It has a trace atmosphere of neon and molecular nitrogen, but the predominant carbon dioxide has long since frozen and fallen to the surface as frost. While Acaeria has a core of heavy metals, the bulk of the planet's volume consists of ice. Several unique forms of long-chain carbon molecules have been recovered on the surface, pushed up from beneath the ice by cryovolcanic processes. Acaeria has a large rocky moon compositionally similar to Luna. Orbital Distance: 1.68 AU; Orbital Period: 4.0 Earth Years; Radius: 6,272 Km; Day Length: 36.2 Earth Hours; Atmospheric Pressure: Trace; Surface Temperature: -178 Celsius; Surface Gravity: 0.38 G.

Maisuth	Ocean/Ice	Good	None	Moderate	Rich	Moderate

Description: Farthest from the dim red dwarf Ondeste, the ice dwarf Maisuth has attracted no interest beyond a cursory flyby by automated probe in 1874. No significant resources were noted. Orbital Distance: 2.35 AU; Orbital Period: 6.6 Earth Years; Radius: 3,893 Km; Day Length: 54.7 Earth Hours; Atmospheric Pressure: Trace; Surface Temperature: -194 Celsius; Surface Gravity: 0.25 G.

Zesmeni	Desert	Rich	None	Moderate	Moderate	Rich

Description: Cold, dim, and shrouded by a methane-ammonia atmosphere, Zesmeni has nevertheless attracted development by asari mining concerns that service military industries. There are significant lodes of valuable light metals present, including titanium and lithium. Titanium is the primary material used in mass accelerator slugs, and lithium is used in the military-grade "droplet" heat radiators used aboard warships. Population: 620; Orbital Distance: 0.8 AU; Orbital Period: 1.3 Earth Years; Radius: 5,806 Km; Day Length: 37.6 Earth Hours; Atmospheric Pressure: 0.64 Earth Atmospheres; Surface Temperature: -119 Celsius; Surface Gravity: 0.66 G.

Tasale *

Planet	World Type	Richness	Element Zero	Iridium	Platinum	Palladium
Beregale	Desert	Rich	None	Moderate	Moderate	Rich

Description: While not a classical "hothouse" world like Venus, Beregale is scarcely more hospitable. In addition to being closest to the star Tasale, its core contains many radioactives and other heavy elements. These increase the heat of the planets and drive volcanism. Beregale's crust is too rigid for plate tectonics to function, and the planet will go through cycles in which the pressure builds to a massive super-volcanic eruption. These spew ejecta over thousands of kilometers, leave caldera a hundred kilometers across, and spew enough molten material to repave entire continents. The last such event was 812,000 years ago; the current rate of outgassing from volcanic hot spots suggests another will occur within the next 10 millennia. Orbital Distance: 0.6 AU; Orbital Period: 0.5 Earth Years; Radius: 10,640 Km; Day Length: 45.7 Earth Hours; Atmospheric Pressure: 2.0 Earth Atmospheres; Surface Temperature: 232 Celsius; Surface Gravity: 2.1 G.

Planet	World Type	Richness	Element Zero	Iridium	Platinum	Palladium
Illium	Not Minable	—	—	—	—	—

Description: Illium is a classic garden world developed to serve as entrepot between the Terminus Systems and the Asari Republics. To abet this trade the normally stringent customs laws of Council space on product-safety-proscribed materials and sapient trafficking are relaxed. Officially, Illium is not an asari world; it is colonized and operated by asari corporate interests. This gives it the same legal latitude enjoyed by the human corporate research enclaves of Noveria. Illium is one of the youngest asari colonies settled during the 7th Expansion Wave. The first child born on the world is only now reaching her middle age. The world is hot and massive; ground settlement is only possible at the higher polar latitudes. In more equatorial locations the population is housed in arcology skyscrapers to escape the heat of the surface. Colony Founded: 1617; Population (Surface): 84,900,000; Population (L4 and L5 stations): 80,300; Capital: Nos Astra; Orbital Distance: 1.3 AU; Orbital Period: 1.5 Earth Years; Radius: 7,431 Km; Day Length: 25 Earth Hours; Atmospheric Pressure: 1.15 Earth Atmospheres; Surface Temperature: 63 Celsius; Surface Gravity: 1.2 G.

Planet	World Type	Richness	Element Zero	Iridium	Platinum	Palladium
Naxell	Giant Ice	Moderate	None	Poor	Moderate	Poor

Description: Naxell is an ammonia-methane ice giant. Several smaller energy corporations shut out of the big market in the Faia gateway system are attempting to develop a local helium-3 fuel mining infrastructure to service Illium. The leading investor is the human corporation Eldfell-Ashland Energy. Their efforts have been hampered by the extralegal pressure the "H-3 Cartels" in Faia system can bring to bear, from simple price undercuts to bureaucratic obstructions (denied permits and constant "health and safety" inspections). Population: 6700; Capital: EAE Krafla; Orbital Distance: 9.37 AU; Orbital Period: 28.8 Earth Years; Radius: 22,981 Km; Day Length: 10.1 Earth Hours.

Planet	World Type	Richness	Element Zero	Iridium	Platinum	Palladium
Ponolus	Desert	Rich	None	Moderate	Moderate	Rich

Description: A fairly typical Venusian "hothouse," Ponolus seems almost tame compared to the violent volcanic outbursts of the inner world Beregale. In contrast, Ponolus is nearly inert, with no active volcanoes or plate tectonics. The most dramatic event in the last million years was the foundering of the asari aerostat research platform Alviusic in 2092, which fell after being holed by an improbably unlucky meteor. Most of the crew successfully reached escape capsules, but six were lost. The crushed wreck of the platform now lies on the Kriusite Plain in the southern hemisphere. Orbital Distance: 2.08 AU; Orbital Period: 3.0 Earth Years; Radius: 5,489 Km; Day Length: 36.2 Earth Hours; Atmospheric Pressure: 96.6 Earth Atmospheres; Surface Temperature: 539 Celsius; Surface Gravity: 0.78 G.

Planet	World Type	Richness	Element Zero	Iridium	Platinum	Palladium
Thail	Giant Jovian	Moderate	None	Poor	Poor	Poor

Description: Thail is a typical hydrogen-helium gas giant. Its complex system of rings is unstable, dating back only a few million years. They are thought to be the shattered remains of a comet. Orbital Distance: 4.46 AU; Orbital Period: 9.4 Earth Years; Radius: 55,263 Km Day Length: 15.5 Earth Hours.

Zelene

Planet	World Type	Richness	Element Zero	Iridium	Platinum	Palladium
Epho	Desert	Rich	None	Moderate	Poor	Rich

Description: Epho is a rocky world with an atmosphere of oxygen and carbon dioxide. There are large craters scattered across its surface, obviously from hypervelocity kinetic impactors. Stretching between these locations are the shattered remains of magnetic levitation rail lines, which strongly suggests that the craters represent the former locations of arthenni mining outposts or other settlements. The equatorial region contains an extensive network of canyons formed by the planet's abundant liquid water. TRAVEL ADVISORY: Epho's atmosphere is approximately 41 percent carbon dioxide at sea level. This is four to six times the level necessary to render most species unconscious within a few minutes of breathing it. Breathing masks must be worn at all times when on the surface of Epho. Orbital Distance: 1.56 AU; Orbital Period: 2.22 Earth Years; Radius: 8,031 Km; Day Length: 70 Earth Hours; Atmospheric Pressure: 0.98 Earth Atmospheres; Surface Temperature: -41 Celsius (12 equator); Surface Gravity: 1.0 G.

Planet	World Type	Richness	Element Zero	Iridium	Platinum	Palladium
Gaelon	Giant Jovian	Moderate	None	Poor	Poor	Moderate

Description: Gaelon is surrounded by an extensive ring system. The inner rings are composed of pulverized nano-manufactured carbon materials thought to be the remains of an arthenni helium-3 mining infrastructure. The few pieces of larger debris found indicate a materials technology at least equal to the current galactic state of the art. The outer rings consist of ice, silicate dust, and the odd bit of rock. Analysis of the debris often shows shock damage and evidence of rapid heating. Some para-historical theorists insist that the outer rings represent debris from a moon or moons destroyed by mass accelerator bombardment. This has been rejected by every reputable xenoarchaeologist; while it is theoretically possible to destroy a small moon utterly with dreadnought bombardment, no species sees a compelling reason to do so. Orbital Distance: 2.96 AU; Orbital Period: 5.7 Earth Years; Radius: 63,539 Km; Day Length: 8.9 Earth Hours.

Planet	World Type	Richness	Element Zero	Iridium	Platinum	Palladium
Helyme	Post-Garden	Moderate	Moderate	Moderate	Moderate	Moderate

Description: Helyme is a post-garden world that once enjoyed an Earth-like oxygen-nitrogen atmosphere. It is still blessed with plentiful water but a generally cold climate (and extreme seasonal shifts courtesy of a 38-degree axial tilt). Helyme is thought to be the homeworld of the arthenni, a space-faring species that disappeared approximately 300,000 years ago. Precisely what happened to Helyme is still under debate. It appears a global extinction occurred, wiping out all native animal life forms more complex than zooplankton. Plant forms were not affected, but the lack of oxygen-breathing life caused oxygenation of the atmosphere. Plant life was reduced after lightning storms ignited global wildfires. The leading theory for Helyme's devastation is an out-of-control biological weapon. For this reason landing is strictly prohibited. The corporations of Illium have emplaced a network of quarantine satellites to dissuade would-be looters from landing in the crumbling cities. Orbital Distance: 1.2 AU; Orbital Period: 1.5 Earth Years; Radius: 5,522 Km; Day Length: 44.4 Earth Hours; Atmospheric Pressure: 0.84 Earth Atmospheres; Surface Temperature: -15 Celsius; Surface Gravity: 0.87 G.

Introduction · Training · Upgrades and Research · Walkthrough · Special Assignments · Planetary Database · Appendix

Zelene (continued)						
Planet	World Type	Richness	Element Zero	Iridium	Platinum	Palladium
Nepyma	Rock	Rich	None	Rich	Poor	Moderate

Description: Tidally locked to the star Zelene, Nepyma has the expected "hot pole" and "cold pole." Along the terminator is a thin band of nearly habitable terrain. Unfortunately, the local biosphere is based on a chlorinated oxygen atmosphere. It is not sophisticated, but it has proven highly dangerous. The asari surveyor Verallas landed on Nepyma in 1684 to study the local ecology. Unbeknownst to the crew, a handful of native chlorine-fixing microbes passed through biohazard screening and entered the ship. The Verallas returned to the port of Nos Parnalo on Illium, where the Nepyman microbes escaped into a temperate environment with plentiful unused chorine. The microbes devoured the chlorides in the earth; as metabolic byproducts they produced toxic polychlorinated biphenyls (PCBs). By the time the infestation was contained an area of nearly 30 square kilometers had been effectively turned into a toxic waste dump. Nos Parnalo had to be abandoned, accelerating the development of Nos Astra. Orbital Distance: 0.8 AU; Orbital Period: 0.8 Earth Years; Radius: 4,456 Km; Day Length: 40.4 Earth Hours; Atmospheric Pressure: 0.55 Earth Atmospheres; Surface Temperature: 32 Celsius; Surface Gravity: 0.57 G.

Eagle Nebula

Amun						
Planet	World Type	Richness	Element Zero	Iridium	Platinum	Palladium
Anhur	Garden	Rich	Rich	Poor	Rich	Moderate

Description: A garden world with heavy populations of humans and batarians, Anhur was home to one of the ugliest violations of sapient rights in modern human history. A consortium of corporations and corrupt politicians, fearing batarian economic competition due to their custom of legal slavery, passed a resolution that abolished the minimum wage—effectively relegalizing slavery on a human-dominated world. Opponents of the motion quickly turned to activism and violence. A civil war erupted as one side sought to end slavery throughout the system and the other, primarily a batarian faction called the Na'hesit, sought to keep the slaves they had. The Anhur Rebellions raged from 2176 to 2178. The Na'hesit had a significant advantage in ships, labor, and weapons, forcing the Anhur militias to hire mercenary companies to even the odds. In the end the abolitionists won out, though at the cost of much of their infrastructure. Though Anhur today still has significant natural wealth, it is economically depressed save for the reconstruction industry. Population: 208,587,000; Colony Founded: 2165; Capital: New Thebes; Orbital Distance: 1.7 AU; Orbital Period: 2.2 Earth Years; Radius: 6,829 Km; Day Length: 18.0 Earth Hours; Atmospheric Pressure: 0.6 Earth Atmospheres; Surface Temperature: 7 Celsius; Surface Gravity: 1.3 G.

Bast	Giant Jovian	Poor	None	Poor	Poor	Poor

Description: A small hydrogen-nitrogen gas giant, Bast and its moons served as the Eclipse mercenary company's fallback position after their defeat on Neith. Once they had gathered their strength they leaked a false position to the Na'hesit consortium to lure them into a trap, which devolved into a pitched battle. Both sides claimed victory   Na'hesit lost more ships but could afford the setback in a way Eclipse could not. Orbital Distance: 7.0 AU; Orbital Period: 18.6 Earth Years; Radius: 18,557 Km; Day Length: 13.6 Earth Hours.

Neith	Desert	Rich	None	Moderate	Moderate	Rich

Description: Cold and dry, Neith has a thin nitrogen atmosphere and vast salt flats at its equator, which is warm enough for liquid water to pool during the summer period. The revealed salt is collected and sold to sodium-poor planets for agricultural purposes. During the Anhur Rebellions, Neith was a staging ground for Eclipse ships and was the site of their first defeat when enemy Na'hesit surprised and routed them with a superior force. Some wreckage from the battle can still be found on the planet today. Orbital Distance: 3.4; AU Orbital Period: 6.3 Earth Years; Radius: 7,008 Km; Day Length: 54.7 Earth Hours; Atmospheric Pressure: 0.7 Earth Atmospheres; Surface Temperature: -25 Celsius; Surface Gravity: 1.4 G.

Sekhmet	Giant Jovian	Moderate	Moderate	Poor	Moderate	Poor

Description: A hydrogen-helium gas giant believed to have entered Amun's system within the last billion years, Sekhmet was the site of an important battle in the Anhur Rebellions. When the Eclipse mercenary company sought to capture the refueling stations to deny the rebels supplies, a fighter wing hiding in Sekhmet's rings ambushed them. Eclipse suffered heavy initial losses but destroyed two rebel carriers and forced them to retreat into FTL. This was considered the "high water mark" of the rebellion: At no point after the battle of Sekhmet did the rebels have a victory. Today Sekhmet is home to refueling stations and a small war memorial in orbit at the planet's L5 Lagrange point. Orbital Distance: 0.4 AU; Orbital Period: 0.3 Earth Years; Radius: 38,347 Km; Day Length: 9.0 Earth Hours.

Sobek	Giant Jovian	Moderate	None	Poor	Moderate	Poor

Description: Sobek is a hydrogen-nitrogen gas giant believed to be an extrasolar capture. Its low-G moons were the sites of many batarian labor camps during the Anhur Rebellions, generating raw materials for the war. When the slaves were finally liberated by Eclipse the mercenaries found abysmal conditions, including whole camps that lacked mass effect fields to keep the gravity at habitable levels. The widespread bone loss among the slaves was part of their masters' final degredation—it would cripple them if they ever left for a standard-gravity world. The plight of the slaves soon garnered galactic media attention, and several charities sprang up to pay for their physical therapy and find them gainful employment. Eclipse mercenaries, normally reviled for their cutthroat tactics and criminal employees, found themselves painted as heroes. The mercenary company still retains an office on Sobek's moon Heqet, out of nostalgia as much as a business strategy. Orbital Distance: 0.8 AU; Orbital Period: 0.7 Earth Years; Radius: 72,530 Km; Day Length: 12.4 Earth Hours.

Imir *						
Planet	World Type	Richness	Element Zero	Iridium	Platinum	Palladium
Gregas	Rock	Rich	None	Rich	Moderate	Moderate

Description: Cold and distant, Gregas is currently 65 percent rock by mass and 35 percent frozen methane and nitrogen ices. In the planet's "summer years" these percentages change as the sun heats its ice and it evaporates into a thin atmosphere. Its calcium-heavy crust has been scouted by countless Korlus surveying teams, most of whom came back empty-handed. Orbital Distance: 10.0 AU; Orbital Period: 31.7 Earth Years; Radius: 5,240 Km; Day Length: 69.9 Earth Hours; Atmospheric Pressure: Trace; Surface Temperature: -170 Celsius; Surface Gravity: 0.7 G.

Imir (continued)

Planet	World Type	Richness	Element Zero	Iridium	Platinum	Palladium
Korlus	Not Minable	—	—	—	—	—

Description: A garbage scow with a climate was how one Citadel Council member described Korlus at the turn of the century, and ever since then the Korlus Tourist Bureau has been attempting to re-brand their planet. It hasn't worked—though they have tried calling it "the recycling center of the galaxy," corruption scandals and a staggering murder rate ensure that Korlus's image is permanently stained. Korlus's biggest business is the recycling of decommissioned or junked spacecraft into their component parts. While the invention of omni-gel has made this process significantly cleaner it is still a dirty business that chokes Korlus's sky with smog and fills its ports with megatons of scrap. A shady hospitality industry and a scavenger underclass round out the spectacle of urban decay. TRAVEL ADVISORY: Korlus ranks second in murder per capita in the Terminus Systems and first in offworlder murder. Civilian traffic is encouraged to employ security professionals when visiting. Population: 3,800,000,000 (est.); Colony Founded: 1781 CE; Capital: Choquo (disputed); Orbital Distance: 1.3 AU; Orbital Period: 1.5 Earth Years; Radius: 6,850 Km; Day Length: 28.9 Earth Hours; Atmospheric Pressure: 1.5 Earth Atmospheres; Surface Temperature: 28 Celsius; Surface Gravity: 1.3 G.

Osalri	Brown Dwarf	Moderate	None	Poor	Moderate	Moderate

Description: Osalri (which means "fire maiden") is a boiling hot dwarf planet close to the G-class star Imir. Too hot for lucrative exploitation, its only satellites are defunct solar arrays destroyed by pirates long ago. Orbital Distance: 0.6 AU; Orbital Period: 0.5 Earth Years; Radius: 2,622 Km; Day Length: 33.4 Earth Hours; Atmospheric Pressure: 1.86 Earth Atmospheres; Surface Temperature: 229 Celsius; Surface Gravity: 0.1 G.

Quodis	Giant Jovian	Moderate	None	Poor	Moderate	Poor

Description: A hydrogen-helium gas giant, Quodis is used by countless spaceships to discharge their drive cores after coming into the system. Commercial vessels restock on their supplies of helium-3 from one of its many orbital platforms. TRAVEL ADVISORY: Piracy at helium-3 refueling stations is common in the Imir system. Visitors are encouraged to use the escorts provided by the Korlus Security Fleet to and from the system's mass relay. To prevent escort fraud always ask for identification from the escort ships and compare them to those found on the Korlus Security Fleet's extranet sites. Orbital Distance: 5.0 AU; Orbital Period: 11.2 Earth Years; Radius: 48,918 Km; Day Length: 13.3 Earth Hours.

Malgus

Planet	World Type	Richness	Element Zero	Iridium	Platinum	Palladium
Flett	Desert	Rich	None	Moderate	Moderate	Rich

Description: Uninhabitable by most species, Flett is home to the Blood Pack's vorcha training and breeding grounds. The thick atmosphere is nearly all nitrogen and lacks oxygen, which poses no hazard to the vorcha. Needing little but imports of food and water, vorcha mercenaries and mercenaries-to-be train religiously to overpower and kill whoever the company is at war with this time. TRAVEL ADVISORY: Flett's spaceports are wholly owned subsidiaries of the Blood Pack mercenary company, a corporation undergoing numerous criminal investigations for capital crimes. Civilian traffic to Flett is strongly discouraged. Orbital Distance: 1.2 AU; Orbital Period: 1.5 Earth Years; Radius: 5,623 Km; Day Length: 48.2 Earth Hours; Atmospheric Pressure: 2.49 Earth Atmospheres; Surface Temperature: 16 Celsius; Surface Gravity: 0.7 G.

Uzin	Giant Pegasid	Moderate	None	Poor	Moderate	Moderate

Description: Named for one of many krogan gods of vengeance, Uzin is a gas giant close enough to its orange sun that none of its moons are considered habitable. Its composition is largely hydrogen and methane, with traces of xenon that the krogan collect for use in ion drives. Uzin is well within the "frost line" where gas giants usually do not form, leading astronomers to believe that its orbit used to be farther from the star. If so this would indicate a seriously unstable orbit, and the planet may plunge into its star within a few million years. Orbital Distance: 0.3 AU; Orbital Period: 0.2 Earth Years; Radius: 74,137 Km; Day Length: 12.4 Earth Hours.

Wrill	Desert	Rich	None	Poor	Moderate	Rich

Description: A planet only a vorcha could love, Wrill is notable for its "near miss" climate: punishing heat and a thin toxic methane-ethane atmosphere. Its surface is dotted with krogan and vorcha habitats eking out a meager living off the planet's tin and copper deposits and killing anyone who cuts into their profits. TRAVEL ADVISORY: Krogan can survive in the heat with the use of a breathing mask. All other species require environmental suits to avoid heat exhaustion and burns. Liquid water can be found in large lakes on the surface. This can be used for thermoregulation, but it is not potable without processing. ALLIANCE BULLETIN: Large-scale gang warfare is a regular occurence on Wrill. Civilian travel is not advised. Orbital Distance: 0.6 AU; Orbital Period: 0.5 Earth Years; Radius: 5,999 Km; Day Length: 30.1 Earth Hours; Atmospheric Pressure: Trace; Surface Temperature: 56 Celsius; Surface Gravity: 0.9 G.

Relic

Planet	World Type	Richness	Element Zero	Iridium	Platinum	Palladium
Beach Thunder	Rock	Rich	None	Rich	Moderate	Poor

Description: Beach Thunder lives and dies on the price of titanium—the metal being the only reason to come to this frozen rock. A best-selling e-novel, "The Hard Stuff," has popularized the story of the miners on the planet. It follows the hanar and drell robo-miners competing with krogan and vorcha, who simply put on environmental suits and lase the titanium out more or less by hand. As the novel's promotional screed says "accidents are frequent, rivalry is fierce, and vengeance served up fast." Orbital Distance: 33.0 AU; Orbital Period: 190.2 Earth Years; Radius: 8,058 Km; Day Length: 54.1 Earth Hours; Atmospheric Pressure: 1.25 Earth Atmospheres; Surface Temperature: -157 Celsius; Surface Gravity: 2.1 G.

First Land	Giant Jovian	Moderate	None	Poor	Moderate	Poor

Description: A hydrogen-helium gas giant believed to be an extrasolar capture, First Land is home to many space stations supporting the ubiquitous refueling platforms. A thriving community of drell and hanar make their homes in orbit here, giving the solar system's robo-miners somewhere to go when the 50-hour days and nights are driving them mad. Orbital Distance: 2.1 AU; Orbital Period: 3.4 Earth Years; Radius: 53,826 Km; Day Length: 10.9 Earth Hours.

Introduction

Training

Upgrades and Research

Walkthrough

Special Assignments

Planetary Database

Appendix

Relic (continued)

Planet	World Type	Richness	Element Zero	Iridium	Platinum	Palladium
Fitful Current	Rock	Rich	None	Rich	Poor	Poor

Description: Fitful Current was so named because it orbits in retrograde, indicating that it may have been an extrasolar planet that was captured by the Relic System's gravity well. Large for a rock planet, Fitful Current has only traces of hydrogen in its extremely thin atmosphere. Hanar robo-miners have recovered some uranium and thorium deposits from its depths. Orbital Distance: 1.2 AU; Orbital Period: 1.5 Earth Years; Radius: 9,260 Km; Day Length: 41.9 Earth Hours; Atmospheric Pressure: Trace; Surface Temperature: -47 Celsius; Surface Gravity: 3.1 G.

Planet	World Type	Richness	Element Zero	Iridium	Platinum	Palladium
Island Wind	Giant Jovian	Moderate	None	Poor	Moderate	Poor

Description: A large hydrogen-nitrogen gas giant, Island Wind is named for the sweet-smelling land breezes that come off of the archipelagos of Kahje in the evening. As tumultuous as any other Jovian giant, Island Wind has cyclones that span tens of thousands of kilometers. Orbital Distance: 3.9 AU Orbital Period: 7.7 Earth Years; Radius: 73,088 Km; Day Length: 17.0 Earth Hours.

Planet	World Type	Richness	Element Zero	Iridium	Platinum	Palladium
Murky Water	Desert	Rich	None	Moderate	Moderate	Rich

Description: Despite the name, Murky Water has yet to show any signs of having any water whatsoever. Its name is a literal translation from the original hanar, who consider murky water a sign of danger. Murky Water has a hazy crushing atmosphere of carbon dioxide and methane that brings the surface heat to boiling levels. It remains unexploited—its gravity and temperature are too high to bother. Orbital Distance: 0.7 AU; Orbital Period: 0.7 Earth Years; Radius: 10,551 Km; Day Length: 53.9 Earth Hours; Atmospheric Pressure: 19.46 Earth Atmospheres; Surface Temperature: 225 Celsius; Surface Gravity: 4.6 G.

Planet	World Type	Richness	Element Zero	Iridium	Platinum	Palladium
Preying Mouth	Giant Jovian	Moderate	Rich	Poor	Poor	Poor

Description: A hydrogen-helium gas giant, Preying Mouth is a ship-killing enigma—the Bermuda Triangle of the Terminus Systems. There are many theories why ships never return from there: undetectable space debris; old disruptor torpedoes and magnetic mines from a long-forgotten war; even miniature black holes. But what is clear is that too many ships have been lost there for it to be happenstance. TRAVEL ADVISORY: Due to the large number of ships lost when attempting to discharge their drive cores in Preying Mouth, the Relic system highly recommends using First Land's complimentary discharge stations instead. Orbital Distance: 16.0 AU; Orbital Period: 64.2 Earth Years; Radius: 40,775 Km; Day Length: 11.7 Earth Hours.

Planet	World Type	Richness	Element Zero	Iridium	Platinum	Palladium
Rough Tide	Rock	Rich	None	Poor	Rich	Rich

Description: A dwarf planet with a shroud of carbon monoxide and dioxide that keeps it warm, Rough Tide was so named when large veins of platinum and palladium were struck and miners from all over the cluster came in to stake their claims. Hanar police and their drell enforcers clashed with krogan and vorcha in an ugly series of race riots in the late 2170s, and the planet has only grudgingly kept a shaky peace since then. Orbital Distance: 7.8 AU; Orbital Period: 21.8 Earth Years; Radius: 2,125 Km; Day Length: 67.7 Earth Hours; Atmospheric Pressure: 7.89 Earth Atmospheres; Surface Temperature: 1 Celsius; Surface Gravity: 0.1 G.

Strabo

Planet	World Type	Richness	Element Zero	Iridium	Platinum	Palladium
Antigar	Giant Jovian	Moderate	None	Poor	Moderate	Poor

Description: Charted by a salarian mining expedition that went off course due to computer error, Antigar is a hydrogen and helium gas giant with 11 known moons and dusty rings. Orbital Distance: 4.0 AU; Orbital Period: 8.0 Earth Years; Radius: 24,193 Km; Day Length: 11.2 Earth Hours.

Planet	World Type	Richness	Element Zero	Iridium	Platinum	Palladium
Jarrahe Station	Not Minable	—	—	—	—	—

Description: There is little public information to be had about this station. It has a salarian name and orbits Antigar at its second Lagrange point. It is not listed in the Alliance directory of helium-3 refueling stations. Orbital Distance: 2.02 AU; Orbital Period: 2.2 Earth Years; Length: 1.5 Km; Population: 33; Gross Weight: 385 metric tons.

Far Rim

Dholen

Planet	World Type	Richness	Element Zero	Iridium	Platinum	Palladium
Charoum	Giant Jovian	Moderate	None	Poor	Poor	Poor

Description: Once a starship refueling station for the quarians, Charoum has expanded under geth rule. Thousands of orbital platforms surround the planet and its many moons, refining helium into helium-3. A vast geth fleet comes and goes between Charoum and Haestrom, preventing all but the most stealthy of spy drones from discovering any information about it. Current estimates place the geth fleet numbers between 5,000 and 10,000 ships, with unknown levels of armament. TRAVEL ADVISORY: Most intelligence estimates state that approaching Charoum is tantamount to suicide. All civilian traffic is prohibited. Population: 250,000–500,000 platforms; Colony Occupied: 1895 CE; Largest Station: "Hell's Hive" (Dina Station); Orbital Distance: 2.9 AU; Orbital Period: 4.9 Earth Years; Radius: 54,532 Km; Day Length: 11.3 Earth Hours; Atmospheric Pressure: 1.37 Earth Atmospheres.

Planet	World Type	Richness	Element Zero	Iridium	Platinum	Palladium
Gotha	Desert	Rich	Moderate	Moderate	Moderate	Rich

Description: A dwarf planet, Gotha has a pressure-cooker atmosphere that brings its surface temperature to a scorching level. Carbon dioxide and ethane are plentiful in the planet's hazy atmosphere. There has been some speculation in the mining community about whether all of the precious metals were mined by the quarians before they fled the system some three centuries ago. Rumors abound that anyone who could brave the geth in the system could find lodes of naturally occuring diamonds on Gotha, but this is likely just a starship legend. TRAVEL ADVISORY: Gotha is in geth space. All civilian traffic is prohibited. Orbital Distance: 1.5 AU; Orbital Period: 1.8 Earth Years; Radius: 1056 Km; Day Length: 66.4 Earth Hours; Atmospheric Pressure: 99.64 Earth Atmospheres; Surface Temperature: 590 Celsius; Surface Gravity: 0.1 G.

Dholen (continued)

Planet	World Type	Richness	Element Zero	Iridium	Platinum	Palladium
Haestrom	Not Minable	—	—	—	—	—

Description: Formerly a quarian colony, Haestrom was established to observe the phenomena on Dholen, the system's parent star. Dholen appeared to be unstable, with a high possibility of erupting prematurely into a red giant. Haestrom was lost to the geth in 1896 CE. Soon after, all communication from the planet and its attendant space stations ceased. The geth have shown no signs of treating Dholen as a threat over the past three centuries, other than establishing several space stations near it. Dholen's magnetic eruptions and solar output overwhelm most communications near it, and it is unclear how the geth have compensated. Today spy probe scans indicate extensive orbital construction around Haestrom, housing thousands of geth platforms and an unknown number of geth software "minds." It is not known how many geth are on the planet's surface: Spy probes face interference from Dholen, making remote scanning difficult. Resource estimations based on geth mining, refining, and fabricating practices suggest that the planet has at least 20 more years of use before it is exhausted. Intelligence experts speculate that the geth have not exploited all of their resources because they wish to keep some in reserve for repairs. TRAVEL ADVISORY: Haestrom is a geth stronghold. Military spy drones using cutting-edge stealth technology are the only vehicles that have returned unharmed from geth space. All civilian traffic is prohibited. Orbital Distance: 6.3 AU; Orbital Period: 15.8 Earth Years; Radius: 6,721 Km; Day Length: 18.5 Earth Hours; Atmospheric Pressure: 0.0 Earth Atmospheres; Surface Temperature: -107 Celsius; Surface Gravity: 1.2 G.

Ma-at

Planet	World Type	Richness	Element Zero	Iridium	Platinum	Palladium
Ammut	Giant Jovian	Moderate	None	Poor	Moderate	Poor

Description: Ammut is an enormous hydrogen-helium giant with a mass approximately nine times that of Jupiter and nearly 2,900 times that of Earth. Despite massive pressure its core has failed to ignite in a fusion reaction, qualifying it as a failed star. It is believed to have captured all other planet-sized bodies in the solar system as moons or in impact events leading to its name, which means "Devourer." Unintimidated by this phenomena, the geth have colonized many of Ammut's moons and skim the hydrogen from Ammut's upper atmosphere. TRAVEL ADVISORY: Ammut is in geth space. All civilian traffic is prohibited. Orbital Distance: 102.1 AU; Orbital Period: 1036.0 Earth Years; Radius: 92,430 Km; Day Length: 12.2 Earth Hours.

Hades Nexus

Hekate *

Planet	World Type	Richness	Element Zero	Iridium	Platinum	Palladium
Asteria	Desert	Rich	Poor	Moderate	Poor	Rich

Description: A habitable planet known for its arid sulfurous deserts, Asteria is colonized near the poles to avoid the uncomfortable temperatures that can reach 65 degrees Celsius in more southern latitudes. While the seas contain primitive animal life, little of it can live on land, leaving the soil to hardy plants that can survive in the extreme heat. Asteria is home to thriving human and asari agrarian colonies but little in the way of manufacturing or mining. TRAVEL ADVISORY: Carbon dioxide concentrations can reach 2,500 parts per million in Asteria's atmosphere. Citizens should carry supplemental oxygen for children and the elderly. Consult with local governments to discuss animal companion detection systems or other preparatory measures. ALLIANCE BULLETIN: Geth have been encountered in the Hekate system. All civilian traffic is prohibited. Colony Founded: 2044 CE; Population: 188,003,870; Capital: Blackdamp; Orbital Distance: 1.3 AU; Orbital Period: 1.5 Earth Years; Radius: 5,900 Km; Day Length: 21.4 Earth Hours; Atmospheric Pressure: 1.2 Earth Atmospheres; Surface Temperature: 25 Celsius (habitable zone); Surface Gravity: 0.8 G.

Planet	World Type	Richness	Element Zero	Iridium	Platinum	Palladium
Bothros	Ocean/Ice	Rich	Poor	Poor	Rich	Moderate

Description: A rock and ice planet, Bothros is home to a scientific curiosity. Evidence of a primate-like spacefaring civilization was found frozen in its equatorial ice, ranging from melted fragments of metal to preserved remains of the creatures still wearing suits for extravehicular activity. Further exploration revealed that their habitation centers were vaporized by orbital bombardments from railgun-like weapons hitting with a force of approximately 120 kilotons of TNT. Only those that fled or happened to be away from the habitats were preserved in the ice, where they died of asphyxiation. This unknown species did not come from Asteria, but scientific teams are looking for evidence that they visited there. It is difficult to believe they would colonize a frozen rock like Bothros and ignore a lush garden world. Their world of origin is also a mystery. ALLIANCE BULLETIN: Geth have been encountered in the Hekate system. All civilian traffic is prohibited. Orbital Distance: 8.5 AU; Orbital Period: 24.8 Earth Years; Radius: 7,191 Km; Day Length: 51.0 Earth Hours; Atmospheric Pressure: Trace; Surface Temperature: -142 Celsius; Surface Gravity: 1.5 G.

Planet	World Type	Richness	Element Zero	Iridium	Platinum	Palladium
Ker	Desert	Rich	None	Moderate	Moderate	Rich

Description: A dry desolate planet, Ker is temperate but supports little life above the microscopic level. Its Earth-like temperatures and gravity make it an appealing place to build habitation hideaways, attracting batarian slavers and criminals who can't afford more luxurious safehouses on other planets. Its forgiving nitrogen-helium atmosphere makes EVAs possible with a minimal amount of equipment; a breathing mask and warm clothing are usually sufficient. Mining and other legitimate activities are few and far between on Ker: The planet's crust is largely free of precious metals, instead producing kilometers upon kilometers of dolomitic limestone calcite and gypsum. ALLIANCE BULLETIN: Geth have been encountered in the Hekate system. All civilian traffic is prohibited. Orbital Distance: 2.2 AU; Orbital Period: 3.3 Earth Years; Radius: 6,420 Km; Day Length: 61.7 Earth Hours; Atmospheric Pressure: 1.2 Earth Atmospheres; Surface Temperature: -4 Celsius; Surface Gravity: 1.1 G.

Planet	World Type	Richness	Element Zero	Iridium	Platinum	Palladium
Triodia	Giant Ice	Moderate	None	Poor	Moderate	Poor

Description: A modestly sized gas giant with an icy core, Triodia has an hydrogen and methane atmosphere that gives it a bluish color. It has 14 moons named after asari virtues. ALLIANCE BULLETIN: Geth have been encountered in the Hekate system. All civilian traffic is prohibited. Orbital Distance: 4.8 AU; Orbital Period: 10.5 Earth Years; Radius: 27,206 Km; Day Length: 18.7 Earth Hours.

Introduction

Training

Upgrades and Research

Walkthrough

Special Assignments

Planetary Database

Appendix

Pamyat

Planet	World Type	Richness	Element Zero	Iridium	Platinum	Palladium
Dobrovolski	Rock	Rich	Moderate	Rich	Moderate	Moderate

Description: Another near-Earth-sized rock planet without much atmosphere to speak of, Dobrovolski is home to Altai Mineral Works, a local extraction company noted for its success in eezo refining. The planet itself provides aluminum for local fabricators, which are churning out habitats at an astonishing rate for a system that has no garden planets. With its ore supply coming all the way from the Sheol system Dobrovolski is held up as the proof of the miner's cliche: "Where there's eezo there's an economy." Orbital Distance: 2.3 AU; Orbital Period: 3.5 Earth Years; Radius: 6,972 Km; Day Length: 59.1 Earth Hours; Atmospheric Pressure: 0.21 Earth Atmospheres; Surface Temperature: -46 Celsius; Surface Gravity: 0.9 G.

Komarov	Rock	Rich	None	Rich	Poor	Poor

Description: First charted by the asari but colonized by humans, the Pamyat system is home to Komarov, an Earth-sized body near the star. It has little atmosphere to speak of, but this has not stopped exploration by robo-miners, who have recovered iridium from the planet's crust. Orbital Distance: 1.0 AU; Orbital Period: 1.0 Earth Years; Radius: 6,861 Km; Day Length: 39.6 Earth Hours; Atmosphere: Trace; Surface Temperature: 55 Celsius; Surface Gravity: 1.3 G.

Patsayev	Ocean/Ice	Rich	None	Moderate	Rich	Moderate

Description: A rock planet encased in frozen oceans, Patsayev is notable for the largest written message ever created by a human being. Andrei Kobzar, a disgruntled miner whose fortunes were spent prospecting for eezo, used the mass accelerator cannon of a local mercenary group's A-61 Mantis gunship to carve a 208-kilometer-long message in the ice saying "Zdes' nichego net," which is Russian for "There's nothing here." The message can easily be seen from space. Ironically, the message itself, intended to discourage future colonists, now draws small tourist crowds. Orbital Distance: 4.2 AU; Orbital Period: 8.6 Earth Years; Radius: 6,351 Km; Day Length: 18.9 Earth Hours; Atmospheric Pressure: Trace; Surface Temperature: -118 Celsius; Surface Gravity: 1.0 G.

Volkov	Rock	Rich	None	Rich	Poor	Poor

Description: A dwarf planet, Volkov has a thick atmosphere of nitrogen and krypton. Home to a thriving iridium mining community, Volkov has a reputation that is summed up as "rich but dangerous." Pirates often lurk behind Volkov's two moonlets, Zenevieva and Alena, and cripple freighters leaving the atmosphere. To make matters worse, Volkov sits in the Chazov Belt, a field of asteroids and other small bodies that leads to frequent meteor strikes on the planet. Meteor-related casualties remain rare, but on Volkov the chances of such a death are high enough that they are factored into insurance premiums. Population: 3,800; Orbital Distance: 8.5 AU; Orbital Period: 24.8 Earth Years; Radius: 1,705 Km; Day Length: 68.2 Earth Hours; Atmospheric Pressure: 3.75 Earth Atmospheres; Surface Temperature: -59 Celsius; Surface Gravity: 0.1 G.

Sheol

Planet	World Type	Richness	Element Zero	Iridium	Platinum	Palladium
Gei Hinnom	Desert	Rich	Moderate	Moderate	Rich	—

Description: A nearly atmosphere-less, tidally locked planet orbiting a red dwarf star, Gei Hinnom was the first place human explorers discovered a dedicated Prothean burial ground. While a few sites were saved for posterity, Eldfell-Ashland Mining successfully lobbied to scout the rest of the planet for element zero and soon was embroiled in a scandal. Mining teams were looting gravesites searching for eezo and other treasures, and many got rich off the so-called "cemetery business." While EAM officially brought a stop to the looting, its mining teams remain on the planet prospecting the unclaimed territory and taking their ore to the Pamyat system for refining. TRAVEL ADVISORY: Armed conflicts have broken out between miners and scientists staking claims to Prothean ruins. Visitors are advised to employ security while exploring unknown regions of the planet. Population: 11,503; Orbital Distance: 0.83 AU; Orbital Period: 0.8 Earth Years; Radius: 2,379 Km; Day Length: 0.8 Earth Years; Atmospheric Pressure: Trace Surface Temperature: 35 Celsius (habitable zone), 108 Celsius/-120 Celsius (nonhabitable); Surface Gravity: 0.1 G.

Hawking Eta

Century

Planet	World Type	Richness	Element Zero	Iridium	Platinum	Palladium
Cantra	Desert	Rich	None	Moderate	Poor	Rich

Description: A terrestrial world of average size, Cantra has an atmosphere composed of nitrogen and argon. Its frozen surface is mainly composed of tin with deposits of calcium. Aside from some spectacular formations of ice at the poles the planet has little to recommend it. Orbital Distance: 14.3 AU; Orbital Period: 60.6 Earth Years; Radius: 5,471 Km; Day Length: 66.7 Earth Hours; Atmospheric Pressure: 0.83 Earth Atmospheres; Surface Temperature: -175 Celsius; Surface Gravity: 0.7 G.

Klendagon	Desert	Rich	None	Moderate	Moderate	Rich

Description: Klendagon is an arid terrestrial planet slightly larger than Earth but with a lower density that reflects its relative lack of heavier elements. The crust is composed of tin and aluminum with wide deserts of dust-fine sand that are easily stirred by the wind. Klendagon's most striking feature is the Great Rift valley, which stretches across the southern hemisphere. What is most fascinating about the Rift is that it does not appear to be natural. The geological record suggests it is the result of a "glancing blow" by a mass accelerator round of unimaginable destructive power. This occurred some 37 million years ago. Orbital Period: 2.3 Earth Years; Radius: 7,377 Km; Day Length: 53.6 Earth Hours; Atmospheric Pressure: 0.64 Earth Atmospheres; Surface Temperature: -53 Celsius; Surface Gravity: 0.88 G.

Tamahera	Desert	Rich	None	Moderate	Moderate	Rich

Description: Tamahera has a thin atmosphere of carbon dioxide and xenon. The surface is icy and composed of sodium oxide with deposits of calcium. It contains a few unremarkable metals but mainly consists of rock. The presence of canyons and flood plains indicates that liquid water once existed, suggesting Tamahera had a thicker insulating atmosphere in the past. Orbital Period: 1.4 Earth Years; Radius: 6,302 Km; Day Length: 40.1 Earth Hours; Atmospheric Pressure: 0.34 Earth Atmospheres; Surface Temperature: -30 Celsius; Surface Gravity: 0.66 G.

Century (continued)

Planet	World Type	Richness	Element Zero	Iridium	Platinum	Palladium
Tharopto	Giant Ice	Moderate	None	Poor	Moderate	Poor

Description: Tharopto is a typical ice gas giant with traces of chlorine and sulphur in its atmosphere. It has over 100 moons and an extensive ring system composed of pulverized rock, presumably the debris from shattered moons. Orbital Distance: 29.4 AU; Orbital Period: 128.2 Earth Years; Radius: 68,714 Km; Day Length: 17.5 Earth Hours.

Chandrasekhar *

Planet	World Type	Richness	Element Zero	Iridium	Platinum	Palladium
Hebat	Giant Ice	Moderate	None	Poor	Moderate	Moderate

Description: Hebat is a methane-ammonia ice giant. When Heavy Metals Exomining of China won the bidding rights to develop the moon of Presrop in the Century system it began by establishing a helium-3 refueling facility on Hebat. The station completed this year is considered a model facility by the executives of the state-run company. Though the station produces more than enough fuel to supply the HMEC ships running to and from Century, it has a crew of only a dozen for maintenance and oversight. Nearly all the day-to-day operations are automated. Orbital Distance: 1.35 AU; Orbital Period: 2.9 Earth Years; Radius: 36,257 Km; Day Length: 17.1 Earth Hours.

Teshub	Giant Jovian	Moderate	None	Poor	Moderate	Poor

Description: The first and larger of the two gas giants in the Hawking Eta gateway system, Teshub is composed mainly of hydrogen and helium. The brown and orange coloration in its upper cloud decks is caused by the upwelling of sulfur from lower levels of the atmosphere. Orbital Distance: 0.9 AU; Orbital Period: 1.6 Earth Years; Radius: 63,568 Km; Day Length: 16.6 Earth Hours.

Schwarzschild

Planet	World Type	Richness	Element Zero	Iridium	Platinum	Palladium
Atahil	Rock	Rich	None	Rich	Moderate	Moderate

Description: A typical Venusian "greenhouse" world, Atahil is only of note for a few scattered craters. Though flattened by millions of years of high pressure the marks of orbital bombardment strikes are unmistakable. It is generally accepted among academics that whoever hailed from or settled Schwarzschild's second planet, Etamis, must have had outposts on Atahil as well. Orbital Distance: 0.9 AU; Orbital Period: 1 Earth Year; Radius: 5,230 Km; Day Length: 28.8 Earth Hours; Atmospheric Pressure: 62 Earth Atmospheres; Surface Temperature: 348 Celsius; Surface Gravity: 0.79 G.

Etamis	Post-Garden	Good	Rich	Moderate	Rich	Moderate

Description: Etamis is a superterrestrial world a third larger than Earth. It is in a "post-garden" state that clearly shows evidence of attack from space. While it's now waterless, the shores of former oceans show patterns of cratering too regular to be anything but saturation bombardment by dreadnought-class kinetic weapons, although it is unclear how most of the atmosphere has been lost. Archaeologists have found little of note. It appears that all settled regions were touched by the global bombardment. The few relics found suggest an advanced spacefaring culture thrived on the world from approximately 20 to 40 million years ago. The level of antiquity makes it impossible to estimate the world's former population or guess whether it was the race's homeworld or a colony. Orbital Distance: 1.35 AU; Orbital Period: 1.6 Earth Years; Radius: 9,577 Km; Day Length: 51.6 Earth Hours; Atmospheric Pressure: 0.2 Earth Atmospheres; Surface Temperature: -49.6 Celsius; Surface Gravity: 3.4 G.

Linossa	Giant Ice	Moderate	None	Poor	Moderate	Poor

Description: Linossa is a hydrogen-helium gas giant. It is surrounded by several thin rings of debris. Analysis of this debris has been difficult due to its extreme age and fragility, but several apparently nano-manufactured materials have been identified. The leading theory is that the inhabitants of Etamis mined the atmosphere for helium-3. Orbital Distance: 3.34 AU; Orbital Period: 6.8 Earth Years; Radius: 55,806 Km; Day Length: 17.8 Earth Hours.

Rihali	Giant Jovian	Moderate	None	Poor	Moderate	Poor

Description: Rihali is a typical hydrogen-helium gas giant. It is notable because none of its moons is larger than 12 kilometers in diameter, a rare trait among the charted gas giants of the galaxy. Orbital Distance: 6.34 AU; Orbital Period: 17.9 Earth Years; Radius: 70,778 Km; Day Length: 15.4 Earth Hours.

Thorne

Planet	World Type	Richness	Element Zero	Iridium	Platinum	Palladium
Derelict Reaper	Not Minable	—	—	—	—	—

Description: Orbiting Mnemosyne is a two-kilometer-long ship with the unmistakable profile of a Reaper. It is giving off power signatures in localized areas, but they are far weaker than a ship this size would indicate. The Reaper seems to maintain a mass effect field that has kept it from falling into the failed star, but massive holes have been blasted and melted into parts of the hull and remain unrepaired. The only logical conclusion is that the Reaper "died" or was at least reduced to minimal functioning a long time ago.

Lethe	Desert	Rich	None	Poor	Moderate	Rich

Description: Lethe is the largest moon of Mnemosyne massive enough to retain its own thin atmosphere of methane and nitrogen and heated by the brown dwarf to relatively moderate temperatures. While nearly the size of Earth, its overall density is low, suggesting a paucity of valuable heavy metals. It is tidally locked to Mnemosyne, with one hemisphere always bathed in the brown dwarf's heat and dim red light. The moon experiences constant weak tectonic activity, driven by the tidal fluxes of Mnemosyne's gravity rather than Lethe's own internal heat. Several large ancient volcanoes release wide-ranging flows of molten silicate. Orbital Distance: 2,323,500 Km (from Mnemosyne); Orbital Period: 16.4 Earth Days; Radius: 5,663 Km; Day Length: 16.4 Earth Days; Atmospheric Pressure: 0.58 Earth Atmospheres; Surface Temperature: 31 Celsius; Surface Gravity: 0.59 G.

Introduction
Training
Upgrades and Research
Walkthrough
Special Assignments
Planetary Database
Appendix

Thorne (continued)						
Planet	**World Type**	**Richness**	**Element Zero**	**Iridium**	**Platinum**	**Palladium**
Mnemosyne	Brown Dwarf	Moderate	None	Poor	Moderate	Moderate

Description: Mnemosyne is a brown dwarf of approximately 37 Jupiter-masses. It is young enough that some nuclear fusion still occurs within its depths. It is luminous and radiates more heat than it receives from the star, Thorne, with an atmospheric temperature in excess of 1,800 degrees Kelvin (1,500 degrees Celsius). Early probes of Thorne showed evidence of a minor gravitic anomaly in the northern hemisphere. This area of unexpectedly low mass did not move with the prevailing wind patterns. While an investigation was planned by the Besaral Institute of Planetary Science, the school ultimately sent an expedition to study the famed "deep anomalies" of the gas giant Ploba instead. Orbital Distance: 0.81 AU; Orbital Period: 0.8 Earth Years; Radius: 72,541 Km; Day Length: 18.7 Earth Hours.

Hourglass Nebula

Faryar						
Planet	**World Type**	**Richness**	**Element Zero**	**Iridium**	**Platinum**	**Palladium**
Alingon	Desert	Rich	None	Moderate	Moderate	Rich

Description: Alingon (which means "deceptive") was so named by salarian scouts because as their probes landed on the planet their instruments started going awry. This turned out to be due to the high concentration of magnetically active periclase (magnesia) in the core and crust of the planet. This interferes with scans and broadcasts, which has given rise to countless spacer stories of pirates lying in wait in Alingon's magnetosphere or crashed ships with untold fortunes stranded on the surface. In reality, any pirates would have a hard time locating prey amid all the interference and would live lives cut off from the rest of the galaxy because the magnetosphere kills extraplanetary communication. Alingon's other natural features are a thin atmosphere of carbon dioxide, spectacular dry ice formations, and xenon gas, which can be skimmed from the upper atmosphere and used in ion thrusters. Orbital Distance: 10.1 AU; Orbital Period: 31.7 Earth Years; Radius: 3,085 Km; Day Length: 56.3 Earth Hours; Atmospheric Pressure: 0.04 Earth Atmospheres; Surface Temperature: -166 Celsius; Surface Gravity: 0.5 G.

Antictra	Rock	Rich	None	Rich	Poor	Moderate

Description: Antictra (which means "fused metal") is so named because of its spectacular craters. A planet high in various grades of iron oxide, Antictra is regularly pummeled by loose asteroids in the nearby belt between it and Wenrum. The iron melted and fused by the incoming meteors makes for spectacular landscape shots that look alien no matter what part of the galaxy you may be from. However, due to frequent meteor impacts exploration is considered highly dangerous even to those with advanced kinetic barriers. Orbital Distance: 12.3 AU; Orbital Period: 43.3 Earth Years; Radius: 5,658 Km; Day Length: 21.1 Earth Hours; Atmospheric Pressure: 0 Earth Atmospheres; Surface Temperature: -180 Celsius; Surface Gravity: 0.8 G.

Asteroid Belt	Not Minable	—	—	—	—	—

Description: N/A

Daratar	Post-Garden	Good	Rich	Moderate	Rich	Moderate

Description: Though ancient riverbeds crisscross the plains of Daratar, photodissociation has long since dried up the world. There are indications of ancient mining operations, but any structures have long since been buried or worn away by the planet's seasonal dust storms. Orbital Distance: 0.9 AU; Orbital Period: 0.9 Earth Years; Radius: 3,937 Km; Day Length: 62.8 Earth Hours; Atmospheric Pressure: 0.49 Earth Atmospheres; Surface Temperature: -66 Celsius; Surface Gravity: 0.5 G.

Nephros	Giant Jovian	Moderate	None	Moderate	Poor	Poor

Description: Nephros (which means "restless sleep") is a relatively small hydrogen-nitrogen gas giant. Its atmosphere is home to spectacular winds of up to 350 kilometers/hour and electrical storms up to 700 times the power of those on Earth, which indicate that its hydrogen clouds contain moderate amounts of water vapor. Orbital Distance: 7.5 AU; Orbital Period: 20.6 Earth Years; Radius: 44,750 Km; Day Length: 11.9 Earth Hours.

Quarem	Rock	Rich	None	Rich	Moderate	Poor

Description: A scorchingly hot planet close to its parent star, Quarem was bombarded by comets and asteroids during its earliest geological periods. As the solar system stabilized, these occurences leveled off until the planet became geologically inactive. Its nitrogen and helium atmosphere is extremely thick due to heavy metals making the planet's core very dense. Unfortunately, these metals are deep below the crust making mining impractical. Orbital Distance: 0.2 AU; Orbital Period: 0.1 Earth Years; Radius: 3,137 Km; Day Length: 53.1 Earth Hours; Atmospheric Pressure: 2.22 Earth Atmospheres; Surface Temperature: 558 Celsius; Surface Gravity: 3.5 G.

Tunfigel	Desert	Rich	None	Moderate	Moderate	Rich

Description: First charted by the salarians, Tunfigel (which means "hard heart") is noted for its platinum and uranium deposits, making robo-mining a lucrative activity. While the surface temperature is well within the range of a comfortable EVA excursion, the extremely dense Tunfigel generates a dangerous gravitational pull five times that of Earth. The salarian miners exploiting the planet derisively nickname planets such as these "elcor tourist traps." Orbital Distance: 1.8 AU; Orbital Period: 2.4 Earth Years; Radius: 10,772 Km; Day Length: 35.5 Earth Hours; Atmospheric Pressure: 0.03 Earth Atmospheres; Surface Temperature: -31 Celsius; Surface Gravity: 5.1 G.

Wenrum	Desert	Rich	None	Moderate	Moderate	Rich

Description: Wenrum ("white knight") takes its name from a salarian story in the Romantic period of a knight who refused all temptation to riches, carnality, and even flavorful food until justice was served to the poor and oppressed. The planet is so named because of its white, highly reflective surface, composed mainly of titanium dioxide and ice and no atmosphere to speak of to dim its albedo. Orbital Distance: 11.8 AU; Orbital Period: 40.6 Earth Years; Radius: 1,574 Km; Day Length: 59.3 Earth Hours; Atmospheric Pressure: 0 Earth Atmospheres; Surface Temperature: -178 Celsius; Surface Gravity: 0.1 G.

Osun *

Planet	World Type	Richness	Element Zero	Iridium	Platinum	Palladium
Aganju	Desert	Good	None	Moderate	Moderate	Rich

Description: Aganju is an extremely large rock planet with a thin atmosphere of hydrogen and carbon monoxide. Abundant in both copper and platinum, the crust has been scanned by mining bots from Erinle, but the specialized equipment to work in Aganju's heavy gravity (more than 5 Gs) has created prohibitive costs, and so Aganju is largely unexploited. Orbital Distance: 3.2 AU; Orbital Period: 5.7 Earth Years; Radius: 10;008 Km; Day Length: 23.3 Earth Hours; Atmospheric Pressure: 0.02 Earth Atmospheres; Surface Temperature: -93 Celsius; Surface Gravity: 5.3 G.

Planet	World Type	Richness	Element Zero	Iridium	Platinum	Palladium
Erinle	Garden	Good	Rich	Poor	Rich	Moderate

Description: Erinle is a garden world in its last stages of habitability. While its soil still supports agriculture, its animal biodiversity has fallen to record lows, and the most successful remaining life forms are toxic blue-green algae and insect-like pest species. A large salarian colony is trying to restore biodiversity to the planet, but setbacks are a fact of life. Mineral and fuel mining remains lucrative, however, and Erinle has a thriving spaceport that refuels many ships passing into the Terminus Systems. Orbital Distance: 0.95 AU; Orbital Period: 0.9 Earth Years; Radius: 6,711 Km; Day Length: 32.4 Earth Hours; Atmospheric Pressure: 1.1 Earth Atmospheres; Surface Temperature: 32 Celsius; Surface Gravity: 1.1 G.

Planet	World Type	Richness	Element Zero	Iridium	Platinum	Palladium
Olokun	Giant Jovian	Moderate	None	Poor	Poor	Moderate

Description: Olokun (which means "sky harvest") is a standard gas giant composed of hydrogen and helium. The spacefarers from Erinle gather helium-3 from here rather than Orunmila because its atmosphere is much more predictable. Orbital Distance: 6.0 AU; Orbital Period: 14.7 Earth Years; Radius: 64,718 Km; Day Length: 11.9 Earth Hours.

Planet	World Type	Richness	Element Zero	Iridium	Platinum	Palladium
Orunmila	Giant Jovian	Moderate	None	Poor	Poor	Poor

Description: A medium-sized gas giant, Orunmila is close enough to its parent star to suffer massive changes in temperature during its day and night periods. This leads to powerful convection currents and storms throughout its hydrogen/helium atmosphere. Gathering helium-3 to refuel is possible for the hardiest of exploration craft, but lesser ships are nearly always lost in the attempt. Orunmila is within the "frost line" of its solar system, where icy-cored gas giants do not usually form. For this reason it is believed to be an extrasolar planet captured by its star's gravity. Orbital Distance: 0.5 AU; Orbital Period: 0.3 Earth Years; Radius: 34,653 Km; Day Length: 13.7 Earth Hours.

Planet	World Type	Richness	Element Zero	Iridium	Platinum	Palladium
Prison Ship Purgatory	Not Minable	—	—	—	—	—

Description: Owned by the notorious Blue Suns mercenary company, the Purgatory was once an "ark ship" used to hold agricultural animals. Now it is used to hold prisoners, whether taken in battle or sold by unscrupulous politicians under the name of subcontracting and outsourcing. Rumors abound that the Blue Suns turn skilled or fit prisoners over to batarian slavers, but few have ever seen the transactions and lived to tell about it. Its population is listed at 4,350 but independent journalists estimate it is nearly three times that in periods of overcrowding.

Ploitari

Planet	World Type	Richness	Element Zero	Iridium	Platinum	Palladium
Aigela	Rock	Rich	None	Rich	Moderate	Moderate

Description: Only known from scan data picked up by space probes, Aigela is currently classified as a dwarf planet. A warm barren rock, its thin atmosphere is composed of carbon dioxide and oxygen. Significant alumina deposits in its crust make its density and gravity very low indeed. Orbital Distance: 0.7 AU; Orbital Period: 0.6 Earth Years; Radius: 1,511 Km; Day Length: 19.3 Earth Hours; Atmospheric Pressure: 0.03 Earth Atmospheres; Surface Temperature: 125 Celsius; Surface Gravity: 0.1 G.

Planet	World Type	Richness	Element Zero	Iridium	Platinum	Palladium
Synalus	Desert	Rich	None	Moderate	Moderate	Rich

Description: Space probes indicate that Synalus is nowhere near as hospitable as its neighbor, Zanethu. Synalus's hydrogen-argon atmosphere is thought to be anathema to life, but the presence of borax on the surface, spawned by a boron-heavy core, indicates the planet may once have had water. Orbital Distance: 2.2 AU; Orbital Period: 3.3 Earth Years; Radius: 5,391 Km; Day Length: 66.8 Earth Hours; Atmospheric Pressure: 1.23 Earth Atmospheres; Surface Temperature: -3 Celsius; Surface Gravity: 0.84 G.

Planet	World Type	Richness	Element Zero	Iridium	Platinum	Palladium
Thegan	Desert	Rich	Moderate	Moderate	Moderate	Rich

Description: Thegan rounds out the trio of planets scouted only by space probe in this backwater solar system. A frozen ball with significant amounts of tin in its crust, Thegan has a fractional atmosphere with trace amounts of carbon dioxide and carbon monoxide. Strange radiation emissions have been charted coming off of Thegan, but it is unknown if these are from radioactive elements or merely a star's radiation reflected by a high-albedo surface. Orbital Distance: 4.1 AU; Orbital Period: 8.3 Earth Years ;Radius: 3,581 Km; Day Length: 28.5 Earth Hours; Atmospheric Pressure: 0.05 Earth Atmospheres; Surface Temperature: -116 Celsius; Surface Gravity: 0.56 G.

Planet	World Type	Richness	Element Zero	Iridium	Platinum	Palladium
Zanethu	Rock	Good	None	Rich	Moderate	Moderate

Description: Believed to be a post-garden world, Zanethu has large deposits of calcium carbonate in its sedimentary rocks, indicating it may have once had plate tectonics and even plant life. Its swirling clouds of dust and snow may have occured more recently and blocked the sun, creating a mass-extinction event. Its surface gravity is comfortable and its temperature tolerable by most sapient species. Orbital Distance: 1.9 AU; Orbital Period: 2.6 Earth Years; Radius: 6,619 Km; Day Length: 53.6 Earth Hours; Atmospheric Pressure: 0.38 Earth Atmospheres; Surface Temperature: -16 Celsius; Surface Gravity: 1.2 G.

Introduction | Training | Upgrades and Research | Walkthrough | Special Assignments | Planetary Database | Appendix

Krogan DMZ

Aralakh *						
Planet	**World Type**	**Richness**	**Element Zero**	**Iridium**	**Platinum**	**Palladium**
Durak	Rock	Rich	None	Rich	Moderate	Moderate

Description: Durak is a small, heat-blasted rock lost in the blinding glare of the star Aralakh. It occasionally traps a trace atmosphere of gases blown in on Aralakh's powerful solar wind, which inevitably blows the gases back out again. The planetoid has a few valuable lodes of heavy metals, which were sporadically mined by the krogan at the height of their power. In the closing years of the Rebellions the five clans working the planetoid fell to fighting over a particularly rich deposit of iridium. All five clan warlords agreed to a Crush (a meeting at a neutral location) to negotiate a truce. Unfortunately, all five arrived planning to betray their fellows. While the leaders and their seconds met, all their bases were destroyed by simultaneous hypervelocity cannon strikes. Left with only the food, water, and air in their hardsuits and with no way to call for rescue the warlords apparently fought each other to the death. The survivors of the five "Durak clans" on Tuchanka still argue about which clan's warlord was the last one standing. Orbital Distance: 0.83 AU; Orbital Period: 0.6 Earth Years; Radius: 1,972 Km; Atmospheric Pressure: Trace; Surface Temperature: 348 Celsius; Surface Gravity: 0.22 G.

Kanin	Rock	Moderate	None	Moderate	Poor	Poor

Description: One of Kanin's hemispheres contains an impact crater 700 kilometers in diameter. Dubbed the Renkat Basin, it was mined for light metals in the interbellum between the Rachni War and Krogan Rebellions. Any obvious resource concentrations have long since been stripped. Orbital Distance: 1.66 AU; Orbital Period: 1.6 Earth Years; Radius: 3,312 Km; Atmospheric Pressure: Trace; Surface Temperature: 155 Celsius; Surface Gravity: 0.28 G.

Kruban	Desert	Rich	None	Poor	Moderate	Rich

Description: Kruban is a tidally locked Venusian hothouse. Its surface is perpetually obscured by clouds of sulfur and carbon dioxide. The first group of krogan brought into orbit by the salarian uplift teams requested a trip to Kruban. The salarians at first thought the krogan were confused about the nature of Kruban's environment; the planet is named for a krogan mythological paradise in which honorable warriors feast on the internal organs of their enemies. In fact, krogan astronomers had correctly deduced the nature of Kruban in the years before the global holocaust. In the two millennia since Kruban had come to be thought of as an ideal test of one's toughness. Every year a few krogan attempt to land on Kruban and exit their ships naked in an attempt to prove their "kroganhood." The planet's surface is littered with the crushed, corroded remains of their ships. Only one, Shath Norda, is known to have returned from the surface alive, albeit with most of his bones crushed and all four of his lungs damaged by sulfuric gas. Norda recovered from his trial to earn the adulation of his people. Until he died in 1943 he could lie with any fertile female he wished. Orbital Distance: 3.31 AU; Orbital Period: 4.6 Earth Years; Radius: 5,443 Km; Atmospheric Pressure: 47.3 Earth Atmospheres; Surface Temperature: 728 Celsius; Surface Gravity: 0.7 G.

Ruam	Giant Jovian	Poor	None	Poor	Poor	Poor

Description: The smaller of Aralakh's hydrogen-helium gas giants maintains a small helium-3 recovery infrastructure. Although the depth of Ruam's gravity well makes it inefficient to export, visitors to the Aralakh system often "top off" their fuel tanks at Ruam's stations. The Council Demilitarization Enforcement Mission (CDEM) maintains a token garrison to monitor any potential sale of fuel to known subversives and terrorists. Population: 1,040; CDEM Garrison: 20; Orbital Distance: 11.1 AU; Orbital Period: 28.4 Earth Years; Radius: 67,154 Km; Day Length: 13.8 Earth Hours.

Tuchanka	Not Minable	—	—	—	—	—

Description: Scarred by bombardment craters, radioactive rubble, choking ash, salt flats, and alkaline seas, Tuchanka can barely support life. Thousands of years ago life grew in fierce abundance under the F-class star Aralakh (a Raik clan word meaning "Eye of Wrath"). Tree analogs grew in thick jungles, their roots growing out of shallow silty seas. Life fed upon life in an evolutionary crucible. This world died in nuclear firestorms after the krogan split the atom. A "little ice age" of nuclear winter killed off much of the remaining plant life. In recent centuries many krogan have returned to their homeworld. The reduced albedo has caused global temperatures to rise. In order to maintain livable temperatures, a vast shroud was assembled at the L1 Lagrange point. It is maintained by the Council Demilitarization Enforcement Mission (CDEM), which is based on orbiting battlestations. CDEM ADVISORY: Visitors to Tuchanka land at their own risk. The CDEM will not attempt to extract citizens threatened by clan warfare. TRAVEL ADVISORY: The ecology of Tuchanka is deadly. Nearly every native species engages in some predatory behavior; even the remaining vegetation is carnivorous. Travel beyond guarded areas is strongly discouraged. Population: 2.1 billion; Capital: Currently Urdnot (since 2183); CDEM Garrison: 2,400 (in orbital battlestations); Orbital Distance: 5.3 AU; Orbital Period: 16.7 Earth Years; Radius: 8,293 Km; Day Length: 21.4 Earth Hours; Atmospheric Pressure: 1.1 Earth Atmospheres; Surface Temperature: 72 Celsius (36 in shrouded areas); Surface Gravity: 1.14 G.

Vaul	Giant Jovian	Moderate	None	Poor	Poor	Poor

Description: Vaul is a hydrogen-helium gas giant named for an ancient krogan deity that stood watch for enemies of his pantheon. The gas giant's moons are named after some of Vaul's myriad eyes and ears. The only reason to visit the Vaul system is scientific curiosity, which the krogan lack. Orbital Distance: 17.8 AU; Orbital Period: 57.8 Earth Years; Radius: 73,944 Km; Day Length: 12.1 Earth Hours.

Nith						
Planet	**World Type**	**Richness**	**Element Zero**	**Iridium**	**Platinum**	**Palladium**
Mantun	Rock	Rich	Moderate	Rich	Moderate	Moderate

Description: The class-B blue giant Nith was once the most strategically valuable system within krogan territory. Though far too hot for habitation, Nith emits thousands of times the energy of a main sequence star like Earth's Sol. With help from salarian uplift teams, the krogan constructed a chain of solar power collector stations in orbit around Nith. These vast arrays beamed power to particle accelerators on the surface of Mantun, which manufactured antiproton fuel for warship thrusters. In the Krogan Rebellions the Spectre agents managed to get a virus into the computers of the solar power arrays; every fifth array suddenly applied braking thrusters. The arrays behind them "piled up," and all were reduced to wreckage. This has since dispersed into a relatively stable ring system. The krogan never had the resources to rebuild the solar arrays, depriving them of their fleet's main fuel supply for the remainder of the war. The particle accelerators still exist on Mantun but have not been used in thousands of years. Orbital Distance: 57.2 AU; Orbital Period: 112.1 Earth Years; Radius: 2,150 Km; Orbital Period: 112.1 Earth Years; Atmospheric Pressure: Trace; Surface Temperature: 641 Celsius; Surface Gravity: 0.28 G.

Nith (continued)

Planet	World Type	Richness	Element Zero	Iridium	Platinum	Palladium
Tula	Giant Ice	Poor	None	Poor	Moderate	Poor

Description: Tula's methane-ammonia atmosphere traps the blistering heat of Nith, driving dayside temperatures up over 1,000 degrees. While some lodes of useful metals are present, the planet's incredible heat makes mining impractical. Orbital Distance: 108.7 AU; Orbital Period: 293.9 Earth Years; Radius: 5,204 Km; Day Length: 59.7 Earth Hours; Atmospheric Pressure: 0.54 Earth Atmospheres; Surface Temperature: 1,036 Celsius Surface; Gravity: 0.55 G.

Planet	World Type	Richness	Element Zero	Iridium	Platinum	Palladium
Vard	Giant Ice	Moderate	None	Poor	Moderate	Poor

Description: Vard is a methane-ammonia ice giant. Until the Krogan Rebellions it had a sizable helium-3 fuel-refining infrastructure. Once the solar arrays orbiting Nith were destroyed, the constant flow of antiproton tankers visiting the system disappeared. There was little point to maintaining the facilities, so they were shut down and abandoned. Today, transients, criminals, and outcasts are squatting in the ancient stations. Although few of the stations are safe for habitation, neither the krogan nor the Council Demilitarization Enforcement Mission patrols care if the squatters take their chances. Population: 2,072; Orbital Distance: 195.6 AU; Orbital Period: 709.6 Earth Years; Radius: 36,670 Km; Day Length: 18.0 Earth Hours.

Minos Wasteland

Caestus

Planet	World Type	Richness	Element Zero	Iridium	Platinum	Palladium
Invictus	Garden	Rich	Moderate	Moderate	Rich	Moderate

Description: Home to dextro-amino-acid-based life, Invictus has temperate zones that were settled by a turian population that initially fell prey to a bewildering number of diseases. Two decades after its first colony was founded its population had been reduced by half due to fatalities and a large colonist exodus. But when the Primarchs considered ceding the planet to robo-mining interests, the turian statesman Shastina Emperus ambitiously declared that she would start her own colony and double its population within five years. This effort succeeded, largely due to the colonies' location in deserts with a minimal number of pest species. The image of Shastina's triumph in the frontier made for good political theater, and the turian population poured in. The planet's tropical belt still remains largely unexplored as its aggressive organic life still wreaks havoc on turian biology. A "house in an Invictus jungle" is a modern turian phrase for an idea that seems like a good idea but only to the one who came up with it. Invictus's atmosphere is primarily nitrogen and oxygen, and its surface crust varies but has high concentrations of alumina and silver. Because it can support life easily, criminals from throughout the Terminus Systems hide out on Invictus. Its official population is estimated to be half the number of sapients that are actually on the planet. Colony Founded: 1939 CE; Population: 320,535,000 (est. 640,000,000 with illegals); Capital: Shastinasio; Orbital Distance: 1.3 AU; Orbital Period: 1.5 Earth Years; Radius: 7,260 Km; Day Length: 31.6 Earth Hours; Atmospheric Pressure: 1.15 Earth Atmospheres; Surface Temperature: 30 Celsius; Surface Gravity: 1.5 G.

Planet	World Type	Richness	Element Zero	Iridium	Platinum	Palladium
Temerarus	Rock	Rich	None	Rich	Poor	Moderate

Description: Visible in Invictus's night sky is Temerarus, a planet named for the turian spirit said to have inspired the crew of their first manned moon launch. A boiling hot rock planet, Temerarus is much hotter than its temperate neighbor due to a thick atmosphere rich in carbon dioxide and helium. Its hot surface is largely composed of boron. Surrounded by a thick dust cloud, Temerarus is often struck by small meteors, making exploration dangerous. Orbital Distance: 3.4 AU; Orbital Period: 6.3 Earth Years; Radius: 3,321 Km; Day Length: 66.4 Earth Hours; Atmospheric Pressure: 15.86 Earth Atmospheres; Surface Temperature: 131 Celsius; Surface Gravity: 0.2 G.

Fortis

Planet	World Type	Richness	Element Zero	Iridium	Platinum	Palladium
Aequitas	Desert	Rich	None	Moderate	Moderate	Rich

Description: Home to the famous Iron Canyons, Aequitas has reddish iron oxide dust (hematite) covering much of its surface and significant blue cobalt deposits that freckle the terrain. Turian explorers have discovered hot springs in the polar ice caps, heated by magma in the planet's crust. In a strange combination of science and hucksterism a small facility exports water from these springs, which is bottled and sold as having medicinal properties. The funds are then used to maintain a research station, which has discovered some fossil evidence that Aequitas once harbored microscopic life, based on deoxyribonucleic acids in these springs. Orbital Distance: 4.0 AU; Orbital Period: 8.0 Earth Years; Radius: 7,437 Km; Day Length: 51.6 Earth Hours; Atmospheric Pressure: 0.49 Earth Atmospheres; Surface Temperature: -85 Celsius; Surface Gravity: 1.6 G.

Planet	World Type	Richness	Element Zero	Iridium	Platinum	Palladium
Pietas	Desert	Rich	None	Moderate	Moderate	Rich

Description: Though Pietas has a combination of features that make terraforming a possibility, the rights to the planet have been tied up in Citadel Council courts for the past eight years. The running joke is that by the time the Council finally gives the go-ahead to colonize the planet, Pietas will have evolved life of its own. Home to comfortable temperatures and a mild atmosphere of mostly nitrogen and argon, Pietas could be habitable with the addition of oxygen-producing cyanobacteria. Its crust is high in silicates and carbon, allowing for easy fabrication of construction materials. Smugglers, pirates, and other unregistered starships sometimes touch down on Pietas to lay low or make repairs. Civilian travel is not advised. Orbital Distance: 1.8 AU; Orbital Period: 2.4 Earth Years; Radius: 5,430 Km; Day Length: 26.5 Earth Hours; Atmospheric Pressure: 1.26 Earth Atmospheres; Surface Temperature: 21 Celsius; Surface Gravity: 0.7 G.

Planet	World Type	Richness	Element Zero	Iridium	Platinum	Palladium
Vir	Desert	Good	None	Moderate	Moderate	Rich

Description: A pressure-cooker planet with a thick, nitrogen-heavy atmosphere, Vir is largely ignored by the galactic community. Probes have revealed a crust of nickel and scorched carbon, both of which can be found in abundance elsewhere at far lower temperatures. Orbital Distance: 0.6 AU; Orbital Period: 0.5 Earth Years; Radius: 8,162 Km; Day Length: 44.4 Earth Hours; Atmospheric Pressure: 106.22 Earth Atmospheres; Surface Temperature: 778 Celsius; Surface Gravity: 2.1 G.

Introduction · Training · Upgrades and Research · Walkthrough · Special Assignments · Planetary Database · Appendix

Nubian Expanse

Dakka *						
Planet	**World Type**	**Richness**	**Element Zero**	**Iridium**	**Platinum**	**Palladium**
Alkonost	Giant Ice	Moderate	None	Poor	Moderate	Poor

Description: Alkonost is a standard ice giant with a methane-ammonia atmosphere. It has an unusually strong magnetic field, which is occasionally useful when ships need to discharge their drives. Orbital Distance: 2.47 AU; Orbital Period: 3.9 Earth Years; Radius: 17,946 Km; Day Length: 18.8 Earth Hours.

Bannik	Desert	Rich	None	Moderate	Rich	Rich

Description: Bannik is a large, superterrestrial "hothouse" with a crushing carbon dioxide atmosphere. A high average density of over 7 grams per cubic centimeter indicates that Bannik is a mineralogical treasure trove. If only there were some way to safely reach its seas of molten metal and lodes of radioactives. The planet's mass is so great that trace amounts of helium and molecular hydrogen can be found in the atmosphere. Orbital Distance: 0.73 AU; Orbital Period: 0.6 Earth Years; Radius: 7,963 Km; Day Length: 54.8 Earth Hours; Atmospheric Pressure: 65.4 Earth Atmospheres; Surface Temperature: 599 Celsius; Surface Gravity: 1.6 G.

Gamayun	Giant Jovian	Poor	None	Poor	Moderate	Poor

Description: Gamayun is a hydrogen-helium gas giant with six large, icy moons. The outermost one, Gigula, is of note for a well-preserved wreckage of an ancient starship that was recovered by a turian military surveyor. Little information has been released to the public on the vessel, aside from a scholarly paper regarding how the internal layout suggests a horizontally oriented race. Orbital Distance: 5.19 AU; Orbital Period: 11.8 Earth Years; Radius: 50,875 Km; Day Length: 65.6 Earth Hours.

Pragia	Not Minable	—	—	—	—	—

Description: The jungle-planet Pragia is overrun by choking hypergrowth caused by industrially mutated plant species. This, combined with its relative isolation and lack of population, has made Pragia an occasional base of operations for drug runners, weapons smugglers, pirates, mercenaries, terrorists, and intelligence agents seeking secrecy. Sustained habitation on Pragia is extremely difficult; mutant and even poisonous plant life can overgrow colonies in days instead of years. Orbital Distance: 1.3 AU; Orbital Period: 1.5 Earth Years; Radius: 5,137 Km; Day Length: 29.6 Earth Hours; Atmospheric Pressure: 0.84 Earth Atmospheres; Surface Temperature: 54 Celsius; Surface Gravity: 0.87 G.

Zirnitra	Ocean/Ice	Rich	None	Poor	Rich	Moderate

Description: Cold, distant Zirnitra has an extremely low density and is thought to be mainly ice around a small rocky core. It has little to recommend it. Orbital Distance: 7.78 AU; Orbital Period: 21.8 Earth Years; Radius: 2,683 Km; Day Length: 44.9 Earth Hours; Atmospheric Pressure: Trace; Surface Temperature: -158 Celsius; Surface Gravity: 0.16 G.

Kalabsha						
Planet	**World Type**	**Richness**	**Element Zero**	**Iridium**	**Platinum**	**Palladium**
Tefnut	Giant Jovian	Poor	None	Poor	Moderate	Poor

Description: A hydrogen-helium gas giant, Tefnut is home to a helium-3 collection and the refueling facility nearest to the Nubian Expanse's mass relay. As such it is a major gateway to the Verge and Terminus Systems and has become famous for its hospitality industry. Tefnut's motto is known throughout the galaxy: "Like home, only better." Visitors here can stay at expansive resort stations, watch locally produced entertainment, buy mind-affecting substances not welcome in Citadel space, and rent companionship. Resources are shipped in from Yamm at substantial discounts, allowing the small space stations to have surprising luxuries, such as edible arthropods and large amounts of fresh water. Population: 33,810 spread across five space stations; Orbital Distance: 4.1 AU; Orbital Period: 8.3 Earth Years; Radius: 57,010 Km; Day Length: 8.8 Earth Hours.

Yamm	Post-Garden	Moderate	Moderate	Moderate	Moderate	Moderate

Description: With over 90 percent of its surface covered in oceans, Yamm is a habitable nitrogen-oxygen world, but its extremes can be quite hostile to sapient life. The heat from its extremely long days reaches dangerous levels ranging from 24 Celsius at night to 53 in the afternoon in the temperate zones. Hurricanes run unchecked across the oceans, with winds reaching up to 250 kilometers per hour. While there are some arthropod-like animals, the predominant forms of life are various kinds of toxic algae blooms that stretch hundreds of kilometers across. However, other biohydrocarbon algae blooms are suitable for use as biofuel, and farming the "green gold" forms the backbone of Yamm's economy. Colony Founded: 2170 CE; Population: 488,504; Capital: New Karnak; Orbital Distance: 2.0 AU; Orbital Period: 2.8 Earth Years; Radius: 6,501 Km; Day Length: 69.6 Earth Hours; Atmospheric Pressure: 1.8 Earth Atmospheres; Surface Temperature: 34 Celsius (temperate zone); Surface Gravity: 1.1 G.

Qertassi						
Planet	**World Type**	**Richness**	**Element Zero**	**Iridium**	**Platinum**	**Palladium**
Norehsa	Giant Ice	Moderate	None	Poor	Moderate	Poor

Description: Norehsa is an unremarkable methane-ammonia ice giant with a small family of icy moons. It is likely that the Qertassi system had additional worlds earlier in its history, but these have been swallowed by the aging giant star. Qertassi is an elderly metal-poor Population II star broadly similar to Arcturus. Orbital Distance: 6.17 AU; Orbital Period: 2.4 Earth Years; Radius: 42,214 Km; Day Length: 19.2 Earth Hours.

Omega Nebula

Arinlarkan

Planet	World Type	Richness	Element Zero	Iridium	Platinum	Palladium
MSV Strontium Mule	Not Minable	—	—	—	—	—

Description: Detecting a derelict freighter that has sustained heavy damage. Blue Suns communications detected aboard the ship.

| Utha | Ocean/Ice | Rich | None | Poor | Rich | Moderate |

Description: Punished with UV and gamma radiation from the Class F star it orbits, Utha is no one's first choice for a planet to land on. Covered in seawater, Utha has a hydrosphere and ozone layer similar to Earth's, but that simply isn't enough to ward off the life-killing radiation. Its nitrogen-rich oxygen-poor atmosphere goes unchanged by the few proteins that have managed to form in the ocean depths. Utha, however, has served as a way station for slaves escaping their batarian masters. What little land it has is tectonically stable, and its considerable radiation belt and electrical storms grant cover from many common types of sensors. Fleeing ships typically hide on Utha long enough to discharge their drive cores and stock up on deuterium before trying to make it to the cluster's mass relay. Orbital Distance: 4.0 AU; Orbital Period: 6.1 Earth Years; Radius: 6,050 Km; Day Length: 49.4 Earth Hours; Atmospheric Pressure: 1.2 Earth Atmospheres; Surface Temperature: 40 Celsius. Surface Gravity: 0.8 G.

Batalla

Planet	World Type	Richness	Element Zero	Iridium	Platinum	Palladium
Logasiri	Desert	Moderate	None	Poor	Poor	Rich

Description: A step above a carbonaceous asteroid, Logasiri is a planet with a carbon-heavy crust and a trace atmosphere of CO2 and helium. Its surface is cool enough to have liquid water, but it is rapidly drying out as it has lost the critical mass to have a self-sustaining hydrologic cycle. Nevertheless, the batarians have colonized the world, forcing slaves to work in their mines and agri-habitats. The labor is hot, endless, and backbreaking, even in the low-G environment. Every horror story told by slaves elsewhere in the cluster seems to be topped by one from Logasiri. The most famous is that of the slaver Silparon, who worked to death 420 slaves over the course of a galactic standard year and ground up their bodies for compost in his greenhouses. He was eventually poisoned by his wife, but his shadow—and his business model—still hangs over the miserable planet. Orbital Distance: 0.6 AU; Orbital Period: 0.5 Earth Years; Radius: 5,017 Km; Day Length: 49.7 Earth Hours; Atmospheric Pressure: Trace; Surface Temperature: 56 Celsius; Surface Gravity: 0.5 G.

| Nearog | Giant Ice | Moderate | Moderate | Poor | Moderate | Poor |

Description: Nearog is a hydrogen-methane gas giant whose moons were once home to Essul, a batarian warlord who terrorized the Terminus Systems. Attempting to unite a pirate army under his banner, he successfully conducted a rapid blitz against 11 habitable planets. Fortunately for the rest of the galaxy, Essul's crimes caught the attention of the Spectres, who deduced his hidden location and assassinated him. Essul's empire, built on a hyperextended army, soon came crashing down. His lost stockpiles of element zero have become something of a legend, and foolish spacers have spent countless amounts of time and money searching the Batalla system, convinced they will be the ones that finally strike it rich. Orbital Distance: 4.8 AU; Orbital Period: 11.8 Earth Years; Radius: 19,976 Km; Day Length: 16.5 Earth Hours.

| Thunawanuro | Garden | Good | Rich | Poor | Rich | Moderate |

Description: A strange island of peace in the lawless Terminus Systems, Thunawanuro is a planet of crushing gravity but abundant life. As its ponderous name indicates, it was colonized by the elcor, who have several booming industries on the planet. Hydroelectric dams and biofuels from tough woody algae provide much of the planet's energy. Mines export uranium, thorium, and gold taken to space with generous use of mass effect fields. Of course, pirates target the elcor's shipping as soon as it leaves orbit, but the elcor's deals with mercenary companies keep away all but the most foolhardy of attackers. Population: 3,769,400; Colony Founded: 2035 CE; Capital: Nurhemathun; Orbital Distance: 1.1 AU; Orbital Period: 1.3 Earth Years; Radius: 11,993 Km; Day Length: 51.7 Earth Hours; Atmospheric Pressure: 2.86 Earth Atmospheres; Surface Temperature: 32 Celsius; Surface Gravity: 6.7 G.

Fathar

Planet	World Type	Richness	Element Zero	Iridium	Platinum	Palladium
Dorgal	Ocean/Ice	Rich	None	Poor	Rich	Moderate

Description: The surface of Dorgal is an ethane-soaked mush. The planet hovers near the boiling point of the hydrocarbon and supports a diverse if simple and slow-moving carbon-based ecology. The planet's gravity is strong enough to retain an atmosphere of molecular nitrogen and carbon monoxide, but the methane that dominated billions of years ago has long since been lost. Orbital Distance: 0.54 AU; Orbital Period: 0.7 Earth Years; Radius: 3,521 Km; Day Length: 51.4 Earth Hours; Atmospheric Pressure: 0.43 Earth Atmospheres; Surface Temperature: -88 Celsius; Surface Gravity: 0.44 G.

| Korar | Rock | Good | None | Rich | Moderate | Moderate |

Description: Korar is a small, lifeless rock blessed with significant deposits of thorium, which is used in radiation shielding and the manufacture of spaceframe alloys. A few miners eke out an existence on the surface, selling their ore at Lorek and praying that the intermittent raids by the Terminus pirate clans will pass their homestead by. There have been no children born on Korar since the infamous pirate raid of 2047, when every child on the planet was rounded up and taken as a slave. Any couple finding themselves pregnant preemptively moves offworld. Population: 2,400; Orbital Distance: 0.32 AU; Orbital Period: 0.3 Earth Years; Radius: 1,919 Km; Atmospheric Pressure: Trace; Surface Temperature: -40 Celsius; Surface Gravity: 0.19 G.

Introduction / Training / Upgrades and Research / Walkthrough / Special Assignments / Planetary Database / Appendix

Fathar (continued)						
Planet	**World Type**	**Richness**	**Element Zero**	**Iridium**	**Platinum**	**Palladium**
Lorek	Ocean/Ice	Rich	None	Moderate	Rich	Moderate

Description: Lorek is an extremely rare example of a habitable world circling a red dwarf star. Originally an independent asari colony named Esan, it was annexed by the Batarian Hegemony in 1913, causing a minor galactic incident. Despite several attempts, the local Terminus warlords have never been able to take Lorek for themselves. Lorek is a low-density world composed of rock, light metals, and a water-based crust. It is tidally locked to Fathar with a sunward "hot pole" and shadowed "cold pole." Water on the sunward side evaporates quickly, traveling over the islands of the habitable terminator zone in the form of massive fast-moving thunderstorms and finally settling as snow on the frozen dark side. There are fears that the buildup of ice cap mass on the far side may cause axial reorientation over the course of several million years, but batarian officials dismiss the idea as an irresponsible theory disseminated by counter-hegemonist subversives. Colony Founded: 1,764; Population: 4,700,000; Capital: Jalnor; Orbital Distance: 0.2 AU; Orbital Period: 59.6 Earth Days; Radius: 6,754 Km; Atmospheric Pressure: 0.4 Earth Atmospheres; Surface Temperature: 40 Celsius; Surface Gravity: 0.6 G.

Kairavamori						
Planet	**World Type**	**Richness**	**Element Zero**	**Iridium**	**Platinum**	**Palladium**
Sehtor	Rock	Rich	None	Rich	Moderate	Moderate

Description: A rocky planet with a crushing atmosphere, Sehtor has been scanned from orbit but largely left unexplored due to its sweltering conditions. Its atmosphere contains nitrogen but also an unusually high percentage of ethane, which can coalesce in pockets near the surface. The alumina-heavy crust of the planet can reach glowing-hot temperatures during the daytime, reaching the ethane's auto-ignition temperature and creating pockets of flame across the landscape. For this reason extra-vehicular activities are discouraged on Sehtor, and no company has been willing to invest in exploration. Orbital Distance: 0.7 AU; Orbital Period: 0.7 Earth Years; Radius: 5,810 Km; Day Length: 47.8 Earth Hours; Atmospheric Pressure: 47.73 Earth Atmospheres; Surface Temperature: 470 Celsius; Surface Gravity: 0.8 G.

Uwan Oche	Rock	Rich	None	Rich	Moderate	Moderate

Description: Uwan Oche ("Uwan Prime") is a stony planet encased in ice under a methane-heavy sky. Named for the Uwan Consortium, the batarian manufacturing firm that financed its exploration, Uwan Oche's crust provides much of the boron allotropes used in omni-gel throughout the Terminus Systems. The area has naturally become a haven for pirates, who attempt to steal the refined gel or its ingredients as soon as the cargo ships leave the atmosphere. Orbital Distance: 2.7 AU; Orbital Period: 5.0 Earth Years; Radius: 6,529 Km; Day Length: 57.5 Earth Hours; Atmospheric Pressure: Trace; Surface Temperature: -126 Celsius; Surface Gravity: 1.1 G.

Vatar	Rock	Rich	None	Rich	Moderate	Moderate

Description: Located within the life zone of a dimming orange sun, Vatar would be habitable except for its carbon-dioxide atmosphere and an icy surface that kills most oxygen-producing bacteria. Nonetheless, mercenary companies and slavers have numerous strongholds on the planet, out of reach of any galactic authority. TRAVEL ADVISORY: A statistically significant number of distress signals have originated within the 1-million-kilometer mark of Vatar. Civilian travel is not advised. Orbital Distance: 1.4 AU; Orbital Period: 1.9 Earth Years; Radius: 6,352 Km; Day Length: 18.0 Earth Hours; Atmospheric Pressure: 0.77 Earth Atmospheres; Surface Temperature: -35 Celsius; Surface Gravity: 1.0 G.

Sahrabarik *						
Planet	**World Type**	**Richness**	**Element Zero**	**Iridium**	**Platinum**	**Palladium**
Bindur	Ocean/Ice	Rich	None	Poor	Rich	Moderate

Description: If it were closer to Sahrabarik, Bindur would have an atmosphere of carbon dioxide and ethane. In the deep cold of the outer solar system, however, both elements have long since frozen to the ground. Orbital Distance: 6.12 AU; Orbital Period: 27.7 Earth Years; Radius: 4,907 Km; Day Length: 53.3 Earth Hours; Atmospheric Pressure: Trace; Surface Temperature: -224 Celsius; Surface Gravity: 0.55 G.

Imorkan	Giant Ice	Moderate	None	Poor	Moderate	Poor

Description: A standard methane-ammonia gas giant, Imorkan is the main source of helium-3 fuel for ships coming to or from Omega. Most of its fueling stations are run by criminal cartels that engage in cutthroat (sometimes literally) pricing wars. Imorkan is also widely known for its layover stations, where pirates in a hurry can find fuel, ammunition, intoxicants, gambling, and sexual companionship at any hour. Orbital Distance: 3.4 AU; Orbital Period: 11.5 Earth Years; Radius: 53,491 Km; Day Length: 18.7 Earth Hours.

Omega	Not Minable	—	—	—	—	—

Description: Built in the mined-out husk of a metallic asteroid, Omega has been a haven for criminals, terrorists, and malcontents for thousands of years. At times the station has lain idle and abandoned for centuries, only to be reactivated by a new group of outlaws seeking a fresh start. The space station's original elegant design has given way to haphazard expansion by scrabbling factions of every species. There is no central government or unifying authority on Omega, and nobody can recall a time there ever was one. Population: 7.8 million; Orbital Distance: 2.43 AU; Orbital Period: 6.9 Earth Years; Total Length: 44.7 Km.

Omega 4 Relay	Not Minable	—	—	—	—	—

Description: The Omega 4 relay is surrounded by hazard beacons and automated warnings. Over the last thousand years many ships have attempted to pass through it, but none have returned. The only ones to pass freely back and forth through the relay are the mysterious Collectors. There are many theories as to why ships never return from Omega 4. Some say there is a black hole at the far end; others (mostly the impoverished underclass of Omega) believe there is some form of earthly paradise. Most, however, simply think that the Collectors capture or destroy those passing through the relay.

Sahrabarik (continued)

Planet	World Type	Richness	Element Zero	Iridium	Platinum	Palladium
Urdak	Brown Dwarf	Moderate	None	Poor	Moderate	Moderate

Description: Urdak is a close-orbiting brown dwarf; most red-brown dwarf binary systems have an average separation of 8 AU. The Sahrabarik system is about 12 billion years old, and it has long since used up the deuterium used to fuel fusion, so Urdak is not luminous like some brown dwarfs are. Urdak is a class L brown dwarf with a relatively low temperature of 1,300 degrees Celsius, but its heat and gravity have made it unpopular for development. There are rumors that the heads of several of Omega's crime syndicates maintain private residences on various moons. Whatever the truth of the matter, battles between syndicate vessels are often observed around the ring plane. News outlets on Omega maintain satellites at Urdak's Lagrange points for real-time coverage of these battles, which garner high viewer ratings. Orbital Distance: 0.8 AU; Orbital Period: 1.3 Earth Years; Radius: 72,512 Km; Day Length: 19.2 Earth Hours.

The Phoenix Massing

Salahiel

Planet	World Type	Richness	Element Zero	Iridium	Platinum	Palladium
Ekuna	Rock	Rich	Moderate	Rich	Moderate	Moderate

Description: First discovered by the quarians at the turn of the century, Ekuna is habitable but a second-tier choice for most species. Circling an orange sun, Ekuna averages below freezing temperatures. This led development firms to colonize at the planet's equator, where the climate is tolerable for agriculture. The quarians, seeking a homeworld of their own, petitioned the Citadel Council for the right to take over Ekuna, but they had already settled a few hundred thousand quarians on the planet before approaching the Council. Seeing this occupation as an illegal act, the Council turned a deaf ear to quarian pleas and gave the world to the elcor, who could withstand the high gravity of the world far better. The quarians squatting on the planet were given one galactic standard month to leave, at which point their colonies would be bombarded. The junk left behind by the fleeing quarians clogs up portions of the landscape to this day. Non-elcor visitors to Ekuna are advised to use personal or vehicular mass effect fields to lighten the pressure, as the surface gravity will otherwise cause health and mechanical problems. Colony Founded: 2103 CE; Population: 221,256,200; Capital: Bel Shadii (elcor: Durawunafon); Orbital Distance: 1.6 AU; Orbital Period: 2.3 Earth Years; Radius: 10,206 Km; Day Length: 36.4 Earth Hours; Atmospheric Pressure: 1.4 Earth Atmospheres; Surface Temperature: -37 Celsius (equator mean temperature 15 Celsius); Surface Gravity: 4.1 G.

The Sea of Storms

Planet	World Type	Richness	Element Zero	Iridium	Platinum	Palladium
Heretic Station	Not Minable	—	—	—	—	—

Description: Once called Haratar by the quarians, this space station was stripped of its useful technology by the fleeing Migrant Fleet when they left the Perseus Veil 300 years ago. Little more than a cold metal superstructure floating in the void, the station was removed from star charts by 2050 CE. Scans indicate the station was reconstructed and upgraded in a massive effort that must have taken at least 10 years, implying that there may have been some geth outside the Veil before their infamous attack on Eden Prime. Needing little but a fuel source it could have been hidden here for much longer without attracting attention from the barren worlds around Tassrah or the clueless elcor in the Salahiel system. Heretic Station, as Legion refers to it, is home to a geth data core capable of broadcasting vast distances through tightbeam projection. Approximately 6.6 million copies of geth software are stored in the station, the majority of which are kept bodiless in servers and downloaded to legged platforms when needed. The station's "population" of legged platforms is approximately 2.4 million. Total Length: 20.5 Km; Total Width: 11.3 Km; Total Height: 11.3 Km; Exterior Armor Thickness: 8 M; Gross Weight: 1.55 Billion Metric Tons; Population: 6.6 Million Copies; 2.4 Million Platforms (1 million of which are in storage).

Tassrah *

Planet	World Type	Richness	Element Zero	Iridium	Platinum	Palladium
Ishassara	Giant Jovian	Poor	None	Poor	Poor	Moderate

Description: A gas giant, Ishassara is composed mostly of hydrogen and nitrogen. Its orbit in recent years has taken it close to the mass relay in this system, making it a popular stop for "scoop ships" to refuel the hydrogen in their thrusters before moving on. Orbital Distance: 3.8 AU; Orbital Period: 5.7 Earth Years; Radius: 22,769 Km; Day Length: 14.0 Earth Hours.

Pahhur	Rock	Rich	None	Rich	Moderate	Moderate

Description: By normal standards a large rock planet, Pahhur (which means "fiery") is constantly scorched by the white bright giant it orbits. A dense atmosphere featuring hydrogen, helium, and clouds of vaporized magnesium floats over its iron-rich core, making for a truly hellish landscape. Its spectacular temperature prevents any practical exploitation. Orbital Distance: 0.6 AU; Orbital Period: 0.4 Earth Years; Radius: 10,560 Km; Day Length: 46.0 Earth Hours; Atmospheric Pressure: 90.59 Earth Atmospheres; Surface Temperature: 1,445 Celsius; Surface Gravity: 4.6 G.

Sarapai	Desert	Rich	None	Poor	Moderate	Rich

Description: Sarapai (which means "ever upward") is the second planet orbiting the white star Tassrah. Sarapai's pressure-cooker atmosphere of carbon dioxide and ethane serves as a greenhouse to an already boiling-hot surface. Cobalt compounds are frequently found on its crust, giving spectacular blue tinges to its land. Scans from orbital probes indicate its crust contains deposits of platinum likely to be as unexploited as those on its sister planet Pahhur. Orbital Distance: 1.7 AU; Orbital Period: 1.7 Earth Years; Radius: 6,016 Km; Day Length: 60.8 Earth Hours; Atmospheric Pressure: 118.08 Earth Atmospheres; Surface Temperature: 1271 Celsius; Surface Gravity: 0.9 G.

Introduction · Training · Upgrades and Research · Walkthrough · Special Assignments · Planetary Database · Appendix

Pylos Nebula

Dirada						
Planet	**World Type**	**Richness**	**Element Zero**	**Iridium**	**Platinum**	**Palladium**
Canalus	Desert	Rich	None	Moderate	Moderate	Rich

Description: Canalus is smaller than Earth but has unusually high density. The high level of tectonic activity indicates that the density is caused by an abundance of radioactive materials in the core. These, combined with the planet's unusually high rate of spin, raise the planet's internal temperature and cause volcanism. While several companies performed mineral assays in the late 2170s, the world's geological instability precluded development. Orbital Distance: 46.3 AU; Orbital Period: 176.8 Earth Years; Radius: 4,618 Km; Day Length: 9.8 Earth Hours; Atmospheric Pressure: 0.83 Earth Atmospheres; Surface Temperature: 99 Celsius; Surface Gravity: 0.85 G.

Siano	Rock	Rich	Moderate	Rich	Moderate	Moderate

Description: Siano, named for an ancient asari philosopher known for being a contrarian, orbits Dirada at a retrograde. It is believed to be an object that fell into the system millions of years ago from parts unknown. The outermost of Dirada's two inner asteroid belts is thought to have been a small planetoid that was broken up by Siano's passage into the system. Siano is formed of low-density rock and is tidally locked to Dirada; the same hemisphere always faces the star. There is evidence that a complex of artificial structures once existed in the north of the sunward-facing hemisphere, but they have been badly degraded by millennia of heat and radiation. Several bunkers of radioactive waste, apparently byproducts of primitive fission plants, have been discovered on the far side. Orbital Distance: 12.9 AU; Orbital Period: 26 Earth Years; Radius: 4,925 Km; Day Length: 26 Earth Years; Atmospheric Pressure: Trace; Surface Temperature: 79 Celsius; Surface Gravity: 0.47 G.

Sineus	Giant Jovian	Poor	None	Poor	Poor	Poor

Description: A standard hydrogen-helium gas giant, Sineus has more than 80 moons. Orbital Distance: 138.9 AU; Orbital Period: 919.2 Earth Years; Radius: 63,748 Km; Day Length: 16.4 Earth Hours.

Thenusi	Rock	Rich	None	Rich	Poor	Moderate

Description: Thenusi is a small barren rock. Though there is evidence that it once had an atmosphere of carbon dioxide, only trace amounts of krypton and xenon remain. Like Siano it is tidally locked to Dirada. Orbital Distance: 25.7 AU; Orbital Period: 73.1 Earth Years; Radius: 3,602 Km; Day Length: 73.1 Earth Years; Atmospheric Pressure: Trace; Surface Temperature: -10 Celsius; Surface Gravity: 0.33 G.

Vioresa	Giant Ice	Poor	None	Poor	Moderate	Poor

Description: With an orbital period nearly two millennia long, the cold and distant Vioresa was actually missed in the initial asari survey of the system. Only a follow-up mineral assay sent to Canalus by a volus mining concern noticed its subtle movement across the stars. Vioresa is a methane-ammonia ice giant circled by a retinue of deep-frozen moons. Its remoteness makes it a popular drive discharge point for pirates working the Pylos Nebula cluster. In the last two years several dozen ships have disappeared while passing through the Dirada system. As Pylos is currently unclaimed by any sovereign power, Council naval patrols are few and far between. Thus far none of the pirates responsible have been apprehended. Orbital Distance: 222.2 AU; Orbital Period: 1,860.4 Earth Years; Radius: 26,566 Km; Day Length: 12.7 Earth Hours.

Zeth	Giant Jovian	Moderate	None	Poor	Poor	Poor

Description: Zeth is a common hydrogen-helium gas giant. An abundance of sulfur in the upper atmosphere gives it a distinct yellow color. Orbital Distance: 69.5 AU; Orbital Period: 325.2 Earth Years; Radius: 60,327 Km; Day Length: 14.8 Earth Hours.

Kriseroi						
Planet	**World Type**	**Richness**	**Element Zero**	**Iridium**	**Platinum**	**Palladium**
Geus	Giant Ice	Moderate	None	Poor	Moderate	Poor

Description: Geus is a methane-ammonia gas giant very similar to its near-twin, Uzin. It presents a nearly featureless robin's-egg-blue face to the universe. Orbital Distance: 0.64 AU; Orbital Period: 0.9 Earth Years; Radius: 33,036 Km; Day Length: 9.9 Earth Hours.

Neidus	Post-Garden	Moderate	None	Moderate	Moderate	Moderate

Description: Neidus lies improbably close to the red dwarf Kriseroi. This allows it to approach habitability though it is quite frigid. It is tidally locked, with a "hot pole" and a "cold pole." Along the terminator the temperature averages just above freezing. On the lee side the temperatures are well below freezing. Neidus has developed a limited native ecology. Much of it clusters permanently attached around geothermal vents. There are, however, more advanced forms of life. Several arthropodal herbivore species wander back and forth across the terminator because they require nutrients available in both environments for sustenance. More dangerous are the omnivorous predator species that devour the arthropods. Most animal life on Neidus has limited vision but a finely developed thermal sense. Orbital Distance: 0.1 AU; Orbital Period: 0.1 Earth Years; Radius: 4,875 Km; Day Length: 0.1 Earth Years; Atmospheric Pressure: 0.84 Earth Atmospheres; Surface Temperature: 2 Celsius; Surface Gravity: 0.87 G.

Tenoth	Giant Ice	Moderate	None	Poor	Moderate	Poor

Description: Tenoth is little more than a glorified "ice dwarf" that has drifted inwards from Kriseroi's Oort Cloud over the millennia. Its extremely elliptical orbit is ultimately unstable. Computer projections suggest it will impact the atmosphere of Geus in a few billion years. Orbital Distance: 1.86 AU; Orbital Period: 2.6 Earth Years; Radius: 1,411 Km; Day Length: 17.9 Earth Hours; Atmospheric Pressure: Trace; Surface Temperature: -220 Celsius; Surface Gravity: .09 G.

Theonax	Ocean/Ice	Rich	None	Moderate	Rich	Moderate

Description: Theonax's surface is covered by water and ammonia-hydrate ices, which are constantly repaved by cryovolcanic processes. The world's size and density suggest the core contains heavier elements and retains much of the heat of the system's formation. Orbital Distance: 0.18 AU; Orbital Period: 0.1 Earth Years; Radius: 10,442 Km; Day Length: 69.9 Earth Hours; Atmospheric Pressure: 1.3 Earth Atmospheres; Surface Temperature: -70 Celsius; Surface Gravity: 1.3 G.

Kriseroi (continued)

Planet	World Type	Richness	Element Zero	Iridium	Platinum	Palladium
Uzin	Giant Ice	Moderate	None	Poor	Moderate	Poor

Description: A typical methane-ammonia ice giant, Uzin has 37 moons of various sizes. Chithess, one of the largest, orbits at a retrograde, suggesting it was a planetesimal that was captured by the gas giant gravity well. The planet itself is believed to be an extrasolar capture as well, though millions of years before Chithess came on the scene. Evidence collected by planetary geologists suggest that Chithess was for many centuries a water-world heated by tidal flexing as its orbit circularized around Uzin. The planetary ocean, once hundreds of kilometers deep, must now be frozen solid. Some have recommended drilling test bores to see if life ever developed in Uzin's seas, but the question is considered academic. Orbital Distance: 0.31 AU; Orbital Period: 0.3 Earth Years; Radius: 31,982 Km; Day Length: 15.2 Earth Hours.

Nariph *

Planet	World Type	Richness	Element Zero	Iridium	Platinum	Palladium
Isale	Giant Jovian	Moderate	None	Poor	Poor	Poor

Description: Isale is a standard hydrogen-helium gas giant. Though gas giants are known for their powerful magnetic fields, Isale's field is stronger than current models predict. Within the "frost line" of its solar system, where gas giants do not usually form, Isale is believed to have once been extrasolar. Orbital Distance: 0.5 AU; Orbital Period: 0.6 Earth Years; Radius: 64,005 Km; Day Length: 17.7 Earth Hours.

Jonus	Giant Ice	Moderate	None	Poor	Poor	Poor

Description: Jonus, a methane-ammonia ice giant, is being developed as a fuel depot serving the Pylos Cluster. Eldfell-Ashland Energy has established a base on one of its moons to crack ice into hydrogen and oxygen and skim helium-3 from its atmosphere. Jonus is also believed to be an extrasolar planet captured by its star. From orbit, *Normandy's* sensors can pick out a hand-painted sign some waggish employee has left outside the complex: "Last chance fuel for 100 light years." Orbital Distance: 0.65 AU; Orbital Period: 1 Earth Year; Radius: 20,312 Km; Day Length: 15.1 Earth Hours.

MSV Broken Arrow	Not Minable	—	—	—	—	—

Description: This cruiser is barreling at high speed across the solar system. Its trajectory will take it directly to the fuel infrastructure on Jonus.

Satent

Planet	World Type	Richness	Element Zero	Iridium	Platinum	Palladium
Anedia	Ocean/Ice	Rich	None	Moderate	Rich	Moderate

Description: Anedia is a small ice body with very low density; its mass is only 4 percent that of Earth. It appears to be composed mainly of carbon and water ice, but over the millennia it has accrued a trace atmosphere of krypton and xenon. While Anedia's gravity is weak enough that a cruiser could land on it safely, there is no particular reason one would want to. Pirates have been known to land to recover ice for cracking into hydrogen and oxygen. One area in the southern hemisphere, the so-called "Anedian Scrapes," is so frequently used for this purpose that higher-albedo raw ice can be easily seen from orbit. Orbital Distance: 1.14 AU; Orbital Period: 1.4 Earth Years; Radius: 2,949 Km; Day Length: 38.6 Earth Hours; Atmospheric Pressure: Trace; Surface Temperature: -41 Celsius; Surface Gravity: 0.19 G.

Boro	Ocean/Ice	Rich	Rich	Moderate	Rich	Moderate

Description: Boro is a young volus colony world settled in defiance of a threat by Terminus pirate groups. The pirates, who can't use the world themselves, have "suggested" that the volus "hire" them to protect the colony. The volus responded by requesting military protection from their turian allies. Although uncomfortably hot by volus standards, Boro has the rare combination of high pressure and ammonia, an ecology the volus require. Development of the colony is proceeding rapidly. Colony Founded: 2180; Population: 1,617; Capital: Yila; Orbital Distance: 2.1 AU; Orbital Period: 3.4 Earth Years; Radius: 10,573 Km; Day Length: 31.0 Earth Hours; Atmospheric Pressure: 1.6 Earth Atmospheres; Surface Temperature: -57 Celsius; Surface Gravity: 1.66 G.

Nataisa	Giant Ice	Moderate	None	Poor	Moderate	Poor

Description: An unremarkable methane-ammonia gas giant, Nataisa would be of no consequence if it weren't the only approachable gas giant in the Satent system. Boro's volus colony has set up a few automated ice cracking stations around the planet, and Narhu Combine has been contracted to set up a helium-3 extraction facility. Construction has lagged due to the CEO's arrest in a kickback scandal that reaches to the highest levels of the Vol Ministry of the Frontier. Orbital Distance: 4.1 AU; Orbital Period: 8.3 Earth Years; Radius: 23,623 Km; Day Length: 8.9 Earth Hours.

Raisaris	Rock	Rich	Rich	Rich	Moderate	Moderate

Description: An airless rock of mixed light ores, Raisaris is only of note for the Teryinu impact crater. It was a relatively recent asteroid strike (within the last million years), and the core of the object was partly composed of element zero. It struck at a low enough velocity that the eezo remained near the surface. Over the years many pirates and "wildcat" miners have attempted to extract the ore. It is believed that the Teryinu debris originated in the pulsar system AAP34211+19. The supernova that formed the pulsar also created the red emission nebula that human spacers have unofficially named the Sakura Nebula. Orbital Distance: 0.6 AU; Orbital Period: 0.5 Earth Years; Radius: 3,790 Km; Day Length: 66.3 Earth Hours; Atmospheric Pressure: Trace; Surface Temperature: 56 Celsius; Surface Gravity: 0.24 G.

Rescel	Giant Pegasid	Moderate	None	Poor	Poor	Moderate

Description: Rescel is a massive "hot Jupiter" gas giant that whips around the star Satent once every four and a half days. Like most planets of its type it migrated inwards from its initial position in the system (thought to be around 0.3 AU). Rescel is one of the few close-orbiting gas giants to show a marked temperature difference in its sun-facing and dark-side hemispheres. The atmosphere absorbs and re-radiates Satent's heat too quickly for winds to carry the heat to the dark side. There is a temperature difference of over 1,000 degrees between the gas giant's "hot" and "cold" poles. Orbital Distance: 0.02 AU; Orbital Period: 4.56 Earth Days; Radius: 69,155 Km; Day Length: 4.56 Earth Days.

Rosetta Nebula

Alpha Draconis

Planet	World Type	Richness	Element Zero	Iridium	Platinum	Palladium
2175 Aeia	Garden	Rich	Moderate	Poor	Rich	Moderate

Description: Named after an asari scientist, this remote planet appears to have been on the list of forbidden mass relays that led to uncharted space. The little data available comes from one far-off probe flyby that reports two planets orbiting a white dwarf star. Your own scans yield far more interesting results. The planet is within the habitable zone of the star. It has oceans of liquid water and a thin nitrogen-oxygen atmosphere consistent with carbon-based plant life. It is possible this is an as-yet-unexplored garden world. Orbital Distance: 4.5 AU; Orbital Period: 7.3 Earth Years; Radius: 6,521 Km; Day Length: 31.6 Earth Hours; Atmospheric Pressure: 0.72 Earth Atmospheres; Surface Temperature: 16 Celsius; Surface Gravity: 1.1 G.

Planet	World Type	Richness	Element Zero	Iridium	Platinum	Palladium
2175 AR2	Giant Jovian	Poor	None	Poor	Poor	Moderate

Description: Still formally unnamed, this planet is a hydrogen-helium gas giant with 21 moon-sized objects. Orbital Distance: 9.3 AU; Orbital Period: 28.4 Earth Years; Radius: 62,775 Km; Day Length: 14.0 Earth Hours.

Enoch *

Planet	World Type	Richness	Element Zero	Iridium	Platinum	Palladium
Goliath	Giant Jovian	Moderate	None	Poor	Moderate	Poor

Description: A hydrogen-helium gas giant, Goliath's orbit takes it near the system's mass relay, a useful event for drive core discharges and automated helium-3 refueling platforms. Unfortunately, its orbit is currently taking it away from the relay, and it will continue this inconvenience for the next three galactic standard years. Orbital Distance: 4.8 AU; Orbital Period: 10.5 Earth Years; Radius: 74,985 Km; Day Length: 14.1 Earth Hours.

Planet	World Type	Richness	Element Zero	Iridium	Platinum	Palladium
Joab	Post-Garden	Good	Rich	Moderate	Rich	Poor

Description: Joab is a two-mooned habitable planet that is most well known for its mass extinction event. Thousands of years ago Joab was home to a primate-like spacefaring civilization as well as abundant flora and fauna. However, this can only be deduced from time capsules put into the ground well outside habitation centers—all cities and detectable dwellings were targeted in a massive orbital bombardment that turned them into vapor. The resulting dust shroud killed all photosynthetic life and all fauna dependent on it. Today, humans have recolonized the planet and are rapidly introducing their own species, beginning with cyanobacteria and heterotrophic bacteria, to bring a suitable level of oxygen and nitrogen for respiration. TRAVEL ADVISORY: Atmospheric pressure at sea level on Joab is double that of Earth. Visitors with upper-respiratory infections, emphesyma, cancer, or a history of thoracic surgery should consult their physician before landing on Joab. Population: 21,553,000; Colony Founded: 2171; Capital: New Jericho; Orbital Distance: 2.3 AU; Orbital Period: 3.5 Earth Years; Radius: 6,709 Km; Day Length: 25.6 Earth Hours; Atmospheric Pressure: 2.18 Earth Atmospheres; Surface Temperature: 14 Celsius; Surface Gravity: 1.2 G.

Planet	World Type	Richness	Element Zero	Iridium	Platinum	Palladium
Laban	Desert	Rich	Moderate	Rich	Poor	Moderate

Description: Laban is a desert world with sea upon sea of scorching hot iron oxide wearing away marbleized cliffs. Its atmosphere is thick and layered with significant levels of oxygen trapped under an upper helium layer. Initially, surveyors detected traces of iridium from orbit, only to find a surprising archaeological discovery—the iridium came from bunkers on the surface that were blown apart by a dreadnought-class weapon. The logical conclusion was that the civilization on Joab had reached Laban and its outposts here were destroyed to make their extermination complete. Orbital Distance: 0.6 AU; Orbital Period: 0.5 Earth Years; Radius: 7,658 Km; Day Length: 24.3 Earth Hours; Atmospheric Pressure: 14.91 Earth Atmospheres; Surface Temperature: 384 Celsius; Surface Gravity: 1.8 G.

Planet	World Type	Richness	Element Zero	Iridium	Platinum	Palladium
Mizraim	Giant Ice	Good	Rich	Poor	Moderate	Poor

Description: A small gas giant, Mizraim is primarily hydrogen and methane around a rocky core. There is no remaining trace of the civilization from Joab on Mizraim itself, but debris orbiting the planet indicates that artificial satellites were once in place before being destroyed. Orbital Distance: 1.2 AU; Orbital Period: 1.3 Earth Years; Radius: 17,932 Km; Day Length: 10.9 Earth Hours; Atmospheric Pressure: 1.9 Earth Atmospheres.

Phi Clio

Planet	World Type	Richness	Element Zero	Iridium	Platinum	Palladium
Cyllene	Giant Jovian	Poor	None	Poor	Poor	Poor

Description: A mid-sized hydrogen-helium gas giant, Cyllene has an automated helium-3 refueling station, indicating that this remote system was once inhabited. Its distance from the mass relay and archaic design of the fuel station suggest that this system was mapped by someone who did not go through the relay but discovered it in independent FTL exploration. Cyllene is within the "frost line" of its parent star, where gas giants do not normally form. For this reason Cyllene is believed to be an extrasolar capture. Orbital Distance: 0.5 AU; Orbital Period: 0.4 Earth Years; Radius: 38,920 Km; Day Length: 12.8 Earth Hours.

Planet	World Type	Richness	Element Zero	Iridium	Platinum	Palladium
Parnassus	Rock	Rich	None	Rich	Moderate	Poor

Description: A boiling hot rock planet with extreme tectonic activity, Parnassus is home to many volcanic mountains. Surface scans reveal several geothermal and solar power stations tapping the planet's abundant energy. There is no history of the planet or its government in Citadel Council records. Given its proximity to a mapped and recorded planet like Cyllene, someone must have deleted Parnassus from the database. Orbital Distance: 1.1 AU; Orbital Period: 1.2 Earth Years; Radius: 5,850 Km; Day Length: 50.2 Earth Hours; Atmospheric Pressure: 4.71 Earth Atmospheres; Surface Temperature: 158 Celsius; Surface Gravity: 0.8 G.

Shadow Sea

Iera

Planet	World Type	Richness	Element Zero	Iridium	Platinum	Palladium
Horizon	Not Minable	—	—	—	—	—

Description: A temperate world that has hit the "sweet spot" for carbon-based life, Horizon has a nitrogen-oxygen atmosphere maintained by abundant indigenous photosynthetic plants and bacteria. While the native plants are not very palatable to humans, the soil conditions are such that a handful of introduced Earth species have flourished, and the colonists must take strict care to prevent ecological disasters. Genetically engineered "terminator seeds" that grow nutritious but sterile crops to minimize outbreaks are the rule rather than the exception. Animals on Horizon appear to be exploding in diversity similar to during Earth's Cambrian period. Large flying insect analogs take advantage of the thicker-than-Earth atmosphere and low gravity to grow enormous. Microbial life has proven relatively benign; a series of vaccinations for the most virulent strains of soil-borne diseases is all that is required for a visit. Population: 654,390; Colony Founded: 2168; Capital: Discovery; Orbital Distance: 2.1 AU; Orbital Period: 3.0 Earth Years; Radius: 5,402 Km; Day Length: 37.8 Earth Hours; Atmospheric Pressure: 1.68 Earth Atmospheres; Surface Temperature: 13 Celsius; Surface Gravity: 0.7 G.

Planet	World Type	Richness	Element Zero	Iridium	Platinum	Palladium
Prospect	Giant Jovian	Poor	Poor	Poor	Poor	Poor

Description: Prospect is a hydrogen-nitrogen gas giant with 13 known moons, most of which seemed to have dense heavy metal deposits on first scan, starting a resource rush by the colonists from nearby Horizon. In a tragic turn of events, a galactic uranium surplus drove half the mining firms out of business, and the surfaces of some moons are littered with the bodies of executives who committed suicide by airlock. Today's mining corporations have reached a much more palatable equilibrium and hold more diversified and sustainable portfolios. Prospect is within the "frost line" of its solar system, where ice giants do not normally form. For this reason it is believed to have been an extrasolar capture. Orbital Distance: 1.2 AU; Orbital Period: 1.3 Earth Years; Radius: 45,277 Km; Day Length: 18.1 Earth Hours.

Planet	World Type	Richness	Element Zero	Iridium	Platinum	Palladium
Venture	Desert	Rich	None	Moderate	Moderate	Rich

Description: A pressure-cooker of a planet, Venture has a thick nitrogen-based atmosphere that is also the source of wealth for a small colonist industry. While Venture's high temperatures are brutal, the primordial soup is not as acidic as on other hothouse planets, and xenon can be readily collected and isolated from the lower troposphere by recovery bots. This xenon is then sold for use in ion drives and some electric lights. Venture's gravity is relatively low for a planet of its size, making the recovery more economical than would otherwise be expected. Orbital Distance: 0.7 AU; Orbital Period: 0.6 Earth Years; Radius: 10,659 Km; Day Length: 26.1 Earth Hours; Atmospheric Pressure: 21.76 Earth Atmospheres; Surface Temperature: 398 Celsius; Surface Gravity: 2.9 G .

Planet	World Type	Richness	Element Zero	Iridium	Platinum	Palladium
Watchman	Rock	Moderate	None	Rich	Poor	Poor

Description: Perched on the outer edge of Iera's small solar system, Watchman is a mid-sized rock and ice planet that has picked up a dozen moon-sized objects. Its nitrogen-oxygen atmosphere is too thin to support life, with solid ice covering its calcium-heavy rocky core. Footprints of the first surveying teams to come to the planet can still be seen on its practically airless surface. The planet, devoid of valuable resources, has seen few visitors since. Orbital Distance: 4.1 AU; Orbital Period: 8.3 Earth Years; Radius: 5,728 Km; Day Length: 28.6 Earth Hours; Atmospheric Pressure: Trace; Surface Temperature: -116 Celsius; Surface Gravity: 0.8 G.

The Shrike Abyssal

Urla Rast

Planet	World Type	Richness	Element Zero	Iridium	Platinum	Palladium
Bovis Tor	Desert	Rich	None	Moderate	Moderate	Rich

Description: Named "the shining sea" in an old volus language, Bovis Tor is so named for its boiling surface rich in glowing-hot alumina flecked with dark ridges of carbon. Its thick atmosphere of nitrogen and oxygen is no indicator of life since the temperatures are simply too high. Orbital Distance: 0.7 AU; Orbital Period: 0.6 Earth Years; Radius: 7,307 Km; Day Length: 33.5 Earth Hours; Atmospheric Pressure: 8.39 Earth Atmospheres; Surface Temperature: 253 Celsius; Surface Gravity: 1.6 G.

Planet	World Type	Richness	Element Zero	Iridium	Platinum	Palladium
Doz Atab	Giant Ice	Moderate	None	Poor	Moderate	Poor

Description: An ice giant, Doz Atab ("sky warden") has a bluish tinge from its hydrogen-methane atmosphere. Its axial tilt causes its seasons to vary wildly in temperature. Orbital Distance: 3.1 AU; Orbital Period: 5.5 Earth Years; Radius: 47,428 Km; Day Length: 10.3 Earth Hours.

Planet	World Type	Richness	Element Zero	Iridium	Platinum	Palladium
Rosh	Rock	Rich	None	Moderate	Rich	Moderate

Description: A recently colonized asteroid large enough to be considered a dwarf planet, Rosh is mined for its platinum deposits for use in hydrogen fuel cells. With wide open spaces and few restrictions on construction or immigration, Rosh is like much of the Terminus Systems—a good place to build a habitat and get lost for a few decades. Colony Founded: 2175 CE; Population: 2250; Capital: Suu Piz; Orbital Distance: 6.9 AU; Orbital Period: 18.2 Earth Years; Radius: 1,360 Km; Day Length: 67.4 Earth Hours; Atmospheric Pressure: Trace; Surface Temperature: -147 Celsius; Surface Gravity: 0.3 G.

Planet	World Type	Richness	Element Zero	Iridium	Platinum	Palladium
Talis Fia	Garden	Good	Moderate	Poor	Rich	Moderate

Description: Talis Fia is a planet capable of supporting life—if that life happens to breathe ammonia. Discovered by asari explorers, the planet was used as a bargaining chip by the Citadel Council, who quickly drafted a colonization agreement with its wealthy client race, the volus. The Council would fund the volus colonization effort in return for massive trade benefits. With uncharacteristic enthusiasm, an enormous volus influx ensued, and the Council reaped the economic benefits for a dozen years before the colonization bubble burst. Today the economic good times on Talis Fia are long gone, and modern volus businesses are cutthroat operations. Piracy is a grave threat to shipping, as well-armed criminals see the volus as easy prey. Colony Founded: 385 CE; Population: 3,800,000,000; Capital: Usra Dao; Orbital Distance: 1.6 AU; Orbital Period: 2.0 Earth Years; Radius: 7,550 Km; Day Length: 33.8 Earth Hours; Atmospheric Pressure: 6.15 Earth Atmospheres; Surface Temperature: -25 Celsius; Surface Gravity: 1.7 G.

Introduction

Training

Upgrades and Research

Walkthrough

Special Assignments

Planetary Database

Appendix

Xe Cha *

Planet	World Type	Richness	Element Zero	Iridium	Platinum	Palladium
Aphras	Post-Garden	Moderate	None	Moderate	Moderate	Moderate

Description: A unique discovery, Aphras is a "heavenly twin"—a planet in a star system that has not one but two worlds of sufficient mass to retain an nitrogen-oxygen atmosphere within the habitable life zone of its parent star. Fossil evidence shows abundant vertebrates and evidence of a sapient terrestrial avian species in its Bronze Age. However, the only trace of contemporary life on the planet is that of single-celled organisms in its seas. All else has suffered from an extinction event—a series of massive impacts that vaporized vast quantities of water and lofted dust into its atmosphere. Early theories that this event was a collision with a fragmenting asteroid have now been discounted—the impact craters were aimed directly at habitation centers. Orbital Distance: 1.4 AU; Orbital Period: 2.0 Earth Years; Radius: 4,530 Km; Day Length: 31.3 Earth Hours; Atmospheric Pressure: 2.32 Earth Atmospheres; Surface Temperature: 33 Celsius; Surface Gravity: 0.7 G.

Tosal Nym	Rock	Rich	Rich	Rich	Poor	Moderate

Description: The sister tragedy to the extinction event on Aphras, Tosal Nym was the rarest of jewels; a second garden planet within the same life zone as Aphras. Not as old as its sister planet, its fossil evidence indicates it was home to abundant invertebrate sea life. However, similar craters to those on Aphras created a dust shroud that killed 99 percent of biota on the planet. The even spacing of the craters indicates a coordinated simultaneous attack from points around the globe rather than an asteroid collision or supervolcanic scenario. Orbital Distance: 2.1 AU; Orbital Period: 3.0 Earth Years; Radius: 6,930 Km; Day Length: 19.8 Earth Hours; Atmospheric Pressure: 1.86 Earth Atmospheres; Surface Temperature: 18 Celsius; Surface Gravity: 1.3 G.

Vem Osca	Giant Jovian	Moderate	None	Poor	Moderate	Poor

Description: A Jovian gas giant, Vem Osca ("weeping witness" in Iperian Volus) is a low-density hydrogen-helium planet with 35 moons. Later this year, 33 of the moons will be visible from the planet's surface, an event that will be recorded by space probes from all over the galaxy. Orbital Distance: 4.6 AU; Orbital Period: 9.9 Earth Years; Radius: 64,826 Km; Day Length: 11.9 Earth Hours.

Zada Ban	Desert	Rich	Rich	Moderate	Moderate	Rich

Description: Zada Ban is a large dense planet named for a volus god of punishment. Its crust is rich in uranium, eroded by winds to create large radioactive dust storms across its surface. The volus of Talis Fia have explored the planet thoroughly with space probes and telepresent robo-mining machines and discovered they are not the first to exploit the planet. Plastics from a mining station approximately 50,000 years old can be found near the planet's equator. Curiously, the mines nearby were not tapped out of uranium ore; they were instead abandoned at the height of their operation. Colony Founded: 2154; Population: 22,500 (in orbital stations); Capital: None (largest station is Dolo Station); Orbital Distance: 0.7 AU; Orbital Period: 0.9 Earth Years; Radius: 7,594 Km; Day Length: 70.0 Earth Hours; Atmospheric Pressure: 0.0 Earth Atmospheres; Surface Temperature: 94 Celsius; Surface Gravity: 1.5 G.

Sigurd's Cradle

Decoris

Planet	World Type	Richness	Element Zero	Iridium	Platinum	Palladium
Laena	Desert	Rich	None	Poor	Moderate	Rich

Description: Laena (which means "cloaked") is a methane-clouded hothouse planet. Its lack of a metal-rich core and significant magnetosphere allows for an easy scan, which reveals mining equipment on its surface. It can be deduced that this mining occured within the last five years—any longer and the machines would have been worn down to nothing by the excessive heat and dust storms of hot iron oxide. Orbital Distance: 1.4 AU; Orbital Period: 1.7 Earth Years; Radius: 6,197 Km; Day Length: 36.2 Earth Hours; Atmospheric Pressure: 37.64 Earth Atmospheres; Surface Temperature: 365 Celsius; Surface Gravity: 1.0 G.

Sanctum	Garden	Good	Moderate	Poor	Rich	Moderate

Description: Sanctum is proof of the old spacer adage "just because it's called a garden world doesn't mean it's a picnic." Freezing ice storms cover the poles and temperate zones, leaving a narrow strip of habitable land at the equator. Dry but windy, this area is home to Sanctum's minimal terrestrial plant life. The planet has yet to develop land-based animals, though invertebrates grow quite large in its pelagic seas. Mining referred to as "ice cracking" at anywhere but the equator is a common employment on Sanctum. The planet is rich in platinum and palladium deposits as well as boron, which is locally used in semiconductor doping. TRAVEL ADVISORY: Carbon dioxide levels on Sanctum can reach 5,000 parts per million during thermal inversions. Travelers should carry a breath mask at all times and consult the Sanctum World Weather Service for warnings. TRAVEL ADVISORY: Piracy is at a 14-year global high on Sanctum. Visitors should take appropriate security precautions. Population: 257,300; Colony Founded: 2169; Capital: Vulpes; Orbital Distance: 2.6 AU; Orbital Period: 4.2 Earth Years; Radius: 6,651 Km; Day Length: 69.4 Earth Hours; Atmospheric Pressure: 0.4 Earth Atmospheres; Surface Temperature: -50 Celsius (mean), 4 Celsius (equator). Surface Gravity: 1.2 G.

Skepsis *

Planet	World Type	Richness	Element Zero	Iridium	Platinum	Palladium
Crick	Rock	Rich	None	Rich	Moderate	Moderate

Description: Known for its spectacular geysers that can be seen from orbit, Crick is a rock planet with expansive frozen oceans. Though it is within the temperature and pressure range for human habitation, its thick atmosphere is largely carbon dioxide and monoxide, making breath masks or environmental suits mandatory. The most abundant resources for exploitation are the potassium salts found in its seabeds, which fetch good prices on terraforming worlds. Orbital Distance: 4.3 AU; Orbital Period: 8.9 Earth Years; Radius: 4,738 Km; Day Length: 60.7 Earth Hours; Atmospheric Pressure: 2.77 Earth Atmospheres; Surface Temperature: -32 Celsius; Surface Gravity: 0.6 G.

Skepsis (continued)						
Planet	World Type	Richness	Element Zero	Iridium	Platinum	Palladium
Darwin	Rock	Good	None	Rich	Moderate	Moderate

Description: A mid-sized rock planet, Darwin is ironically named, being one of the worst places for life in the galaxy. Its atmosphere is punishing, its temperature boiling, its chemical makeup toxic. Carbon monoxide and methane wrap the planet in an unyielding haze, and scans of its surface show only silicates and molten tin. Its daily thermal fluctuations lead to hurricane-level vortices, two at each pole, forming "eyes" that can be seen from orbit. Despite all this Darwin is still used by spacers as a drive core discharge point—hydrogen pierces the clouds in the upper atmosphere, making for a relatively benign approach. Orbital Distance: 0.9 AU; Orbital Period: 0.9 Earth Years; Radius: 6,771 Km; Day Length: 37.3 Earth Hours; Atmospheric Pressure: 112.06 Earth Atmospheres; Surface Temperature: 710 Celsius; Surface Gravity: 1.2 G.

Franklin	Rock	Rich	None	Rich	Moderate	Poor

Description: A large moon, Franklin retains a trace atmosphere of carbon dioxide, but its desolate surface holds no signs of water or life. In order to defend Watson from the pirates of the Terminus Systems, Franklin is home to two Alliance spaceports and naval bases capable of fielding six fighter squadrons each and a classified number of interplanetary ballistic missiles. Mass effect fields keep the gravity in its installations at a comfortable level for long-term living. Orbital Distance: 2.1 AU; Orbital Period: 33 Earth Days (around Watson), 3.0 Earth Years (around Skepsis); Radius: 2,405 Km; Day Length: 33 Earth Days; Atmospheric Pressure: Trace; Surface Temperature: -116 Celsius; Surface Gravity: 0.1 G.

Keimowitz	Ocean/Ice	Rich	None	Poor	Rich	Poor

Description: Named for the 21st century pioneer of groundwater remediation techniques, Keimowitz is an impressive layer of ice over a stony metallic core. Despite its size it has only one moon, Noa, which shares its carbonaceous composition, leading astronomers to believe it formed following a giant impact. Iridium deposits have attracted miners to the planet; they must work through robots and telepresence because of the planet's strong gravity. Orbital Distance: 16.8 AU; Orbital Period: 69.1 Earth Years; Radius: 9,586 Km; Day Length: 29.7 Earth Hours; Atmospheric Pressure: Trace; Surface Temperature: -190 Celsius; Surface Gravity: 3.4 G.

Pauling	Giant Ice	Poor	None	Poor	Moderate	Poor

Description: A hydrogen-methane gas giant, Pauling's gravitational field is believed to have cleared most of what would otherwise have been a sizable asteroid belt. The 2163 mission of the space probe Ultimate gave the inhabitants of Watson reams of data reinforcing this theory, giving the colonists an accurate count of its moons (66), rings, moonlike ring objects, and more than 200 visible impact craters on its pockmarked surface. Ultimate has since been retrieved for re-use on subsequent missions within the solar system. Orbital Distance: 4.3 AU; Orbital Period: 8.9 Earth Years; Radius: 4,738 Km; Day Length: 60.7 Earth Hours; Atmospheric Pressure: 2.77 Earth Atmospheres; Surface Temperature: -32 Celsius; Surface Gravity: 0.6 G.

Wallace	Giant Pegasid	Moderate	None	Poor	Moderate	Moderate

Description: An unusually small Pegasid or "hot Jupiter," Wallace was originally an extrasolar planet that entered this system and was captured by the gravity well of the G-class star Skepsis. Tidally locked, Wallace's "hot side" reaches temperatures over 2,500 degrees Celsius. While not large enough proportionate to the star to cause eclipses visible from Watson, it is easily seen at dawn or dusk as one of the brightest objects in the sky. Orbital Distance: 0.04 AU; Orbital Period: 11 Earth Days; Radius: 39,459 Km; Day Length: 11 Earth Days.

Watson	Garden	Good	Rich	Poor	Rich	Moderate

Description: Watson is known in human media for two things—its spectacular tides brought on by a large moon and the bureaucratic snafu over which Earth nations got to settle there first. Watson is a garden world first discovered in 2165 CE with credit claimed by the Chinese People's Federation, the United North American States, and the European Union. The Systems Alliance brokered the infamous "Reykjavik Compromise," allowing limited colonization from each coalition in cities comprised of populations from each nation. Watson itself trends colder than Earth, with a temperate zone measuring about 30 degrees latitude in either direction from the equator. Its life does not easily map to Earth's evolutionary eras—some islands have species that resemble terrestrial placental mammals, while others are overrun by arthropods. It is estimated that at least two more generations of xenozoologists will be needed to properly classify all the species of the planet. Orbital Distance: 2.1 AU; Orbital Period: 3.0 Earth Years; Radius: 6,733 Km; Day Length: 37.8 Earth Hours; Atmospheric Pressure: 0.6 Earth Atmospheres; Surface Temperature: -18 Celsius (mean), 25 Celsius (habitable zone); Surface Gravity: 1.2 G.

Solar System

Sol						
Planet	World Type	Richness	Element Zero	Iridium	Platinum	Palladium
Earth	Not Minable	—	—	—	—	—

Description: For detailed information please refer to the standard issue Alliance Galactic Codex. Earth's orbit is riddled with debris generated by "bootstrap" space development; use of kinetic barriers is recommended at altitudes over 85 kilometers. Population (Surface): 11.4 billion; Population (L4 and L5 stations): 250,000, Orbital Distance: 1 AU; Orbital Period: 1 Earth Year; Radius: 6,378 Km; Day Length: 23.9 Earth Hours; Atmospheric Pressure: 1 Earth Atmosphere; Surface Temperature: 23 Celsius; Surface Gravity: 1.0 G.

Jupiter	Giant Jovian	Moderate	None	Poor	Poor	Moderate

Description: Jupiter's deep gravity well and lethal radiation have kept its moons from being significantly exploited. The largest outpost is Binary Helix Corporation's Nautilus facility, attached to the underside of Europa's ice sheet. Population (all moons): 9,100; Orbital Distance: 5.2 AU; Orbital Period: 11.7 Earth Years; Radius: 71,492 Km; Day Length: 9.93 Earth Hours.

Mars	Not Minable	—	—	—	—	—

Description: Once considered a prospect for terraforming and colonization, Mars turned into a quiet backwater after the discovery of faster-than-light travel. Its southern pole is a historical preserve centered on the Prothean ruins found there. Immigration and development are restricted as the search for Prothean artifacts continues. Orbital Distance: 1.52 AU; Orbital Period: 1.88 Earth Years; Radius: 3,402 Km; Day Length: 24.6 Earth Hours; Atmospheric Pressure: Trace; Surface Temperature: -138 Celsius; Surface Gravity: 0.38 G.

Introduction
Training
Upgrades and Research
Walkthrough
Special Assignments
Planetary Database
Appendix

Sol (continued)						
Planet	World Type	Richness	Element Zero	Iridium	Platinum	Palladium
Mercury	Rock	Moderate	None	Rich	Moderate	Poor

Description: A handful of solar power stations exist on "peaks of eternal light" at the north and south poles of Mercury. The difficulties imposed by the planet's proximity to the sun and high orbital velocity have limited development. Population: 340; Orbital Distance: 0.39 AU; Orbital Period: 88 Earth Days; Radius: 2,240 Km; Day Length: 58.7 Earth Days; Atmospheric Pressure: Trace; Surface Temperature: 430 Celsius; Surface Gravity: 0.38 G.

Neptune	Giant Ice	Poor	None	Poor	Moderate	Poor

Description: Though Neptune, like Uranus, has plentiful helium, its remoteness made it an unpromising target for mining before the development of mass effect drive. With Uranus cheaper to exploit it has never seen extensive development. The only permanent human presence is a small research facility on Triton. Population (Triton): 70; Orbital Distance: 29.1 AU; Orbital Period: 164.8 Earth Years; Radius: 24,764 Km; Day Length: 16.1 Earth Hours.

Pluto	Rock	Moderate	None	Rich	Poor	Poor

Description: Pluto is one of Sol's numerous "ice dwarf" worlds. It is mainly of note for being the gravitational "anchor" for the mass relay to Arcturus. Pluto and the Charon relay (formerly encased in ice and considered a moon) orbit each other. Pluto's orbit was circularized in 2157 as a side effect of the Charon mass relay recovery operations. Population (gateway stations): 9,300; Orbital Distance: 39.5 AU; Orbital Period: 247.7 Earth Years; Radius: 1,151 Km; Day Length: 9.4 Earth Hours; Atmospheric Pressure: Trace; Surface Temperature: -229 Celsius; Surface Gravity: 0.06 G.

Saturn	Jovian	Good	None	Moderate	Moderate	Moderate

Description: Saturn has been a major source of helium-3 fuel for fusion plants since the 2150s. The moon of Titan is mined for hydrocarbons and used as a hostile environment training facility for Alliance Marines. Population (orbitals and Titan): 117,000; Capital: Huygens Dome; Orbital Distance: 9.5 AU; Orbital Period: 29.5 Earth Years; Radius: 60,268 Km; Day Length: 10.3 Earth Hours.

Uranus	Giant Ice	Depleted	None	Poor	Poor	Poor

Description: After the development of mass effect FTL drive, distant Uranus was the target of a "land rush" to exploit its combination of plentiful helium-3 fuel and shallow (for a gas giant) gravity well. Today Uranus is the largest producer of helium-3 in Alliance space. Population: 371,000; Capital: Sakharov Station; Orbital Distance: 19.2 AU; Orbital Period: 84.3 Earth Years; Radius: 25,559 Km; Day Length: 17.3 Earth Hours.

Venus	Post-Garden	Good	None	Moderate	Moderate	Rich

Description: With its molten temperatures, sulfuric acid clouds, and crushing carbon dioxide atmosphere, Venus has only a handful of aerostat research outposts. Population: 800; Orbital Distance: 0.72 AU; Orbital Period: 224.7 Earth Days; Radius: 6,052 Km; Day Length: 243 Earth Days; Atmospheric Pressure: 90 Earth Atmospheres; Surface Temperature: 465 Celsius; Surface Gravity: 0.88 G.

Titan Nebula

Haskins						
Planet	World Type	Richness	Element Zero	Iridium	Platinum	Palladium
Capek	Rock	Rich	Moderate	Rich	Poor	Rich

Description: Baked in the fierce heat of a white sun, Capek is a rocky waterless world wrapped in a haze of hydrogen and ethane. Sulfur and iron give yellowish and black tinges to much of the planet's surface. No registered settlements appear in the records, though there are clearly metallic anomalies that indicate roofed structures. Orbital Distance: 4.4 AU; Orbital Period: 7.1 Earth Years; Radius: 5,899 Km; Day Length: 18.7 Earth Hours; Atmospheric Pressure: 0.95 Earth Atmospheres; Surface Temperature: 65 Celsius; Surface Gravity: 0.8 G.

Valhallan Threshhold

Micah						
Planet	World Type	Richness	Element Zero	Iridium	Platinum	Palladium
Dumah	Giant Jovian	Moderate	None	Poor	Poor	Poor

Description: Home to 51 moons, including the prebiotic moon Anafiel, Dumah is a standard hydrogen-helium gas giant with violent surface winds exceeding 1,900 kph. Like its sister planet Elohi, it is believed to be an extrasolar capture. Orbital Distance: 1.6 AU; Orbital Period: 2.0 Earth Years; Radius: 59,152 Km; Day Length: 10.0 Earth Hours, Atmospheric Pressure: 1.05 Earth Atmospheres.

Elohi	Giant Jovian	Moderate	None	Poor	Moderate	Moderate

Description: A small hydrogen-helium gas giant formed around a metallic hydrogen core, Elohi will be the site of a rare astronomical event later this year. The comet Asaro will come in on its orbit of 70 galactic standard years and travel so close to the giant that it is predicted to be captured as a moon. Dozens of space probes from around the galaxy have been launched into the Raheel system to record this moment. Elohi is within the "frost line" of its parent star, where gas giants do not usually form. For this reason it is believed to be an extrasolar capture. TRAVEL ADVISORY: A statistically significant number of distress signals have come from the 1-million-kilometer mark around Elohi. Pirates are believed to be working the area. In-person tourism is not advised. Orbital Distance: 0.6 AU; Orbital Period: 0.5 Earth Years; Radius: 38,119 Km; Day Length: 11.8 Earth Hours; Atmospheric Pressure: 0.97 Earth Atmospheres.

Introduction

Training

Upgrades and Research

Walkthrough

Special Assignments

Planetary Database

Appendix

Micah (continued)

Planet	World Type	Richness	Element Zero	Iridium	Platinum	Palladium
Farlas	Rock	Rich	Moderate	Rich	Poor	Moderate

Description: One of a trio of asteroids formed around an element zero core, Farlas is the easiest to mine for low-yield eezo. A carbonaceous asteroid, Farlas has a trace of water-bearing minerals and organic carbon in the form of kerogen. Currently the asteroid is surrounded by quarian mining ships extracting fuel for the flotilla. Orbital Distance: 4.1 AU; Orbital Period: 8.3 Earth Years; Radius: 540 Km; Day Length: 24.1 Earth Hours; Atmospheric Pressure: 0.0 Earth Atmospheres; Surface Temperature: -116 Celsius; Surface Gravity: 0.1 G.

Israfil	Rock	Rich	Moderate	Rich	Moderate	Poor

Description: Largest of the "eezo trio," Israfil is a silicate-heavy carbonaceous asteroid. It is home to approximately 40 species of microorganisms in its liquid water and was blamed as the source of the prion-based biowarfare agent EHE (exotic humanoid encephalopathy) used by the terrorist group Totenkopf in their attack on Gagarin Station in 2184. While many in the scientific community protested that Israfil did not have sufficient atmosphere or evolutionary history to sustain life at the prion level, the asteroid and its eezo miners were nevertheless quarantined to reassure the public that the Systems Alliance was taking action. Though no evidence has yet been found that EHE originated from Israfil or was even synthesized in a local lab, the SSV Manila and a team of epidemiologists maintain watch over the asteroid's ship traffic for now. Population: 1006; Orbital Distance: 4.3 AU; Orbital Period: 8.9 Earth Years; Radius: 905 Km; Day Length: 68.6 Earth Hours; Atmospheric Pressure: Trace; Surface Temperature: -100 Celsius; Surface Gravity: 0.3 G.

Kakabel	Rock	Rich	Moderate	Rich	Poor	Rich

Description: The second asteroid in the system formed around an element zero core, Kakabel is another carbonaceous asteroid with a surface made of hydrated minerals such as carbonates and clays. Beneath its icy surface is liquid water with some amino acids. The surface of Kakabel is pitted and scarred with strip-mining stations, where the quarians took as much eezo as possible before moving on. Orbital Distance: 4.2 AU; Orbital Period: 8.6 Earth Years; Radius: 470 Km; Day Length: 68.3 Earth Hours; Atmospheric Pressure: 0.0 Earth Atmospheres; Surface Temperature: -118 Celsius; Surface Gravity: 0.1 G.

Paz

Planet	World Type	Richness	Element Zero	Iridium	Platinum	Palladium
Garvug	Post-Garden	Good	Rich	Poor	Moderate	Moderate

Description: In 354 CE Gorvug was considered a "bargain world" given to the krogan to placate them because no one else wanted to live on such a frozen rock. Technically a life-bearing world, Gorvug had a small farm belt around its equator and well-insulated marine life in its seas. By the turn of the century the krogan had completely adapted, breeding hundreds of younglings per family in vast underground bunkers. By the turn of the next century Gorvug's narrow strips of coral reef had been destroyed by overfishing and pollutants, and excess krogan took to the stars to find another planet to consume. Gorvug was treated as an object lesson by the Citadel Council—the krogan could not be trusted to check their own numbers. Today Gorvug is a frozen wasteland home to corporate ecoengineering efforts trying to implement sustainable agri- and aqua-culture practices. Krogan and vorcha packs are a constant threat, and the corporations pay mercenaries well to keep their operations safe. Orbital Distance: 4.0 AU; Orbital Period: 6.1 Earth Years; Radius: 6,200 Km; Day Length: 27.0 Earth Hours; Atmospheric Pressure: 1.2 Earth Atmospheres; Surface Temperature: -30 Celsius (5 at the equator); Surface Gravity: 1.0 G.

Raheel-Leyya *

Planet	World Type	Richness	Element Zero	Iridium	Platinum	Palladium
Leyya	Binary Sun	—	—	—	—	—

Description: The smaller pair of the binary giant system, Leyya is a young star, a BIII blue bright giant approximately 13 times the mass of Sol and 27,500 degrees Celsius. Too hot to have any planets formed around it, Leyya will most likely nova within a short period—a few million years.

Susskind Station	Not Minable	—	—	—	—	—

Description: Originally a small scientific research outpost with living modules for only 20 people, Susskind Station is a triumph of modern "snap-on" modular engineering for space station expansion. Now with facilities for over 2,000 visitors and docking for over 50 starships, Susskind serves as a spaceport for those wishing to study the Raheel-Leyya binary blue giant. Population: 1,550 (3,550 including visitors); TRAVEL ADVISORY: Due to the quarian fleet occupying the system, all docks at Susskind Station are currently filled. Local authorities predict this condition for the foreseeable future until such time as the flotilla departs.

The Migrant Fleet	Not Minable	—	—	—	—	—

Description: A fleet of 50,000 craft holding over 17 million quarians, the Migrant Fleet is the largest array of spacefaring vessels in the known galaxy. Though quarians on Pilgrimage have visited most settled worlds in the galaxy, few outsiders have ever stepped foot inside the quarians' ships.

APPENDIX
XBOX 360 ACHIEVEMENTS

Mission Achievements

Icon	Achievement	Description	Gamer Pts.
	Missing in Action	Save your crew from an overwhelming attack.	5
	Very Elusive	Return to active duty.	10
	The Convict	Successfully recruit the biotic convict.	10
	The Krogan	Successfully recruit the krogan.	10
	The Archangel	Successfully recruit Archangel.	10
	The Professor	Successfully recruit the professor.	10
	The Quarian	Successfully recruit the quarian.	10
	The Justicar	Successfully recruit the justicar.	10
	The Assassin	Successfully recruit the assassin.	10
	Colony Defense	Defend a human colony from attack.	25
	The Prodigal	Gain the loyalty of the Cerberus officer.	15
	Ghost of the Father	Gain the loyalty of the Cerberus operative.	15
	Catharsis	Gain the loyalty of the biotic convict.	15
	Battlemaster	Gain the loyalty of the krogan.	15
	Fade Away	Gain the loyalty of Archangel.	15
	The Cure	Gain the loyalty of the professor.	15
	Treason	Gain the loyalty of the quarian.	15
	Doppelganger	Help the justicar resolve her mission.	15
	Cat's in the Cradle	Gain the loyalty of the assassin.	15
	Friend or Foe	Obtain geth technology.	10

Mission Achievements

Icon	Achievement	Description	Gamer Pts.
	A House Divided	Hack a geth collective.	15
	Ghost Ship	Complete the investigation of a derelict alien vessel.	25
	Suicide Mission	Use the Omega 4 relay.	50
	Paramour	Successfully pursue a relationship with a teammate.	50

Completion Achievements

Icon	Achievement	Description	Gamer Pts.
	Mission Accomplished	Save humanity throughout the galaxy from certain annihilation.	100
	Against All Odds	Survive the suicide mission.	50
	Insanity	Complete the game on the "insanity" difficulty level without changing the setting.	75
	No One Left Behind	Keep your team alive through the suicide mission.	50
	Long Service Medal	Complete *Mass Effect 2* twice, or complete it once with a character imported from *Mass Effect*.	50

Combat Achievements

Icon	Achievement	Description	Gamer Pts.
	Head Hunter	Perform 30 headshot kills with any weapon on humanoid targets.	10
	Brawler	Shoot 20 enemies while they're knocked back by a punch.	10
	Big Game Hunter	Defeat a thresher maw.	10
	Tactician	Hit 20 different targets with multiple biotic powers to combine the effects.	10
	Master at Arms	Kill enemies with five different heavy weapons during the game.	10
	Merciless	Make 20 enemies scream as they fall or are set on fire.	10
	Overload Specialist	Disrupt the shields of 25 enemies.	15
	Warp Specialist	Warp the barriers of 25 enemies.	15

Combat Achievements

Icon	Achievement	Description	Gamer Pts.
	Incineration Specialist	Incinerate the armor of 25 enemies.	15
	Highly Trained	View all advanced combat training videos at Shepard's private terminal.	5

Exploration Achievements

Icon	Achievement	Description	Gamer Pts.
	Operative	Complete a mission discovered by scanning an unexplored world.	10
	Agent	Complete five missions discovered by scanning unexplored worlds.	50
	Prospector	Retrieve mineral resources by scanning and probing a planet in the galaxy map.	5
	Explorer	Visit 100% of the planets in an unexplored cluster.	10

Progression Achievements

Icon	Achievement	Description	Gamer Pts.
	Power Gamer	Reach level 30 with one character.	25
	Scholar	Unlock 15 new *Mass Effect 2* codex entries.	15
	Technician	Obtain 10 technology upgrades.	15
	Weapon Specialist	Fully upgrade a weapon.	15
	Scientist	Complete any research project in the *Normandy*'s laboratory.	5
	Fashionista	Personalize your armor in your quarters on the *Normandy*.	5
	Power Full	Evolve any power.	15

SHOP INVENTORIES

Use these inventories to keep track of the goods offered in all shops across the galaxy.

Omega

Omega's a rough place, but with a little charm or intimidation, you can score great deals.

Kenn's Salvage

Item	Description
Microfusion Array	Increases heavy weapon ammo capacity.
FBA Couplings	Satisfies engineers' special assignment aboard *Normandy*.
Synchronized Pulsar	Increases shotgun damage.

Harrot's Emporium

Item	Description
N7 Visor	New armor piece. Increases headshot damage by 10%.
Model Ship—Geth	Small ship model for captain's quarters.

Harrot's Emporium

Item	Description
Capacitor Chestplate	New armor piece. Reduces shield delay by 10%.
Predictive Display	Doubles time limit for hacking.
Ordnance Pack	New armor piece. Increase spare heavy weapon ammo by 10%..

Omega Market

Item	Description
Stimulator Conduits	New armor piece. Increases storm speed.
Model Ship—Turian Cruiser	Small ship model for captain's quarters.
Scram Pulsar	Increases sniper rifle damage.
Fornax	Titillating alien magazine…
Strength Boost Pads	New armor piece. Increases melee damage by 5%.
Stabilizing Gauntlets	New armor piece. Increases weapon damage by 5%.

Illium

Without buying the star charts from Beria's Frontiers, you cannot find all of the N7 assignments.

Serrice Technology	
Item	**Description**
Hyper Amp	Increases biotic damage.
Quantum Threading	Doubles time limit for security bypass.
Microscanner	Increases medi-gel capacity by 1.

Gateway Personal Defense	
Item	**Description**
Lattice Shunting	Increases Shepard's health.
Microfield Pulsar	Increases submachine gun damage.
Kinetic Pulsar	Increases assault rifle damage.
Amplifier Plates	New armor piece. Increases shields by 5%.

Baria Frontiers	
Item	**Description**
Hades Nexus	New star chart—reveals cluster on galaxy map.
Minos Wasteland	New star chart—reveals cluster on galaxy map.
Pylos Nebula	New star chart—reveals cluster on galaxy map.
Shrike Abyssal	New star chart—reveals cluster on galaxy map.

Memories of Illium	
Item	**Description**
Prejek Paddle Fish	Decoration for captain's quarters.
Model Ship—Alliance Cruiser	Small ship model for captain's quarters.
Model Ship—Athabasca Class Freighter	Small ship model for captain's quarters.

Tuchanka

Don't skip Forack's Database. The krogan scientist has some awesome upgrades. But they are spendy. You may have to come back multiple times to score them all. The N7 assignments are a great way to pick up extra cash for these upgrades.

Ratch's Wares	
Item	**Description**
Microfusion Array	Increases heavy weapon ammo capacity.
Stabilizing Gauntlets	New armor piece. Increases shields by 5%.
Asymmetric Defense Layer	New armor piece. Increases health by 5%.
Shield Harness	New armor piece. Increases shields by 5%.
Pyjak Meat	A varren delicacy.
Serrice Ice Brandy	A favorite of Dr. Chakwas.

Fortack's Database	
Item	**Description**
Kinetic Pulsar	Increases assault rifle damage.
Hyper Amp	Increases biotic damage.
Titan Pulsar	Increases heavy pistol damage.
Synchronized Pulsar	Increases shotgun damage.

The Citadel

Although visiting the Citadel is entirely optional, missing out on its great shopping will deny you some great upgrades and extra items.

Citadel Souvenirs	
Item	**Description**
Space Hamster	Decoration for captain's quarters.
Illium Skald Fish	Decoration for captain's quarters.
Thessian Sunfish	Decoration for captain's quarters.
Model Ship—*Normandy SR1*	Small ship model for captain's quarters.
Model Ship—*Destiny Ascension*	Small ship model for captain's quarters.
Model Ship—*Sovereign*	Small ship model for captain's quarters.

Zakera Café	
Item	**Description**
High-Grade Provisions	Quality cuisine satisfies mess hall cook's special assignment.
Ascension Novel	Historical novel.
Revelations Novel	Historical novel.

Rodam Expeditions	
Item	**Description**
Scram Pulsar	Increases sniper rifle damage.
Titan Pulsar	Increases heavy pistol damage.
Microfield Pulsar	Increases submachine gun damage.
Off-Hand Ammo Pack	New armor piece. Increases spare ammo capacity by 10%.
Aegis Vest	New armor piece. Increases health by 5%.

Saronis Applications	
Item	**Description**
Microcore Amplifier	Increases tech power damage.
Ablative VI	Upgrades shields, barriers, and armor for squad.

Cirta Foundation	
Item	**Description**
Microscanner	Increases medi-gel capacity by 1.
Life Support Webbing	New armor piece. Increases health by 5%.

OMEGA.

IN THE LANGUAGE OF THE HUMANS, THE TURIANS, THE ASARI, OR ANY OF THE OTHER SPECIES OF THE CITADEL, IT HAS THE SAME NAME --

-- THE END OF ALL THINGS.

OMEGA, A STATION CARVED FROM AN ASTEROID IN THE TERMINUS SYSTEMS, FAR FROM CITADEL CONTROL --

-- ANCIENT, CONTESTED GROUND FOR THE MANY SPECIES THAT NOW COEXIST UNEASILY INSIDE ITS PRESSURIZED WALLS.

MASS
E F F E C T
REDEMPTION

story MAC WALTERS
script JOHN JACKSON MILLER
art OMAR FRANCIA
colors MICHAEL ATIYEH
letters MICHAEL HEISLER

OMEGA -- FINAL DESTINATION FOR SO MANY DESPERATE BEINGS WHOSE HOPES HAVE FAILED.

PROVIDING, OF COURSE, THAT THEY CAN GET THERE ALIVE...

WE'RE HERE. A LONG WAY TO BRING ONE PERSON --

MASS EFFECT 2 COLLECTORS' EDITION
BONUS MATERIAL

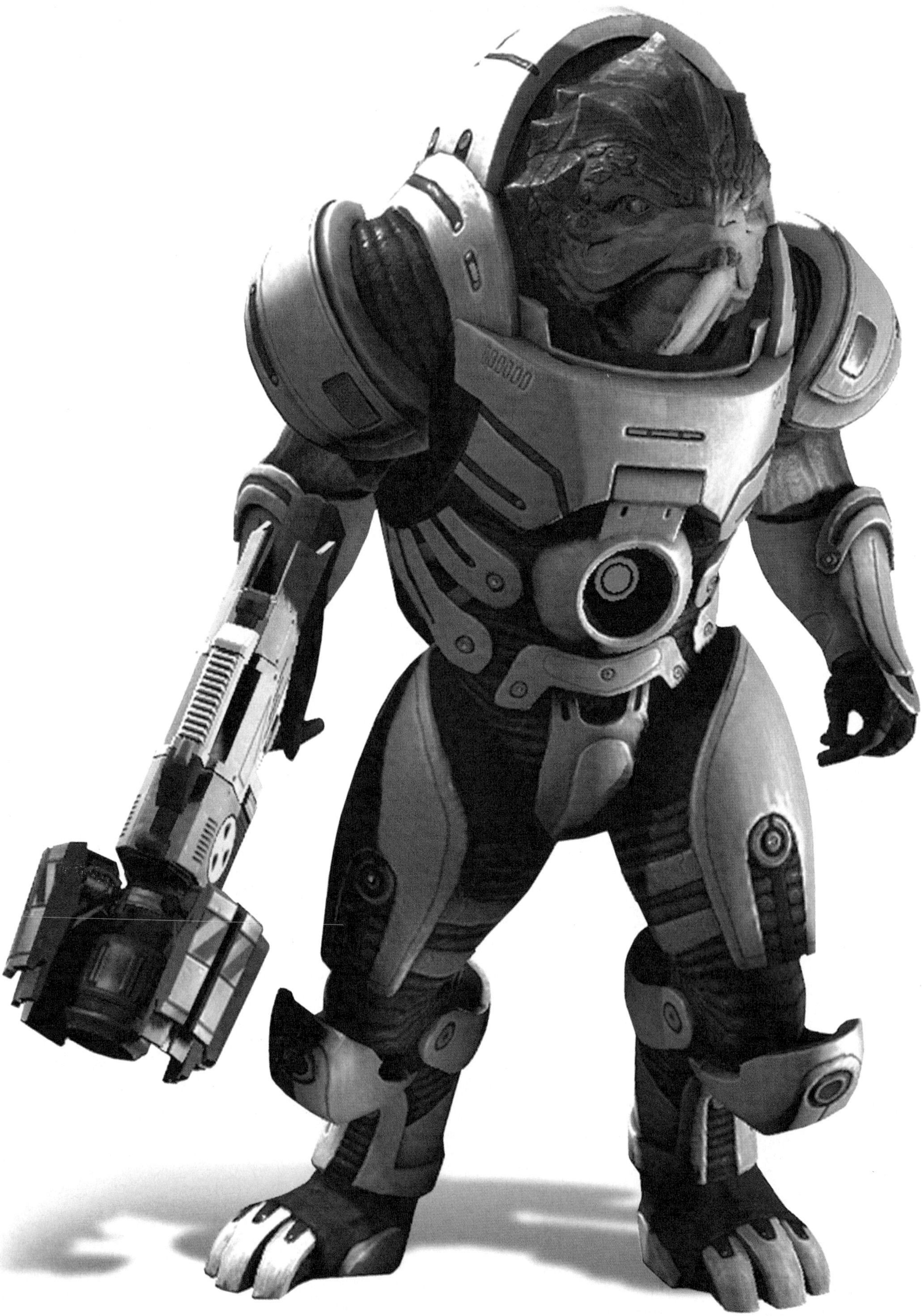

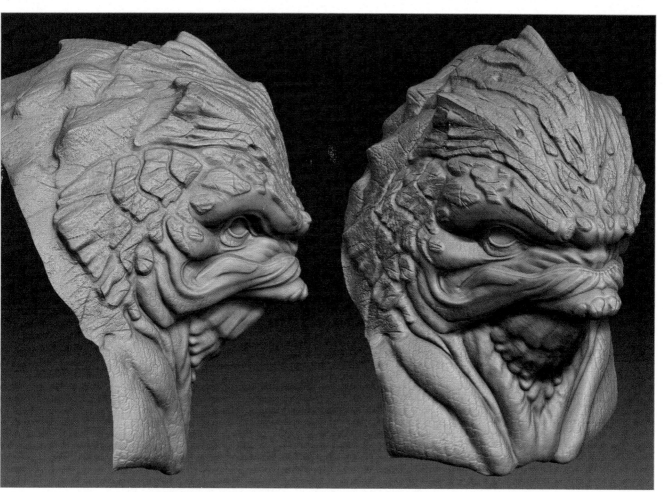

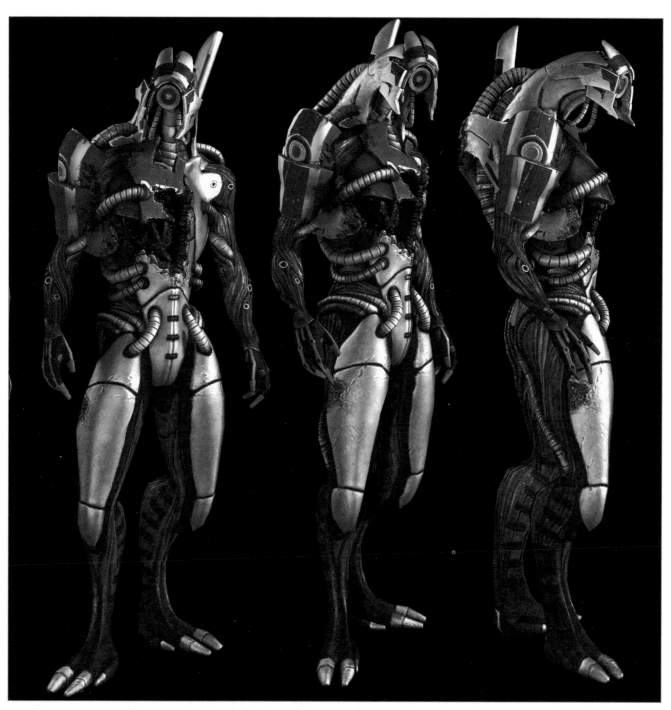

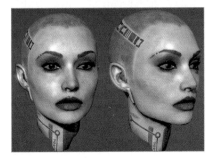

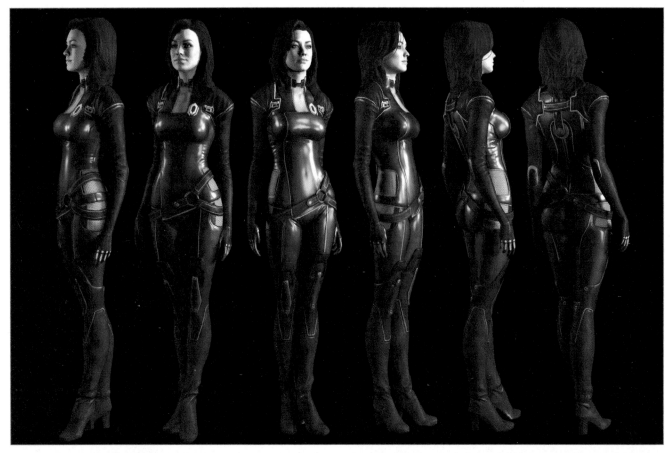

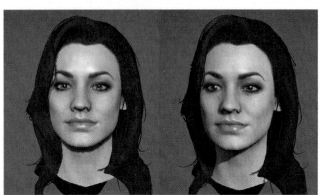

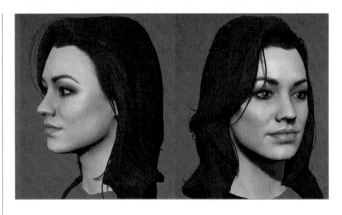

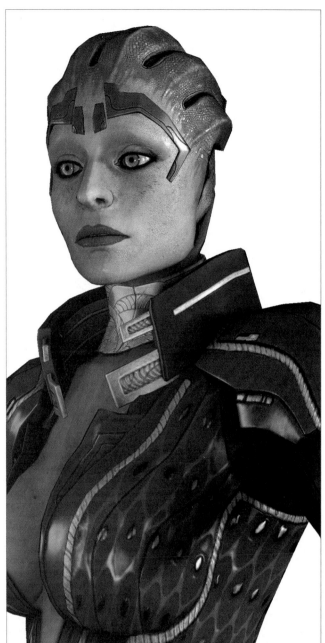

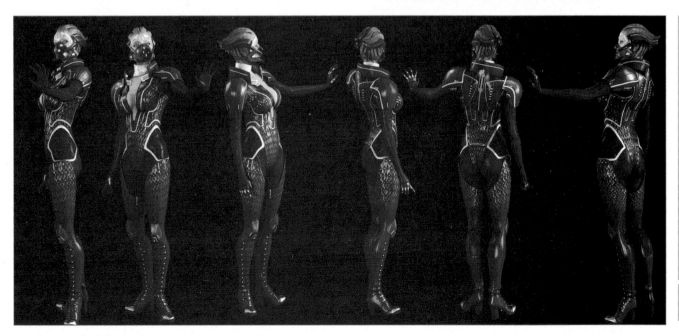

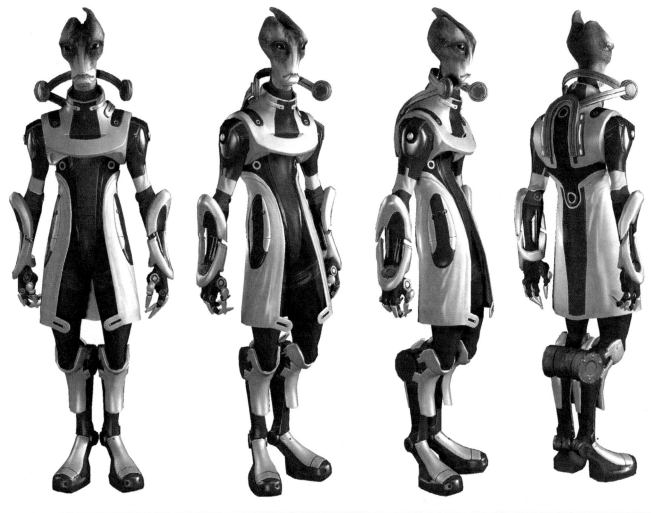

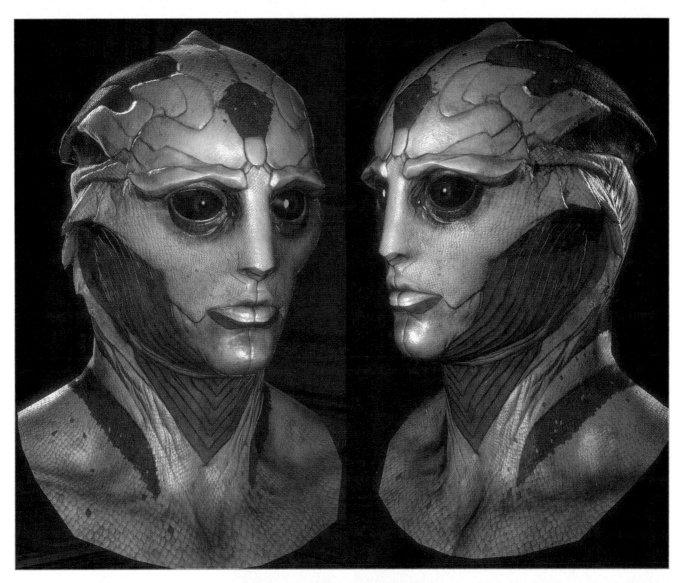

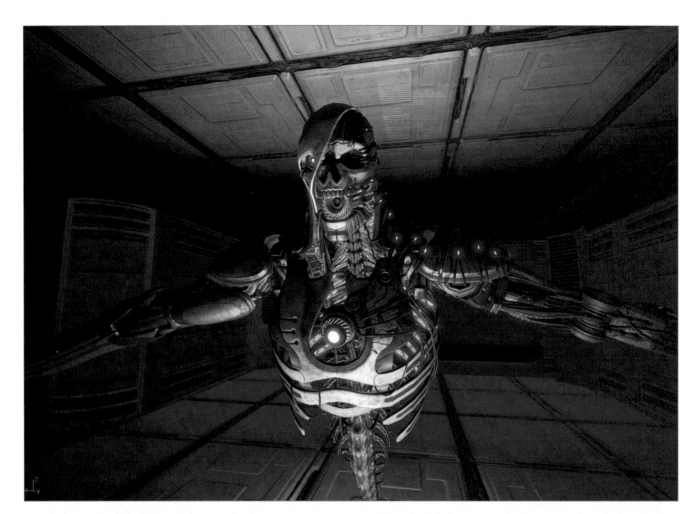

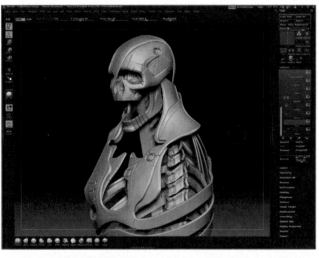

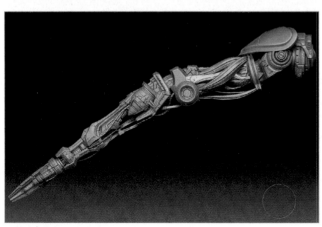

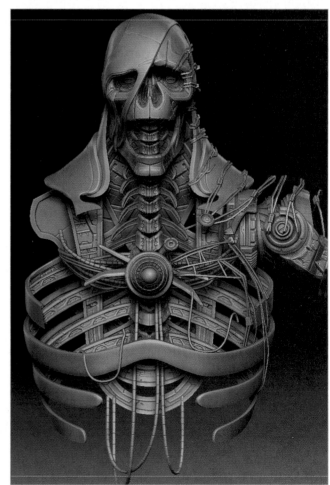

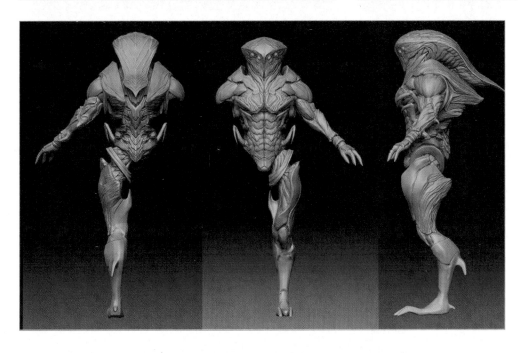

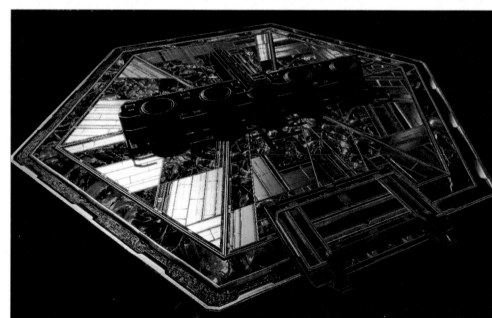

Proto Reaper

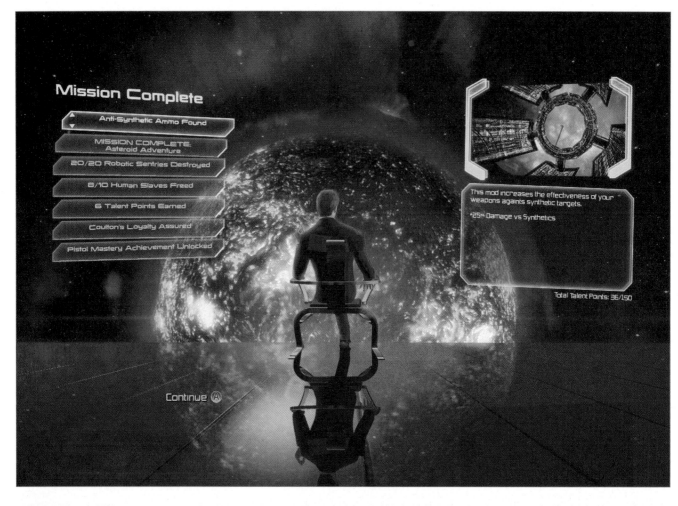

Mission Complete

- Anti-Synthetic Ammo Found
- MISSION COMPLETE Asteroid Adventure
- 20/20 Robotic Sentries Destroyed
- 8/10 Human Slaves Freed
- 6 Talent Points Earned
- Coulton's Loyalty Assured
- Pistol Mastery Achievement Unlocked

Continue Ⓐ

This mod increases the effectiveness of your weapons againts synthetic targets.

+25% Damage vs Synthetics

Total Talent Points: 36/150

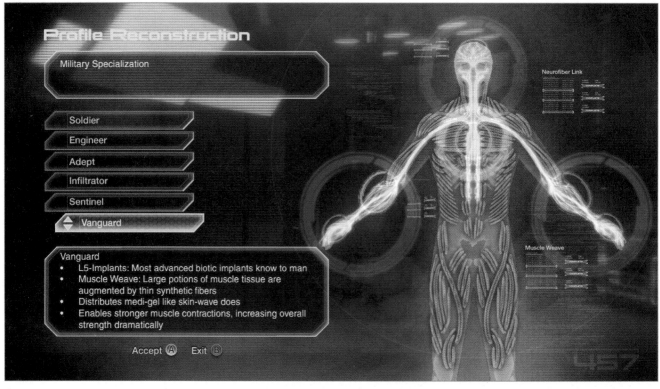

Profile Reconstruction

Military Specialization

- Soldier
- Engineer
- Adept
- Infiltrator
- Sentinel
- Vanguard

Neurofiber Link

Muscle Weave

457

Vanguard
- L5-Implants: Most advanced biotic implants know to man
- Muscle Weave: Large potions of muscle tissue are augmented by thin synthetic fibers
- Distributes medi-gel like skin-wave does
- Enables stronger muscle contractions, increasing overall strength dramatically

Accept Ⓐ   Exit Ⓑ

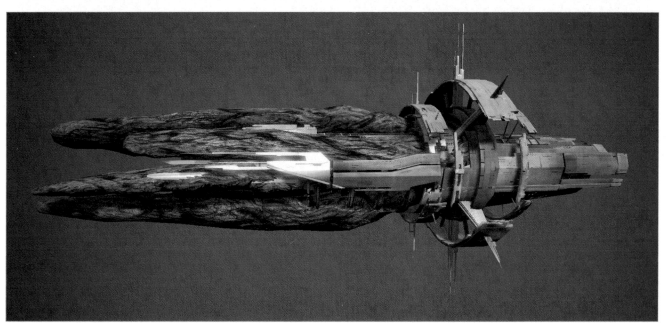

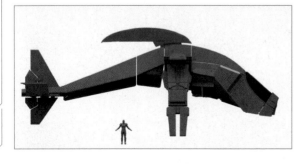

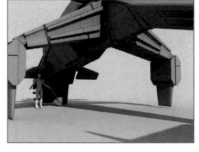

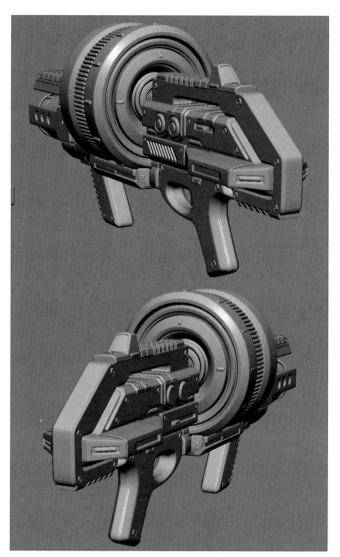

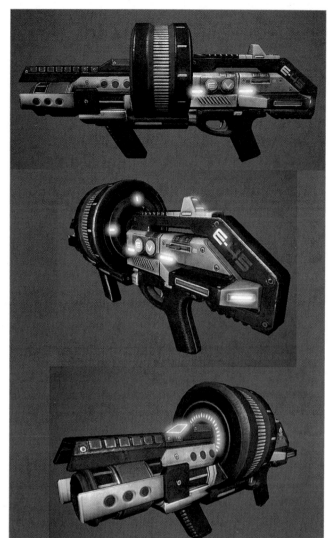

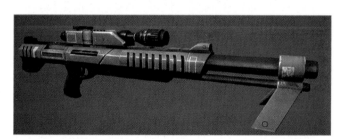

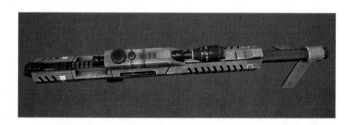

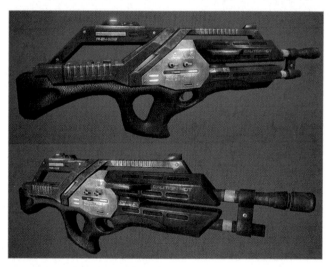

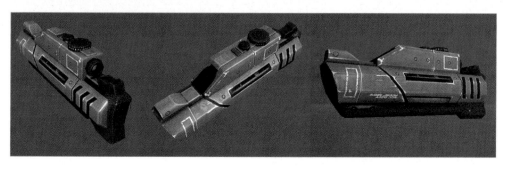

MASS EFFECT 2: THE LORE IS MY SHEPARD

Mass Effect was always planned as a trilogy. The first chapter set the board. The power center of the galaxy, the Citadel, was under attack by one of its own agents, the rogue Spectre Saren, who was himself only a pawn of the real threat: the Reapers. As Commander Shepard, humanity's best foot forward in a cosmos that regarded us with a mixture of skepticism and hostility, you had to dismantle Saren's plot, stop the Reaper attack, and save the Citadel. Nothing short of an epic adventure filled with larger than life personalities. How do you top that?

You do it by going lean and mean. The danger in Mass Effect 2 is no less lethal; the Reapers are back and have a new client, the Collectors. But instead of tearing across the stars to unravel the sinister true history of the galaxy to get at the core of the Reaper threat, you now know exactly what you need to do. You need to take the fight to the Collector homeworld on the other side of a mass relay no other ship has ever returned from. Without help from the Council, which has convinced itself that the attack on the Citadel was a lone event, it is a suicide mission of singular purpose. The chance of success is as low as the danger is high. But nobody should

Casey Hudson,
Executive Producer

ever put Shepard's back to the wall and not expect the commander to go down without a hell of a fight.

Executive Producer **Casey Hudson** looks back on the genesis of Mass Effect 2's suicide mission in the immediate aftermath of the original game's release. "We started work

on Mass Effect 2 around November 2007, the same month as the release of the first game. We had some early ideas about features we wanted to add and technology we wanted to improve. We also had the high-level arc of the trilogy carved out as part of developing the story for the first game, so we had a good initial idea of where we would start and end the story for the sequel. It would be a story that centered on the preparation and execution of a mission that you're not expected to survive. The squad members themselves would become the story, and their recruitment, loyalty, and specialization would be the basis for the missions in the game—thus tying many subplots into the final goal."

Bioware succeeded in creating a supporting cast for the original Mass Effect that players loved, from the gruff krogan Urdnot Wrex to the no-nonsense Ashley Williams. Topping this crew for Mass Effect 2's story of a disparate band united was no easy task, but Bioware did so by casting a wider net and pulling in new faces from different races, such as the mile-a-minute salarian thinker Mordin Solus and the introduction of a new species, the drell, which is represented by the calm assassin Thane. But each character is not only defined by their sometimes otherworldly skin. Team mates have unique personalities and drives that are revealed as Shepard spends more time with them on the Normandy. Look for these personalities to not only reveal themselves on the battlefield, but in the quiet moments, too. Staring death in the face reveals the core truth about a person.

Miranda starts out as cold and calculating, but as you get to know her through conversations on the Normandy, she begins to let her guard down. However, at no point is she more vulnerable than when you agree to help her with a family problem that she has obviously shared with nobody until speaking with you. If you listen to each squad member –really listen–that vulnerability is what makes them so real and sympathetic. Who doesn't grapple with regret like Mordin? Or suffer under the burden of hate like Garrus?

Hudson points to his favorite in the Mass Effect 2 cast, Subject Zero, as an example how a strong backstory told through subtlety and not bombast makes for a great character. "She was the most difficult to discuss prior to launch because her story is full of twists and surprises," says Hudson. " Like her experience in the game world, Subject Zero was a character that people initially revolted against, but as they got to know more about her they realized she was really interesting. And in the game, the way she reveals her vulnerable side to you feels very real and is hard to ignore on an emotional level."

You really get to that vulnerability by accept her loyalty mission the quest to destroy the Cerberus facility on Pragia where she believes she was tortured as a child. "I wasn't prepared for how much compassion I suddenly felt for her when she finally revealed a bit of vulnerability, after maintaining a tough exterior up to that point," says Hudson. "As tough as she was, I suddenly felt like she needed to be protected."

Other team mates may necessarily foster a need for protection or nurturing, but undertaking their loyalty missions definitely completes then as a real being. And loyalty missions are two-way streets. Why wouldn't you feel an added degree of comfort or loyalty to Tali after guiding her through her gut-wrenching test at the mercy of the quarian conclave?

Strong backstory will take a character only so far, though. To fully connect with the player, the character's performance must be equally strong. This comes in both the form of the voice actors hired to portray the characters, such as Martin Sheen ("The West Wing," "Apocalypse Now") as the Illusive Man. He brings an immediate danger to the part, as his voice as an edge to it that makes you only surrender 80-percent of your trust. You're just waiting for him to take advantage of you, which is why you hold back on the remainder.

According to Lead Writer Mac Walters, with so much dialogue in Mass Effect 2, "often actors come in for multiple reads simply due to the length of the scripts. Occasionally actors are brought back due to changes in the script or performance requirements."

The other half of the performance is the actual look and movement of the character. While all of Shepard's compatriots are expertly acted, Hudson points to the lone non-organic member of the team as a real testament to the power of an animator's ability to coax a performance out of a digital model. "With Legion, the articulation of his face allows him to speak with great expression, which is emotionally compelling and yet still appropriate for a machine." It's true. Watch the flaps above Legion's single eye as it explains the geth heretics to Shepard. With a simple raise of a flap, you get the emphasis Legion would put on the words if the geth was actually programmed to speak with the same inflection as a human.

Walters points out that it's not just the main cast of Mass Effects 2 that offer compelling performances. Every denizen of this galaxy is loaded with backstory, culture, and agendas that shape their behavior in events of Mass Effect 2. This is best exemplified by the newest race in the galaxy, the vorcha. "Originally, we thought they might be another simple, non-speaking enemy like the geth. But over time we decided that they were in fact a bit more vocal, if no more friendly than the geth," says Walters. "We soon added cultural narrative, suggesting how the Vorcha tend to be pack-based; working in groups, they are fierce, one-on-one, they're easily intimidated."

There are additional characters in Mass Effect 2 beyond the beings that Shepard interacts with over the course of the adventure. Setting can have character, too. The planets of Mass Effect 2 offer a host of personalities, from the ravaged Tuchanka that you cannot help but feel sorrow for after you really get your head around the devastation of the genophage. Not only was this burnt-out planet once a magnificent garden world that sustained life, but now it is a scene of violence and sadness. You only see the hard face of the krogan on Tuchanka, but you know that out of sight, Tuchanka is the graveyard of millions of krogan children that never got a chance at life.

"My favorite place in Mass Effect 2 is Omega," says Hudson. "One of the things I like most about playing games or watching movies is when they create a place that I'd like to live in, or wish I could go to in real life. Omega and the Afterlife bar have that effect on me." Omega's rough-and-tumble nature as an outpost for villainy is seen in the sleazy neon that crawls down skyscrapers and the back alleys that you just know have seen a thousand murders. No den of unsavory characters, though, is complete without a bar to call its own, like Afterlife. "Inside the Afterlife bar, the music and atmosphere make me wish I could go there for real and see what it would be like to spend an evening amongst turians and batarians, with Aria looking down from her VIP balcony above."

Art Director Derek Watts is just as pleased with both the scope and personality of Mass Effect 2's galaxy. "I can't think of another game that has gone to so many places with their own distinct architecture and culture, from the utopian world of Illium to the blasted flat planet of Tuchanka. It's the attention to detail that makes all of them come alive and why you become completely engrossed in the experience," says Watts.

The personality of these planets is expressed not just by general atmosphere, but by the specific architecture, too. Bioware's artists looked to the different expressions of culture through architecture on this planet when designing the skylines across Mass Effect's cosmos. "We dove into architecture books and magazines to scour the world for the latest and greatest contemporary architecture, from Zaha Hadid to Arthur Erickson. One example that stood out was the pyramid-shaped building on Tuchanka," says Watts. "It was based on an actual building in North Korea. It's 100 stories high and is completely abandoned. They built the structure with substandard concrete and it's just sitting there casting a shadow over the whole city. Nobody can use it because it's too dangerous. It's awesome."

BIOWARE: DOCTORING THE GAME

BioWare didn't start out as a game powerhouse. Originally, BioWare was formed as a medical education software developer in 1990 by former medical classmates Dr. Ray Muzyka, Dr. Greg Zeschuk and Dr. Augustine Yip. However, after discovering that medical software wasn't exactly their game, the trio turned to, well, games. BioWare was formally founded in 1995, but by that point, the developer was already working on its first game: Shattered Steel. Dr. Yip departed from BioWare in 1997, prior to the launch of the studio's ground-breaking Baldur's Gate, the PC adventure that catapulted them into prime time. Over the years, BioWare's headliners have included: Jade Empire, MDK2, Star Wars: Knights of the Old Republic, and the recently-released Dragon Age: Origins. BioWare remained an independent developer until 2007, when it was acquired by publisher/developer Electronic Arts, just before the release of the original Mass Effect for the Xbox 360.

Ray Muzyka,
BioWare Co-Founder

Greg Zeschuk,
BioWare Co-Founder

Prima had an opportunity to ask founders Muzyka and Zeschuk about the early days of the company, the philosophy that guides it, and what the future holds in a post-Mass Effect 2 world.

Prima: How did BioWare come to be?

Muzyka and Zeschuk: All three founders had a desire to pursue something more 'creative' than medicine. While medicine is a noble and exciting career, people generally don't appreciate a creative doctor! Ray and Greg both practiced for a number of years while building BioWare, but eventually decided that, instead of shaking up the medical establishment, we wanted try our hand at building high quality videogames, a subject near and dear to our hearts. We had all been addicted to videogames from a very young age and had never before really seriously considered building a videogames studio as a potential career, but when the opportunity presented itself after we graduated from medical school, we jumped at it. It's fair to say that we didn't really know what we were doing at the time and one could argue that continues until this present day, as every day at BioWare is a new adventure full of life-long learning and amazingly passionate, creative people to work with! We had tremendous passion for games, and managed to gather a team that not only shared that passion, but also backed it up with tremendous skill. Fifteen-plus years later, we're honored that so many of those great people from the early days of BioWare are still with us.

Prima: Are there any stories that everyone at the company knows even if they weren't involved/working for BioWare at the time it happened?

Muzyka and Zeschuk: The company has grown so much over the years that there are literally hundreds of "legendary" BioWare stories. There are some amusing tales from the early years of younger employees who ran headlong into their first open martini and cigar bars at our Christmas parties, sometimes with mixed results... Since then, the stories have evolved to include huge family barbeques on beautiful summer days with our ever-growing staff and their ever-growing families, exciting Dragon Boat races where our BioWarriors have won numerous medals, relaxing winter ski trips to Banff, and our festive game-release celebrations —now at multiple locations, including BioWare Edmonton, BioWare Austin, BioWare Montreal and Mythic in Virginia.

Prima: What is the prevailing atmosphere of the studio? Casual brainstorming? Disciplined achievement?

Muzyka and Zeschuk: The office atmosphere is very relaxed, so much so that some people who visit don't understand how work gets done. However, hidden under the easygoing demeanor of our employees, there is tremendous passion, skill, and a burning desire to make the world's best games, each one better than the last. We like to work hard, and we like to play hard. Most of the people at the company have many good friends in the office and they work together each and every day to deliver great entertainment to our fans, striving to fulfill our studio group vision of genuine emotional engagement in our games.

Prima: What was the watershed moment in BioWare's history?

Muzyka and Zeschuk: Without a doubt the biggest moment in BioWare's life is the arrival of a new game on store shelves (or digitally delivered to your hard-drive in today's world). PR and accolades from magazines, websites, and tradeshows are great, but the biggest reward comes from knowing we've actually been successful in taking an idea from inception all the way to being a real product and that our fans will finally be able to play it and tell us what they think. We really care what our fans think of the games and we want them to be completely satisfied and happy with what we've made for them—one of our goals is to never break the trust with our fans that every one of our games will be of extremely high quality. It's exciting running into people who've played our games; usually they're effusively happy, but we also get a lot of constructive advice, which we then fashion into knowledge that we apply to our next games. It's great being able to create entertainment for people that makes a genuine positive difference in their lives.

Prima: Is there a BioWare mission statement? Or philosophy that drives the BioWare game development?

Muzyka and Zeschuk: We have a set of core values that we've been living since the beginning of BioWare. They've undergone occasional refinement and a few added dimensions, but generally they've helped guide us to be

successful over the last 15 years. BioWare's Core Values are: Quality in our products, quality in our workplace, and entrepreneurship, all in the context of humility and integrity.

These might seem really straightforward, but keeping them truly balanced—and living them each day in every decision we make-is not. That is our biggest secret in building both great games and a great company; by keeping the core values balanced and ensuring all your key stakeholders (Employees, Customers and Investors) are happy, you have the potential to reach a superb state where employees are happy making great games, which in turn make the fans happy, which causes them to buy lots of copies, which makes our investors happy—resulting in a vibrant, sustainable business long-term. We try to remain humble and maintain integrity, as we believe it's always important to treat everyone fairly and to always be open to improvements in making our games and managing our studio group, now a successful division of Electronic Arts for the past couple of years.

Prima: Are there any projects that were started but never finished? Or are there some that were conceived of near the beginning of BioWare's life but still haven't been realized?

Muzyka and Zeschuk: We have tried a number of different ideas over the years, some of which haven't seen the light of day, and others that have morphed into new projects. As you've probably seen in the last couple years, we've also been doing a few more "experimental" projects, such as Gift of the Yeti game on Facebook. That's clearly not a BioWare game in the traditional sense, but it does represent us exploring new directions in social gaming. Don't worry, though! We're going to continue making the story-driven adventures that people love, but you might also start seeing some interesting new things in our future games as we focus on direct to consumer and social gaming features in addition to epic stories, choice with emotionally engaging consequences, amazing worlds to explore, tactical and strategic choices in combat, rich personalization and customization, and high-quality gameplay throughout!